PATH OF
DESTRUCTION

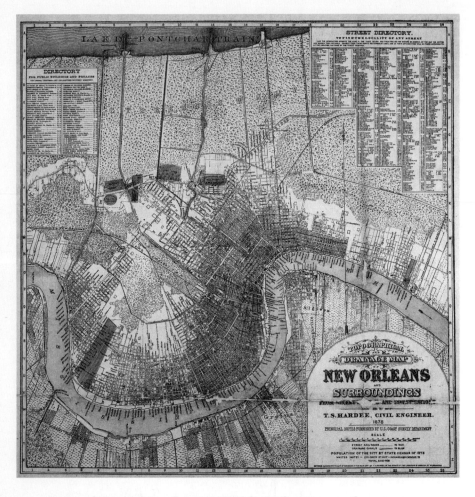

A map of New Orleans drawn in 1878 by civil engineer and surveyor Thomas S. Hardee shows the city occupying a crescent of high ground along the bank of the Mississippi River. Streets trailed off into a cypress swamp, crisscrossed by low ridges, that stretched north to the shore of Lake Pontchartrain. Over the next hundred years, developers gradually filled in the swamp and built the neighborhoods of modern New Orleans on top of it. But those newer areas were mostly below sea level, and they all flooded when Hurricane Katrina's storm surge struck the city in August 2005. Only the older settled areas along the river in Hardee's map remained dry and intact. More than a century of progress and development was undone in a day. Courtesy of the Louisiana State Museum.

PATH OF DESTRUCTION

THE DEVASTATION OF NEW ORLEANS AND THE COMING AGE OF SUPERSTORMS

JOHN McQUAID AND MARK SCHLEIFSTEIN

LITTLE, BROWN AND COMPANY
New York   Boston   London

Little, Brown and Company
Hachette Book Group USA
1271 Avenue of the Americas, New York, NY 10020
Visit our Web site at www.HachetteBookGroupUSA.com

First Edition: August 2006

Map of the New Orleans levee systems by Emmett Mayer III

The authors are grateful for permission to reprint the following: "When the Levee Breaks," by Joe McCoy. Used by permission of Edwin H. Morris & Company, a division of MPL Music Publishing, Inc. Topographical and Drainage Map of New Orleans and Surroundings courtesy of the Louisiana State Museum

Library of Congress Cataloging-in-Publication Data

McQuaid, John.
    Path of destruction : the devastation of New Orleans and the coming age of superstorms / John McQuaid and Mark Schleifstein.—1st ed.
        p. cm.
    Includes bibliographical references.
    ISBN-10: 0-316-01642-X
    ISBN-13: 978-0-316-01642-1
    1. Hurricane Katrina, 2005.   2. Emergency management—Louisiana—New Orleans Metropolitan Area.   3. Disaster relief—Louisiana—New Orleans Metropolitan Area.   4. Intergovernmental cooperation—Louisiana—New Orleans Metropolitan Area.   5. Natural disasters—Louisiana—New Orleans Metropolitan Area.   6. Environmental degradation—Louisiana—New Orleans Metropolitan Area.
I. Schleifstein, Mark.   II. Title.
HV6362005.L8 M37 2006
976.3'35064—dc22   2006018762

10 9 8 7 6 5 4 3 2 1

Q-FF

Printed in the United States of America

*TO THE PEOPLE OF NEW ORLEANS, AND TO THE MANY
FRIENDS AND STRANGERS WHO HELPED THEM THROUGH
KATRINA AND ITS AFTERMATH*

CONTENTS

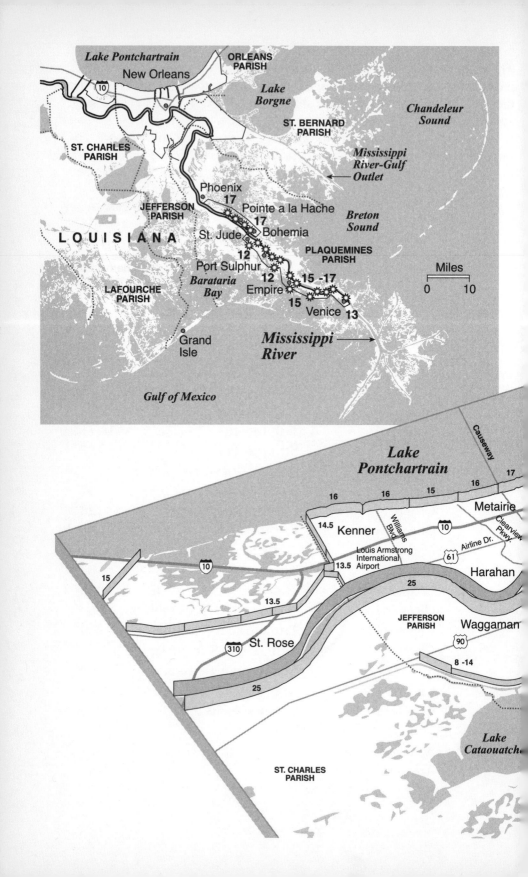

The complex array of earthen levees, levee walls (the heights of which are indicated in the maps), and drainage canals designed to protect the New Orleans metropolitan area from hurricane storm surge was a "system in name only," according to the Army Corps of Engineers panel tasked to investigate its failure in the aftermath of Hurricane Katrina. Some levees were still not complete, more than forty years after construction on the system had begun. Others were not built to mandated heights or had sunk below authorized levels. Several levee walls were improperly designed and were pushed over by Katrina's surge. Some levees were built with substandard materials and washed away.

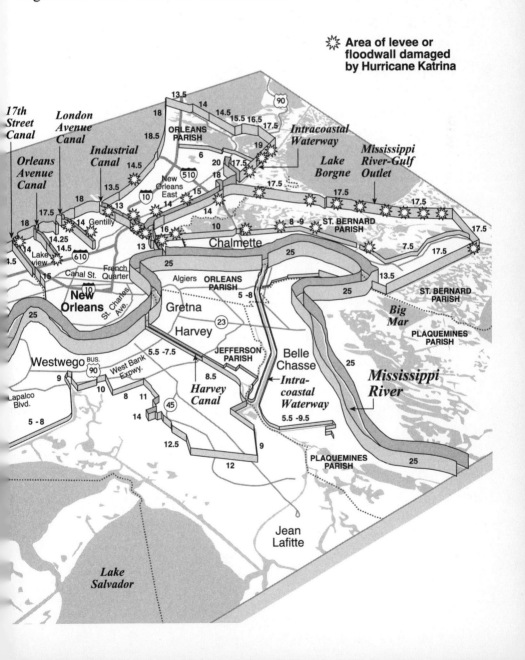

INTRODUCTION

I N 2002, WE WROTE a series for the *Times-Picayune* that explored New Orleans's unique vulnerability to hurricanes, especially the enormous storm surge waves they generate. Our reporting explored an obvious but little-acknowledged fact: here was a city that, for the six months of every hurricane season, lived with a substantial risk of utter annihilation. New Orleans's predicament seemed to fly in the face of sound government policy, not to mention basic common sense: much of the city was built on top of a swamp, below sea level and gradually sinking. The hurricane levees around it formed a shallow bowl that, if breached or overtopped by a storm surge, would fill with water. Anyone there would be trapped by quickly rising floodwaters, their escape routes cut off. As streets became rivers and neighborhoods lakes, hundreds, maybe thousands, would drown.

Such horrors seemed unimaginable to most Americans, and remote even to New Orleans residents who had heard scientists and emergency managers describe them each summer. Hadn't the city already survived for almost three hundred years? Didn't it have a full guarantee of protection from the U.S. government, in the form of levees designed by the Army Corps of Engineers, with its two centuries of experience and gold-plated reputation?

The fine print acknowledged the danger. The Corps of Engineers claimed its levees could protect the city only from the storm surge waves produced by relatively weak hurricanes, those in Categories 1 and 2, and some of those in Category 3 (on the Saffir-Simpson scale, used to measure hurricane strength). If a more powerful storm struck the city, the levees would fail—end of story. That dark fate was the result of decisions made long ago by Congress that no one seemed interested in revisiting. In Washington, those in power had other constituencies requiring immediate attention, and in Louisiana the salvation of New Orleans was surprisingly low on the to-do list. After all, New Orleans had thus far avoided the Big One. And its citizens and the nation thus essentially agreed to gamble that, as hurricanes roared over the Gulf of Mexico each year, it would keep lucking out again and again.

There was no rescue strategy for the city itself. If New Orleans got hit, the plan was simply to let it be destroyed, then clean up the mess.

So, when Hurricane Katrina struck and submerged most of New Orleans on August 29, 2005, we were stunned and horrified, but not surprised. Afterward, as we—along with hundreds of others of journalists, congressional investigators, and forensic engineers—began to examine what had gone wrong, the outlines of an even greater tragedy emerged. The levee system had been much weaker than originally advertised. In some places, the Corps had made serious design errors, engineering screwups of historic dimensions. The levees were not the only problem; the city of New Orleans had essentially given up trying to figure out how to evacuate residents with no transportation, and the federal government reorganization that followed the terrorist attacks of September 11, 2001, had, somehow, actually weakened the nation's ability to respond to a catastrophe. Initially it had been easy to blame the destruction of this great American city on Mother Nature. But the more we investigated, the more obvious it was that man had set the stage.

There has always been an element of folly in mankind's attempts to control or outsmart nature. The self-important activities of human society are brief flickers of a candle flame compared to the mighty forces driving the rise of mountains, the shifting of river courses, and the fury of hurricanes. Occasionally, nature erupts in some entirely predictable way—a hurricane thrashes the coast, a river overflows into towns on its banks, a mudslide carries off a neighborhood—and stunned citizens and their leaders collectively remark, "What the hell just happened?" Yet after a few years, the disaster is forgotten, and people fall back into the patterns of living that tempt another, even worse catastrophe.

Of course, life requires some risk-taking, and there is no such thing as perfect security. But this cycle of disaster is so obvious, and so stubbornly repetitive, that the pattern suggests it may be hardwired into the human brain. Humans tend to be optimists even when facts tell them otherwise, like the title character in John Irving's *The World According to Garp,* who buys a house after watching a plane crash into the upper story, figuring the property has used up its quota of bad luck.

Americans are especially stubborn this way, and indeed, America would not exist if countless explorers, patriots, and homesteaders had not taken on grave risks. But today, technology and the trappings of modern life mislead us; they can create the appearance of security, making still-dangerous places feel positively cozy. And as the twenty-first century has dawned, new perils have arisen, among them a disturbing increase in the number of powerful hurricanes around the globe, possibly spawned by man-made global warming.

A loose-knit group of scientists and emergency managers was the only thing standing between New Orleans and its eventual fate. They devoted entire careers to studying hurricanes and storm surges, and raced desperately against the doomsday clock, hitting countless bureaucratic walls along the way, doing their best to push New Orleans's predicament into the public eye. But they were small voices calling attention to ingrained, systemic problems. That their heroic efforts ultimately failed is the result of ignorance, bad decisions, and a sorry lack of leadership. It is too late to save the New Orleans that once was. But it may not be too late to do something about the storms to come.

PATH OF
DESTRUCTION

Chapter 1

CITY ON THE DELTA

ELEVEN HUNDRED YEARS AGO, several small bands of Indians had settled in the vast muddy delta where the Mississippi River flows out into the Gulf of Mexico. Day to day, it was a decent, if not always comfortable, place to live. Molded by the river and the sea, the delta wetlands sprawled for hundreds of miles. Fields of yellow green, reedy grass rustled under hazy sunshine, stirred by gentle summer breezes and beaten flat by evening thunderstorms. The Indians hunted deer and fished clams, crab, spot, and drum from lakes and bayous, nursing frequent bites from swarms of mosquitoes and taking care to avoid snakes and alligators. Their mud-and-bark cabins, roofed with cypress bark and palmetto leaves, sat on the delta's only high ground—an intricate lace pattern of ridges and the banks of rivers and bayous (from the Choctaw *bayuk,* for the area's slow, meandering streams). Near their settlements they left middens made of discarded clamshells and other debris. Groups of Indians had expanded their settlements and built more robust trade routes, part of a cultural emergence that stretched as far as a thousand miles to the north, up and down the river valley. They worshipped at temples and burial mounds that sat near open plazas. They built low earthen walls to protect their homes from flooding. The peaty soil was ideal for planting corn and potatoes.

One day the sky turned gray. Puffy clouds hung low, and the wind gusted hard out of the east. Rain began to pelt the Indians' cabins. The wind soon turned into a steady, howling gale. It tore roofs off, then began shredding walls and toppling trees. Stores of food and clothing scattered and blew away. Snapped branches and driftwood smashed into obstacles with loud cracks.

Then, though the Indians were far inland, water from the Gulf began to rise around them. Nearby bayous flowed backward and spilled over their banks.

Suddenly, the river itself began to flow backward.

One minute the flood was ankle deep, the next, up to a man's neck. The churning waters swallowed villages and carried the Indians away. People gasped for air, reaching for stray branches or anything that might keep them afloat. The salt water stung their eyes, nostrils, and throats. Many were pulled under or struck by debris and drowned. Bodies and debris floated in silty water, shoved to and fro by the wind. Soon an eerie quiet settled over the marshes. The wind stopped and the sun came out and dappled a new sea that stretched for miles in every direction, with only the boldest of treetops reaching out of the water. Then the rain and wind began again, before finally dying down. The water began to recede.

Only settlements built on the highest ground remained. As dazed survivors surveyed the damage, the vistas were unrecognizable: they saw a broken landscape of fallen trees and ragged marshes, everything covered with a layer of fine gray sand swept miles inland from the floor of the Gulf. Bayous had shifted course. Some banks and ridges were higher. Others had completely disappeared.

The remaining Indians set about rebuilding their settlements, never so sure again of their own security.

A few hundred years later, the giant hurricane was nothing more than a fading legend among the Indians when the delta then turned upside down again.

Every spring for as long as the Indians had known, the Mississippi—from an Ojibwe Indian phrase for "gathering of great waters"—had welled up and overflowed its banks, depositing silt and muck for miles on either side, building land mile by mile out into the Gulf. The river seeks the Gulf by the shortest, steepest path. As its course grew out into a longer and gentler incline and silt built up along the riverbed, every thousand years or so the Mississippi would find that shorter and faster way to the Gulf. Such was the case about six hundred years ago. For years, more and more flow had been diverting into a modest tributary about thirty miles northeast of the river, less and less through the river itself. As the delta spread, the flows reached a tipping point, divided more or less equally. Then came a swift reaction, over a blink of geological time: the Mississippi changed course. All of its forty thousand tons of water per second began coursing down the shorter route out into the Gulf. At the point where the two channels previously split, the old river outlet was sealed off with muck.

Villages along the river's new course flooded, while those Indians living along its old course suddenly found themselves sipping salt water. Those who viewed the river as a constantly changing yet permanent fixture may have interpreted the change as a sign of wrath from their spirits. Once again, they would bury the dead and rebuild.

Today, civilization enfolds us like a great security blanket. Homes, offices, roadways, and bridges are engineered to exacting standards. Cars have air bags, alarms, and satellite links to keep people from getting lost. Every child's toy has a warning label. But in many ways we're no safer than were the Indians of the Mississippi delta centuries ago—and in some ways we're even less secure.

New Orleans, which straddles the riverbanks those Indians once occupied, sits atop a lower Mississippi delta that stretches out past the edge of the North American continent, fading from hard ground to a distinctive Rorschach blot of mud, grass, and water. It's a malleable, changeable place without clear boundaries, "a land between earth and sea—belonging to neither and alternately claimed by both," Army Corps of Engineers geologists wrote in a seminal 1958 study. Most of the time, earth and sea exist in a state of low-level flux. Waves pound, earth sinks, marshes and dunes change shape. But every so often, the water erupts: a hurricane pushes the sea far inland, or the river brings a whole winter's worth of cold rain and melting snow coursing down from the north. Wherever it comes from, the flow sweeps away obstacles. It drowns, soaks, and rots. Some things it merely ruins. Some it vanishes.

Despite that constant danger, the river and the delta's proximity to the sea have long lured waves of settlers—first Indians, then Europeans from France, Spain, and England, and, later, people from around the world. Many prospered, picking up a dogged affection for the place as they faced down floods, drenching rains, searing heat, mosquitoes, and palmetto bugs. Each generation of settlers engineered defenses against high water, only to see them washed away and their homes wrecked. Then—whether because they wanted to defy nature, or prove their ingenuity, or because they simply forgot about the risks after a few years—they started over.

By the start of the twenty-first century, those fixes had morphed the delta into a strange hybrid of the man-made and natural. Levees had locked the river into its course. The water-and-mud landscape was carved up and channelized like a huge jigsaw puzzle, embedded with concrete, steel, pipes, and electronics. Suburbs and outlying towns stretched for miles, south to the point where the river split into three channels resembling a bird's foot, upriver past open marshes, and along the shores of Lake Pontchartrain. Around this urban blotch sat hundreds of miles of towering earthen levees, concrete-and-steel floodwalls, gates, and locks—their heights carefully calculated to repel all but the highest floods. The walls worked in tandem with an intricate web of canals, pipelines, and pumps built to expel any water that got in.

None of this destroyed the ancient dance between the delta and the sea—it just distorted it. Underneath homes, skyscrapers, streets, and the flood defenses that protected them, the marshes were sinking. Closer to the Gulf, where reeds and grass still grew, they were dissolving. With fewer natural obstacles, hurricane floods moved farther and farther inland. Levees had turned the city and suburbs into a set of giant soup bowls—low-lying, sinking areas rimmed by walls. Centuries earlier, a hurricane washed a flood over a place and the water would be gone in a day. Now it would be trapped.

Still, New Orleans residents had other perks of civilization backstopping them. If disaster did strike, the most powerful nation on earth was poised to intervene, rescue, and rebuild. Emergency management pros working for dozens of government agencies had trained precisely for just such a catastrophe. The whole nation knew the president as a man of decisive action thanks to his response to a terrorist attack—a disaster of a different kind, but a disaster nevertheless. He'd spent four years overseeing the biggest government reorganization ever. Its goal was protecting citizens. Its bottom line: be ready.

But on August 29, 2005, those systems—flood defenses, government agencies, plans, and preparations—all failed. Hurricane Katrina sent another huge wave washing over the delta. Though much smaller than the one that hit 1,100 years ago, it rose over marshes and into lakes abutting the city. It flowed into canals next to homes and streets. It poured over levees. It pressed against floodwalls and they fell like dominoes. Water flowed through the streets, submerging homes, schools, convenience stores, gas stations, and cars. A thousand people drowned. Tens of thousands more were caught by surprise, suddenly trapped in attics and on rooftops. Battered survivors struggled through a week of hell awaiting rescue, and government officials from the president on down seemed indifferent or clueless. Many residents surveyed the wreckage and wondered if their beloved city could ever be rebuilt, its color and spirit restored. For now, it was little more than a ruined shell. The flood wrecked not only homes and lives but all the systems that make modern society hum—freshwater pipelines and pumps, electric and phone lines, cell phone towers, and Internet servers.

In the space of a few hours, the storm stripped away the security blanket. Twenty-first-century America's awesome computational power, its accumulated knowledge of science and history, its engineering wizardry, its love of gadgetry and instantaneous communications, its military's proven ability to move people and materiel anywhere in the blink of an eye—none of these could save New Orleans, or even rally to save trapped flood victims afterward. Instead, chaos and stupidity ruled the day. The Indians were living in the dark and got swept away. But America knew all about hurricanes and New Orleans was swept away anyway. In the aftermath, only a narrow rim along the natural high ground of the riverbank was still inhabited and functioning—the approximate boundaries of New Orleans in the mid-1800s. Refugees dispersed around the United States in the largest diaspora since the Dust Bowl of the 1930s.

In 1999, a computer scientist at MIT named Alan Wexelblat posted a message to the Listserv of the Viridian movement—a virtual community devoted to a futuristic melding of ecology, technology, and design. "I don't have a word for this form of disaster, but I bet we see a lot of them in the '00s," he wrote, adding a link to an article headlined "Fecal Explosion Threatens City." It recounted how, in 1998, Hurricane Mitch had damaged the sewage system of Tegucigalpa, Honduras, causing cracks in culverts and buildups of shit and gas. Sewage was bubbling up into the streets in spots. Nobody knew what to do—except maybe junk the system and start from scratch.

This type of breakdown was distinct from an old-fashioned natural disaster, Wexelblat wrote. "These Viridian Disaster events will be infrastructural in nature, rather than merely external. They'll be collapse, implosion, failure type events, rather than explosive, razing type events. The technical system will tie itself in knots, because the planet really is *much* bigger/more powerful than these systems were designed to accept."

Wexelblat's thesis was that our decades-long back-and-forth between nature and modern technology would create weird feedbacks that would explode in our faces. We're shortsighted in engineering our technological systems, and stupid when it comes to taking the measure of nature. Now the two are engaged in a destructive, possibly apocalyptic dance. "Humans have a very hard time thinking and operating on geological time scales," Wexelblat said. "If you think about ways we treat some of our systems, we think only about short term effects: The Mississippi is flooding—let's build some concrete along it." Wexelblat disasters, as they came to be known, happen in slow motion, without anyone noticing for years. When they do, it's too late.

A hurricane is a heat engine packing unimaginable energy. At the height of its strength, it can release the equivalent of a ten-megaton nuclear bomb exploding every twenty minutes. That's a concentrated energy output five times greater than the world's power plants generate in a day. (This means that stopping a hurricane is probably beyond mankind's technological reach.) It takes just a fraction of the storm's power to drive the winds that shriek at racecar speeds around the eye and can toss a man like a rag doll.

Hurricanes have pummeled the Mississippi delta regularly over its more than five-thousand-year lifespan. The delta sits at the end of the one of the world's biggest hurricane alleys, exposed on three sides to shallow sea warmed all summer by the tropical sun, a cauldron for brewing storms. In most places, where beaches fringe higher, harder ground, a storm surge—a massive energy pulse moving through the water—is brutal but brief: the wave rises as it comes ashore and washes inland, obliterating most everything in its path before quickly receding. But a surge striking the flat, open Mississippi delta can inundate thousands of square miles. As annual river floods built up the delta over thousands of years, repeated hurricane strikes helped mold that land, reworking the soft superstructure of marsh fringes, ridges, and natural levees in violent, at times strangely beautiful ways.

The study of these ancient storms is called paleotempestology. Louisiana State University geologist Kam-biu Liu is one of the field's pioneers. Liu had an interesting insight when he began studying the geological evidence of ancient hurricanes in the 1980s. Storm surges picked up sand from the floor of the Gulf and carried it over dunes and coastal ridges, then dumped it miles inland, spread out in the pattern of a giant fan. Hurricanes thus left sand where it otherwise would never be found.

If scientists dug deep enough in the right inland spots, they might find anomalous sand layers sandwiched between other soils. Since only a powerful hurricane with a high storm surge could wash sand past the coastline, those ancient sand layers would be the fingerprints of the biggest hurricanes of the past, Category 4 or 5 storms as measured by today's Saffir-Simpson scale.

Liu and a group of colleagues staked out five sites along the Gulf Coast, including the Pearl River basin just northeast of New Orleans. Some were lakebeds—ideal for getting a read on the past because they tended to be stable, unaffected by tides or floods. Others were marshes, which contain a tree-ring-type pattern showing annual layers of deposits, including silt and clays from the river. Taking soil borings extending down fifty feet or more, Liu's teams tested the samples to discern squishy organic soils from dense, granular sand. When imaged and graphed, sand layers leaped out in a clear light band.

Those patterns of light and dark that Liu observed helped him piece together a history of superstorms over the past five thousand years. It was necessarily incomplete—there aren't that many sites where telltale sand layers can still be found—but it was revealing. Liu's research showed the Gulf Coast to be a violent place: giant storms hit regularly over the centuries. The results also indicated that the past thousand years or so had been pretty quiet, with only a handful of big hurricane strikes. During the three thousand years before that, giant storms had barreled ashore three times as often. This history suggests that the settlement of the Gulf Coast over the past millennium by Indians and then Europeans had come about thanks in part to dumb luck: people arrived during a lull in the action.

The night of September 12, 1722, a hurricane nearly destroyed the French colonial outpost of La Nouvelle Orleans, then just over four years old. The storm swept across marshlands, French ships sheltering in bayous, and remote Indian settlements before it reached the colony's distinctive crescent bend in the Mississippi. The camp sat on the riverbank, surrounded by wooden palisades built to repel enemies, drainage ditches, and a four-foot earthen levee fronting the river. Once there, the storm pounded the fragile settlement of about a hundred barracks, including one housing a hospital and another where the St. Louis chapel shared space with a warehouse. The wind grew steadily stronger as morning approached, blowing many crude shacks away.

"Towards ten o'clock in the evening there sprang up the most terrible hurricane which has been seen in these quarters," Diron d'Artaguette, the inspector general for the Company of the West, which ran the colony for the French Crown, wrote in his diary. "At New Orleans thirty-four houses were destroyed as well as sheds, including the church, the parsonage and the hospital. In the hospital were some people sick with wounds. All the other houses were damaged about the roofs or the walls." The storm surge pushed the river eight feet above normal. Colonists watched in amazement and thanked God that it was late summer, so the river was low. It didn't overflow.

Fortunately, the hurricane had delivered a glancing blow— wind did more damage than water—though it made many of the 250 colonists think about heading back to France. The next afternoon, as settlers and traders straggled back to the camp, d'Artaguette received reports of crops destroyed, houses knocked down, and many pirogues—canoelike boats that were the principal form of transportation—disappeared. One enterprising trader, a man named Poussin on his way to New Orleans to sell fowl, Indian corn, and other goods, had been swept away in his pirogue. It was assumed he had met an unfortunate end.

Stunned at the hurricane's fury and frustrated at the hardships they now faced, some colonists began talking of desertion, d'Artaguette wrote. They planned to head downriver and seize the *Kerliazou,* a passenger ship anchored there, but an informer tipped off Governor Jean-Baptiste Le Moyne de Bienville, who alerted French soldiers to be on the lookout. The plan was aborted, but disquiet continued. Workers complained a couple of days later that they were being forced to rebuild the home of one of the colony's leaders "when they did not have there a church in which to put God under cover . . . nor a hospital in which to put the sick."

Europeans had come to the Mississippi delta, and if it hadn't been before, it was now clear that they were in for a rough time.

As the Indians before them had discovered, even without the storms, the delta was a harsh place, a dicey spot to make a life. Huts and fortifications sank in the mud. Navigation was treacherous. The alligators that plied the bayous could suddenly rise from slumber and snatch a man below in a single violent spasm. Some Indians were hostile to outsiders. Pirate ships prowled the Gulf Coast, preying on ships foolish enough to hug the shore or get stuck in the sand. The climate was unbearably hot in the summer and prone to freezes in the winter, limiting the crops that could be cultivated for profit.

The biggest challenge was staying dry. The Mississippi delta was a damp place surrounded by bodies of water that regularly overflowed. Each spring, the river would rise over its banks at various spots, temporarily turning dry areas into lakes, leaving puddles as it receded. Without levees, the river gently unfurled over the land, then withdrew—expanding and contracting like pulses of blood through an artery. Hurricane flooding tended to be mild, too. La Nouvelle Orleans was ringed by miles of robust marshlands and cypress forests. At the outermost edges sat barrier islands with dunes at least ten feet high. They couldn't stop a storm surge, but they could cut it down to size, and as a wave pushed over the marshes and trees, it would lose momentum and dissipate. There were serious dangers, to be sure. A storm surge pushing Gulf water up the river could easily overflow the banks, washing away homes and crops. Storm surges could also flow into Lake Pontchartrain through two channels, but five miles of swampland and forest stood between the lake and the high ground on which the outpost could be found.

The English and Spanish had established thriving colonies along the Atlantic and Gulf coasts and down in Mexico and in Central and South America, but the Mississippi delta remained mostly unexplored, a mystery, the hostile conditions there delaying settlement there a full two hundred years past Europeans' arrival in the New World.

Yet the Mississippi beckoned. It was—potentially—an economic and strategic asset without peer, providing access to the vast, unexplored American interior. The French had already set up forts and some trading posts along the river up to its territories in Canada. The outlet into the Gulf was a prize in the contest for continental dominance, neatly interposed between Spanish colonies to the west and in Florida, and English ones to the northeast. It provided refuge for ships and places to dig in and repel enemies. The short-term economic picture was less promising, but manageable. The land had little of value—no precious metals to mine—but the soil was fertile, if soggy. (It also sat over resources that would later prove even more important than any eighteenth-century colonist could imagine—oil and natural gas.) The emerging Enlightenment view stated that with reason, science, and determination, mankind could understand nature and control it. Those who built New Orleans set out to prove this faith true and abiding, to claim the delta not just for France, but for the future.

Forty years before the 1722 hurricane, nobleman and explorer René Robert Cavelier de la Salle had claimed all land around the Mississippi for France. After exploring the Great Lakes and canoeing downriver from an Illinois fort, de la Salle erected a cross and a plaque near the mouth of the Mississippi, somewhere southeast of present-day New Orleans. He christened the territory Louisiana for King Louis XIV. Two years later, he returned with four ships and three hundred would-be colonists via the Gulf of Mexico to build the first European settlement along the lower Mississippi. The mission went awry when his navigators could not distinguish the river's mouth among the confounding delta tidal flats. De la Salle ended up far to the west in Matagorda Bay, Texas, and after three failed marches east to find the correct river outlet, his own men murdered him and left his body behind.

More than a decade later, two young brothers, Jean-Baptiste

Le Moyne de Bienville and Pierre Le Moyne d'Iberville, set out on a mission to explore Louisiana and set up colonies if they could. They sailed upriver as far as Baton Rouge and eventually set up a provisional capital on Mobile Bay. Iberville died of yellow fever while on a military mission in Havana in 1706, and Bienville continued as governor.

During the first years of the eighteenth century, the British controlled the seas, and Louisiana—then just a handful of settlements along the Gulf—was all but cut off from France. As a result, settlers eked out an existence by trading with local Indians. Later, with a tenuous peace established and France looking to make some money, Bienville decided the capital should best be sited inland along the river—a logical way station for shipping. An earlier settlement to the south was vulnerable to flooding, so in 1717 Bienville sent a letter to the company describing a crescent bend in the river that he believed would be safe from tidal flux and hurricane flooding. The following February, he set out from Dauphin Island on Mobile Bay with a convoy of small boats and made his way upriver to the bend he had described, which lay due south of Lake Pontchartrain. A thick forest covered it, home to alligators, muskrats, and mosquitoes. A well-worn Indian portage ran across a cypress swamp to the north, and the remains of an Indian village sat nearby.

New Orleans was founded in 1718 at a high spot on the riverbank in the current location of the French Quarter; the settlement was named for the French regent Philip II, the Duke of Orleans. The first official settlers arrived early in the year. Bienville's party reached the site in June with six heavily provisioned vessels. "There were thirty workmen, all convicts; six carpenters and four Canadians," wrote Jonathan Darby, an Englishman sent to manage one French concession along the river. "M. de Bienville cut the first cane. Mssers Pradel and Dreux the second . . . to open a passage through the dense canebrake from the river to the place where the barracks were to be. . . . The whole locality was a dense canebrake with only a small pathway leading from the Mississippi to the Bayou [now St. John] communicating with Lake Pontchartrain." One man stuck his knife into the soil underfoot and rousted an alligator. It rose, thrashing, out of the muck and terrified the party.

In 1721, French military engineer Adrien de Pauger laid out the settlement in a distinctive grid pattern built around a central square, the Place d'Armes—an attempt to impose some order on the chaotic surroundings.

It's not too harsh to say that the history of New Orleans and the delta region is a story of one kind of raw economic exploitation—often by distant powers—followed by another, interrupted by war and natural disasters, with only Mardi Gras to take the edge off. Humans develop complex relationships with the land. They shape and exploit it. More often than not they trash it. When the Europeans brought their rapacious economic empires to the lower Mississippi, they began a troubled and abusive relationship—one intertwined with New Orleans's long flirtation with disaster. Hurricanes and floods forced history, the economy, and the culture in new directions.

John Law, a notorious rake and gambler, was the first of a parade of speculators, businessmen, and corporate entities with designs on Louisiana's resources. In 1694, Law, a brilliant though dissolute twenty-two-year-old heir to a Scottish banking family, shot and killed a romantic rival in a duel in London's Bloomsbury Square. He was convicted of murder, imprisoned, and sentenced to death, but the authorities let him off, deciding to fine him instead. When the dead man's brother set about getting that decision overturned, Law fled to Amsterdam, and from there ambled about Europe for two decades, gambling and womanizing and ginning up financial schemes. But Law truly came into his own after moving to Paris in 1715. Thanks to his close friendship with the Duke of Orleans, Law embarked on a remarkable career.

First, Law devised a way to liquidate the heavy debts incurred by the late, free-spending Louis XIV via a bank, the Banque Generale, which he established to sell shares and issue credit. The duke was so pleased at the result that he put Law in charge of Louisiana. In 1717, Law bought out the firm overseeing trade in the colony and founded the Company of the West. In exchange for the monopoly, Law agreed to maintain French troops and to, essentially, summon from thin air a fully manned, smooth-running colony, transporting six thousand colonists and three thousand African slaves over the next twenty-five years.

Embarking on a feverish campaign to raise money and re- cruit colonists, Law painted the delta as a land of plenty in in- ternational advertising campaigns well ahead of their time. Thousands came, including groups of Germans from the Rhineland, tired of war with the French. When the flow dimin- ished, authorities in France resorted to another, more efficient recruiting technique: they conscripted criminals, reprobates, military deserters, prostitutes, and the poor and shipped them off to a place where they would likely never be heard from again—if they weren't killed by disease or drowned in a storm or a shipwreck. "By 1719, deportation to Louisiana had become a convenient way to get rid of troublesome neighbors or family members," historian Gwendolyn Midlo Hall wrote in the book *Africans in Colonial Louisiana*. "Some families asked for the de- portation of incorrigible sons, daughters, and nephews. Persons from all social milieux were denounced for their conduct, and police inquiries were held. Comments found in police files in- cluded, 'Here is a true subject for Louisiana.'"

Law's so-called Mississippi Scheme created a speculative bubble—one of the modern world's first. Law sold shares in the company for cash—and to the government in exchange for low- interest bonds. In the space of two years, the price of company shares shot from five hundred to fifteen thousand livres. Law took the capital inflows and expanded: he bought up rival trad- ing companies, forming a new venture, the Company of the In- dies. But later in the year, with results lacking, the shares' value plummeted, then collapsed. The Duke of Orleans dismissed Law and kicked him out of the country in 1721. He died penni- less in Venice in 1729.

Hurricanes struck and flooded the settlement in 1719, 1721, and 1722. Following the last of these, New Orleans and its surrounding communities—some dozens of miles away, a difficult journey by pirogue through swamps and cypress stands—were a mess. Huts could be rebuilt easily enough, but crops were destroyed during a time when the colonists were mightily struggling to make anything grow—let alone turn the profit that the company was demanding. Colonists in other Gulf Coast settlements grumbled that it had been a mistake to relocate the capital to such a dangerous spot.

Upriver along what was nicknamed the "German coast" because of its concentration of Rhinelanders, settlers were plowing up muck to plant vegetables to be sold downriver in New Orleans. The company had given them only a few crude tools and they could barely grow enough to feed themselves. But Louisiana's administrators had a solution. "The soil is so unrelenting in the lower portion of the colony that one must always have a hoe ready. The weeds grow so fast and so thick that, after a short time, it looks as if no work has been accomplished. The land is covered with tree trunks and stumps, and these people have no draft animals," read a 1724 census. "If these German families, the survivors of a much greater number, are not helped by Negroes in their work gradually they will perish."

Slaves from Africa and later Haiti and other Caribbean islands were the dominant presence in New Orleans from its earliest days, thanks to the desperate need for labor. The Company of the Indies had been reconstituted after Law's departure, and from 1721 to 1732, Louisiana's slave population increased from 533 to about 3,600, while the population of Europeans grew much more slowly, from 1,082 to 1,720. The French stopped the slave trade in 1730, but the Spanish revived it when they took over the colony in 1763. By 1788, a census showed there were 21,465 slaves in the region—half the population.

Meanwhile, after a decades-long lull in storm activity, hurricanes thrashed the Mississippi delta six times in ten years— 1772, 1778, twice in 1779, 1780, and 1781. The first storm drove ships at the mouth of the river aground in the marshes and cut new channels through eastern barrier islands protecting the city. The second wrecked small settlements south of the city along the river. The third, in June 1779, ripped off roofs and damaged most standing structures.

The fourth, on the morning of August 18, 1779, had, in its way, an international impact. The British—looking for any toehold they could find in North America to help put down the Revolution—had established a fort at Baton Rouge. Spain was determined to push them out. Governor Bernardo de Galvez had assembled a small armada and planned to sail upriver and attack on the twenty-second. But as the hurricane storm surge moved up the river, it picked up de Galvez's ships and smashed them against the riverbanks. Some floated clear into the marshes and cypress forests. Only one survived.

"Although the wind and the rain began on the night of the 17th, it was not until three o'clock in the morning that it attained its full violence, keeping its strength continually until ten o'clock in the morning, then it began to lose its force a little, but not until all the houses, barges, boats and pirogues were demolished, some with many people from these settlements," de Galvez wrote the day after the storm in a letter to a colleague.

> Others have gone aground, half destroyed and useless, stranded in the woods and finally, there are others of whose fate we are still ignorant. To aggravate the situation, the schooners and gunboats have also sunk. The village presents the most pitiful sight. There are but few houses which have not been destroyed, and there are so many wrecked to pieces; the fields have been leveled; the houses of the near villages, which are the only ones from which I have heard to this time, are all on the ground, in one word, crops, stock, provisions are all lost.

Though New Orleans was a wreck, de Galvez decided to move forward with his military plans. The colonists were unaware that de Galvez had just received confirmation that his provisional appointment as governor was to be made permanent. De Galvez went to the Place d'Armes and stood in front of the St. Louis Cathedral. According to one account, he announced this to a hastily assembled crowd: "I shall defend the province; but, although I am disposed to shed the last drop of my blood for Louisiana and for my king, I cannot take an oath which I may be expected to violate, because I do not know whether you will help me in resisting the ambitious designs of the English. What do you say? Shall I take the oath of governor? Shall I swear to defend Louisiana? Will you stand by me, and conquer or die with your governor and for your king?" He pulled out his new royal commission with a flourish and hoisted his sword—to thunderous cheers. De Galvez had his support, and ordered boats raised from the bottom of the lake and river, repaired, and restocked.

The Spanish mission launched only a week late and, drawing on farmer-soldiers from the German and Acadian coasts, drove the British from Baton Rouge a few weeks later. Nevertheless, de Galvez and his bosses were discouraged. The 1779 storm and those of the next two years were a familiar story: acres upon acres of tilled fields drowned, no structure left undamaged, a dazed population wondering if it was worth it. There was the usual second-guessing in customs houses, trading firms, and royal courts around the world. During the city's colonial period, levees (from the French word *lever,* to raise) were a local matter. Among the first things settlers did after the city's founding was to build a three-foot river levee. The colony later took on the responsibility of upkeep and raising the levee as needed. But outside New Orleans, the region's flood defenses were a patchwork. Colonial administrators assigned the task to private property owners, many of whom didn't do a good job. Still, by this time, many settlers had invested decades of their lives and weren't going easily.

In 1795, two events occurred that would conspire to turn the land around New Orleans into an agro-industrial zone—and make remolding the landscape to control floods essential.

That spring, a group of slaves on a sugar plantation in Pointe Coupee, upriver from Baton Rouge, spent months plotting a rebellion in the woods that surrounded the cane, rice, and indigo fields. Louisiana's slaves had developed a hidden culture in the area's woodlands and swamps. Sometimes with the leave of their owners, sometimes without, many traveled freely along backwoods paths and bayous, trading with the Indians, pirates, trappers, and freedmen who lived beyond the fringes of settlements. On this robust black market, slaves could get food, animals, and tools for their gardens, and find fellowship outside strict plantation rules. They could also trade news and information. The biggest news of the day was the French Revolution, begun in 1789. A slave revolt in Haiti was also underway. To someone living under the double yoke of slavery and colonial rule, revolution was a thrilling idea. Along with a small group of white supporters, the Pointe Coupee plotters aimed to abolish slavery in Spanish-ruled Louisiana.

Unfortunately for them, the rebellion was a bust. They torched some small buildings, but the plan was quickly foiled and all would-be revolutionaries arrested. Twenty-three slaves were hanged. Governor Francisco Luis Hector de Carondelet ordered their heads cut off and displayed on pikes at intervals downriver to New Orleans. After that, the governor cracked down, forbidding slaves to travel without permission from their masters. The revolt, along with several others around the same time, gave Louisiana's white leaders and their foreign overseers pause. Slaves, after all, outnumbered freemen.

Sixteen years later, a Haitian slave named Charles Deslondes led another rebellion just upriver from New Orleans. It was the biggest slave revolt in American history, involving about 140 men, most of them Haitians—and it was also crushed. As slaves marched along the River Road, setting sugarcane fields and plantation buildings on fire, planters called out their militia, who were joined by vigilantes. (A militia of black freemen also volunteered to help put down the revolt.) The two sides clashed outside New Orleans. With few guns, the slaves got the worst of it—sixty-six were killed, compared to only two whites. The heads of the captured rebels again ended up on pikes.

The Louisiana slave revolts became part of the mythos of

the Old South. White parents used the stories of them to strike fear into the hearts of their children. Plantation owners used them as a tool and an excuse for tightening the grip on slaves and expanding the harsh proto-industrial plantation system.

The same year as the failed Pointe Coupee revolt, a New Orleans gentleman planter named Jean Etienne de Bore reached the end of his patience—and his considerable fortune. For two years, de Bore had watched as insects devoured the indigo crop he was growing in neat rows in the reclaimed swamp outside New Orleans. Indigo was profitable but unreliable, and for de Bore this was the last straw. His response was an even bolder gamble: plant sugarcane on every square inch of his land.

It was a crazy scheme, and de Bore's wife, friends, and business associates told him so. Once cane was harvested and crushed, yielding a sweet, opaque juice, there was no quick and easy way to granulate sugar out of it—and thus no way to store it. But de Bore had hired an expert sugar maker from Haiti named Antoine Morin, and through trial and error, they found a way to boil the juice in a vacuum pan and condense granules from it. After the 1796 harvest, de Bore sold a hundred thousand pounds of sugar and some molasses for an astonishing twelve-thousand-dollar profit.

De Bore's invention turned the riverscape into an industrial engine for sugar. By dint of its economies of scale and its strategic location, Louisiana had a lock on the American sugar market. Within a decade, Louisiana had created the nation's first agro-industrial economy, richer and more sophisticated than the rival cotton industry. The sugar crop, of course, also depended entirely on slave labor. Louisiana's slave population tripled to more than one hundred thousand between 1810 and 1830, outpacing the white population. Slaves worked in punishing, difficult jobs that could ruin a man in the space of a few years. Cane had to be cut with a knife, and a missed slash could slice off a thumb or a limb and even kill a man. Crushing and refining machinery frequently broke down, sometimes exploding and spraying molten syrup and metal in every direction. Louisiana's sugar plantations were seen as the worst lot for a slave, and spawned the phrase "sold down the river."

The nineteenth century's first major storm struck as the United States—New Orleans's latest overseer, following the 1803 Louisiana Purchase—was preparing for another war with the British. New Orleans was no longer just a remote and tenuous foothold in the swamp. It had triumphed over its disadvantages to become something more: one of the biggest and boldest cities in America, a leaping-off point between the unexplored interior and the wider, civilized world. But it was also on edge. The British coveted their former colonies and were a constant presence in North American seas and waterways. As war began in June 1812, residents fretted that the British would try to seize the city with their far superior navy.

The first hurricane, in June, sideswiped the city. The second was a killer.

The winds began rattling the rafters around eleven o'clock the night of August 19. The river quickly rose. Though the city now had a substantial earthen levee, the great mass of water from the surge washed a section of it out and gushed through muddy streets, rising over dozens of newly constructed homes and shops. (As the city expanded, prime real estate along the river had been settled, and the new neighborhoods sat in low-lying areas.) The floodwaters ran downhill into the swamp that remained between the city and the lake, then flowed north and eastward around the back of the French Quarter. Much of the city flooded, except for the Quarter and the settled bank of the Mississippi upriver along the crescent.

The flood left the city wide open to enemy ships or boats. The storm pummeled and scattered American naval forces in the river and Lake Pontchartrain and in outlying lakes and bayous. Rumors spread that the British had seized Fort St. Philip, the principal American outpost near the mouth of the river—though it too was under water.

Luckily for the city, British ships in the Gulf were widely dispersed and they took losses during the storm as well. Occupied elsewhere, the British held back and did not try to seize New Orleans for another two years. Troops led by Andrew Jackson turned them back in the Battle of New Orleans, which actually took place a few miles downriver from the city, in Chalmette.

In spite of the risks, sugar and river traffic continued to bring money and people to Louisiana. The river was a busy thoroughfare—rowboats, pirogues, sailing ships, and barges, then steam-driven paddle wheelers and ferries, all plied its waters. Waves of immigrants—blacks from Haiti and the Caribbean, Cajuns from French Canada, and later the Irish—created a unique, at times volatile mixture. Voodoo cults practiced openly, and concerned city officials tried regulating them rather than trying to stamp them out. Ritual dances were restricted to a single spot at the edge of the French Quarter that became known as Congo Square. The city's multiracial mélange—created by a century of French, Spanish, Caribbean, and African residents living in close quarters—made for odd hierarchies. Light-skinned free women of color were the prize at Quadroon Balls, where white men could meet them and select one to be a mistress luxuriously maintained in a French Quarter apartment. The women had to be just the right shade of café au lait: no one with more than a quarter African descent could participate in the balls. Carnival, which had been celebrated since the French arrived, evolved into a bigger, grander affair, with sumptuous masked balls and parades through the streets by secretive social clubs called krewes. Members of the city's white business elite founded the first, the Mistick Krewe of Comus, in 1856 and staged their first parade the next year.

Even before Bienville's arrival, fishermen and trappers had been building shacks on ridges and along bayous, homesteading on the marshy prairies. Soon the marshes had a new purpose: recreation. Wealthy plantation owners and the New Orleans elite—its bankers and shippers—began building vacation homes and resorts to the south of the city. Most of these spots could be reached only by boat. They offered cooler breezes and quiet in the summertime, and access to the delta's few beaches.

The places had a dreamy quality, the wedding-cake filigrees of their porches and balconies rising out of the flat blue green marshes, their crisply dressed Negro staffs offering vacationers all the comforts of the big city.

Marshes provided New Orleans with some protection, but closer to the Gulf that buffer all but disappeared. The night of August 10, 1856, an enormous hurricane struck Last Island, a resort on the outermost lip of the delta, due south of New Orleans. For several days, Last Island's four hundred vacationers had been transfixed by unsettled yet undeniably pleasant weather—bright sunshine, gusty winds, big swells, and a heavy chop on the normally placid Gulf waters. The hurricane—probably a Category 4 with sustained winds above 135 mph and one of the strongest ever to strike the United States—whipped the village with rain and wind all day Sunday. Overnight, the storm surge rolled over the island, turning its placid shell-lined streets into a raging maelstrom, washing out the road and the mud and sand underneath it, cleaving the island in two within hours. Almost two hundred people drowned or were crushed by wreckage propelled through the water by hundred-mile-per-hour winds. According to one account, a boat sent to evacuate guests foundered and capsized, though some people survived by climbing up onto its shipwrecked hull. By morning, the storm was gone—and with it the island itself.

Reverend Robert McAllister, a twenty-five-year-old assistant pastor at a Presbyterian church in Thibodaux, about twenty miles northwest of the island, was staying in a guesthouse. He and eleven others crouched in the center hallway as the winds rose. They huddled as the roof and walls disintegrated around them and blew away, then lay there for hours in the driving rain. A maid, who had earlier denied accusations of stealing, confessed: above the wind she screamed out a list of items she had pinched, including coffee, lard, liver, and hams. After nightfall they saw water approaching from the south and the north, so they crawled to a nearby levee and grabbed on to a decaying wooden frame of a child's windmill and rode out the flood. When they staggered back to the village the next morning, nothing remained except scraps of wood and half-buried bodies. McAllister wrote:

> The jewelled and lily hand of a woman was seen pro-
> truding from the sand, and pointing toward heaven; farther,
> peered out from the ground, as if looking up to us, the regu-
> lar features of a beautiful girl who had, no doubt, but a few
> hours before, blushed at the praise of her own loveliness,
> and again, the dead bodies of husband and wife, so relatively
> placed as to show that constant until death did them part,
> the one had struggled to save the other. And, more affecting
> still, there was the form of a sweet babe even yet embraced
> by the stiff and bloodless arms of a mother. Sights like these
> suddenly presented, gave a shock never to be forgotten, and
> called up certain feelings which no language can describe.
> There were about one hundred houses on the island; not one
> was left, nay not a sill nor sleeper, not any part of their foun-
> dations to indicate that buildings had once been there.

What remained were memories of what had been, and perhaps a sign of what was to come. According to one account,
maybe apocryphal, guests at the island's hotel staged an elaborate dance as the storm raged outside. Last Island would thus
live on after the storm—a symbol of the waning days of the ante-
bellum South, its traditions and self-absorption about to be
swept away.

Chapter 2

RIVER AND STORM

HURRICANES POUNDED NEW ORLEANS again and again during its early years. Other misfortunes struck, too—in 1788, three quarters of the town burned down. But as the nineteenth century dawned, New Orleans was still there. It wasn't so much the courage of its inhabitants as basic logistics: there just wasn't much to destroy. In its early years, New Orleans consisted of four shell-lined mud tracks running parallel to the river and nine perpendicular, bounded by the river and the forest. If a storm hit, the city could be repaired and rebuilt within months, usually better than ever.

But that soon changed. After the 1803 Louisiana Purchase, that soupy backwater grew into one of the largest and greatest cities in America. Its population swelled from eight thousand to almost three hundred thousand and its neighborhoods spread west along the riverbank and then north into the cypress swamps. The newly settled areas lay low and flooded easily. As the river rose every spring, New Orleanians got the jitters.

On May 5, 1816, a break in a plantation river levee upriver sent water gushing into New Orleans. It spread for miles, inundating newer neighborhoods before stopping at Dauphine Street at the edge of the old city. A later map of the flood shows much of New Orleans under water, the curving line of the flood stopping just a few blocks short of the high ground along the riverbank. Another levee broke upriver on May 4, 1849, and over the next ten days the water crept slowly eastward, covering two hundred city blocks and forcing twelve thousand people to evacuate. During that flood, when the water had reached the levee along one of the city's main drainage canals, residents realized the water would start to pool next to the earthen wall and rise over their homes. Already snakes and alligators were slithering through the streets. People gathered shovels and picks and prepared to break the wall open, hoping they could drain the backlog. Before the still-dry neighbors across the canal could do anything, the levee collapsed on its own.

Clearly, something had to be done. The job fell to the Army Corps of Engineers.

The Corps was the nation's engineering brain trust—a place where science, ingenuity, and Manifest Destiny butted up against America's geographical sweep and the power of nature. Its number-one mission was navigation: river channels had to be wide and deep enough to allow ships and barges to pass. The Mississippi posed the most famous of the Corps's confrontations. For tens of thousands of years the river had done what it pleased, shifting its course this way and that, carving out new channels, building new delta lobes. But by the nineteenth century, the nation's future depended on bringing those forces to heel. If ports were going to stay open for business, the flooding that plagued New Orleans and other cities along the river had to be stopped.

The Corps had an august history dating to the Revolutionary War. George Washington believed that his army's success depended on the ability to design and build fortifications to repel larger enemy forces. In June 1775, Congress authorized the appointment of a chief engineer and two assistants when it created the Continental Army. The following February, Washington besieged the British at Boston. He and his war council decided to seize Dorchester Heights across from Boston Harbor—the high ground that would let them bombard the city. Their plan depended on surprise. In a single night, the Continental forces snuck over to the heights and erected a fort, constructing wood frames filled with bundles of sticks designed by Colonel Rufus Putnam, the chief engineer. When the British awoke the next day, they were stunned to find themselves staring down the barrels of rebel cannon. They soon gave up and left Boston, humiliated.

Four years later, Congress created the Army Corps of Engineers, recruiting many of its experts from France. The modern organization was formally established in 1802 and given the job overseeing the new military academy at West Point. In the decades that followed, the Corps took on new, distinctly nonmilitary tasks. It would fortify a vast country's borders in war, but also ease navigation and stimulate commerce, protect coastal settlements from the sea and river ports from spring floods.

In Louisiana, Corps engineers hired civilian contractors to build defenses at strategic sites around New Orleans and began looking at ways to improve river navigation. Congress had initially resisted getting involved in levee construction, correctly fearing it would end up paying through the nose for generations. But New Orleans and other growing ports were demanding action, as were shipping and trade firms. In 1811, the first steamboat arrived in New Orleans. By 1850, there were 187 of them operating on the lower Mississippi. In September of that year, Congress set aside fifty-thousand dollars for a "topographical and hydrographical survey of the Delta of the Mississippi, with such investigations as may lead to determine the most practicable plan for securing it from inundation."

The river levees, it turned out, were a big part of the problem. They constrained the river flow, so spring floods rose higher. They also cut off the regular deposits of sediment that spread over the delta each spring. Instead, silt was building up in the passes out to the Gulf. Oceangoing steamships that tried to reach New Orleans were running aground on the sandbars—forty alone in 1852. Congress also wanted a permanent, twenty-foot-deep channel, if it could be constructed and maintained.

The assignment was split between two men—Andrew A. Humphreys of the Corps and Charles S. Ellet Jr., an independent civilian engineer. Ellet turned in his assessment fewer than two years after getting the job. Though sketchy—he had not bothered to collect much data—his report contained a brilliant intuitive leap. Ellet suggested treating the river gingerly. Levees should be fortified, he wrote, but should be supplemented with diversions and reservoirs to take some of the pressure off during high water.

Humphreys, scion of an aristocratic family of engineers (his grandfather had designed the revolutionary vessel "Old Ironsides"), was brilliant, ambitious, and arrogant, and had been looking for a career-making assignment. Now, with one finally at hand, Ellet had beaten him to the punch. But the assignment offered Humphreys the last word and he decided that word must refute Ellet—utterly. So Humphreys devoted years to the project. Aided by a young engineer, Henry Abbott, Humphreys ultimately spent eleven years visiting sites along the river, sampling the muck, calculating. His final recommendation was simpler than Ellet's. He believed levees alone could solve the problem.

If levees were high enough, and fortified enough, Humphreys argued, they could stop flooding. That would direct more water downstream, and the river would rise higher and flow faster. The extra drag on the bottom would wash the channel clear—solving the navigation problem. The most obvious drawback was that higher levees also meant the water between them could rise higher—making for a potentially more dangerous flood season. And if a crevasse formed, the game was up. (Humphreys also wanted to build a channel bypassing the river mouth altogether—a plan that became a reality a century later.)

The competing plans were put on hold during the Civil War. Humphreys's reckless thirst for enemy blood and battle turned him into a war hero, and in 1866 he was appointed commander of the Corps. Ellet was killed in the war, and with his passing, his plans—far ahead of their time—were left with no support. Humphreys was also doomed to be frustrated, though. He was again supplanted, this time by James Buchanan Eads, civilian engineer, who proposed building jetties along the Mississippi's southwest pass—making the channel even narrower and faster. He was awarded the contract over Humphreys's objections.

Humphreys soon retired into obscurity. But his "levees-only" theory would reverberate for more than a century. Since 1850, when the government had given the green light to states to sell off swampland to pay for levee construction, levees had been good business. Developers filled in swamps and turned them into farmland, then demanded higher levees to protect the fields. More swamps were developed. Damming off tributaries and locking up the river behind ever-higher walls accelerated the cycle. With taller walls and fewer outlets, the river crested higher every year. But because of the short-term financial incentives, the levees-only movement had the backing of every farm and business interest in the Mississippi Valley.

The river levees were hulking walls of earth, thirty feet high in spots, with gentle grassy slopes falling away from a flat crown, sometimes spanning a width of two hundred feet. A wide buffer zone called a *batture* sat between the levee's base and the river, typically planted with trees to reduce scour during high water. In the early years, slave labor built the levees. After the Civil War black laborers continued to do most of the work, often in appalling conditions. During high water in 1912, an engineer in Mississippi ran out of sandbags. He ordered his workers, Negro convicts, to lie along the top of the levee. "The black men obeyed, and although spray frequently dashed over them, they prevented the overflow that might have developed into an ugly crevasse," the *New York Times* reported approvingly. "For an hour and a half this lasted, until the additional sandbags arrived."

The levees' simple appearance was deceptive. They were the result of a meticulous engineering process that took many possible contingencies into account: the maximum anticipated high water; the speed and force a flood stage would apply to the levee surface; a flood's possible months-long duration. Engineers studied and fortified each bend in the river, knowing that shifting momentum would press the flowing river against the outer bank, making the water flow higher and faster, exerting tremendous force. They paid special attention to the density and character of the soil, which they dug from the riverbank. Floodwater not only pressed against a levee, it penetrated and saturated it, weakening the structure at its core. Weeks of high water would gradually soften and wear away at a levee until pieces were sloughing off. Small, hard-to-find irregularities—stray bits of rotting wood, animal carcasses—could provide avenues for river water that would start bubbling up to the soil's surface on the other side. Soon the flow would begin to carry off soil particles from inside the levee. Then with a rumble a large section would shift, soil sliding over soil along a plane or an arc. The river would blast through the gap with a roar, taking tons of soil with it as it opened a widening crevasse.

Understanding the dynamics of river flooding seemed an ideal challenge for nineteenth-century engineers. It was, after all, a mechanistic problem, with variables that could be measured: rainfall, river flow, the deposition of sediments in the Gulf, the progress of a flood crest as it moved downstream. Those numbers could in turn be plugged into equations to shape levees and dredge channels. But the arithmetic could go only so far. To people without satellites, computers, or even reliable measures of wind and waves, hurricanes were acts of God, impossible to anticipate or control. Cyclones roared in off the sea without warning. Winds blew in one direction, then another, then stopped, then started again. And in New Orleans, water could rise suddenly anywhere around the city—in Lake Pontchartrain, Lake Borgne to the east, over the southern marshes—or in the river itself. Prediction seemed impossible.

Institutions and entire fields of study sprang up around river flooding. But before the twentieth century, hurricanes belonged to no single discipline, not even meteorology. Over the centuries, the subject of storms attracted more seafarers, civil servants, and amateur scientists than PhDs. Slowly, at times only through luck, they developed a picture of how intense weather worked and how raging, whirling cyclones behaved. It took another intuitive leap to understand storm surges—and the destruction of another great American city, Galveston—before scientists and governments could begin to devise a possible defense against them.

In October 1743, thirty-seven-year-old Benjamin Franklin was a printer and pamphleteer, the publisher of *Poor Richard's*

Almanack, the newly appointed postmaster of Philadelphia, and—though he had not yet begun his experiments with electricity—an avid scientist. The evening of October 21, a nor'easter thwarted Franklin's plan to observe a lunar eclipse. "Before 8 a Storm blew up at N.E. and continued violent all Night and all next Day, the Sky thick clouded, dark and rainy, so that neither Moon nor Stars could be seen. The Storm did a great deal of Damage all along the Coast," he wrote to his friend Jared Eliot, fellow Revolutionary-era polymath—a clergyman, physician, agronomist, and scientist—in 1750.

Franklin was puzzled when he read later newspaper accounts of the eclipse, and wrote his brother in Boston for clarification. He confirmed that astronomers there had indeed observed the eclipse at nine p.m. and that the storm arrived about an hour later. In the 1700s, people thought clouds, storms, and fair weather moved only along the same pathways and direction as the wind. Franklin's data made no sense: a nor'easter should move southwest, with its prevailing winds, not north. It should have struck Boston before Philadelphia.

In his later letter to Eliot, Franklin attempted to make sense of the seemingly inconsistent observations. He rapidly sketched the basic ideas that animate every TV weather forecast today— that hot air rises and denser cool air falls, that pressure gradients make wind move independently of a storm's path:

> Suppose a great Tract of Country, Land and Sea, to wit Florida and the Bay of Mexico, to have clear Weather for several Days, and to be heated by the Sun and its Air thereby exceedingly rarified; Suppose the Country North Eastward, as Pensilvania, New England, Nova Scotia, Newfoundland, &c. to be at the same time cover'd with Clouds, and its Air chill'd and condens'd. The rarified Air being lighter must rise, and the Dense Air next to it will press into its Place; that will be follow'd by the next denser Air, that by the next, and so on. Thus when I have a Fire in my Chimney, there is a Current of Air constantly flowing from the Door to the Chimney: but the beginning of the Motion was at the Chim-

ney, where the Air being rarified by the Fire, rising, its Place
was supply'd by the cooler Air that was next to it, and the
Place of that by the next, and so on to the Door.

In one paragraph, Franklin debunked the idea of a storm as
a kind of supernatural entity with its wind and rain moving along
a straight line, as if blown by a heavenly mouth with fat cheeks.
His image of a storm as a heat pump anticipated the modern
understanding of hurricanes. But with limited meteorologic
tools, the insight was more theoretical than practical.

William Dunbar, a Scottish explorer, farmer, and scientist, took
notes of his observations as he hunkered down in New Orleans
during the hurricane of 1779—the storm that sank Governor
Galvez's fleet. The wind and rain went on for hours, Dunbar
wrote later,

> after which succeeded all at once a most profound and awful
> calm, so inconceivably terrific that the stoutest heart stood ap-
> palled and could not look upon it without feeling a secret hor-
> ror, as if nature were preparing to resolve herself again into
> chaos. . . . [Then] in 5 or 6 minutes, perhaps less, the hurri-
> cane began to blow from the opposite point of the compass
> and very speedily regained a degree of fury and impetuosity
> equal if not superior to what it had before possessed.

Dunbar had, of course, been in the eye of the storm. Piecing
his observations together, he envisioned the storm as a huge
whirlwind moving along a path. "It is probable that as similar observations are made upon all hurricanes, tornadoes and whirlwinds, they will be found universally to consist of a vortex with a
central spot in a state of profound calm, which spot will probably be greater or less according to the magnitude of the vortex,"
he wrote in an 1801 paper, one of the first to describe the true
form of a hurricane. Dunbar didn't get everything right. His paper speculated that the eye formed when mysterious "electrical
fluid" was wicked away from it, forming a kind of vacuum. But

Dunbar's insight was a piece of a puzzle that scientists, military strategists, and ship's captains were slowly assembling. With armadas and merchant vessels crowding the shipping lanes, success and survival depended on divining the "law of storms." Greater understanding couldn't come too soon: a year after Dunbar's leap, the deadliest hurricane in history tore across the Caribbean, smashing many ships to kindling. Some twenty-two thousand people died, perhaps eight thousand on ships. The British fleet, jousting with French ships in the Antilles, lost twelve ships; more than one hundred British merchant vessels also sank. An English scout sent to Barbados to inspect the wreckage assumed an earthquake had accompanied the hurricane. Later the same month, three more storms killed thousands more.

With meticulous observation and deduction, William Redfield clarified things further. Redfield, another amateur scientist, whose day jobs included apprentice saddlemaker, door-to-door salesman, and businessman, was traveling in Connecticut in the summer of 1821 when a hurricane blew through. Redfield noticed that trees and branches felled by the wind pointed in different directions depending on what part of the state he was visiting. That anomalous fact stuck in his head. A decade later, following a chance conversation on the subject with Yale scientist Denison Olmstead on a ferry plying Long Island Sound, he tried to solve the mystery. Using books, newspaper accounts, and interviews, Redfield reconstructed the course of the 1821 storm. He traced the storm from its Caribbean origins along its course shadowing the East Coast, then over New York City and into Connecticut. He held off from publicizing his findings until he had more evidence, which he got by meticulously reconstructing a second storm, this time using the logbooks of 164 ships.

"All violent gales or hurricanes are great whirlwinds, in which the wind blows in circuits round an axis; that the winds move not in horizontal circles, but rather in spirals," he wrote in a paper published in the *American Journal of Science*. "That the velocity of rotation increases from the margin toward the center of a storm. That the whole body of air is, at the same time, moving forward in a path, at a variable rate, but always with a velocity much less than its velocity of rotation."

As Redfield was outlining the dynamic shape of a hurricane, meteorologist James Espy identified some of the internal dynamics. Like Franklin, Espy saw the storm as a heat pump: as he explained in his *Philosophy of Storms,* water, warmed by the sun and entering the atmosphere, gets caught in a kind of self-reinforcing, amplifying loop. As it evaporates from the surface of the ocean, it cools off and begins condensing into rain. But this cooling releases energy, which warms up the air again, causing more evaporation. Under the tropical sun and with the right combination of breezes, warm water vapor feeds into this system and it grows into a hurricane. (Espy and Redfield tangled over the nature of hurricane winds. Espy argued they blew straight into the center of the vortex. Redfield correctly countered that they spun around it, never reaching the center.)

Redfield's idea bounced quickly around the seagoing world, where it sparked shocks of recognition. Colonel William Reid of the British Royal Engineers began writing to Redfield after he was dispatched to Barbados to help reconstruct colonial settlements in the wake of an 1831 storm that killed 1,477 people. Frustrated at the lack of data about the hurricane, Reid followed Redfield's example and set about gathering more. He read local government records and ships' logs, trying to extract stray bits of information on timing, wind direction, and flooding. In 1841 he published a book called *The Law of Storms* that included, among other things, a detailed reconstruction of the Great Hurricane of 1780.

Reid's book was, in turn, the talk of the South Seas. It inspired ship's captain Henry Piddington to write *The Sailor's Horn Book for the Law of Storms.* Piddington, who coined the term "cyclone" for storms with winds blowing around an eye, offered practical advice for sailors, suggesting a storm's outermost winds could put a fresh breeze in their sails that they could ride to safety. He identified a hurricane's right front quadrant as its most dangerous area. There, the direction of winds blowing around the center coincides with the storm's forward motion. If the wind speed of the storm is 100 mph, and the storm is moving forward at 20 mph, then the speeds along its right quadrant will be added together, making a total of 120 mph.

Despite these advances, predicting a hurricane remained an impossible task. That began to change in 1844, when Samuel F. B. Morse and a partner demonstrated the telegraph for the first time in America. Morse's telegraph involved physically breaking an electric circuit at one end of a wire to produce observable changes at the other end. Suddenly, information could travel almost instantly over great distances. Monitoring the weather in real time would finally be possible.

Ten years later, a major storm struck the Black Sea, where the French and British were laying siege to the Russian fleet at Sebastopol. Huge waves wrecked thirty-seven ships and left the attacking forces short of clothing and food as a harsh winter set in. The next year, French emperor Napoleon III dispatched his chief astronomer, Urbain Le Verrier, a brilliant scientist who had postulated the existence of the then-undiscovered Neptune by observing a slight wobble in the orbits of other planets. He was to study the disaster and figure out ways to avoid a repeat. With surprising speed, he gathered data from ships' logs and drew what he called a "synoptic map"—a detailed picture of the storm over several days. The map resembled a modern weather map, with intensifying pressure gradients drawn tightly together and winds circulating around a low.

Le Verrier figured that if the behavior of weather could be observed in such detail, then it could be analyzed and predicted. Napoleon III agreed. Telegraph cables were being laid and stations were sprouting up around Europe, and he commissioned a telegraph system devoted to the weather. Within two years it covered much of Europe. In 1860, a Dutch meteorologist issued the first weather warning based on information from this telegraph web for a North Sea storm.

In the midst of the Civil War, the United States took a while longer to get its own weather warning systems up and running. By 1869, Cleveland Abbe, the director of the Mitchell Astronomical Observatory in Cincinnati, set up the nation's first weather telegraphy service and made the first semiofficial weather forecast. Abbe's "probabilities," issued for the eastern states, weren't that reliable, but they were better than nothing. ("It is probable that the low pressure in Missouri will make itself felt decidedly tomorrow with northerly winds and clouds on the Lakes, and brisk southerly winds on the Gulf," read one of his first.) And with them, a line had been crossed: prediction of the weather was now officially deemed possible, with increased accuracy assumed to be on the horizon.

By the start of the twentieth century, meteorology had established its scientific legitimacy and the U.S. Weather Bureau had set up posts around the United States. But forecasting hurricanes was still hit or miss. Some experts, such as Cuban priest and academic Benito Vines, drew on detailed histories to predict where storms might go. But most of the time, hurricanes still seemed to have minds of their own, and their most unpredictable element and greatest threat was a storm surge. Nineteenth-century hydrologists knew a lot about waves. But a storm surge was no ordinary wave, as the residents of Galveston found out in September 1900.

They thought they knew hurricanes. After all, Galveston's fortunes had risen when one struck the nearby port city of Indianola in 1875. They rose further when another hit the same spot eleven years later, driving many Indianola residents out for good. Galveston picked up the slack and became a bustling port for cotton and other goods, with dozens of ships calling each week; its traffic was second only to New Orleans's. Galveston's population reached thirty-five thousand as the end of the nineteenth century approached, all living on the tip of a barrier island on the Gulf at the entrance to a large bay, with an elevation no more than nine feet above sea level at its highest point.

The 1875 and 1886 storms had caused some flooding in town, and some residents had pushed to build a seawall to protect the city from storm waves. But in July 1891, days after a tropical storm flooded city streets, Weather Bureau meteorolo-

gist Isaac Cline brought the best scientific knowledge of the day
to bear on the problem in two articles published by the *Galveston News*. A seawall was unnecessary, he declared, explaining
that "the opinion held by some, which are unacquainted with
the actual conditions of things, that Galveston will at some time
be seriously damaged by some such disturbance, is simply an
absurd delusion and can only have its origin in imagination and
not from reasoning. . . . It would be impossible for any cyclone
to create a storm wave which could materially injure the city."

Cline was an industrious Victorian-era scientist, a hoarder of
weather data and relentless seeker of insights into the way the
world worked. He had been an early recruit to the Army Signal
Corps's weather service, joining after graduating from medical
school. He had found that weather and its public health effects
were more interesting to him than treating patients. He became
a rising star in the Weather Bureau, determined to make better,
faster forecasts. After postings in the Texas towns of Fort Con-
cho and Abilene, he had moved to Galveston in 1888 to take
over the newly established weather observation post.

Cline felt that the Texas coast was safe because hurricanes
barreling into the Gulf from the West Indies would weaken well
before they reached Texas. If one did strike, he reasoned, the island's beaches and the gradual slope of the Gulf floor would
dampen the storm surge. Whatever washed into the town would
then recede like water off a duck's back, running into the bay
and the flat Texas lowlands.

In early September 1900, a powerful storm—now believed to be
a Category 4 hurricane with winds exceeding 135 mph—moved
west toward Texas. The Weather Bureau received sketchy reports about a tropical storm in the Gulf, but had no clear picture
of its location or course. As the storm passed the Mississippi
delta on September 6, the steamship *Louisiana* ran into high
winds and seas and its barometer plummeted. The captain estimated that the winds had hit 150 mph. Forecasters disagreed
about what would happen next, with some maintaining that the

storm would head to the northeast, and others predicting a westward course. The bureau issued storm warnings for the coast down to Galveston.

Few worried in Galveston, where all appeared normal until the early morning hours of September 8, when water began creeping up the beach against a stiff offshore breeze. Summoned to the beach at about five a.m. by his brother Joseph, who worked for him, Cline saw that if the wind shifted and the water kept rising, the city would be threatened. "Unusually heavy swells from the southeast, intervals of one to five minutes, overflowing low places south portion of city three to four blocks from beach. Such high water with opposing winds never observed previously," he telegrammed his bosses in Washington.

Cline later wrote that he hitched up a horse to a two-wheeled cart and rolled through the streets, warning residents to move to higher ground. He claimed to have saved six thousand people, but given Cline's long-standing skepticism about the risk of storm surges, this account has been questioned. Author Erik Larson wrote in *Isaac's Storm* that he could find no eyewitness accounts of Cline's urgent warnings to townspeople, and that he had stubbornly clung to his original assertion about the city's safety until it was too late. In any case, the fault was not the Cline brothers' alone: they had sent reports to Washington every two hours, but the Weather Bureau never issued a hurricane warning. At three thirty p.m. the telegraph lines went out, but Joseph used the last working telephone line to relay information to a telegraph station in Houston. Then that line went dead.

Isaac, meanwhile, waded through hip-deep water back to his own house. He had fortified his home against hurricane winds, and about fifty neighbors had taken refuge there. But by evening, the water was neck deep in the street when Joseph returned and urged the neighbors to escape to the relative high ground at the city's center. Across the city, thousands were facing the same choice—risk drowning by moving through the streets, or be crushed by wreckage as homes ripped apart.

At about seven thirty the water suddenly rose an additional four feet in the space of a few seconds. "I was standing at my front door, which was partly open, watching the water, which was flowing with great rapidity from east to west," Isaac wrote. "The water at this time was about eight inches deep in my residence, and the sudden rise of 4 feet brought it above my waist before I could change my position." Houses dislodged from their foundations broke up and floated by. A piece of railroad trestle a quarter-mile long lodged against Isaac's home and swells began pounding it against the wall, again and again. The house broke up around them. Cline's wife, Cora, was pulled underneath the wreckage and drowned. The storm surge had raised the water to a height of fifteen feet above sea level, more than enough to cover Galveston. Cline, his three daughters, and his brother clung to floating timbers for the next three hours. They thought they'd be swept out to sea, but they came to rest on a piece of high ground about three hundred yards away. The city was destroyed.

The water receded, but the storm itself did not stop—weakened, it veered sharply northeastward across the country, eventually hitting Lake Erie, where it sank two ships. By September 12 it had moved out toward the North Atlantic, where it thrashed Canada's Maritime provinces, killing as many as one hundred people, then continued east, where dozens of ships sank, including nine schooners from the tiny French islands of St. Pierre et Miquelon, off the coast of Newfoundland, drowning 120—every fisherman.

All told, more than eight thousand people died in Galveston. The vast majority drowned. Others were crushed in the maelstrom of water and wreckage. Some were buried alive under huge piles of debris, but with 3,600 homes wrecked, rescuers reached few of these victims in time. The huge number of bodies presented major public health problems. At first the dead were dumped out at sea. But then the bodies began washing back ashore, and authorities resorted to burning the dead and debris together. Funeral pyres dotted the city for months afterward, turning the air black and acrid.

In a September 28 report, Cline admitted he had been wrong about the danger of storm surges and the need for a seawall: "I believe that a sea wall, which would have broken the swells, would have saved much loss of both life and property. I base this view upon observations which I have made in the extreme northeastern portion of the city, which is practically protected by the south jetty; this part of the city did not suffer more than half the damage that other similarly located districts, without protection, sustained."

Less than a year later, Cline was promoted and transferred to New Orleans. There, he took charge of the new Gulf states office of the Weather Bureau, one of only three regional offices. In his autobiography, Cline wrote that the transfer also had something to do with the fact that the New Orleans *Times-Democrat* had been publishing a daily column comparing the previous day's forecast to the actual weather—mocking the Weather Bureau for its failures. After his arrival the forecasts improved and the newspaper spiked the column. Cline quickly settled into life in the city, riding the St. Charles Avenue streetcar to work and opening a small shop on St. Peters Street in the French Quarter called the Art House, where he indulged his hobby of collecting paintings, glassware, and historical knick-knacks, and spent his spare time restoring paintings.

Cline tried to put his Galveston experience to use and began to study the unique problems New Orleans faced: river floods and storm surges. With more observations, he believed he could develop an accurate picture of a hurricane's effects on the sea.

Like all beachgoers, he knew big waves cannot abide the shallows: when they come near the shore they break and recede. Though this looks intuitively obvious, it depends on a subtle dynamic between water, wind, and the ocean bottom. As wind blows across the surface of the ocean, its friction kicks up waves—pulses of energy moving through the sea, making the water bob up and down. A wave runs out of space as it moves into the shallows. Like someone tripping on a landing, it tips forward and starts dragging along the bottom. Under normal conditions, the wave breaks and the water it has carried to shore flows back out. But when a hurricane pushes a wave toward shore, there isn't enough time or space for it all to flow back out. In such cases, the sea level rises, a phenomenon called wave setup. In the Gulf's shallow waters, though, wave setup wasn't a huge factor, so clearly something else was going on to bring so much water into Galveston so quickly.

In 1915, after much additional observation and theorizing, Cline got to test some of his new ideas. Those intervening years had seen the invention and spread of another new technology—radio—and forecasters could now use hundreds of additional nodes in the information web. Unlike telegraph stations, radios could move around. Ships at sea could send information about storms in real time to their brethren and forecasters. That meant creating an accurate map of a hurricane as it developed was possible. Shipboard radio rooms equipped with the latest spark-gap transmitters had become mandatory after the *Titanic* sank in 1912. (The wireless operator on the SS *Californian,* a nearby ship, had attempted to warn *Titanic* about ice ahead, but the doomed ship's radio man was busy contacting a land station. The *Californian's* operator went off duty at eleven p.m., forty minutes before the *Titanic* struck an iceberg. Thus the only ship close enough to save *Titanic* passengers was out of radio communication until the next morning, hours after most had drowned or died of hypothermia.)

With this ever-expanding trove of data and his own observations, Cline arrived at a clearer understanding of hurricanes, realizing that a storm surge was something different from the wind-driven waves he had once thought inconsequential. A storm surge was an entity unto itself—a giant wave that moved over open water with the storm. Cline hypothesized that a storm surge formed to the right of a hurricane's eye in its northeastern quadrant—the area where whirlwinds and forward speed work together. Over open water, the surge would be barely detectable. But when it moved closer to shore, it could rise up by a dozen feet or more, depending on the lay of the land. This gradual process begins in the days before a storm makes landfall, and Cline believed that such abnormal storm tides would allow him to pinpoint where a hurricane would come ashore.

In late September 1915, the strongest hurricane since 1900 entered the eastern Gulf. Cline sifted through weather reports

passed on to him from the Weather Bureau, but was more interested in the differences in tidal data at gauge stations all along
the Gulf Coast and from two instrumentation stations he had
personally installed on Swan Island, off the coast of Honduras,
and Cape San Antonio, on the coast of Cuba. The gauge stations
showed the tide had risen and then fallen at Galveston, but that
it was continuing to rise along the Louisiana coast.

Cline calculated that the storm was a major hurricane and
that it was bearing straight for New Orleans by way of Barataria
Bay due south of the city. He was right; the eye of the storm
passed directly overhead, and the lowest barometric reading
(the atmospheric pressure, inversely proportional to a storm's
strength) from a hurricane at that time, 28.11, was recorded at
Tulane University. Homes in the Bucktown settlement at Lake
Pontchartrain were inundated, and the *Times-Picayune* reported
that the surge had carved a new outlet for the 17th Street
drainage canal. Cline later reported that the storm produced a
surge of thirteen feet in western Lake Pontchartrain and nine to
eleven feet along the Mississippi coast. Local newspapers and
the Weather Bureau proclaimed Cline a hero for sending mes-
sengers by boat and horseback to coastal communities in southeast Louisiana, warning of the hurricane's imminent landfall.

While Cline's insights into storm surges were basically right,
they could be used to predict hurricanes only in ideal circumstances. The 1915 storm had run a course headlong toward
New Orleans, meaning its surge rolled ashore in a predictable
fashion. But hurricanes are usually more temperamental—they
can aim for a spot on the coast and veer off at the last minute,
foiling anyone using tidal gauges to predict landfall. Some
storms are compact, yet powerful, so their storm surge arrives
later and more quickly. Some park themselves off the coast for
days, pushing a tidal surge before kicking that up another notch.
Cline had gotten lucky—as future storms would reveal.

Chapter 3
1927 AND 1965

I N THE SPRING OF 1927, nature exposed the folly of the Corps's levees-only strategy, laying bare all the fault lines in American society. It also pushed a would-be president to invent modern emergency management.

The previous autumn, heavy rains and snowstorms blanketed the North American midsection. Once the melt set in, rivers swelled with more water than ever in recorded history, flooding a half-dozen states. As the water flowed south, it poured into the Mississippi, contained by the Corps's levees. The river started to rise, cresting at Cairo, Illinois, on January 1, 1927—earlier than ever before. The Cairo overflow was the first of a series of crests that winter and spring, and the flow threw tremendous force against the Corps's trapezoidal earthen walls. Millions of tons of water eroded levee slopes and percolated through the soil inside and underneath them, straining and weakening the levees to the point of collapse in dozens of places.

The Mississippi River Commission, the agency set up in 1879 to smooth commerce and prevent flood disasters (and closely aligned with the Corps), assured people that the levees would hold. Nevertheless, from Illinois to Louisiana efforts began—some with forcibly conscripted black laborers—to shore up weak points in the system. Guards were posted to foil dynamite-wielding saboteurs who knew a crevasse in one place would ease the pressure elsewhere.

In New Orleans, a tight-knit cabal of bankers and business-men fretted that a flood would destroy their city. Even if that could be avoided, panic might take hold as news spread of levee breaks upriver, wrecking the city's economy in the process. Still in his Weather Bureau post in New Orleans after more than a quarter century, Isaac Cline followed the progress of the flood. Though he believed crevasses upstream from New Orleans would spare the city, he wasn't taking chances. He issued a se-ries of cautionary flood bulletins, but the local papers—the *States,* the *Item,* and the *Times-Picayune*—ignored them. On April 14, Cline scolded reporters at his office. There was noth-ing they could do, they told him—a committee was censoring all news on the river.

Cline was aghast. "The greatest flood in history is approach-ing and your action in suppressing flood information and warn-ings . . . is jeopardizing the lives of men, women and children," he lectured one of the censors over the telephone. "I am telling you now, the people of the lower Mississippi Valley are going to get the warnings from the Weather Bureau. You may control the press, but we have the mails, the telegraph, the telephone, and the radio and you cannot suppress the distribution of flood warnings and information through these channels."

Business leaders offered Cline assurances that his bulletins would get out. In any case, it was impossible to conceal the ob-vious: the muddy brown river was rising against the city's levees, carrying debris from upstream—logs, branches, dead animals. Soon, residents began to flee. The city hadn't flooded since 1849, and since then its population had more than doubled and its neighborhoods had spread out across the swamp toward the lake, east into St. Bernard Parish and west into Metairie. Its ex-panding waterways—especially the Industrial Canal connecting the river to Lake Pontchartrain, completed four years earlier—were not fortified against flooding. If New Orleans went under, it might never recover, so the poobahs hatched a plan. James Thomson, the owner and publisher of the *Item,* was the first to suggest it: dynamite the levee downriver and relieve the pres-sure on the city, preserving its safety. Of course, such an action would also destroy St. Bernard and much of Plaquemines Parish and leave ten thousand people homeless. But that seemed preferable to the alternative, at least to elites like Thomson who, not surprisingly, did not live in St. Bernard or Plaquemines Parish.

On April 15, Good Friday, heavy rainstorms drenched the Mississippi Valley from stem to stern. "The roaring Mississippi River, bank and levee full from St. Louis to New Orleans, is believed to be on its mightiest rampage. . . . All along the Mississippi considerable fear is felt over the prospects for the greatest flood in history," noted an article in the Memphis *Commercial Appeal,* adding that "Government engineers are confident that the government levees will withstand the floodwaters."

Privately, those engineers were preparing for the worst. The flood was clearly going to overwhelm the levees at one or more weak points—the question was where and when. They didn't have to wait much longer for an answer. On April 16, a 1,200-foot levee section collapsed south of Cairo at Dorena, Missouri—the first of a cascade of breaks down the river. At eight a.m. on April 21, another levee collapsed at Mounds Landing, Mississippi. Thousands of African American men had been shoveling earth at that location through the night, desperately trying to fortify the wall. Many were swept away and drowned when the wall gave way with a thunderous rumble. Floodwaters poured south through the gash toward Greenville.

"Levee broke at ferry landing Mounds, Mississippi eight a.m. Crevasse will overflow the entire Mississippi Delta," read a telegram from Major John Lee, the Corps district engineer, to Corps chief General Edgar Jadwin.

New Orleans businessmen spent the next two weeks lobbying politicians in back rooms to get political support and legal cover for dynamiting the levee. Cline's scientific imprimatur was key to the effort. "The people of New Orleans are in such a panic that all who can do so are leaving the city and it is ruining business," banker Lem Pool pleaded to him over the phone. But

Cline saw no reason to support the idea, believing the city wouldn't flood. After more cajoling, though, he came around. People were panicking, even though his forecasts stated clearly that New Orleans was not in danger. "The opening of the levee appeared to be the only solution that would restore confidence," he wrote later. So he called Pool back and offered a scientific fudge. "You may go to Governor Simpson," Cline said, "and tell him that there is another rise in the river on its way here and that if the levee is going to be opened to relieve the situation it should be opened at once."

The businessmen behind the plan then secured the backing of the president, the governor, and the leaders of the affected parishes, the latter by offering vague promises of reparations and a two-million-dollar loan fund to tide residents over. On Friday, April 29, dynamite was used to blow a gash in the levee at Caernarvon, a short distance from a crevasse that had flooded the parishes only five years earlier. The first blast did little, and the dynamiting took more than a week. But in the end the river gushed through a gap, spreading water, mud, and silt over the towns, hamlets, and bayou camps of St. Bernard and Plaquemines, which had mostly emptied out as word spread of the plans. Refugees with nowhere else to stay were housed in New Orleans warehouses, segregated by race. "We're letting 'em do it because we can't stop 'em," St. Bernard sheriff L. A. Meraux told reporters at the site of the breach. "You can't fight the Government. . . . And we haven't got a line in writing of any guarantee that we're going to get anything back."

Days before, a levee at Glasscock, north of Baton Rouge, had begun to break. The day after the dynamiting began, it gave way. Water gushed west into the Atchafalaya River basin and the Mississippi crest fell. With that, blowing up the St. Bernard levee turned out to have been unnecessary. When it came time to settle up months later, residents of the two parishes were screwed. Many of their claims—which totaled thirty-five million dollars—were rejected by the reparations committee, which authorized only $2.9 million in payments, the amount left over after the one-million-dollar cost of feeding and housing refugees was deducted. Of that, only eight hundred thousand dollars went to 2,089 individual claimants—an average of $284 each.

More than four hundred miles upriver (about 240 miles as the crow flies), the initial flood through the Mounds Landing crevasse put Greenville and much of the Mississippi delta under ten feet of water, creating a vast, churning sea for hundreds of miles around. Tens, then hundreds of thousands of people climbed onto rooftops and up into trees, where most waited for rescue without food or water. Spring rainstorms had spread over the South and temperatures hovered near freezing at times; some of the stranded began dying of exposure. Nearly two hundred thousand people saw their homes disappear under water. Those who didn't drown were left homeless. It didn't end there. Floodwater flowed around and back into the Mississippi, pumping it up again. More breaks flooded large swaths of Arkansas and Louisiana, creating a syncopated series of disasters lasting into May. After that, it took months for the waters to subside.

Survivors gathered on the only remaining dry land: the levees. Thirteen thousand people—almost all of them African American—were stranded on the Greenville levee without food or water, and their numbers kept rising as boats deposited more refugees. Sometimes rescue barges would come and take people away, giving priority to white women and children. "It resembled a war zone, all confusion and noise, chocked with smoke from kitchens, people on litters, squalling children, and a few men with purpose struggling to establish order," John M. Barry wrote in *Rising Tide*. Though Will Percy, the local Red Cross chief and scion of an old, progressive southern family, tried to arrange an evacuation, landowners objected because they were afraid their labor force would never return. Percy's father, LeRoy Percy, sided with them. The blacks were left behind, the men later forced to work by National Guard troops.

The 1927 flood was the nation's first truly modern disaster. Though the official death toll was only 246 (the real number was likely much higher), the flood exceeded any previous American catastrophe in scale and complexity. It wasn't just some flawed levees that had collapsed, but one of the world's premier, supposedly foolproof pieces of infrastructure. Nature had foiled modern technology and human imagination. And as walls broke, they exposed America's most shameful injustices: poorer towns were sacrificed for richer ones. White victims were rescued but not black ones.

The flood held the nation's rapt attention for months. Papers coast to coast wrote up the sorry state of the levees and the plight of refugees. On-scene reports went out over radio. Telegrams flew. People chatted about crevasses on the telephone. As states were overwhelmed one by one, it became clear that a national response of some kind was not only necessary, but expected.

Nevertheless, as the water had risen along the southern length of the river that spring, President Calvin Coolidge had resisted any federal role. Finally, the governors of six affected states begged him to help. Mississippi governor Dennis Murphree wired the president: "unprecedented floods have created a national emergency. . . . This territory will be water covered one to twenty feet in twenty four hours contains population 150,000 . . . Highways covered . . . Railroad operations suspended . . . Beyond capacity local and state agencies to relieve and control."

Coolidge's reluctance had ample precedent. For most of American history, local officials handled local problems. Nobody expected the president to put out fires or rescue people from earthquake rubble. In the nineteenth century, a disaster in New England was worlds away from South Carolina or California, and no one but the locals cared. Even cataclysmic events such as the Galveston flood and the San Francisco earthquake of 1906 had remained mostly local affairs, thanks in part to their geographical compactness.

Afflicted areas did get attention after the dust settled. In 1802, a Christmas fire burned along a central street of Portsmouth, New Hampshire, engulfing 132 buildings in the heart of the city's commercial district. The next year, Congress passed its first disaster relief law, cutting local merchants a break by waiving some taxes on imported goods. After that, Congress cut disaster relief checks again many times over the decades.

Of course, for years America had been so big and empty that many natural terrors went almost unnoticed. Early the morning of December 16, 1811, for example, a tremendous jolt awoke residents of the town of New Madrid, Missouri. It was the first of three enormous earthquakes triggered that winter by a huge fault that runs through the Midwest, starting in Arkansas, skirting St. Louis, and continuing north into Indiana. Townspeople rushed from their beds into the streets and saw the ground shuddering in waves, like a shaken carpet. Fissures opened. Trees and buildings toppled. The Mississippi sloshed around like water in a washbasin. More giant quakes followed through February—all exceeding 8.0 on the Richter scale, bigger than anything the United States had seen before or since. Yet the quakes didn't kill many people. Only one person died in New Madrid, trapped under a fallen roof. The typical property damage was a toppled chimney.

But within decades, great cities were growing all over the United States, including St. Louis, which a similar quake would level today. Soon, there was a lot more that could go wrong in a lot more places.

The morning after the Mounds Landing levee broke, Coolidge yielded, naming Commerce Secretary Herbert Hoover chairman of a special committee of five cabinet secretaries to run the federal disaster response. There was no precedent for the move—committee members would have to improvise and invent as they went along. Hoover, out to raise his profile for a planned presidential run, was a whiz-kid engineer who believed that there was no problem too complex to manage. He had run a mass evacuation of Americans from Europe at the start of World War I and managed a relief organization directing supplies to war-ravaged Belgium. Working for the Wilson administration, he ran a food aid program for Europeans after the war ended. He expected to conquer this new challenge, too.

With Coolidge's support, Hoover became the nation's flood czar—the public and private face of government relief, an avatar of decisive action and competence. The job he did was deeply flawed in many ways, but his accomplishments set a standard that officials struggled to repeat for generations afterward.

Hoover could not get organized quickly enough to make a difference in the first days after the Mounds Landing crevasse, but soon he and his aides—led by Henry Baker, the disaster relief director of the Red Cross—had people jumping. They set up ad hoc rescue teams and arranged for food and temporary housing for refugees. The operation was lean, meticulous, and forward-looking. The commission demanded that every rescue boat be inspected. It arranged for the Corps to relay reports on weak levees to the rescue fleet and to local officials so that boats could get into position and refugees would have a place to go immediately after a breach.

Hoover had unquestioned authority over the entire response, public and private. But he wasn't a general directing a federal army. There were no fat appropriations from Congress, no big mobilization of U.S. troops or other national resources. Instead, Hoover ran a hybrid organization in which the Red Cross and local agencies did most of the work. He had the last word on all decisions, but gave on-the-ground responsibility to Red Cross chapters. The result was, for the time, a nimble structure in which people on the front lines could respond to problems in front of them and Hoover could direct resources where they were needed most.

In all, according to *Rising Tide,* "330,000 people were rescued from rooftops, trees, high ground, levees. There were 154 tent cities in seven states. . . . 325,554 people, the majority African-American, lived in these camps for as long as four months. An additional 311,922 people outside the camps were fed and clothed by the Red Cross. Most of these were white. Of the remaining 300,000 people, most fled."

The reticent Coolidge never said a word publicly on the flood, so Hoover stepped into the void. On April 30, he delivered a speech over the radio from his Memphis headquarters. It was one of the first national addresses—providing a springboard for his successful presidential run the next year. He said,

> I am speaking to you from the temporary headquarters which we have established for the national fight against the most dangerous flood our country has ever known. It is difficult to picture in words the might of the Mississippi in flood. . . . A week ago when it broke the levee [at Mounds Landing], only a quarter of the river went through the hole. Yet in a week it poured water up to twenty feet deep over . . . an area up to 150 miles long and fifty miles wide . . . behind this crevasse lies the ruin of 200,000 people. Thousands still cling to their homes where the upper floors are yet dry. But thousands more have need to be removed in boats and established in great camps on the higher ground. Other thousands are camped upon broken levees. This is the pitiable plight of a lost battle.

Hoover's tenure lasted well past the flooding itself. After the water subsided, the nation faced a wearying set of social problems. Hundreds of thousands of homeless refugees, most of them African Americans, were stuck in camps in appalling conditions. Many were forced into labor. One Greenville man, James Gooden, was shot by a police officer after rejecting an order to return to work after a difficult night shift, and African Americans grew restive. Hoover's oversight of the camps helped shift the black vote from the Republican to the Democratic camp—a factor in his loss to Franklin Roosevelt in the 1932 presidential election.

The 1927 flood reverberated through the nation's culture and unconscious for generations, especially among African Americans. It was one factor in the great northern migration of blacks from the South that began shortly afterward. One song, "When the Levee Breaks," by blues artists Joe McCoy and Memphis Minnie (recorded by Led Zeppelin decades later), captured the sense of helplessness at being caught between nature and flawed man-made structures, with no hope of rescue.

If it keeps on rainin', levee's goin' to break,
If it keeps on rainin', levee's goin' to break,
When the levee breaks I'll have no place to stay.
Mean old levee taught me to weep and moan,
Lord, mean old levee taught me to weep and moan,
Got what it takes to make a mountain man leave his home,
Oh, well, oh, well, oh, well.
Don't it make you feel bad
When you're tryin' to find your way home,
You don't know which way to go?

Like a chorus, history would repeat.

In September 1947, a hurricane blew ashore to the east of New Orleans, crossing the Chandeleur Islands' gentle crescents early the morning of the nineteenth. Water rose eleven feet over St. Bernard and Plaquemines parishes. But the storm damage was less telling than what it had suddenly revealed: the threat of a Gulf storm surge entering Lake Pontchartrain. The lake hadn't risen much. But to the city's west, it sloshed over levees into Jefferson Parish. Moisant International Airport, then in its second year of operation, ended up with two feet of water on its runways. Airline Highway, the main route between New Orleans and Baton Rouge, was also under water. Fifteen thousand homes took on some water. Spooked, the Orleans Levee District spent eight hundred thousand dollars to raise the lakefront levees to nine and a half feet high, and Jefferson Parish embarked on a similar plan. Locals started feeling around for federal funding.

As it had been one hundred years before with the river, Congress was reluctant to take on a new responsibility—one that would require funding more or less forever. But the United States had just won the war and remade the world. Veterans were back making babies and building homes with two-car garages, and the suburban footprint was spreading out from the cities, exposing ever-wider areas to storms, floods, and other disasters. New Orleans got hit again in 1948, and in 1949 Congress ordered a study into a possible federal role in raising the lakefront levees.

Five years later, Hurricane Carol brushed by North Carolina's Outer Banks before making straight for the northeast coast. The Category 3 storm thrashed Connecticut's eastern cities and towns, ripping off part of the roof of New London's city hall, and a storm surge submerged small towns and seaside resorts, washing hundreds of homes away. Narragansett Bay rose thirteen feet. The damage totaled $450 million—about $3 billion in 2005 dollars.

Political leaders rushed to do something—anything. Suddenly it wasn't just New Orleans or Mobile in Mother Nature's crosshairs, but the country's population and power centers: Boston, New York, and Washington. Senator Prescott Bush, a Connecticut Republican (father of President George H. W. Bush and grandfather of President George W. Bush), took up the hurricane cause. He pushed for more hurricane and storm relief. The federal government ought to offer flood insurance, Bush suggested. He also wrote and pushed through a law that put the Corps on a path toward fortifying the entire coastline: the Bush Hurricane Survey Act of 1955.

The Bush Act instructed the Corps to make a survey "of the eastern and southern seaboard of the United States with respect to hurricanes, with particular reference to areas where severe damages have occurred." The study was to include "the securing of data on the behavior and frequency of hurricanes, and the determination of methods of forecasting their paths and improving warning services, and of possible means of preventing loss of human lives and damages to property, with due consideration of the economics of proposed breakwaters, seawalls, dikes, dams, and other structures."

Assigning the task to the Corps made political sense. Hurricanes knew no boundaries. If a local government did a bad job building a levee or a seawall and it failed, the flooding could spread to neighboring jurisdictions. Even if it spent lavishly to protect itself, a town could still end up under water. This was especially true in south Louisiana, where dozens of levee districts butted up against each other—some rich, some poor. Only a national effort with universal standards could knit disparate systems together for safety's sake.

The Corps New Orleans District took up its part of the assignment. In an interim report in 1962, it listed some of its findings. The document was a template for pretty much everything that would happen over the next twenty years. Its very first paragraph described the problem succinctly (even if it was far too rosy about the city's future economic prospects):

> The lowlands in the Lake Pontchartrain tidal basin are subject to tidal overflow. The Greater New Orleans Metropolitan area which lies in this basin will continue its rapid economic development in the near future even though severe damages have resulted from several hurricanes in the recent past. Hurricane damages result from surges . . . intensified by local wind effects, and the combination of waves and surges causes overtopping of the protective works along the shores of the lake. The eastern portion of the area is also subject to flooding by surges and waves that move directly from Lake Borgne and overtop the existing inadequate protective system seaward of the developed land areas. As a result, residences and industrial and commercial establishments suffer damage, business activities are disrupted, lives endangered, and hazards to health created. Hurricanes much more severe than any of record are possible. In the event of the occurrence of such a severe hurricane, catastrophic property damage and loss of human life would be experienced.

In other words, the growing city was on a collision course with disaster.

On the afternoon of September 10, 1965, Louisiana senator Russell Long called the White House. For Long—the son of legendary governor Huey Long and a longtime Washington power broker—the conversation had one goal. He wanted a presidential visit, and quick. Back home, thousands of people sat slumped on rooftops without water or food, baking in the summer heat, waiting to be rescued. Others swam or waded toward high ground in a dreary, sodden procession. Hurricane Betsy had struck New Orleans overnight and pushed a wave from the Gulf of Mexico past all natural and man-made defenses into the neighborhoods of a large American city. The wave had overwhelmed levees, which were breached in several spots. Many people were taken by surprise as water engulfed their homes. One man was slumbering in his easy chair when, he told the *Times-Picayune,* he "felt something cold, looked down and there I was with water in my lap." He climbed onto the roof of his house. "God, it was like one giant swimming pool as far as the eye could see. There were people I knew—women, children, screaming, praying. . . . A woman who lives down the block floated past me, with her two children floating beside her." The rising water forced many people into attics, where they drowned. About eighty were dead altogether. An ad hoc fleet of rescuers in motorboats navigated through floating wreckage, coaxing victims to climb or jump down from the eaves.

Long observed that an old tree had fallen on his own Uptown house and that only by the grace of God had his wife and children not been killed—they had all been in another room. Then he cut to the nub. A Lyndon Johnson visit, he suggested, would have political advantages: a public display of support for New Orleans might help swing a state he had lost in the previous election. (Louisiana was one of only six states Republican Barry Goldwater won in 1964. Five were in the Deep South, where voters were angry over Johnson's stance against segregation. The sixth was Arizona, Goldwater's home state.)

Johnson was noncommittal. "Russell, I sure want to," he said. "I've got a hell of a two days that I've got scheduled. Let me look and see what I can back out of and get into and so on and so forth and let me give you a ring back. If I can't go, I'll put the best man I got there."

"So now listen," Long replied. "We are not the least bit interested in your best man. As far as we're concerned, I'm just a Johnson man." Long continued to wheedle, imagining the news

coverage the visit would get: "The President was very much upset about the horrible destruction and damage done to this city
of New Orleans, lovely town. The town that everybody loves. If
you go there right now, Mr. President, they couldn't beat you if
Eisenhower ran."

Johnson agreed to go and departed that same afternoon, accompanied by a delegation that included Louisiana senator
Allen Ellender and Major General Jackson Graham, the chief of
civil works at the Corps of Engineers. Air Force One arrived at a
battered Moisant Airport at 5:36 p.m., where Johnson met with
Mayor Victor Schiro and other local officials. The president was
supposed to give a press conference and fly out again, but
Schiro pleaded with him to tour the city. Johnson knew and
liked Schiro—and also towered over him, something that
earned Schiro the presidential nickname "Little Mayor." LBJ ac-
ceded and the presidential entourage drove east into the city.

At one point the motorcade stopped at a bridge over the Industrial Canal. Levees on both sides of the waterway had been
topped and broken, and the watery vista stretched for miles
around them. The flood was much deeper on the east side—the
Lower Ninth Ward—where people could still be glimpsed on
rooftops. Johnson got out of the limousine, and aides and reporters scurried after him as he went to meet an extraordinary
procession of refugees trudging over from the Lower Ninth.
"People were walking along the bridge where they had disembarked from the boats that had brought them to dry land," reads
a diary kept by aides. "Many of the people were carrying the
barest of their possessions, and many of them had been sitting
on top of their houses waiting for rescue squads to retrieve the
families and carry them to dry land—and to food and water."

The president chatted with some of the survivors, including
William Marshall, a seventy-four-year-old black man.

"You ever seen anything like this before?" Johnson asked.

"No sir, not in my life. I've seen storms and hurricanes, but
not this much water. Unless of course . . . a cloud burst or
something, and it wasn't nothing like that."

"How come you didn't lose any more lives?"

"Well, God, with the providence of Him. I guess we will see, through His mercy."

Johnson next went to George Washington Elementary School, a few blocks to the west on St. Claude Avenue, where hundreds of refugees, all African Americans, had gathered. The sun had set. Lit only by a few flashlights wielded by aides, Johnson climbed the steps and went into the building. Inside, families were huddled together in the dark on the floors, some eating carrots and cold beans off paper plates. They asked Johnson for water, which had been cut off. "The people all about were bedraggled and homeless . . . thirsty and hungry. It was a most pitiful sight of human and material destruction," the diary reads. Outside, Johnson suggested to Schiro that local soft drink bottlers deliver truckloads of sodas to the refugees. The mayor agreed to look into it.

Cokes were just the beginning. Johnson was obviously touched by what he had seen.

The city was a wreck. Power and phones were out. Thousands were living in emergency shelters. Water would have to be pumped out and breaches repaired. Homes would have to be rebuilt. "I am determined we can help these people in every way that human compassion and effective aid can serve," Johnson declared back at the airport before departing, promising to cut "all red tape" and send food, medicine, and other aid to the city immediately. He ordered Buford Ellington, director of the federal Office of Emergency Planning, the civil defense agency created at the start of the Cold War, to stay behind and coordinate the effort. Johnson told Schiro privately he would do everything he could to help the hurricane victims. When he got back, the president spent several days lining up aid for the city. The *New York Times* reported he had spent the next day, a rainy Sunday, in the Oval Office focused on New Orleans—though there wasn't much for him to do.

Recriminations for the disaster followed soon after. Edward Teller, the nuclear physicist and contributor to the Manhattan Project, came to town September 14 to deliver a speech to the Mid-Continental Oil and Gas Association and attacked city officials for not warning people that a flood was upon them. "It is incredible that people had only twenty minutes between the time they first knew water was rising and the time it reached a height over their heads to get out. Then it's too late," he said. The Junior Chamber of Commerce wrote a letter to city officials the next week asking "why the people in the hardest-hit area were not evacuated" and noting that it was "alarming to awaken to the fact the Civil Defense shelters contained empty water storage cans, that there was no emergency generator at the vital city water supply chlorinator, that shelters were without vital and adequate police protection and that communications broke down following the city's power failure."

Local politicians defended themselves—and then spread the blame around for good measure. Congressman F. Edward Hebert brushed off Teller's remarks, saying that scientists "live in an ivory tower on Cloud Nine, untouched even by space-ships." But, he added, civil defense should get more federal money. Schiro wrote constituent letters explaining his actions. He had advised people to get out, he wrote, but "many did not hear this warning, thus they lacked the knowledge to prepare to evacuate." (Mayor Schiro had appeared on television before power went out at 11 p.m. the night of the storm—a few short hours before the flood. Wearing a civil defense hard hat, he warned people in low-lying areas to evacuate. But no general evacuation was ordered.) But the basic problem was obvious: "the tidal surge . . . was so tremendous the system of levee pro-tection could not possibly contain this surge of water."

The city's vulnerability stunned the nation. It was obvious that if something weren't done to protect New Orleans, it might not survive another blow. Ironically, the principal source of the city's vulnerability was its growth. As it had expanded, upgrades on its already weak hurricane levees hadn't kept pace. Unnoticed by the public until a storm hit, this "levee gap" put hundreds of thousands of residents' lives at risk, and that risk was spiraling gradually higher. If Betsy had struck a few decades earlier, the pattern of damage would have been a lot different—and signifi-cantly smaller. Before the 1920s, there were no big navigation canals running through the city, no floodwalls to breach. The lakefront levees were lower, but the swamp would have tamped down any storm surge coming from the lake.

Now, New Orleans had spread out on top of the swamp. It stretched from the river to the lake—an urban landscape that filled all available space. Its suburbs were expanding west and south. In the city proper, a population of six hundred thousand lived in a bowl that dipped as deep as twelve feet below sea level in spots. The lowest points could be found in the newest, nicest suburbs, nearest the lake, which were built on drained, filled swamplands. Water—lakes, canals, wetlands, the river—now lapped close to homes and businesses at every point on the city's perimeter. Directly or indirectly, all the waterways connected to the Gulf of Mexico.

Lake Pontchartrain posed the biggest threat in a hurricane. Under the right circumstances, a storm surge could flow into the lake, overflow levees, and spill into the city and suburbs, flooding hundreds of square miles. To the city's south and east, St. Bernard Parish and the Lower Ninth Ward were far from Lake Pontchartrain but even more exposed, right next to Lake Borgne, a big lagoon surrounded by marshes and open to the Gulf.

The Corps had raised and fortified the river levees after the 1927 flood, and they easily repelled a ten-foot rise in the Mississippi during Betsy. But all that protected the city from hurricane floods was a haphazard network of earthen levees. And the Corps's navigation improvements had actually made matters worse: the Industrial Canal, completed in 1923, ran north–south through the city from Lake Pontchartrain to the Mississippi. It was linked to the Gulf via the Intracoastal Waterway—a connection dug in the 1940s. Another, a recently completed canal called the Mississippi River-Gulf Outlet (nicknamed the Mr. Go), fed into the Intracoastal. Together, all three channels could carry ships in and out of New Orleans—as well as billions of gallons of water from the Gulf into the heart of the city.

The Corps had been obsessed with controlling the Mississippi for a century, but by 1965, the problem seemed to be—

tenuously, anyway—in hand. After the 1927 flood, Congress responded with the Flood Control Act of 1928. It had given the Corps (which had got the country into the fix to begin with) more money and power. Corps generals got outright control over all federal flood-control projects and a free hand to redesign the levees—which they did. Early on, the Corps dropped "levees only" for a more varied approach. In some spots, it rerouted the river; in others it built diversions, an idea it had previously rejected. One such diversion, the Bonnet Carré Spillway, completed in 1937, sat just upriver from New Orleans at the site of several past crevasses. The spillway consisted of a concrete gate, seven thousand feet across, built into the river levee, and seven thousand creosote-treated wooden slats that contained the river flow. When the time came to open it, a crane moved along a track at the top of the spillway, pulling up the slats and laying them along the top. As much as 250,000 cubic feet per second of river water, contained by guide levees, flowed across six miles of swamp and into Lake Pontchartrain.

The Corps's Old River Control Structure, above Baton Rouge, finished in 1963, was the apotheosis of river management: a giant system of floodgates that locked the Mississippi into its course. For decades the river had been showing signs of a shift to a shorter route one hundred miles west, down the Atchafalaya. The Old River structure stopped that natural process in its tracks. In doing so it kept New Orleans from ending up on a brackish bayou, an economic irrelevancy.

River levees were the Corps's traditional bread and butter: they made trade and port activity possible and aided navigation. But hurricane protection had nothing to do with navigation and had few economic perks—except, of course, preventing catastrophes—so Washington had ignored it. Local governments built hurricane levees, not the Corps.

Betsy had exposed the system's weak spots, turning the city's flood defenses against it. Keeping forecasters guessing, it had done a loop-the-loop in the Atlantic and strafed Florida before entering the Gulf early September 8. At that point the Weather Bureau announced a hurricane watch for the coast from Mississippi to Matagorda Bay, Texas. The next day, the storm veered east toward Mississippi, then toward western Louisiana, then split the difference and headed straight for New Orleans. As Betsy's eye approached, the city was square in the storm's northeast quadrant, where 130-mph winds were the fiercest, blowing from the east. The wind pushed rising Gulf waters across Lake Borgne and into the Intracoastal and the Mr. Go. The water entered the city and crested over the tops of the levees on both sides of the Industrial Canal, taking chunks of wall with it. Water poured onto streets and into backyards, flowing overland and through a ready-made set of sluices: the city's drainage network. It flowed west and north via drainage canals and culverts. In eastern New Orleans—a thinly populated area fronting Lake Pontchartrain—water ponded in an empty area between Louisiana Highway 90 and the levee, but snaked through culverts and eventually poured over the highway into neighborhoods on the other side. Along the river, a torrent flowed into the Lower Ninth Ward—including the Louisiana National Guard headquarters at Jackson Barracks—and St. Bernard Parish, farther east. In some spots the floodwater rose ten feet in as many minutes.

Betsy got Washington's attention—thanks to Louisiana's congressional delegation, which marshaled all its political clout to get it. It was surprising that the state still had much sway, as its economic star had been fading since the late nineteenth century. The port and the growing oil and gas industry were New Orleans's prime economic engines, but the city was a long way from its heyday. The nation's economic focus had moved elsewhere. In 1840, New Orleans had been the third-largest city in the United States. By 1900, it had dropped to twelfth, and sixty years later it was fifteenth, its slow growth outpaced by other cities. After Betsy hit, the city's population began to decline.

But Louisiana's potency in Congress was at its height—the result of decades of seniority, the Democratic Party's grip on power, and the state's well of uncanny political talent. Russell Long held the job of Senate majority whip and a seat on the Appropriations Committee, New Orleans congressman Hale Boggs was majority leader, and Senator Allen Ellender chaired Appropriations. It was also a singular political moment. Johnson and Congress were in an ambitious mood, riding a wave of postwar optimism. Any and all challenges could be tackled with American resources and moxie: racial oppression in the Deep South, Communist insurgencies in Southeast Asia, grinding poverty, space exploration. Building higher and sturdier earthen walls around New Orleans was a modest task by comparison, easily accomplished with enough cash, slide rules, and bulldozers.

On October 21, six weeks after the storm, Congress passed the Flood Control Act of 1965. Among other things, the new law green-lighted a Corps project called the Lake Pontchartrain and Vicinity Hurricane Protection Plan. It was a new levee system guaranteed by the full force of the federal government. It would cost eighty million dollars, be complete by 1980, and promised to keep the city safe for generations.

The Corps's 1962 report had laid out the plan to protect the city in broad brushstrokes: its first choice was to build gates in the passes into Lake Pontchartrain, cutting off entrée of all Gulf surges—but also reducing tidal flows that sustained shrimp, oysters, drum, and other species. If the lake was protected, the city's bowl was safe. (The Corps was less enthusiastic about its alternative, raising lakefront levees.) But the gates would not protect the east side—St. Bernard and the Ninth Ward, including the Industrial Canal—which was still open to the Gulf across dozens of miles. Those areas would need new, much higher levees. There were some stumbling blocks. The city's soil, with its layers of peats and clays, was soft and squishy and difficult to build on. It was also porous—floodwater could saturate the soil and weaken it, just as it did before crevasses formed in the river levees. The delta, and everything on it, was also sinking at varying rates—about five inches to two feet per century—resulting in lower levees and higher floods as the decades went by.

The Corps had social as well as civil engineering in mind. It ambitiously proposed building a levee ring around eastern New Orleans—then a large, thinly populated stretch of swamp along the lake. Such an enclosure would let developers reclaim land and give the city growing room. A later study found that only 21 percent of the land the Corps's new system would enclose was already inhabited. Millions of dollars would be spent protecting empty space.

How the Corps made that decision gives some insight into its approach. Even today, before the Corps builds a levee, it has to answer the question: how high should it be? The question is a lot harder than it sounds. A twenty-foot-high levee costs a lot more than one fifteen feet high—especially if it's hundreds of miles long. But if floods never top fifteen feet, then the extra expense will be wasted. (In theory, the U.S. government could spend hundreds of billions of dollars erecting hundred-foot-high, titanium-and-marble-plated levees along all rivers and coastlines and never worry about flooding again—but that's obviously not practical.) The idea is to find the point where economy and safety are in perfect harmony. Err on the side of economy, and you may end up under water. Err on the side of safety, and you may bust the budget—and never know if it was worth it.

There was another variable, too. As Congress had handed the Corps more responsibilities over the years, it demanded that everything the Corps built yield economic benefits that exceeded costs. Of course, hurricane levees kept people safe. But public safety had never been the Corps's primary mission, and the potential loss of human life—much harder to quantify versus, say, the loss of a factory—played no formal role in its decision making. The focus was infrastructure, and infrastructure was a gold mine. As a result, hundreds of big, sometimes unnecessary projects—locks, dams, dredging—got green-lighted.

Hurricane levees had to be justified using the same formulas, and one way to make the numbers work was to include the swamplands. Corps economists figured that for every dollar spent on new levees, the region would see thirteen dollars in benefits from development. Left out of any equation was the potential loss of human life resulting from insufficient protection and the astronomical economic losses from such a catastrophe.

A week after the Corps lost a tangle with environmentalists over its proposed lake barriers in December 1977, members of Congress met in the French Quarter to take stock of the levees. Bob Livingston, then a freshman Republican congressman from Jefferson Parish, began quizzing Colonel Early Rush III, the Corps's chief engineer in New Orleans. Livingston noted dryly that the Corps was close to finishing most of its levees around the empty swamps in the east. Its own maps, meanwhile, showed that the levees around inhabited areas were only 10 to 20 percent complete.

"It would seem to me that if hurricane protection to the people and properties is the paramount importance, that the portion that you would want to complete first would be those levees surrounding inhabited areas rather than those around uninhabited areas," Livingston said. "Would that not be a priority, sir?"

In fact, using the "build it and they will come" logic, almost any Corps project could be justified; many in Congress and the business community felt that levees were an important draw for shopping malls and subdivisions.

Rush gamely pointed out that some levees around settled areas in St. Bernard had indeed been built up before the eastern levees. But he didn't address Livingston's central point—that the people of New Orleans had somehow ended up way back in the queue.

When the government (or, typically, insurance companies) protect people from risk, that encourages more risky behavior, not less. Economists call this "moral hazard." If you know your insurance company will reimburse you if your house burns down, you're likely to be slightly less fastidious about changing out the batteries in your smoke detectors. On a grander scale, if someone else—in this case, the whole country—pays for levees, it's easier to live in a hurricane zone. The Corps had in essence slapped a big sign on New Orleans and its undeveloped areas saying: "Come on down, we will make these areas safe." Left unsaid was the fact that the Corps had only the sketchiest idea of how much protection it actually provided.

The Corps's grand plan called for an average levee height of about fourteen feet above sea level. That, statisticians figured, would protect against high water that came only once every two or three hundred years. The numbers were precise—the chance of a two-hundred-year flood occurring in a given year equals 0.5 percent. But they were also rough guesses based on the Corps's unscientific cost-benefit analysis and a Swiss cheese of statistics and 1950s-era meteorological knowledge. And the risk for St. Bernard, the Lower Ninth Ward, and eastern New Orleans—poorer outlying areas more exposed to the Gulf—was statistically higher than it was for New Orleans proper and its more affluent suburbs in Jefferson Parish.

River levees were designed to hold back a "Standard Project Flood"—a water height with a calculated risk, based on crunching the statistics from past high-water marks. The Mississippi River levees in New Orleans, for example, averaged twenty-five feet high, enough to repel a Standard Project Flood that came around only once every eight hundred years.

But this approach didn't translate easily. Hurricane floods and river floods both involve lots of water, but otherwise they're quite different. Rivers rise between their banks; a storm surge could rise almost anywhere around New Orleans. A Standard Project Flood could be calculated from the Corps's copious statistics on past river floods; the historical record of storm surge flooding was full of holes. Creating a "Standard Project Hurricane" and its flooding model also posed computational problems much more complex than those of a river flood, impossible to solve in an era when a single electronic computer filled a room, not the corner of a desktop.

Nevertheless, at the Corps's request, Weather Bureau meteorologists gamely proceeded. They created a chimerical storm, a physical impossibility, by cherry-picking elements of past storms—mainly the hurricanes that had dealt damage to New Orleans in 1915 and 1947. Consistency was not a hallmark. Weather satellites were only beginning to provide insights into the structure of hurricanes, and the Saffir-Simpson hurricane scale did not yet exist. The imaginary storm's central barometric pressure was 27.6 inches—something meteorologists later learned was found only in a powerful Category 4 hurricane. But winds reached sustained speeds of only 100 mph—a Category 2 storm.

The Corps then determined how high and how often its fictional storm would push water up around New Orleans. Depending on where you were, the Standard Project Hurricane generated a storm surge height averaging about 11.5 feet. After adding some extra "freeboard" for waves, the Corps came up with a uniform levee height of fourteen feet.

There were other wrinkles in the design process. Some things were done a certain way because the Corps had always done them that way.

Most structures—bridges, buildings, and levees—are over-engineered: they have components stronger than the minimum necessary, or have redundant, fallback systems installed. That means they're designed to take a certain amount of force—plus some extra—so they don't collapse when stresses reach the anticipated maximum.

Engineers gauge the overall strength of a structure with "factors of safety." A safety factor is a unitless number, the ratio of the total stress a structure can withstand, with all its enhancements, to the actual stress designers expect. Building codes, safety regulations, and design manuals lay out clear standards for factors of safety, and design engineers must verify that every structure and all its constituent parts meet them. If something doesn't measure up, the design is changed. The higher its safety factor, the more secure a structure is, both from unexpected external pounding and from flaws or weaknesses that can creep in during design, construction, and aging. When such problems arise, the safety factor—also a rough measure of overall stability—falls. When it drops below 1.0, the structure fails.

The safety factor for Corps levees, outlined in all its engineering manuals, was 1.3. That meant that when the floodwater reached 11.5 feet, the hurricane levees would still have

30 percent more strength to spare. That standard dated back decades, to a time when most levees protected rural areas—cows in pastures, not people in city neighborhoods. Back then, the cost of failure was low. As the years went by, more levees were built around cities, but the Corps safety standard remained unchanged. It was also a lot lower than the corresponding standard for bridges and other structures that millions of lives depended on, which was 2.0 or higher. That meant when the levees were constructed, there would be only the narrowest margin for error.

The levee system was built on such quirky numbers, spun out by teams of contractors and Corps employees in New Orleans, Vicksburg, and Washington using slide rules, pencils, and graph paper. The numbers made little sense from the standpoint of public policy, or even consistency. But one thing was uniform: they all made the system sound a lot safer than it actually was.

The way we perceive danger often diverges from the reality of risk. People go about their business scared of some things and not others, and the difference is based mainly on their own biases. People fret about a terrorist attack on the subway, but think nothing of driving across town. The odds say the drive is far more likely to kill you. With the levees, this kind of misperception became a mass phenomenon—an enormous, shared illusion of safety, signed off on by the highest authorities.

Take the two-hundred-year flood. It comes around once every three human lifespans. But it's a misleading statistic, a danger that looks small in a given year but grows a lot bigger when you're talking decades. The risk of a two-hundred-year storm over the expected forty-year life of New Orleans hurricane levees, for example, is 18 percent. In other words, the project had slightly less than a one-in-five chance of failure—destroying large parts of the city—at some point in its lifetime. This risk was programmed into the project, accepted up and down the line by engineers, politicians, and citizens alike. Perhaps the most glaring example of statistical peculiarity sat under the Corps's New Orleans district office, on the riverbank: the Mississippi's levees were designed for an eight-hundred-year high-water mark. That made them four times safer than hurricane levees.

Hurricane Betsy traumatized neighborhoods that had already been turned into battlegrounds by the nation's rising political flux. Just a few miles from the French Quarter and central business district, the Ninth Ward and St. Bernard belonged to an earlier century. When the Industrial Canal was completed in 1923, it only increased their isolation. The canal had spurred some business growth along St. Claude Avenue, the main road. Small businesses and a sense of pride and community ruled. Many people had built modest homes themselves and owned them outright. But until the 1950s, a single bridge was the only direct connection between the Lower Ninth and the rest of the city ("Lower" referred to its location downriver from the Upper Ninth, across the canal). It felt disconnected in other ways, too. The Lower Ninth's streets trailed off into grass, mud, and bayou inlets.

After the Supreme Court's 1954 *Brown v. Board of Education* decision, Louisiana had gone to war with the federal courts, trying to forestall the inevitable. State legislators had tried to remove the four New Orleans school board members who voted to allow integration to go forward. But a judge had overruled them, and the segregationists ran out of options.

One remaining hurdle was a test the New Orleans school system forced on those children applying to attend white schools. It was an obvious attempt to screen out as many as possible, and only five passed. Six-year-old Ruby Bridges would attend William Frantz Elementary, while Leona Tate, Tessie Prevost, and Gail Etienne would go to McDonogh # 19. (A fifth girl backed out at the end.) The school board had decided that girls would be the first to enroll because they would be harder to attack—and potentially easier to manage as students—than boys. On November 14, 1960, the entire nation was rapt at the unfolding drama.

Bridges entered the school accompanied by four federal marshals. People spat on her and called her names, and outraged white parents ran into classrooms and pulled out their children. Bridges and her mother did nothing that day but sit and wait for something to happen—fortunately, nothing did. The next day, Ruby went back, where she took her place as the only student in the school. She was paired with Barbara Henry, a white teacher, and for most of the academic year they were the only teacher and student in the entire school. After several months, some of the white students returned. But the success of school integration was short-lived. It ignited an immediate white flight out of the Ninth Ward, with most whites relocating to St. Bernard Parish, taking their jobs, their small businesses, and their customers with them. What had once been a mixed working-class neighborhood became overwhelmingly black— and Betsy was the final straw. After the storm, some whites simply abandoned their homes and moved.

With white flight, local politics radically shifted. New Orleans became an overwhelmingly black city as white residents moved en masse to St. Bernard, Metairie, and the West Bank suburbs; the city's black residents, meanwhile, mobilized. Black political organizations—started as neighborhood self-help groups and pumped up by the infusion of federal funding that accompanied Betsy and Great Society programs—launched dozens of local African American politicians into positions of power. SOUL, the Southern Organization for Unified Leadership, was one of a half dozen such organizations. Founded in 1966 at the Battleground Missionary Baptist Church in the Lower Ninth Ward, SOUL was a coalition of local groups aiming to get their own elected to public office. While remarkably successful on the local level, SOUL, like so many urban political machines, became as much about paybacks as progress. For many years, for example, state representative Sherman Copelin, who represented the Lower Ninth Ward, used it as a power base both to mobilize votes and dispense patronage.

Chapter 4

THE LEVEES

A S MEMORIES OF HURRICANE BETSY and the tumult of the 1960s faded, a wondrous contraption of earth, steel, and concrete rose around the city. The Corps and its contractors ranged over every square inch where land met water around New Orleans—or where someday it might. They towed barges, dredges, and pile drivers over lakes and deep into the marshes. They parked them next to shipping lanes and in canals alongside the leafy streets of upscale neighborhoods. They sculpted millions of tons of earth into levees towering as high as seventeen feet. In tight spots where broad levee foundations would never fit, they drove corrugated steel sheet pilings into the muck and fixed concrete slabs on top to make floodwalls. They knit the walls and levees together with locks, gates, seawalls, breakwaters, and bridges. The city's new flood defenses relied on the high tech and the low, on computers and muddy boots. In size and ambition, only the dikes and barriers protecting the similarly waterlogged Netherlands could compare with the New Orleans levees.

But the work took far longer than anyone anticipated. Once the political momentum from Hurricane Betsy faded, the inevitable construction delays began. In 1965, the Corps confidently predicted it would be cutting the ribbon on the Lake Pontchartrain and Vicinity hurricane project in 1982. But 1982 came and went. The system wouldn't be finished by 2005—

forty years later—and by then its cost had ballooned past one billion dollars when inflation was taken into account.

The problems went deeper than funding or logistics. As decades passed, more than the delta landscape was changing: the shape of the city and its expectations, the nation's politics and priorities—these too had evolved. As the levees rose around New Orleans, the absolute and all-seeing dominion the Corps maintained over its big projects began to break down. In 150 years, the Corps had laid a tremendous footprint on the American landscape. It had built big things anywhere it wanted, sowing new business and development—damn the side effects. But soon after it embarked on its New Orleans hurricane project, the world changed.

On January 1, 1970, President Richard Nixon signed the National Environmental Policy Act, the first in a set of sweeping laws written to protect the nation's air, water, and wildlife. Ever since Rachel Carson's *Silent Spring* had dramatized the risks of toxic pollution in 1962, threats to nature had struck a chord in the national psyche. In the foment of the 1960s, environmental groups had grown in size, bankroll, and political clout. The new environmental laws—besides NEPA, they included the Clean Water, Clean Air, and Endangered Species acts—all passed overwhelmingly, and Nixon created the Environmental Protection Agency to enforce them. But NEPA was the most powerful and wide-ranging of the set. It was deceptively simple: henceforth, all federal agencies had to study how their projects would affect the environment and do whatever they could to limit those effects. They'd document their conclusions in an environmental impact statement and invite the public to comment.

NEPA and the Clean Water Act gave the Corps new responsibilities with regard to protecting Louisiana's marshes, whose delicate ecology had been under assault for decades. Problem was, the Corps had led that assault: its customary approach had always been to drain and fill marshes first and ask questions later. Sure enough, it soon entered a series of legal brawls with a tiny group named Save Our Wetlands, founded by a New Orleans lawyer named Luke Fontana with aid from a group of Tulane Law School students. Using NEPA as a cudgel, Save Our Wetlands filed suit against the Corps in 1974 for its work creating a new subdivision on the northeast shore of Lake Pontchartrain. The Corps had dredged navigation channels and green-lighted the filling-in of 2,600 acres of protected wetlands—all without doing a single environmental impact statement or complying with the other new laws. The environmentalists lost that fight on a technicality, but in 1977, Save Our Wetlands and other community groups again filed suit against the Corps, this time challenging its hurricane protection plan for New Orleans.

The Corps had drawn up two grand hurricane protection strategies. Its first and favored choice involved blocking off Lake Pontchartrain. Massive concrete-and-steel gates would be installed across two natural channels into the lake, the Rigolets and Chef Menteur passes. The gates would be shut as a hurricane approached. The plan also envisioned new levees stretching across the wetlands surrounding the gates. Together, they would seal off the lake from Gulf storm surges. This, the engineers argued, would protect most—but not all—of New Orleans and the growing suburbs nearby. The Corps's second choice would leave the lake open; when it filled up during a storm, higher levees along the lakefront would protect New Orleans. They called this secondary option the "high level" plan.

From an engineer's point of view, the barrier plan was the most sensible approach: it blocked flowing water at a narrow area far from neighborhoods, like an army clustering its forces to bottle up a mountain pass instead of spreading out along the long border below it. But that strategy also looked like a potential environmental disaster. Key to the Corps's plans was a new residential development called Orlandia, to be bankrolled by a Texas oil tycoon and built on filled-in wetlands. That, along with the levees and gates, would destroy a big swath of marsh, a habitat for plant life, birds, and fish—including fish caught by sport and commercial fishermen. The crucial issue, though, was how much the hurricane project would attenuate the tidal flow in and out of the lake. Reducing it to a trickle would disrupt webs of life across a wide area, turning an already polluted body of water into a big, poisoned puddle.

Save Our Wetlands sought a federal injunction, arguing that the Corps's environmental impact study didn't measure up. (The Corps had done only a cursory study, based on an out-of-date mathematical model of tidal flow and a phone call with a biologist. And it hadn't even looked at the potential impact of its own second-choice plan.) In a December 1977 hearing before federal judge Charles Schwartz, attorney Fontana and environmental lawyer Jim Tripp brought in experts to pick apart the Corps's science and its cost-benefit studies. Corps attorney Joseph Towers pled safety concerns: a more detailed study of lake biology would take years, time the city might not have.

After three days of testimony, Schwartz said he'd heard enough: Save Our Wetlands had proven its case. He told the Corps to sit down with the group and negotiate a compromise. From the point of view of the Corps and its powerful allies in the business and political worlds, this was akin to a dog sitting down to hash things out with a flea. Not surprisingly, negotiations over the next day went nowhere.

An irritated Schwartz called the principals to a meeting in his chambers at ten o'clock that evening. The assembled group spanned generations, attitudes, and political interests. Judge Schwartz sat at the head of the table, absently chewing the end of an unlit cigar. Besides the attorneys for both sides, Colonel Early Rush III of the Corps was there, dressed in his army uniform, brimming with ribbons. So was a representative of New Orleans's old-line political guard: U.S. Attorney Gerald Gallinghouse, a former president of the Orleans Levee Board. Gallinghouse bluntly told Schwartz to back off.

"Your injunction will kill millions of people!" he lectured Schwartz. If the injunction went forward, he suggested, Congress could be persuaded to exempt the hurricane levees from environmental requirements altogether.

To some of the environmentalists, it looked like Schwartz was wavering. Fontana stood up, wagged his finger at the judge, and declared he was losing respect for him. Stressed out and on his third day without sleep, Fontana began to sob. He gathered up his papers and, cursing, burst out of the judge's chamber.

The next morning, Judge Schwartz issued an injunction stopping all work on the barrier plan. The case was straightforward, he wrote: the Corps had tried to put one over on the public and been caught. "The report is not candid and is in fact misleading," he wrote of the original environmental impact statement. "The EIS actually expresses only a hope that a project can be accomplished in the desired way while on its face it appears that such project and result are a tested fact. As written the EIS actually precludes both public and governmental parties from the opportunity to fairly and adequately analyze the benefits and detriments of the proposed plan and any alternatives to it." He ordered the Corps to redo the environmental impact assessment—and study the second-choice plan, to raise the lakefront levees, too.

Schwartz had humiliated the Corps. A bunch of local community activists had usurped its iron-fisted control over the levees and wetlands. Its ace in the hole—its close relationships with Louisiana politicians, bankers, and developers—had made no difference. Meanwhile, the estimated cost of the project had risen steadily since 1965, and further delay meant an additional ascent. The local levee boards, which were required to pick up 30 percent of the tab, started getting nervous about the up-front expense and the long-term upkeep of giant gates and locks. After the Corps completes a project, local agencies maintain it.

"I was told by scientists it would take approximately ten years to do a scientific study on the inter-transportability of marine organisms between the Gulf and the lake—that's a lot of time," said General Thomas Sands, chief in the New Orleans district from 1978 to 1981. "Second, if you looked at the costs and benefits over the life of the project—the cost of building the high level plan as opposed to cost of barriers—the barrier costs were increasing at a rate faster than the high level plan." On a technical level, the barrier plan made sense. But the environmentalists were right, too: the cost to nature would be enormous. This zero-sum trade-off—that no matter what choice was made, damage would be done—was the price of living where it increasingly made no sense to live. In their attempts to make the delta friendly to human habitation, engineers and politicians and developers ended up making it much more hazardous. Virtually any remedy would be the equivalent of applying a tourniquet.

As the debate progressed, the barrier plan lost the public's support, if it ever had it. "I couldn't understand why there was not a ringing bell sounding that said wait a minute—why are you not going to prevent tidal surge from going into Lake Pontchartrain?" Sands said. "There was no hue and cry related to it, people saying wait, you're abandoning the barrier plan!"

But it was ultimately the Corps's own cost-benefit calculations that killed the project. (It was shelved in 1985.) "The High Level Plan has greater net benefits, is less damaging to the environment, and is more acceptable to the public," a reevaluation concluded in 1984. The new "levees-only" plan echoed the doomed approach imposed on the river a century earlier. But the military analogy was still most apt: it was like spreading soldiers thin along a long border. Letting down your guard at any point would allow the enemy—a catastrophic flood—a chance to break through.

In 1991, Senator Russell Long made a routine tweak in some legislative language at the request of the Orleans Parish Levee Board—one of a hundred favors he did for local pols and other constituents every year. The Levee Board wanted to turn the New Orleans drainage canals into a federal hurricane protection project. The reasons were financial in origin, but to understand the full range of what was at stake one needed to look back to the nineteenth century and the city's long struggle to pump itself dry.

Long's move attempted to legally join Louisiana's two great monuments to engineering technology—the Corps's twentieth-century network of hurricane levees and the city's system of pumps and canals, much of it built in the nineteenth century.

Both were designed for the same purpose: keeping the city safe and dry. Hurricane levees kept water from getting in; the pumps and canals pushed water that got inside back out. Together, they made life in New Orleans possible. Without them, no modern city could exist under the constant threats posed by nature.

Otherwise, though, their functions were distinct, with different agencies and interests controlling them. In the political culture of New Orleans, that was a recipe for trouble.

For more than a century, the canals had been the domain of the Sewerage and Water Board, most of whose fifteen members were appointed by the mayor. As the board's name implied, it was a nuts-and-bolts agency that exerted iron control over the city's sewer systems, pumping stations, and canals.

After Hurricane Betsy, the Orleans Levee Board exerted more control over the canals when it became obvious that they could overflow from storm surges or rainfall. The Board of Commissioners of the Orleans Levee District—the official name of the Levee Board—was a powerful and somewhat mysterious agency, its six members appointed by the governor (the mayor and a member of the city council had ex officio seats). The board's somewhat arcane function belied the power and money at its disposal. Levee commissioners oversaw an empire that included the municipal Lakefront Airport (originally named for board chairman Abraham Shushan, its name was changed after Shushan was sent to prison in a 1930s corruption scandal) and drew copious revenue from marinas, floating casinos, and other ventures that had nothing to do with flood protection.

The drainage canals stretched like delicate fingers from the lake deep into the geographical center of the city. Pumping stations sat at their south ends. When it rained—as it did in torrents during the spring, when thunderstorms sometimes dumped ten inches or more in a few hours—the city's many low spots filled with water. The rainfall drained into sewers, culverts, and narrow waterways that splayed like a spider's web across New Orleans. Giant pumps consolidated the flow from most of the city into three main canals, pushing it out through neighborhoods into Lake Pontchartrain.

Those "outfall" canals started out as ditches dug in the nine-teenth century. Back then, they trailed off downhill into the swamp, away from the neighborhoods that lined the riverbank. As the city expanded northward toward Lake Pontchartrain, the canals were deepened to accommodate extra rainwater running off streets. As the years passed, these arteries helped define the neighborhoods and character of New Orleans. The 17th Street canal ran along the western border with neighboring Metairie (17th Street was renamed in 1894, but the canal kept the name). The Orleans and London Avenue canals lay farther east, one on each side of City Park. Beyond London Avenue sat the Industrial Canal—the shipping channel running through the Ninth Ward, completed in 1923.

As people moved into New Orleans's low-lying areas during the nineteenth century, more and more water had to be pumped upward to get it out of the city—putting a constant strain on primitive, paddle-wheel "drainage machines." Fetid water and stagnant sewage in ditches bred repeated epidemics, including yellow fever, spread by mosquitoes, that killed tens of thousands of New Orleanians—eight thousand residents in 1853 alone. By the turn of the century, it was unclear if the city could continue to grow, or even sustain itself with its current population. Then came A. Baldwin Wood.

Wood was a gifted engineer with a knack for problem solving on the fly. Raised in Uptown New Orleans, he graduated from Tulane University's engineering school in 1899 and got a job at the New Orleans Drainage Commission, which soon merged with the Sewerage and Water Board. There, he quickly made a mark working on the city's creaky pumps and pipes. Wood was a notorious perfectionist—during one of his early as-signments, he ordered brand-new sewage pumps completely re-built after finding small glitches. If he found this sort of a gadget lacking, he would design his way around the problem—sometimes inadvertently inventing a new device.

In 1913, Wood invented a new kind of pump that was bigger and more powerful than the standard models of the day, thanks to its innovative design. At the time, most pumps used big screws to lift water mechanically. The Wood pump used suction from a huge, propellerlike blade. This let it operate smoothly and quietly, and move a lot more water. After building tiny scale models, testing and retesting, the Sewerage and Water Board concluded that using Wood's new pumps would almost double the city's pumping capacity and ordered that eleven be built and installed by 1915. Brick pumping stations—giant pipes sprouting from their sides like the legs of a giant beetle—started going up at key junctures around the city where sewers and underwater aqueducts met larger canals. When a hurricane struck in September 1915, the two completed Wood pumping stations acquitted themselves well.

Wood's devices—augmented by even larger models designed in 1928, and by new "clogless" rotors that became the worldwide standard—allowed even the most sodden swamplands to be pumped dry and kept that way. Roads previously consisting of mud with an overlay of shells could be paved. New lands could be opened to development and farming, and the city expanded north toward the lake, into the now-reclaimed cypress swamp. Even Lake Pontchartrain became a fertile ground for expansion: in 1924, the Levee Board built a stepped concrete seawall at the lakefront, a half mile out into the water, then dredged the bottom and filled in the huge gap behind it, creating what would become the city's priciest neighborhoods, home to marinas, yachts, and the University of New Orleans.

Wood's achievements made him world famous. He was hired to design Chicago's drainage system. "Wood pumps" (as they came to be known) were built in India, Egypt, and China. When the Dutch government—seeking ways to reclaim submerged land to build new cities and farmlands—approached Wood, he declined because he didn't want to leave New Orleans. The Dutch came to him. New Orleans, thanks to Wood, seemed to have all the answers.

There was one problem: if a hurricane storm surge entered the lake, the canals would be a direct conduit for a flood into the heart of the city. City engineers fretted over this for years. In

1871, city surveyor W. H. Bell suggested that pumping stations should be moved to the lakefront because "heavy storms would result in water backup within the canal, culminating in an overflow of the city." The proposal was ignored.

Bell's fears were realized during the 1915 hurricane, when Lake Pontchartrain rose five to seven feet. "On Thursday morning the lake level still maintained its maximum elevation, and there were numerous points along the various navigation and drainage outfall canals and on the rear protection levees where lake water was entering the city in large amount," Sewerage and Water Board superintendent George Earl wrote. But still, decades passed, nothing was done, and the problem got worse. Pumping stations once at the edge of the city soon sat in the midst of the urban landscape, below sea level in many places. The canals were left open to the lake, running through newly built neighborhoods. The Levee Board drove sheet pile (rows of flat, interlocking steel columns) into the low earthen canal levees to hold them in place—but it clearly wasn't enough protection.

Had the Corps's original barrier plan gone forward and blocked storm surges from Lake Pontchartrain, the canals would have been a minor concern. But once the Corps dropped it in favor of a levees-only policy, the canals became vulnerable points. They would have to be protected somehow or it would mean catastrophe. The Corps's solution sounded familiar: more gates, this time across the mouths of the three canals at the lakefront. It was a simple, elegant answer. Unlike in the original barrier plan, the environmental impact in this case would be minimal—the lakefront was already developed. And the same military analogy held: cut off your enemy at the narrowest point. The alternative—building miles of levees along the canals— would expose a wider area to flooding should a levee fail.

The Corps had already ceded some control over the rivers and the marshes to the EPA. But with the new canal plan, the Corps was trespassing on New Orleans's political turf, where patronage ruled and tendrils of political influence stretched everywhere. The Levee Board was in charge of the canal floodwalls. The Sewerage and Water Board owned the pumping stations and the canal bottoms. Backyards sat on either side of the canals—private property, their owners represented by neighborhood associations and sundry political groups.

These groups didn't much like the gate idea when the Corps proposed it in the 1980s. The Sewerage and Water Board was nervous that the new gates would make it impossible to pump water out during a storm—trapping rainfall and flooding the city anyway. Corps officials disagreed, noting that if there was a storm surge in the lake, the high water would block the outflow anyway. "If there is a tidal surge in Lake Pontchartrain, I don't care where the barrier is. You're not going to be able to pump water out into the lake efficiently," said General Sands, who oversaw the development of the second gate plan. The Levee Board's chief concern was more mundane. Under complicated cost-sharing arrangements between the agencies, the board would end up paying a lot more if a gate were constructed (in that case, the official purpose of the floodwalls would be to contain rainfall, not storm surges). But if the Corps built hurricane levees along the canals, the federal government would shoulder most of the costs.

Again, the debate didn't make much difference: the projected costs for the Corps's pricey, complex gates started escalating, just as they'd done with its earlier plan. Congress required choosing the low-cost approach, so the Corps agreed to build floodwalls in the 17th Street canal and held out hope for gates in the other two canals. The flow of water was only one variable. The flow of money was another. The Corps argued that in this case, building floodwalls was a purely local responsibility: the Corps of Engineers didn't do drainage canals. Thus Senator Long's intervention. In an appropriations bill that included hurricane protection, he fiddled with the language so that the canals were explicitly included.

"The Corps didn't know we added this language in there," said Long's then chief of staff Bruce Feingerts, who drafted the relevant wording at the Levee Board's request. "Then they called me and asked why they were being told to build in the canals, and I showed them the page in the conference report. They weren't happy."

The Corps had been defeated again: it would now have to build and pay for floodwalls in the canals. The change was added to a growing mountain of aggravations. Since the defeat of the barrier plan, the agency had adjusted its mission. It was staffing up with biologists, ecologists, and economists to help it negotiate the shoals of expanding environmental regulations, even requiring a senior biologist to take part in every major decision. It was also farming out more and more of its core engineering functions to contractors. As the hurricane levee project dragged into its fourth decade, the regular stream of money from Congress fell off. It was getting harder and harder to finish projects on time, if at all. And, everyone knew, the weather wasn't going to wait forever.

All of these problems conspired to turn a straightforward engineering task—building modest floodwalls in canals—into the single most troubled of the Corps's hurricane projects.

The Corps chose the simplest and cheapest type of floodwall to protect New Orleans. Called an I-wall, it consisted of a sheet pile foundation topped by ten feet of concrete, embedded in a low earthen levee. I-walls weren't the strongest type of barrier—but who needed strength in a canal, where pounding waves wouldn't be a problem? I-walls also took up very little space—unlike a wide earthen levee—so they were perfect for people's backyards, and for keeping complaints to a minimum.

"The problem with the walls along the canals was the difficulty in locating them properly," recalled Fred Bayley, then chief of the New Orleans engineering division. "They ran along through neighborhoods. People were unhappy with any type of construction in that area, and would be unhappy with any expansion into their yards. Their back doors were not far from the canals."

But building in the soil was a challenge. It was, after all, a swamp. Its many layers, squashed under homes and earthen fill, were a museum of the previous thousand years. They contained the decaying remnants of trees, bushes, grasses, fish, and muskrats. Add the castoffs of human activity—huts, tools, railroad ties, and discarded clothing of Indians and European American trappers, fishermen, and pirates. Some layers had deteriorated to peat—rotting organic matter. Some were soft clays with organics mixed in, others harder, drier clays. Farther down sat silt and sand, the remnants of Pine Island, the ancient beach from the time the area fronted the Gulf. Traces of old bayous and channels also sliced through the subterranean landscape.

In the summer of 1994, contractor A. B. Pittman ran into a problem at the 17th Street canal: the floodwalls it was building were tilting a few degrees off the vertical. Pittman's pile drivers had been hammering sheet piles into the muck. Then workers set up molds over the piles and poured concrete into them. When the molds and their support braces were removed, some of the slabs had tipped. The soil, it turned out, was very soft—and driving the piles only made it softer.

If you were a biologist or an archaeologist, the Louisiana muck was fascinating. But it was maddening stuff for engineers. Soil is an engineering wild card even under the best of circumstances. It's made of compressed, tiny particles and water. Making things stand up straight was challenge enough. But ensuring that they stayed upright during the unusual pressures of a flood was even harder. Floodwater rising next to a levee puts pressure on the soil. Most of the time, the soil in a levee remains in place. But if the water pressure rises high enough, the friction and pressure holding the soil in place are overcome: a chunk breaks loose and starts sliding along a broad plane. All it takes is a single weak point to open a levee breach.

Nevertheless, if a levee can be built to the right dimensions, every soil quirk accounted for, it will stand up under the worst of circumstances. Engineers start with a disadvantage: there's no way to get a complete picture of what's underground. The Corps and its contractors had drawn up a subterranean map using soil borings 350 feet apart, most at the centerline of the levee. But in New Orleans, the soil varies yard by yard. Firm areas abut soft, weak ones. Underground debris that never turns up in a boring can provide conduits for floodwater and precipitate a collapse. A boring created when a drill bit grinds through an ancient tree may not contain evidence of a layer of clay a few inches away. Solidity is flecked with weaknesses.

Engineers try to account for such uncertainty by being more conservative in their designs. But the Corps standards for hurricane levees left little room for error. The mandated safety factor—1.3—was already quite low. More generally, because storm surge floods last for only hours or, at most, days, hurricane levees and floodwalls were not required to be as wide or strong as their river counterparts. Those differences downplayed the risk of seeping water. "The belief was that hurricane protection levees didn't have to accommodate long periods of saturated soils as the result of flood stages remaining alongside them," said Randy Hanchey, a former Corps engineer who later went to work for the state of Louisiana. With river levees, he said, "they wanted to contain the seepage . . . but they didn't build the hurricane levees that way."

In 1988, engineers at the Metairie office of Modjeski and Masters—a prestigious century-old design firm with offices around the United States—working with PCs, pencils, paper, and calculators, figured out some basic dimensions for the floodwalls in the 17th Street canal. They had data from soil borings done by Eustis Engineering, a respected local firm. Eustis had squashed samples from each layer in a centrifuge to see how they responded to stress, and written reams of documents with quirky observations on the soil's color and consistency in different layers. The Modjeski and Masters designers plugged that data into a set of formulas provided by the Corps. The equations painted a rough picture of how the soil would behave when stressed.

An I-wall's two components—the concrete-and-steel wall and its earthen levee base—work in concert to keep the whole structure upright. The levee holds up the wall, of course. But the steel sheet pilings, driven deep into the soil, also stabilize the levee, in part by stopping water from seeping through and dislodging the soil.

But if the earthen base alone is deemed stable enough, deep

sheet piling isn't necessary. That was the choice Modjeski and Masters engineers made with the 17th Street canal. They figured the soil's prime weak point was thirty-six feet down, where the swamp muck sat on the layer of sand. They calculated that the girth of the levee and the soil's weight pressing down at that point would resist any incipient failure. That analysis conveniently confirmed that the Corps could go the cheapest route: for much of the wall's length, it could use sheet piles that the Levee Board had already installed, simply driving them down an additional seven feet, to a total depth of seventeen feet.

That analysis effectively ignored layers of soft soils at a depth of about fifteen to twenty feet down. There, a slippery, inch-thick layer of clay sat between a fatter layer embedded with remnants of leaves and twigs (apparently deposited by an ancient hurricane or river flood) and a layer of exceedingly soft peat. Any engineering student could see these layers were a potential weak point; building a wall in it would be like putting bricks on Jell-O. Sheet piles anchored seventeen feet down would not go past the weak layers—or even the bottom of the canal, which the Sewerage and Water Board had recently dredged down to 18.5 feet. To make matters worse, the dredging had shaved soil off the levee base under water in the canal, making a shorter route for water seeping under the wall, and again increasing the odds of failure. (A Modjeski and Masters executive later told the *Times-Picayune* that his firm had at one point recommended a sheet pile depth of thirty-five feet and was rebuffed by the Corps. He did not document the claim.)

The soil analysis technique Modjeski and Masters used dated to the early twentieth century. Other Corps offices had abandoned this type of analysis in favor of more up-to-date soil models, but the New Orleans district had stubbornly stuck with what it knew. The design was approved by the Corps's New Orleans district and by reviewers in the division office in Vicksburg.

Meanwhile, the Corps was cutting corners elsewhere. The New Orleans levees now made a sprawling footprint over the delta. But in some spots, different structures met and didn't quite fit together. In others, where floodwalls dipped under bridges, workers and volunteers had to pile sandbags into gaps when hurricanes approached. Ideas about how to fix the problems came and went. In 1978, when a levee on the London Avenue canal washed out, the Corps proposed building a T-wall, a fortified floodwall that looked like an inverted *T,* anchored with both sheet piling and much longer steel beams. The new design was later abandoned in favor of weaker, cheaper I-walls. Regarding the Orleans canal, the Corps and the Sewerage and Water Board figured if water rose too high against the pumping station, its wall might collapse and destroy the pumps inside. However, they couldn't agree on how to deal with the problem, and funding for a fix ran out. The floodwalls were never connected to the pumping station and gaps remained on both sides, one about eighty feet short of the brick pumping-station wall, the other about thirty yards.

Chapter 5

SINKING FEELING

THE MORNING OF July 18, 1997, a small, temperamental hurricane named Danny wobbled toward the Louisiana coast on an east-northeast course, squeezed in that direction by high-pressure systems on either side. Danny's eye made landfall at about nine a.m. on the eighteenth, to the east of Grand Isle and due south of New Orleans. It moved across the marshes, the Mississippi River, and more marshes, then out over the Gulf again on its way toward Alabama. It came ashore there early the next day.

When a hurricane moves over land, it is cut off from the sea's great well of warmth and moisture. As a result, its massive whorl starts to disintegrate into bands of thunderstorms and unsettled air, which is why a hurricane's strength diminishes as it moves inland. As expected, readings of the air pressure within the eye—an important measure of hurricane strength—rose slightly as Danny moved across the Mississippi delta. But then something strange happened: the pressure began dropping again as Danny crossed the marshes and bays east of the river.

Local hurricane watchers reviewed Danny's behavior with alarm. Windell Curole, who oversees a federal levee in Louisiana's Lafourche Parish—one of the few such redoubts that far south—looked over the barometric pressure and the track afterward and was stunned. "It was crazy," he said later. "What kind of place makes a hurricane get stronger?" Luckily, even a fortified Danny was too weak to cause much damage. But the boost in strength was an ominous sign.

Anyone flying over southeast Louisiana could see the reason. The delta ringing New Orleans was a delicate filigree of blue, green, and brown. Instead of a peninsula, it was a vast multitude of inlets: water jutted into land, creeping around and over it, worming its way in via bayous, canals, and thousands of small cuts people had made over the previous three centuries. The form of this strange hybrid changed hourly with the tides. And in a storm, the entire landmass was submerged and became a shallow sea—suddenly a very good heat sink for a hurricane.

As the Corps embarked on its plan to protect New Orleans with a new levee system, engineers observed a big kink developing: the land around and underneath those levees was sinking into the Gulf. Geologists and coastal scientists had noted this for decades, but government agencies and residents had largely ignored the problem. By the 1970s, however, such a lack of attention became impossible. Changes could be observed year to year. Tides and storms were shaving down barrier islands to narrow dunes and washing salt water farther inland, poisoning the marshes. Savannahs of yellow-green grass were turning brown. Fields of dead cypress resembled monstrous claws reaching into the sky. The cradle of south Louisiana's famed bayou culture—home over the centuries to French and French Canadian fishermen and trappers, Indians, pirates, and, later, immigrants from the Canary Islands, Croatia, and Vietnam— was disappearing along with the land.

In some ways, this change was inevitable: river deltas have limited lifespans, decaying as the sea reclaims them. But once humans tried to stop the Mississippi delta life cycle cold, to stabilize the changeable earth under their feet, the result was one of the world's great engineering follies. The Louisiana marshes weren't just fading away; they were sinking and eroding ten times as fast as normal. And from small bayou hamlets inland to New Orleans, the vanishing delta was undermining the region's hurricane levee protection even as it was being built. The lower the delta sank, the closer deadly storm surges migrated toward the city. There's a famous Chekhov maxim about drama that states that if a gun appears on the wall in Act One, it should go off in Act Three. In Louisiana, the gun was already on the table. Now, by speeding the delta's decline, man had loaded it.

In the early 1800s, as tribal lore has it, a Choctaw named Jean Charles Naquin ran supplies for Jean Lafitte while the famed pirate secreted himself away in the marshes, trading goods and emerging for raids on ships in the Gulf—and, at one point, to join forces with Andrew Jackson in the Battle of New Orleans. Naquin frequented the marshes near the village of Pointe-aux-Chenes, in Terrebonne Parish, about seventy miles southwest of New Orleans. One typical marshy spot, not quite a ridge and not quite an island, made a good campground and way station. It was reachable via a small bayou and reliably dry. Naquin and his sons cleared a passage through the bayou so they could get a decent-sized pirogue through. In 1876, one son, Jean Baptiste Narcisse Naquin, along with three other men, all related by marriage—Antoine Livaudais Dardar, Marcelin Duchils Naquin, and Walker Lovell—bought the ridge. At some point after that, the bayou became known as Bayou Jean Charles. After the Civil War, Jim Crow laws against race mixing were in force throughout the South, even in the remote bayous of Louisiana. The four Indians came from mixed stock—Spanish and French colonists had routinely taken Indians as their wives—and were looking for a place to call their own, away and isolated. When the men brought their families there, they christened the island Isle de Jean Charles.

Needing an easy way in and out, the men took shovels and buckets and widened the bayou some more. They built a makeshift bridge to connect the two halves of the island, and they put up small huts in the traditional style, with clay and moss walls, raised clay floors to keep things dry, and dome-shaped roofs covered in palmetto fronds, with a smoke hole in the center. Marsh stretched out for more than a mile behind their huts. Residents could walk out into their backyards and cut down trees, plow the land, and farm potatoes, beans, corn, and okra. Children wandered off into the woods and the tall grass and pretended to be Lafitte's band. Their fathers scraped up a living off the marshes, trapping muskrats, tending to oyster beds, and shrimping from pirogues and small skiffs, selling their wares in nearby villages. A 1910 census listed seventy-seven residents belonging to sixteen families. In later decades, the population grew to more than two hundred.

Isle de Jean Charles had a tenuous connection to the mainland, and liked it that way. There was a narrow wagon path along an abutting ridge, but it flooded easily. For decades, the children rode pirogues each day to an Indian school set up by the Baptist Church in Pointe-aux-Chenes, until the church set up a one-room schoolhouse on the island. Modernity finally encroached in 1953 in the form of a two-mile dirt track raised over the high-tide mark, though storms still flooded it. After that, successive chiefs succeeded in getting the two-mile road inlaid with shells, then blacktopped in the 1970s.

Then their land started disappearing out from under them.

It was imperceptible at first, but by the 1960s Isle de Jean Charles had become less of a ridge and more of a true island. The grass started dying and the swamps grew muddier. The outer edges of gardens and farms died off, then larger areas became impossible to till. By the 1990s, the high tide was lapping within spitting distance of people's homes. The road often disappeared under high water, and the new chief—a descendant of Jean Naquin named Albert Naquin—made repeated treks to Baton Rouge to persuade the state to raise and repave it. Naquin himself moved off the island to Pointe-aux-Chenes because the daily commute to his job was so unreliable.

Nearly every day, Naquin gets in a pickup and drives across the span to visit his two brothers and sister and other longtime residents, who still hop in boats and ply the marshes, dragging shrimp nets or harvesting oyster leases beyond the edge of the grass, where a small cemetery sits dating back one hundred years. Reverend Roch Naquin, a local Catholic priest, comes in regularly to say masses in people's kitchens.

"It ain't much to look at, but it has some value to society. We've been making a life here. Our ancestors are buried here. We deserve some recognition, some protection," Chief Albert said. "But there's a lot of competition out there. That makes it hard to get the resources you need. Everybody's living under the same threat." That threat is a hurricane. In the early years, a hurricane storm surge rolling over the island was a relatively rare sight, maybe once in a generation—and even then it didn't rise so high. The residents knew their luck could always run out. Past catastrophes were fixed in memory, history, and legend. The 1856 Last Island storm was one cautionary tale. But the worst by far was a hurricane that struck the marshes without warning on October 1, 1893. The storm was only a Category 2, with sustained wind speeds of about 100 mph. But its storm surge washed over dozens of marsh villages with minimal levee protection or none at all. It carried off the homes of fishermen and vacation cottages that dotted the beach at Grand Isle. It destroyed all but two houses in the village of Buras on the riverbank and knocked the Our Lady of Good Harbor Catholic Church off its pillars. Railroad workers clearing the tracks afterward found the bodies of three young sisters from nearby Oyster Bayou, nearly naked and wrapped in barbed wire. Nine men clinging to debris floated for four days, eating what they could by tearing at the bodies of dead animals scooped from the water. Human corpses could be seen for miles around them.

A busy fishing town named Cheniere Caminada (blending the French for the delta's low oak ridges with the Spanish for "pathway") took the brunt of the 1893 storm. Cheniere Caminada consisted of about three hundred modest cottages constructed with Cajun *bousillage,* a mixture of mud and Spanish moss, built close together in two neat lines along a ridge similar to Isle de Jean Charles, facing Caminada Bay and the western end of Grand Isle. As the water rose, hundreds climbed up on rooftops. A report in the *Thibodaux Sentinel* described the terrible scene:

> The first effects of the storm were felt between 4 and 5 p.m. on Sunday. Everyone apprehended that something terrible was about to happen. . . . There was one avenue of safety, and that was to seek the upper stories of the houses, but even that chance for escape was lost when the wind and waves combined shook the frail habitations, which rocked to and fro and creaked and groaned under the repeated attacks of the furious elements. Soon the houses were being demolished, wrecked and carried away. The wind shifted to the southeast, and for hours shrieked with redoubled fury. Above the thundering voice of the hurricane could be heard the despairing cries, the groans and the frantic appeals for help of the unfortunate victims.

The next morning, half the town's population—about eight hundred people—were dead. Across the marshes, the toll was two thousand.

"Dead were everywhere; the odor endured," one account read. "Often coffins and separate graves were unavailable, so bodies were buried where they were found." The authorities dug a mass grave on the site of the village. A few persistent fishermen later tried homesteading the ridge, but a 1915 hurricane wiped out the settlement and no one ever dared settle there again. A small graveyard and memorial were later built by the roadside, where they remain today.

The possibility of a similar end lurked in the back of the minds of everyone who lived on or near Isle de Jean Charles. And the odds were getting shorter. Starting in the 1960s, Isle de Jean Charles had been hit at least once every ten years. Hurricane Hilda put three feet of water over the island in 1964. Ten years later, Hurricane Carmen did the same. In 1985, resident Michel Dardar finally raised his house four feet after Hurricane Danny (another storm, predating the 1997 Danny) flooded the island, but two months later, Hurricane Juan's six-foot storm surge got him anyway. In 1992, Hurricane Andrew did the same. Each time, Dardar returned, dried out his walls and floors, replaced his furniture, and got on with his life, unwilling even to think about leaving.

What had happened to Isle de Jean Charles was happening across the delta. Whether they worked the marshes or not, people in hardscrabble towns like Dulac, Cutoff, Leeville, and Bayou Dularge marked their daily rhythms by the tides and the yellows, greens, and pale lavenders of grass, water, and sky. Those rhythms had become unstable and dangerous. The water was moving farther north, too, encroaching on the suburbs around New Orleans faster than new subdivisions could be built.

What was happening? For one, change is the rule on a delta. People think that geological time is impossibly slow, stretching beyond the boundaries of everyday perception. For the most part, this is correct. We'll never watch a mountain range rise out of the ground. But a delta is a protean creation, changing over centuries, decades, years, and sometimes hours.

The Mississippi delta's origins lie only twenty thousand years back, when glaciers covered much of North America. The oceans had receded—their water was locked up in the ice—and the Gulf of Mexico was about four hundred feet lower than it is today. When the glaciers melted and withdrew, they left behind a bruised landscape of valleys, hollows, and flats, littered with boulders and rock formations. Rivers swelled and seas rose, pushing the coastline back to more or less its current position. There, the river met the sea and began to whip up a layer cake of earth: the sea washed sand upriver and over the low-lying delta plain, creating beaches, dunes, and sandy stretches along the curves of bayous. The river fought back, dumping silt and clay from far upriver along its banks and, during floods, spreading sediment for hundreds of miles around. Each year, spring floods deposited more and more new earth.

When the seas stopped rising about five thousand years ago, the eventual site of New Orleans was mostly under water. Only a sliver of land that geologists dubbed Pine Island stretched along what would become the south shore of Lake Pontchartrain. But soon, due to buildups of silt and muck, the river began darting (in geologic time) back and forth like a loose garden hose, laying the foundation of today's Mississippi delta. The river changed course every thousand years or so, sending torrents through narrow bayous. Over the millennia the Mississippi made seven of these course corrections, so today's delta sits on top of six earlier incarnations. Isle de Jean Charles and other ridges are remnants of past riverbanks that straddle the delta in a fine skeletal structure.

From the time that Indians first arrived in the area around 8,000 BCE to the present day, such ridges have been the prime real estate—the places most likely to stay dry during a flood. In New Orleans, that high ground lies on the riverbanks and on ridges that cut north of the river through Metairie and Gentilly and northwest away from the French Quarter along what is now Esplanade Avenue.

When a river changes course, abandoned delta lobes become geologic has-beens, no longer nourished by floods and deposits of fresh sediment. Centuries of piled-up muck slowly compresses and settles. The sea intrudes where it couldn't before, sloshing its way up abandoned tributaries and insinuating itself into the soil. As the fresh water–salt water balance shifts, the ecological webs that sustain wildlife change as well. Grass and trees die. Some fish disappear, others take their place.

Usually, though, the river is building a new delta lobe somewhere nearby, so life relocates. When the Corps established its tenuous grip on the Mississippi in the nineteenth century, however, the levees radically altered the play of forces between the river's flow, the sea, and the land. With the river locked in place behind ever-higher levees, marsh-building stopped.

Even before the levees, it had slowed. Earlier deltas spread out lazily over the shallows. But the last delta lobe, called the Balize delta, was a mere teardrop in the Gulf compared to the large, messy splotches that preceded it. As the delta's edge approached the continental shelf, where the seafloor dropped three hundred feet, much of the river sediment was already ending up under water—not in new land. The pattern indicated that the Mississippi was contemplating another course change—this time down the Atchafalaya River. Such a shift would have rebuilt marshes to the west of New Orleans. But the river levees and, later, the Corps's Old River Control Structure prevented that, too.

With no new earth building it up, the delta collapsed like a soufflé. A National Geodetic Survey study showed that some places were sinking at an astonishing pace. Between 1966 and 1993, Chauvin, a village a few miles west of Isle de Jean Charles, sank an average of six-tenths of an inch per year—sixteen inches total. In many spots, it was even faster—an inch per year in Humphreys, even more in Franklin. New Orleans was sinking, too. Michoud, in the eastern part of the city, sank nearly an inch a year between 1955 and 1993—almost three feet. In the city's western suburbs and other parts of town, the process was slower. But everything was headed downward—except the sea, which was gradually rising. When sinking land and rising seas were combined, the study found that in south Louisiana, the change amounted to five feet per century.

Meanwhile, people discovered that swampland did have economic value after all, thanks to the delta's other big geological feature: more than one hundred million years ago, a sea covered most of North America, and as it receded it left massive salt deposits behind. Earth and the rotting remains of the rich biological trove—dinosaurs, vegetation, early mammals—built up on top of them. Enormous rock layers pressed downward on this biological gumbo, creating a deep trough of compressed muck on top of the salt, which over time became seams of oil and pockets of natural gas. Sometimes the pressure caused this mix to erupt toward the surface, and Indians and early settlers would spy the telltale rainbow of oil in the marsh and make use of oil tar as pitch for their pirogues.

After the Civil War, sugar lost its economic cachet. Plantations were broken up and the land along the river and elsewhere on the delta was sold off to interests that had other ideas about how to exploit them. Logging companies moved in and chopped down the cypress forests. Then they ran out of trees.

In 1901, Jules Clement, a farmer in the southwestern Louisiana town of Jennings, found bubbles percolating up from the mud in his rice field. Curious, he stuck a section of stovepipe into the muck, lit matches, and tossed them in. The bubbles caught fire. Just a few months earlier, the nation's first oil gusher had been discovered at Spindletop, Texas. It turned out that Clement was sitting on treasure worth more than gold, and soon a consortium of local businessmen had hired a couple of wildcatters, the Heywood brothers, to drill on his property.

Drilling rigs went up throughout Louisiana as multiple pockets of gas and petroleum were found, easily accessed from under the delta's mushy soil. In 1909, John D. Rockefeller made it official and Standard Oil built the state's first refinery, north of Baton Rouge. Thanks to an antitrust ruling, Texas had become a bit hostile to Rockefeller, but the Louisiana political establishment treated businesses with a light hand if they knew how to spread money around. Huey Long began cementing the mutual back-scratching, taxing oil and gas to pay for schoolbooks and fund the state government. Louisiana politicians enriched themselves by playing elaborate shell games with swamplands that ostensibly belonged to the public. Leander H. Perez, the notorious, racist district attorney who held absolute power in Plaquemines Parish, persuaded Long to back a law ceding control of the lands to local governments. Then he had his local politicians lease the lands to his own dummy corporations, which turned them over to oil companies—for a hefty price.

With the Standard Oil refinery as an anchor, a variety of companies built a network of pipelines, roads, and canals to link the drilling with the refining—and ship the product wherever it might be needed. By 1926, 2,610 miles of pipeline covered the southern reaches of the delta. Drawing oil and gas out of the earth aggravated faults and the land sank faster. It also scarred the marshes. The companies leveed off prime drilling sites, creating polluted, stagnant lakes. They dumped chemical and petroleum waste wherever they pleased. They dredged and widened the bayous and cut the marsh into a crosshatched pattern of channels. Once their underground finds dwindled by the 1970s, companies moved drilling operations offshore, where the truly big strikes awaited, leaving the damaged marsh behind, a mere transit point for pipelines and equipment barges.

The Corps took an active hand in this destruction as well. Two of its main missions were, after all, building navigable waterways and stimulating development where none existed. Even after Congress decided wetlands were worthy of protection, it put the Corps in charge of handing out the permits—with predictable results.

The Corps made its single biggest impact in the 1960s, when it built the Mr. Go channel through the marshes to the east of New Orleans. The project cost a whopping sixty-two million dollars—a shade less than the cost of the entire proposed levee system—and more material was dredged from it than had come out of the Panama Canal. But when the dredging started, tides began bringing salt water farther inland than it had ever come before, with disastrous results. The banks of the canal—originally 650 feet across—quickly dissolved, and the canal effectively spread across the marshes. It widened to a half mile across in spots, and it was hard to tell where it left off and the marsh began. Despite the fact that the Mr. Go never caught on as a shipping route—most days, it was lucky to see a single ship—the Corps continued to devotedly service the canal, dredging it year after year.

The destruction of the marshes took tragicomic turns as well. In the 1930s, Louisiana importers hoping to make a killing in the fur business brought a big, hungry South American rodent called the nutria to the Gulf Coast and set up breeding farms. The nutria is about fourteen inches long, with prominent whiskers, bright orange teeth, a voracious appetite, and a gift for reproduction. When the farms failed, nutria began to multiply and spread throughout the marshes. Within a decade they had squeezed out the native muskrats sought by trappers. They were kept in check by fur hunters until the 1970s, when antifur activists caused a worldwide drop in demand for their pelts. Nutria are burrowing animals that savor the root beds of marsh plants. Soon millions of creatures were literally turning the grasslands upside down and devouring them.

As the land sank and water flowed farther inland, these man-made alterations turned the delta into an enormous, waterlogged jigsaw puzzle, each ragged piece separated from the others by salty water. Mathematically speaking, the length of its exposed edges—where salt water was eating into mud and grass—grew geometrically. Marshlands disappeared at a rate of thirty-four square miles per year between 1956 and 2000—though it slowed to twenty-four square miles after 1990—still equivalent to thirteen football fields per day. From the air, Isle de Jean Charles had become a yellow sliver surrounded by blue.

The changes robbed the outlying towns around New Orleans of all their natural flood protection. The waterlogged marshes were lower relative to sea level, so floods were deeper. There were fewer natural obstacles—trees, grass, brush—whose drag could slow a flood moving inland. With nothing in their way but an irregular patchwork of levees, storm surges from even modest hurricanes now flowed across highways, onto school playing fields and parking lots, into drainage canals and strip malls. Weak storms were doing more damage than mighty ones had a few decades earlier. When Hurricane Camille—a monster Category 5 storm that wrecked the Mississippi coast in 1969—roared past to the east of New Orleans, it caused some flooding in Shell Beach, a lonely outpost along the Mr. Go frequented by commercial fishermen and sportsmen. When Hurricane Georges, a Category 2 storm following a similar track, swept through in 1998, natural defenses had all but disappeared and Shell Beach ended up under several feet of water.

In July 1985, the National Geodetic Survey issued a new set of benchmark elevation readings for New Orleans. Most were lower than the numbers that Frederick Chatry, chief engineer for the Corps New Orleans District, had used since 1965 to set the heights for levees under construction. That meant the levees would not do the job they were originally designed to do. The risk of flooding or failure would be higher—incrementally in some places, a lot more in others.

Chatry faced a difficult choice. Applying the updated figures to the levee system would mean raising hundreds of miles of levees, requiring additional planning, design, and construction work. The delays and the price tag—probably in the tens of millions of dollars—would bust his already overstretched budget and enrage Congress and local governments. In its original authorization, Congress had made no allowances for changing conditions.

So Chatry split the difference. The Corps would use the new elevation numbers only for new projects not yet on the drawing board. Those completed or already under way would still be based on the older numbers, meaning some would be more than a foot shorter than the heights mandated by Congress. "The level of precision in the current data and the practical difficulty and cost of changing such projects combine to mandate this course of action at least for the foreseeable future," he wrote in a memo to his bosses in Vicksburg. They concurred.

Geologists had studied subsidence for decades, but few looked at how sinking marshes compounded the damage from storm surges. At LSU, coastal oceanographer Joe Suhayda and computer scientist Vibhas Aravamuthan began studying the relationship in the 1990s. It was a difficult engineering problem—how did a giant wave interact with a nearly flat, yet rough and variable, landscape? And how did that relationship change as the land disappeared? Doing studies on how to repair the ragged, damaged marshes, they'd found that most modelers—including those in the Corps—were using outdated elevation data. In many spots water had intruded to places where maps showed land; the landscape was changing faster than surveyors could update the data.

Suhayda had an insight: if the models could account for the disappearing marshes, they could show changes in storm surge flooding as well. Using topographical data going back more than a century, and some future projections, Suhayda and Arava-muthan created a series of virtual deltas. The oldest, circa 1870, showed a solid marsh stretching out to the barrier islands. The last, circa 2020, showed only an evanescent crochet around New Orleans. Suhayda and Aravamuthan threw virtual storms at these virtual coastlines and the results were striking: the earlier deltas had water building up against barrier islands and the coastline, moving only so far inland. An imaginary Category 3 hurricane left the city of Houma, about forty miles southwest of New Orleans, dry in 1930. But by 2020—with barrier islands virtually gone and only a fragmentary marsh protecting the city—the storm left it surrounded by three feet of water.

The constant battering from hurricanes took a toll on communities as well as the land. Some towns managed to harden themselves. Grand Isle, the barrier island fronting the Gulf—its inhabitants perched on top of a sand dune—tried various engineering schemes to protect itself from the fate of nearby Cheniere Caminada. It built a system of jetties to protect its beach. They failed. It tried a levee. It dissolved. All homes were built on stilts or pilings—the only way to get federal flood insurance. Farther inland, towns that took on six feet of water one year, then double that a few years later, faced slow disintegration. Hurricane Andrew put ten feet of water into the shrimp port of Dulac in 1992. More than a decade later, many businesses—fishing supply outlets, barber shops—sat abandoned. Some streets were lined with empty homes, occupied by transients or used as temporary digs by drug dealers.

Younger people started abandoning Isle de Jean Charles as soon as they graduated from high school, leaving the place populated by a declining older generation and a group of impoverished residents surviving on fishing and government support. In 2002, the Corps made a decision that meant a certain end for the island. A cost-benefit analysis decreed it be left outside a big new hurricane levee that would snake through bayou country. Retired from his job as an inspector with the Minerals Management Service, Chief Albert traveled to New Orleans and

Washington to lobby the Corps. He gathered letters from residents. He put together a history to show the community's cultural value. He pushed for federal recognition for the tribe, and the political cachet that might confer. He failed. Protecting Isle de Jean Charles, the Corps reasoned, would cost more than the place was worth, so it didn't deserve the taxpayers' money. The next year, Chief Albert's sister Denecia and her husband, Wenceslaus Billiot, raised their house from two feet off the ground to thirteen. "I don't know how long we got," he told a reporter. "I don't think we got another twenty years. You never know."

Soon he would find out.

Chapter 6

"WE'RE GOING TO NEED A LOT OF BODY BAGS"

ITH HIS DOCTORATE IN SOCIOLOGY—his PhD dissertation explored the Jesuit philosophy of education, which exhorts students to channel learning into leadership and public service—Walter Maestri seemed an unorthodox choice to direct Jefferson Parish's Office of Emergency Management. In Louisiana, such jobs usually went to ex–military officers, firefighters, or cops, who handled their most important task, orchestrating hurricane evacuations from the New Orleans area, like generals planning troop movements. And Maestri was unlikely for reasons beyond his fancy diploma: he knew trouble was inevitable.

Maestri had been serving as Jefferson's chief of information technology in 1997, trying to persuade government offices to use instant messaging, when Tim Coulon, the parish president, tapped him for the emergency position. Coulon had a new idea for the job: scare people. Cajole them. Drill them on the risks of hurricanes and floods. Anything—just so they left town when an evacuation was declared. Previous evacuations had resulted in fewer than half of the parish's residents actually leaving. Maestri was to become a prophet of doom, a Cassandra in spectacles and a button-down shirt. Seeing it as a chance to save lives and shape public policy at the same time, Maestri pursued the assignment with gusto. A blunt, fast-talking, heavyset man, Maestri seemed to take a certain grim delight in painting a graphic portrait of the watery hell that a hurricane could bring down on Louisiana. He'd spin horrific scenarios: biblical floods that swallowed all of New Orleans. People clawing at attic roofs as water rose past their necks. Thousands of human carcasses floating in the streets, rotting in the summer sun. He'd show slides of the rubble of Richelieu Apartments, a doomed building in Bay St. Louis, Mississippi, where dozens of people died in 1969 when Hurricane Camille's twenty-eight-foot storm surge washed over the coast. He all but stood out on a street corner with a sign that said THE END IS NEAR—though if someone had suggested it, he might have done that, too. Hurricane evacuations were "the rent we pay for living in southeast Louisiana," Maestri told a meeting of the parish's Citizens Drainage Board early in his first hurricane season as emergency director. "If I don't get fifty to sixty percent of the people in Jefferson Parish out, we're going to need a lot of body bags."

Maestri was the most outspoken of a group of scientists and emergency managers who recognized that a catastrophe was certain to strike New Orleans sooner or later. They doggedly pushed government agencies and the public to prepare for the worst, mainly by clearing out of town when a storm strike was imminent—a monster task, given the public's apparent indifference to the threat and the insane logistics of moving more than a million people out of southeast Louisiana in the space of a few days. Like the nineteenth-century debates over river flooding, their work was a product of its time, based on an emerging, highly detailed scientific portrait of a city under water.

It had been clear from the time of Bienville that hurricanes could flood New Orleans, and the Corps of Engineers had later put numerical odds to that risk—albeit imprecise ones. As the Corps's hurricane levees rose around the city, they gave the shallow New Orleans "bowl"—and those of neighboring suburbs like Jefferson—a noticeably higher protective rim. If a hurricane dumped enough water inside the levees, however, the resulting flood could now get quite deep—as much as thirty feet in some spots in the Lakeview neighborhood of New Orleans, thirteen feet below sea level. Betsy's flood had been trapped inside the St. Bernard and the Ninth Ward levees, but the central part of the city had never filled up with water. The very idea seemed abstract, almost unthinkable. It lay only in the realm of actuaries rattling abacuses, not in the five senses or the gut.

Understanding the threat to New Orleans and preparing for it depended on reliably predicting both hurricanes and the storm surges—arts that didn't come into their own until late in the twentieth century.

Ever since Isaac Cline's insights into the 1915 storm, meteorologists had increasingly made use of a growing raft of data. Radio and telephones allowed instant communication of weather information, filling many gaps in the picture of hurricane anatomy. But scientists still couldn't observe a storm as it was happening or divine where it would go with much precision.

One day in 1943, Lieutenant Colonel Joseph Duckworth of the U.S. Army Air Corps changed the rules. Duckworth was training British pilots to fly on instruments out of Bryan Airfield in east Texas, north of Houston. As a hurricane approached the coast one day, the Brits began ribbing Duckworth about the sturdiness of his AT-6 Texans, two-man, single-engine training craft. Duckworth bet them he could fly an AT-6 into the storm and back, then he did just that. Along with a copilot, weather officer Lieutenant Ralph O'Hair, Duckworth passed through choppy air and rainstorms until he reached the eye of the hurricane, then turned and flew back. Then he took a British pilot, Lieutenant William Jones-Burdick, back in with him. Jones-Burdick measured a temperature of seventy-three degrees Fahrenheit at seven thousand feet—proving what meteorologists predicted but had never confirmed, that the eye is a locus for warmth at high altitudes. With Duckworth's flights, hurricane reconnaissance was a reality.

Weather radar soon followed, then the launch of the nation's first weather satellites, starting on February 17, 1959, with the *Vanguard 2*—an aluminum-plated sphere containing two telescopes, two photocells, and transmitters. *Vanguard 2* unfortunately stopped working after nineteen days, but not before scientists realized that the data provided by weather satellites could be revelatory. Satellites allowed the Weather Bureau for the first time to see an entire storm and begin to decipher how it formed, moved, and interacted with the atmosphere around it. The TIROS III satellite, for example, provided a bird's-eye view of Hurricane Carla, which hit western Louisiana in September 1961, clearly showing the jet stream shaping its path and the empty areas between the storm's outer rain bands as it moved ashore.

Scientists began assembling a more nuanced, three-dimensional picture of a storm, and they were often surprised by what they found. On August 5, 1969, a weather satellite named ESSA 9 took pictures of a cloud pattern that looked like an inverted *V* off the coast of Africa—a tropical wave. It would later become Hurricane Camille, and as it approached the Gulf Coast, satellite passes showed it to be a relatively small storm. The conventional wisdom held that the bigger a storm was, the stronger it was. But two days later, a C-130 navy reconnaissance plane showed Camille was the most intense hurricane in the nation's history, with ground-level winds estimated at 200 mph.

Storm surges were another matter. From Cline's bad advice to Galveston to the Corps's Standard Project Hurricanes, scientists struggled unsuccessfully to predict the vagaries of the giant waves. But in the 1970s, computer models had begun to penetrate those mysteries. The early models were crude representations at best—they could show only what happened at the edge of the coastline, where water met land. As a result, in Louisiana, where storm surges rolled for miles over a flat landscape, these primitive models were useless.

But computing power advanced, and scientists at the Corps and National Weather Service kept refining their programs. In 1978, the Weather Service came up with a model it called SLOSH, for Sea, Lake and Overland Surge from Hurricanes (hurricane modelers had a sense of humor—SLOSH supplanted an earlier model named SPLASH). Here, "overland" is the key word—SLOSH could show what would happen when a storm surge moved inland.

SLOSH was deliberately scary. The National Weather Service used it to generate worst-case scenarios so emergency managers and the people running the federal flood insurance program could gauge which tracks were most troublesome. Modelers would create a virtual hurricane and dispatch it against a stretch of coastline again and again at different speeds and angles, generating hundreds of distinct flood patterns. They'd then take the high-water marks from each one and aggregate them all into a single map: the worst of the worst cases. Those maps got people's attention. They illustrated the grave danger New Orleans faced with hard numbers and bold colors: every single point in the city and surrounding areas had the potential to end up under water. A direct hit by a Category 5 storm—the biggest and baddest hurricane, with winds over 155 mph—would bring twenty to thirty feet of water into the city. That was higher than all hurricane levees, higher than even the river levees, making a flood forty feet deep in some spots. A Category 5 flood could also move far inland, swamping outlying towns all the way to Baton Rouge, or along the Mississippi coast.

Category 5 storms were relatively unlikely, but the picture improved only marginally for a Category 4 hurricane: flood heights dropped, but the map showed the city and all its suburbs were still vulnerable—levees couldn't protect any part of New Orleans from a direct blow. The same held for most Category 3 storms. Maps showed the levee system couldn't even stop a flood from a common Category 2 storm. Under the right circumstances, weak storms could top levees and flood parts of St. Bernard Parish, the Ninth Ward, Jefferson Parish, and central New Orleans.

People in local government, not to mention the public, had never comprehended arcana like the Standard Project Hurricane. But everybody with a TV had heard their local meteorologists going on about hurricane categories. It was now obvious that the levee system would not stand up against storms seen in the Gulf every summer. The fog of uncertainty cleared: the city could fill up like a soup bowl and sooner or later, it would.

Scientists at the National Hurricane Center and emergency managers across southeast Louisiana eyeballed evolving versions of these maps with alarm. The city's basic vulnerability had always been obvious, but the models quantified it. And if a weak hurricane could put any point on the map under water, no one was safe. Thousands, maybe tens of thousands, could end up dead. Hundreds of thousands could be trapped on rooftops and second stories, with roads cut off and little hope of a quick rescue. New Orleans itself could be destroyed as its infrastructure stewed for weeks under water. A prestorm mass evacuation was the only solution. The city might be destroyed, but at least lives would be saved.

"Without question, we've felt through the years that New Orleans is one of the most vulnerable places in the United States," hurricane center director Neil Frank told *U.S. News & World Report* in 1981. "Not only does the area have bad hurricanes fairly frequently, but it has a tremendous concentration of people. Many of those people live in low-lying areas that could be severely flooded by a hurricane. They really don't have a workable evacuation plan for that city."

The maps made explicit one of the strangest trade-offs in American history, something only hinted at before in the Corps's dry earlier analyses. Faced with the risk of New Orleans being destroyed, the default policy of the Corps and the U.S. government was to throw up their hands. Local governments could try to save as many lives as possible by evacuation, but the city itself would be sacrificed. Higher, stronger levees could eliminate that terrible risk, or at least substantially reduce it. But that option was not and never would be a priority with the Corps or Congress. The Corps was building its system as originally designed. It hadn't failed yet, and that was good enough.

The details of New Orleans's predicament were unique, but not the underlying problem. As American prosperity bloomed after

World War II, cities grew bigger and suburbs sprawled. Economic and electronic interconnectedness grew. The size, shape, and dynamics of catastrophes changed: with each passing year, when hurricanes and other natural disasters struck, they did more damage, cost more, and sounded louder political, economic, and social reverberations.

In 1998, two researchers—Roger Pielke Jr. of the University of Colorado and Christopher Landsea of the National Hurricane Center—clearly demonstrated that hurricane disasters were getting worse not because the storms were bigger or more frequent, but because there was so much more stuff to destroy. More than half the American population lives in densely packed areas hugging the coastline. As the economy grew, the hurricane-prone south Atlantic and Gulf coasts became magnets for migration—families, young people, and retirees wanted space, views, and fresh air, and they wanted out of cities and declining rural towns. The population of southeast coastal counties grew by 58 percent between 1980 and 2003. Along the Gulf Coast, it swelled by 46 percent. Both easily outpaced the national growth rate, 28 percent. Money poured into new subdivisions, hotels, and businesses. Once-remote fishing villages became scenic detours in the emerging landscape of six-lane strips, fast-food restaurants, and big-box stores. Pielke and Landsea's research showed that the expanding urban blotches along the Atlantic and Gulf coasts had created a giant and very expensive target. A Category 4 hurricane that struck Miami and Alabama in 1926 had cost around one billion in 1995 dollars. Had the same hurricane struck seventy years later, they calculated, it would have racked up seventy-two billion dollars in damage.

The growing Sun Belt helped elect Ronald Reagan president and sped the Republican ascendancy in Washington, with its antipathy toward taxes, regulation, and big government in general. But of course it was that very government that made the Sun Belt expansion possible. While the Corps ringed the swamps of eastern New Orleans with levees for the developers, it was joined by other federal agencies also devoted to subsidizing life along the coast. The Corps fortified and restored beaches, built seawalls and levees along the coastlines. The National Flood Insurance Program, created by Congress in 1968, helped people live on dangerous floodplains, secure in the knowledge they'd be bailed out—in some cases, again and again. A glitzy new gambling business, with casinos and hotels to rival Atlantic City and Las Vegas, sprang up along the Mississippi Gulf Coast that Hurricane Camille ravaged in 1969—placing an all-or-nothing wager with Mother Nature.

Growth and migration were not restricted to the seashore. Americans moved up mountains, into forests, and out along rugged earthquake faults. Their choices reflected the country's age-old flirtation with the edge, and colonizing these areas created a new frontier, an unusual amalgam of the modern and the wild. Its clashing juxtapositions could be seen in the news nearly every day, as mountain lions attacked suburbanites in Colorado and California, and forest fires, earthquakes, and mudslides wrecked subdivisions that hadn't existed twenty years before. Protection—whether it was fortifications against floods or quakes, or the availability of emergency workers, or access to homeowner's insurance—amounted to a frail patchwork that provided an illusion of security that could fall apart in an instant.

After Herbert Hoover's work on the 1927 flood, the disaster-response role devolved to local governments, with an occasional ad hoc role for the feds. During and after World War II, natural disasters were a third-tier national priority behind threats to the whole nation's existence—the Axis powers and global nuclear annihilation.

But, like Coolidge, successive presidents recognized a basic fact: big disasters were ultimately a national problem. Easily overwhelmed by catastrophes, state and local governments increasingly came to rely on the federal government—and the nation—to backstop them. Given the expanding size and reach of the federal bureaucracy, this reliance wasn't surprising. Mayor Victor Schiro summarized the prevailing sentiment after Hurricane Betsy: "We have been more generous with aid to foreign countries. It is about time we say, 'Charity begins at home.'"

Federal assistance could mean many things: sending the military, distributing food and water, offering low-interest loans to rebuild. But the federal government never really mastered the art of disaster response. Each crisis was a thankless minefield. The best a president or his aides could hope for was to avoid screwing up. If they stumbled, they'd have a political as well as a natural disaster on their hands: homeless and storm-battered citizens complaining about incompetent leadership. If everything went well, victims would be too busy cleaning up to show much gratitude. There were few incentives to prepare, and every incentive to cross your fingers and hope it didn't happen on your watch.

President Johnson's impulsive response to Hurricane Betsy had been extraordinary, but throughout the 1960s and 1970s natural disasters became an almost routine national problem. The nation was pounded by hurricanes Carla in 1962, Betsy in 1965, Camille in 1969, and Agnes in 1972. Major earthquakes struck Alaska in 1964 and Southern California in 1971. Dozens of federal agencies took a hand in disaster relief, with confusing, erratic results. Congress took a stab at organizing it in 1974 with the Disaster Relief Act, which authorized the president to formally declare disasters, mobilizing federal help from the top. But President Jimmy Carter decided the act was not enough, and in 1979 he created the Federal Emergency Management Agency after governors appealed to him to organize disaster response under a single agency.

FEMA unified natural-disaster response and preparedness with civil defense, but basically the new agency was a shell. It had about two thousand employees and a small budget. For manpower, it relied on a shifting pool of volunteers— government employees and retirees from around the country with emergency experience who were called up during disasters. This structure had some logic to it: FEMA's job was to juggle the vast resources of the federal government and get other agencies to jump, like Hoover did in 1927. But FEMA never had Hoover's clout. Its small size and unusual mission made it politically weak, subject to the whims of whoever was president. Through the end of Carter's presidency and into the Reagan years, it became a political dumping ground, top-heavy with patronage appointees. Reagan-era director Louis Giuffrida, a close associate of then Attorney General Edwin Meese III, spent years fending off congressional investigators who uncovered a pattern of cronyism and contracting irregularities. Among other things, a contractor had picked up the tab for Giuffrida's tickets to a political dinner for Reagan and Vice President George H. W. Bush, and Republican operatives had persuaded the agency to award a contract to a company whose nuclear accident training course gave faulty advice that health experts said could kill people. Giuffrida resigned in 1985 after investigators issued their report. "This resignation marks the end of a disastrous era for FEMA and brings hope for more competent stewardship," said then Congressman Al Gore, who chaired the investigating committee.

"FEMA wasn't ready" became a common refrain as disasters struck. After Hurricane Hugo hit just north of Charleston in September 1989, FEMA was already overstretched dealing with damage the storm had done a few days before in the Caribbean. South Carolina officials found they didn't have the food, clothing, and money they needed. When aid began coming in from private sources, they had no people to distribute it. Pleas for federal help fell into bureaucratic cracks: a request for emergency generators from the Charleston mayor's office took days to make it to FEMA headquarters because it wasn't properly routed through the governor's office; FEMA then demanded more paperwork to justify the requests. The agency took more than a week to set up two emergency offices in the disaster zone. When one finally opened, people who showed up had to make appointments to return the next week. Senator Fritz Hollings captured the frustration when he called FEMA "the sorriest bunch of bureaucratic jackasses I've ever known" and told them to get the hell out of the way.

Three weeks later, the San Andreas fault slipped at Loma Prieta, California. An earthquake measuring 7.5 on the Richter scale rocked the San Francisco area at 5:04 p.m. on October 17, just as a World Series game was about to get under way between the two local teams, the Oakland Athletics and the San Francisco Giants. It was a fortunate coincidence: fans settling in to watch the 5:30 game at home had left the roads nearly empty during the height of rush hour. The earthquake wave rumbled from one side to the other of Candlestick Park—which suffered only minor damage. After the shaking stopped, some in the crowd began chanting "play ball," but the series was postponed by ten days.

FEMA got better reviews this time out, putting people on the ground within twenty-four hours of the quake. But its image wasn't helped when one key official—Jerry Brown, the chief of FEMA's medical disaster response unit (and not the politician of the same name)—took a vacation the day after the quake with his bosses' OK. And the disaster, which fell far short of a worst-case, nevertheless paralyzed state and local agencies when communications quickly broke down. Just two months earlier, FEMA had sponsored a quake emergency exercise in Sacramento. More than five hundred emergency managers gathered to re-create an 1868 earthquake that had a magnitude of 7.5. The exercise assumed that between three thousand and eight thousand people would die, roads and bridges would collapse, and hospitals and emergency centers would be destroyed. Total damage: forty-four billion dollars. Officials came out of the exercise sobered at the scale of the challenge. Yet when they had a milder, real-life test, many key response systems failed.

Two major disasters in the space of a month had exposed weaknesses at the local, state, and federal levels. And while President George H. W. Bush made some tweaks to FEMA, he'd been largely indifferent, delaying the appointment of a director for more than a year because chief of staff John Sununu reportedly mistrusted the agency, which had delayed approval and forced changes in evacuation plans for New Hampshire's Seabrook nuclear power plant when he was the state's governor. Sununu, a nuclear power advocate who had clashed with protesters and regulators for years, wanted to appoint someone more sympathetic to the nuclear industry. Bush did so, finally appointing a former New Hampshire transportation secretary to the job in August 1990. Even with a director in place, disaster response required political clout and skill, and FEMA had neither, so Bush bypassed it entirely and opted for the Coolidge approach: he appointed high-profile, ad hoc task forces for both disasters.

Bush went the same route when Hurricane Andrew hit south Florida three years later during the height of the 1992 presidential campaign. The Category 4 storm wrecked Homestead, a suburb south of Miami, leaving block after block of shredded houses. (Ten years later, scientists concluded Andrew's winds had actually reached Category 5 strength in south Miami.) More than two hundred thousand people were left homeless and a million more without electricity. With firehouses destroyed, roads blocked, and communications disrupted, local agencies were paralyzed, and thousands of emergency responders wandered signless streets without equipment or resources.

FEMA was supposed to be the cavalry, but it did little for three agonizing days. One problem was administrative—regulations prohibited action until there was a reasonable certainty a storm would hit, defined as just twenty-four hours before landfall. That had given the agency little time to position aid and response teams.

As the week wore on, Kate Hale, Dade County's emergency management director, described her incredulity watching federal officials give press conferences boasting of the help they were sending, while nothing arrived. "For God's sake," she said, "will you please cut it out and help us out down here?" FEMA officials, meanwhile, were at a loss. "Something is wrong. I don't know where things are breaking down. Nobody knows where it's breaking down. I'd like to know myself," a FEMA spokeswoman complained to the media the same day.

As FEMA employees were wringing their hands, politicians were sparring and spinning. Bush aides said that the president had delayed sending federal troops and supplies because Florida governor Lawton Chiles hadn't formally requested help and had even rejected an offer from the president to dispatch federal troops immediately. Chiles aides countered that the governor had asked the Corps of Engineers to bring in bulldozers and cranes to clear debris, but the plea had been rejected because, according to bureaucratic regulations, Chiles hadn't activated all National Guard engineering units. And he didn't recall Bush's offer of troops. Chiles subsequently submitted a general request for help and Bush acted within hours.

On August 26, two days after Andrew hit, Bush appointed an emergency task force headed by Transportation Secretary Andrew Card (later Bush's son's chief of staff). The task force flew down to Miami and met the governor. Chiles accepted a massive federal aid package. That same day, Bush sent in 3,500 army troops to establish order, clear streets, and start bringing in needed supplies. The aid did not begin arriving in bulk until a few days later—six days after the hurricane struck.

But the problems were only beginning. For weeks afterward, old complaints came up again and again: FEMA had too few offices in the devastated area, and when people went to one, they were given an appointment and told to return on a later date. Many in dire need found themselves without necessary assistance. Television crews descended on the scene at a moment that could not have been worse for Bush. Democratic challenger Bill Clinton was ahead in the polls, and Florida's electoral votes made it a key swing state in the upcoming election. While stumping, Clinton talked up his experience with disasters as governor of Arkansas and called for an independent panel to investigate what went wrong in Florida. As Bush struggled to deflect the criticism, recriminations flew. "FEMA may be well-meaning, but they have no clout in the initial phase," Chiles complained. "You've got to loudly and strongly and probably with all kinds of paper tell the White House what you need." Some complained Bush was too focused on international affairs, especially Iraq (a Bush-led international coalition had expelled Iraqi dictator Saddam Hussein's troops from occupied Kuwait, but Hussein was harassing inspectors searching for evidence of weapons programs). Anthony Gonzalez, a construction worker whose home was destroyed, told the *Washington Post,* "I don't believe this. Does President Bush only have a map that has the rest of the world but not the United States on it?" On August 28, ABC's *Nightline* focused on the issue, broadcasting scenes of military vehicles rolling through splintered neighborhoods in Homestead.

"Massive federal relief comes to Florida four days after the disaster," Cokie Roberts intoned. "Now all around him, a nagging question for President Bush."

Soldier: "These people were in dire need of our help. I'm surprised we weren't brought here sooner."

Roberts: "And the man who sent the cavalry takes a defensive posture."

President Bush: "I'm not going to participate in the blame game."

For a major storm, Andrew's death toll was modest: sixty-one people. What surprised the experts was its cost: after a year or two of mounting insurance claims and FEMA expenditures, it amounted to thirty billion dollars—split about evenly between the federal government and insurance companies (which stampeded out of south Florida as the scale of their obligations became clear). Andrew was the first eleven-figure disaster in American history. Two years later, there was a second. An earthquake rocked Northridge, California, a suburban area outside Los Angeles. The cost: forty-four billion dollars.

The totals confounded the number crunchers—no one had anticipated such figures were possible for two disasters that could have been much worse. (Andrew was a strong but fast-moving storm that left mostly wind damage. The quake had measured a moderate 6.7 on the Richter scale and lasted only fifteen seconds.) Both had struck suburban areas, sparing big cities nearby. Kobe, Japan, wasn't so lucky. An earthquake hit the city center in 1995, costing Kobe one hundred billion dollars. This kind of megadisaster was a new phenomenon, peculiar to America, Europe, and Japan—the developed world. Of course, earthquakes were common in Turkey, Iran, India, and Pakistan, as were deadly tsunamis in South Asia. Bangladesh endured periodic storm surges that killed hundreds of thousands of people until charities erected more than a thousand shelters on stilts. U.S.-style megadisasters were less deadly, thanks to superior infrastructure and emergency response. But there was far more expensive wreckage—and a greater global economic and political fallout. The veneer of civilization was thicker, but no less fragile. These were twenty-first-century-style disasters, each a clash between a superpower and nature that nature was bound to win.

Hurricanes, of course, were disasters that could be predicted; once one had been foreseen, the most practical step to take was to get everybody out of the way. As meteorologists honed their hurricane models and coastal towns and cities grew, community leaders began to realize they'd better try to evacuate whenever possible. But the uncertainty of forecasts, along with rising populations, sprawl, and traffic jams, made ordering an evacuation one of the trickiest decisions a mayor, parish president, or county executive had to make. (Legally, evacuations were the responsibility of local authorities.) And just ordering an evacuation didn't necessarily mean people could get out: in 1979, residents of Pascagoula, Mississippi, and Mobile, Alabama, fleeing Hurricane Frederic ended up in a monstrous traffic jam stretching all the way to Jackson, two hundred miles north. Once, it might have been sufficient to roam the streets with a bullhorn, yelling, "Everybody out!" Now, evacuations required meticulous planning and orchestration. Without such plans, the evacuation itself would turn into a disaster.

The first real interest in evacuations in the United States had come during the 1940s and '50s, when cities and towns were girding themselves against German and Japanese bombers, then all-out nuclear war. At the height of the Cold War, an apparatus of earnest bureaucrats devised response plans for a Soviet nuclear attack and possible invasion—how to evacuate cities, where to shelter people, how to preserve power plants and water treatment facilities. To take but one example, in the 1950s, Tennessee authorities drew up a fanciful plan to evacuate the entire population of Memphis—then four hundred thousand people—and relocate it in thirty counties in rural areas of four nearby states in the event of a Soviet attack.

The local civil defense offices set up to carry out plans like Tennessee's later evolved to handle both natural and man-made disasters—and there was no shortage of potential catastrophes to plan for. After the 1979 near meltdown at the Three Mile Island nuclear power plant, near Hershey, Pennsylvania, the Nuclear Regulatory Commission forced the utilities industry and communities with nuclear plants to routinely make evacuation plans. Soon, emergency planners were looking at other threats, including chemical, biological, and nuclear weapons.

Though uniquely exposed, New Orleans and surrounding parishes took a long time to understand the utility of evacuations. Isaac Cline's warnings about the 1915 storm were published in the local newspapers, and he had sent messages out with riders on horseback and by boat to the coast, but beyond that it was every man for himself. Governments did nothing to shelter residents or move them to higher ground. That attitude dominated for decades. When hurricanes approached during the 1960s and '70s, residents were broadcast recommendations based on National Hurricane Center predictions, but these weather forecasts with exclamation points lacked detailed information about what exactly residents should do before a storm hit. As the flood-the-bowl scenario emerged in forecasting and SLOSH maps, however, Louisiana officials realized they had to do more.

Geographically, New Orleans wasn't set up well for evacuation. Interstate 10 was the only major highway, running east-west through the city. A four-lane causeway ran north across Lake Pontchartrain, but it could be dangerous as a storm got close. To get out of the low-lying danger zone, evacuees had to travel at least thirty miles out of town—ideally farther. And it wasn't just New Orleans at risk. A dozen marshy coastal parishes lay around it, most of them halfway submerged already.

South of New Orleans, at the edge of the Gulf, sat Port Four-chon, one of the country's biggest oil and gas terminals—and the leaping-off point for thirteen thousand offshore workers. The only way out of Fourchon was via Louisiana Highway 1, a two-lane road that sat barely a foot above the marsh.

But ignorance and a lack of manpower were even bigger ob-stacles than roads and danger zones. In Louisiana parishes in the early 1980s, most emergency-preparedness officials had no staff. Many had their wives helping out in the office as volun-teers. Madhu Beriwal, an emergency planner, began working on Louisiana's first hurricane evacuation study in the early 1980s. "I was working with surge models and evacuation times and public opinion surveys. We asked, where does this information go and how is it used?" she said. "I found it quite horrifying that there really was no plan for this information. It was not going anywhere. There was a disconnect between the technical, sci-entific information we were producing and how it was utilized for planning and operations. There was just no place to put it. No one was looking at how long it took to evacuate and how much water would come from various storms."

Beriwal's group also polled Louisiana residents. "In the sur-vey we did in nineteen eighty-three–eighty-four, one person said, 'I will leave when the levee behind my house breaks,'" she said. "Some things don't change. People look for an environmen-tal trigger they can recognize, but when the trigger comes, it's too late. The surge models showed water rising four or five feet in a matter of minutes."

Beriwal's study ran out of funds in 1985, before the final report was done, but her team managed to put together an at-las of SLOSH maps for every emergency director in the region. Four years later, Beriwal was working on the problem again as a private consultant, this time for New Orleans and neighbor-ing Jefferson Parish. She came up with a good estimate for a complete evacuation for a Category 5 storm: a dismally slug-gish 106 hours, or about four and a half days. Given the state of hurricane forecasting, that meant the city would be un-der water while cars still sat waiting to get up onto the interstate's on-ramps. Interestingly, that was the only time anyone had ever examined how to evacuate for a worst-case, Category 5 storm.

"This is part of the problem with catastrophe planning: a reluctance to look at the problem head-on," Beriwal recalled. "Everybody wants to look at the problem at a scale that's manageable, but nature doesn't know that. There's something about us in this country. We want just the exactly right amount. We want a paucity of wasted energy. We want exactly the right number of National Guardsmen standing by. Well, my philosophy would be the course of least regret, and then scale it back from there. If you have to overevacuate, say that. Bad things can happen if you don't do that."

President Clinton took office in 1993 with an interesting theory: responding to disasters could be good politics. It fit well with his centrist, third-way approach to policy: if government couldn't solve all your problems—which, when it came to disasters, it clearly could not—it would strive to make your life easier. If that buttressed the fraying compact between the public and the federal government—especially in disaster-prone states with lots of electoral votes, like Florida and California—that would be good for Clinton and the Democratic Party.

Clinton appointed James Lee Witt to head FEMA. Witt had been chief of Arkansas's Office of Emergency Services, the first appointee with state emergency-management experience to run the federal agency. Clinton lavished attention on Witt and FEMA, making his job a cabinet-level post. A FEMA director with the president's ear can get things done, and the changes meant everything for an agency whose principal job was getting other agencies to act together, fast. Witt made FEMA's beleaguered bureaucracy run smoothly: he created a more employee-friendly place to work, tapping the experience of the agency's long-suffering professional staff. FEMA ran more games and simulations with local officials. Its response times improved.

Witt had a far more ambitious aim: ending the American flirtation with disaster. The whole U.S. system, he recognized, was basically constructed backward: people waited until catastrophe struck, then realized the horrible mistakes they'd made. When they rebuilt, they fixed those mistakes. But those fixes were just strong enough to protect against the previous disaster—not the next one. Then the whole cycle started over again. What if, Witt and his aides decided, you invested your money before disaster struck? If homes were moved out of floodplains, for example, then they wouldn't be damaged when the water rose. That would save federal insurance and aid payouts: everybody wins. It was a bold idea—and one that flew in the face of political reality, not to mention human nature. Witt's pride and joy was a program called Project Impact, which gave grants and other incentives to cities for this kind of disaster proofing. It was a modest effort, more of a showpiece than a major policy change. But it was a start.

Hair-raising near misses by hurricanes concentrated the minds of Louisiana's emergency planners during the 1990s. "It became clear we had Category 5 storms, Category 3 levees, and tropical storm support at the state and local level," said LSU coastal scientist Joseph Suhayda.

The planners began to coordinate and upgrade their battle plans. It wasn't a moment too soon—around 1995, hurricane activity began to tick upward, part of a decades-long cyclical swing and possibly the result of global warming, scientists believed. But glitches remained. When Hurricane Andrew crossed into the Gulf and headed for Louisiana after ravaging Florida, state and local officials put their piecemeal evacuation plans into action. They directed most evacuees west to Baton Rouge. That turned out to be directly in the path of the storm, which made landfall in a remote area in Cajun country west of New Orleans and then veered northeast toward the capital.

After Hurricane Andrew, Louisiana created an Office of Emergency Preparedness, run by the National Guard, and made evacuation the centerpiece of its hurricane planning. As emergency managers studied evacuation data from Andrew and previous storms, they noticed something alarming: there was a core population that almost never left, made up mostly of the city's poorer residents—at least one hundred thousand of them—with no access to transportation.

Without it, they'd be trapped. The last-resort fallback for people who stayed behind was called "vertical evacuation"—a retreat above the flood line to the upper floors of high-rise buildings in the city center. But Andrew undercut those plans, too: hurricane winds had blown out windows in tall buildings in Miami. The Burger King International building in Miami had been constructed to the latest hurricane standards, to withstand 150-mph winds. But the National Weather Service had data from dropwindsondes—radio sensors that reconnaissance planes dropped into storms—showing that winds increased by as much as 50 mph above ground level. Wind and driving rain destroyed the executive suites on the Burger King building's upper floors, while a seventeen-foot flood washed through the lower levels. Vertical evacuation would be simply too dangerous in New Orleans except in a narrow zone between the uppermost flood height and the tenth floor.

As Hurricane Georges bore down on the city in September 1998, New Orleans mayor Marc Morial called a voluntary evacuation. Georges was a Category 2 storm, but it was headed straight for the city and forecasted to strengthen, and a direct hit could have overtopped the levees and flooded the bowl. Yet only a third of the population left. Those who did got only aggravation for their trouble: they drove west on the same day as LSU was playing Idaho, filling Tiger Stadium in Baton Rouge with a crowd of 80,466 people from across the region. (LSU won, 53–26.) That put ten thousand extra cars on the road, and as a result, traffic was jammed up from New Orleans to Baton Rouge, a distance of eighty-five miles. For those left behind, the city for the first time opened the Superdome, where 22,000 people gathered. (It housed an additional 7,000 at the convention center, a vacant department store building, and several schools.) At the Dome, people ate cold hot dogs and warm juice served by prisoners. Hundreds protested when the city tried to keep them inside after the storm passed because of a curfew; Mayor Marc Morial relented, and about 4,000 left. No major crimes were reported, though television cameras outside caught some people walking out with bar tools and sofa cushions stolen from suites inside. Afterward, state officials urged their New Orleans counterparts not to open the Superdome as a general refuge, but limit it only to special-needs patients—people needing medical care but not hospitalization.

But there were some positive developments. At LSU, scientists Joe Suhayda and Vibhas Aravamuthan had adapted their storm surge computer model to work in real time to aid an evacuation as a storm approached, pinpointing the spots likely to go under water first as the floodwaters rose. "There was a vacuum," Suhayda said. "State and local emergency managers needed information that the federal government and the state were not providing." (Their efforts also ran into resistance from the National Weather Service. It disapproved of broadcasting such precise flood forecasting, fearing it might deter people from evacuating if it predicted some areas wouldn't go under water.) As the storm approached, the LSU model identified a section of Highway 61, the old main road between New Orleans and Baton Rouge, as likely to flood, and state workers successfully sandbagged it.

The near miss rang alarms in New Orleans, Baton Rouge, and Washington. "After Georges, people began saying, 'We dodged the bullet—we need Category Five protection,'" Suhayda said. The storm pumped a seven-foot storm surge into Lake Pontchartrain—not enough to top the lakefront levees, but enough to smash weekend fishing shacks and wash their debris close to the top. It was a gentle hint of what would happen if a similar storm came in on a slightly different track.

The Corps, as usual, saw it as an opportunity to build. The following year, it unveiled a $1.6 billion plan to extend its hurricane levees for dozens of miles along the coast in concert with a hoped-for effort to restore coastal wetlands. And, Corps officials said, they would embark on a preliminary study to determine how to protect the New Orleans area from a Category 5 hurricane.

The Corps, the Weather Service, the state, and a task force made up of parish emergency managers started coordinating their plans. The Corps studied how to drain the city after a catastrophic flood. Initial estimates showed it could take at least six months to pump out enough water to let the public back in, and some engineers thought it might be a year and a half before people could come back. The agencies worked on how to stage evacuations: the most exposed communities lying to the south of the city would go first. New Orleans and Jefferson would go last—if they went earlier, they'd clog the roads and maybe trap cars trying to get out of the marshes. In 2004, authorities unveiled "Contraflow"—a plan to make the interstate and other main roads one-way out of town during the evacuation. It had its first test that year during Hurricane Ivan. The result: the state waited too long to start, most residents went west on the most congested route, and traffic was badly snarled. Officials swore they'd get it right the next time.

A successful evacuation still depended most on something that was notoriously hard to measure—the public's willingness to listen and act. Officials wrestled with huge logistical problems, but their biggest obstacle was human psychology—their constituents' and their own. Ordering an evacuation was a wrenching decision. In many cases it would be a false alarm, as hurricanes almost always diverted from forecast tracks. Order an evacuation too early, and it was more likely to be wrong and get people angry. Order it too late, and people could die. "It's a tremendous burden that the parish president and mayor had to face," Maestri said, describing the Georges decision. "They were basically asking a million people to get in their cars and leave their homes not knowing when they were coming back or what they were coming back to when they came back." In addition, every evacuation—right or wrong—sucked air out of local economies to the tune of one to fifty million dollars per mile of coastline per day, according to one study. Some businesses didn't hesitate to sue local officials for making the decision.

Would people listen? Historically, calls for evacuation got wildly different responses depending on the urgency of the warnings, the local history with storms, and people's attitudes. One key question was whether to order mandatory evacuations or leave them voluntary. It was mostly a semantic distinction: in the tight time frame of an evacuation, there was no practical way to physically expel people from town. Yet if you wanted to convince skeptics, making something mandatory ratcheted up the pressure. "The idea of ordering, as opposed to recommending, an evacuation is very important," said Don Lewis of Post, Buckley, Schuh and Jernigan, a consulting firm that studied evacuations. "All our data shows that if people think a mandatory evacuation order has been issued and it applies to them, they are much more likely to evacuate than if it's just recommended to them. . . . That's a major policy issue: whether they are arrested or if they aren't, you have to make them feel that it's for real." New Orleans and Jefferson typically did not make evacuation orders mandatory, though outlying parishes did.

Computer models could paint a vivid picture for the people who could read them, but most of the public still didn't grasp the enormity of the threat hanging over them. During the 1990s, a small group of emergency managers and academics—including Maestri, Suhayda, and Windell Curole of Lafourche Parish's federal levee district—started beating the hurricane drum hard.

"You go out and make a stink. Get the public interested," Curole told his colleagues. "That will drive the issue."

The media love doom, so the warnings got attention. At the June start of each hurricane season, one of the authors of this book, Mark Schleifstein, detailed the emerging, alarming picture in the *Times-Picayune*. Since he'd started at the paper covering the environmental beat in 1984, he had grown as alarmed as the experts at the city's odds of mass destruction. By 1992, he was acting as an informal hurricane advisor to editors—whether they wanted the advice or not. He penned a memo warning them against positioning reporters in motels, because gusting wind could easily tear off a roof and cut off phone lines; emergency operations centers were far more secure. That advice was ignored during Hurricane Andrew: a reporter and photographer were at a motel in Morgan City, Louisiana, about eighty miles southwest of New Orleans, when its roof blew off. As a result, they couldn't call in a story until the next day.

By the late 1990s, Schleifstein was pressing the paper's editors to take a deeper, investigative look at hurricane risks. The editors bit, and brought in John McQuaid (the other author of this book) from the Washington bureau. The two reporters had worked on several big projects for the paper, including a Pulitzer Prize–winning series that explored the science, economics, and environmental fallout of the global fisheries crisis. Schleifstein wanted to do a series focusing on the Big One (as emergency managers were now calling it): on what would happen if the New Orleans bowl filled up with water. The once-fanciful scenario had recently acquired a wealth of gory details thanks to those studying the computer models and estimates. They envisioned a hell on earth: hundreds of thousands trapped on rooftops, an untold number of dead. New Orleans would be uninhabitable for months as the Corps pumped water out, and possibly beyond hope of repair. A major American city would, effectively, be turned to swamp and wasteland. The images were so searing that no one quite believed them. Schleifstein, who owned a house in Lakeview, one of the lowest areas of town, had already written it off as a likely loss. Unlike his neighbors, he never boarded up his windows when a storm menaced the city. To him, the yearly hurricane gamble was just the price of living in New Orleans.

The *Times-Picayune* editors worried that if the series focused too much on the worst-case scenario, it would be dismissed as alarmist. "Disaster porn," one called it. And in some ways McQuaid felt that focusing on the Big One would only state the obvious. In local government circles, it was a well-known scenario. Writing about something that might not happen for fifty or one hundred years didn't seem so gripping. Instead, we seized on the link between hurricanes and coastal erosion, the fact that storm surges were penetrating farther inland and hurricanes could now gain strength crossing watery marshes. Within that larger story lurked the shadow of the Big One.

As we studied the worst-case scenario, alarming facts jumped out. The city had pursued a schizophrenic strategy, throwing all its efforts into urging people to leave while giving up on evacuating people without transportation. Instead, it would once again open the Superdome—this time with limited food, water, and support (and no Red Cross assistance)—for anyone remaining who wanted a safe place to stay. For those caught in the flood, the Red Cross estimated that tens of thousands would die in a storm. Ivor van Heerden, the director of LSU's recently formed Center for the Study of Public Health Impacts of Hurricanes, spoke of a "witches' brew" of floodwater, gasoline, and household chemicals that a hurricane might cook up in the New Orleans bowl. Even the giant coastal restoration projects that politicians were contemplating would provide only limited protection against big storms. And the levee system was a lot weaker than the Corps's already-pessimistic numbers indicated it was. The only solution was significantly higher, stronger levees. Suhayda suggested a more fanciful solution: build a wall bisecting the city—compartmentalizing it so that if one area flooded, the other would stay dry. He called the designated dry area a "community haven."

The *Times-Picayune* published our series, titled "Washing Away," in June 2002. It got a lot of attention locally. TV stations splashed it across their screens. Members of Congress used it in their campaign for coastal restoration money. And many people who read it were scared—something that would help spur them to get on the road when the next evacuation came. But on the bigger issues—whether New Orleans should get stronger, better levees—there was no action.

As we were researching the stories, *Scientific American* published an article by Mark Fischetti detailing the "fill the bowl" scenario. The *New York Times* and *Washington Post* followed suit. Later, Daniel Zwerdling of National Public Radio and PBS reported in depth on the problem, and *National Geographic* did its own piece. New Orleans, soup bowl and death trap, thus became a staple of the national media's annual hurricane story (and increasingly, its global warming coverage, too). The question was no longer Did anyone know? but Did anyone care?

Chapter 7

HOMELAND SECURITY

S OON AFTER PRESIDENT George W. Bush was elected in 2000, his newly appointed FEMA director, Joseph Allbaugh, asked his staff to tell him about the agency's plans for the city of New Orleans to recover from a catastrophic hurricane. There were none. This was the case even though the "New Orleans scenario" was one of several megacatastrophes the agency had begun looking at during the 1990s at the urging of the Red Cross. (The others included earthquakes hitting San Francisco or St. Louis and a terror attack on New York City.) The estimates of possible damage were hair-raising: a Red Cross official estimated the number of dead from a catastrophic storm in New Orleans at between twenty-five thousand and one hundred thousand.

"Catastrophic disasters are best defined in that they totally outstrip local and state resources, which is why the federal government needs to play a role," Allbaugh told the *Times-Picayune* in 2002. "There are a half-dozen or so contingencies around the nation that cause me great concern, and one of them is right there in your back yard."

Allbaugh made the worst-cases a personal priority. As it happened, Colonel Michael Brown, the assistant director of Louisiana's Office of Emergency Preparedness, had been talking with FEMA officials in Washington and the regional office in Denton, Texas, suggesting a big exercise that would test the response at all levels of government and see how—or if—the agencies would work together if a hurricane put New Orleans under water. Within months of taking over, Allbaugh decided this was a good idea and launched just such a study. The contract went to Madhu Beriwal, who had worked on the issue for two decades. Louisiana officials were thrilled. They'd been pushing for this kind of attention for years. They gave FEMA a twenty-nine-page outline of issues they wanted addressed—including identifying stretches of elevated interstate wide enough to land rescue helicopters and locating enough small boats for rescue efforts. The Corps already had begun working on a plan to "unwater" the city—to drain it of as much as thirty feet of water even if the pumps were disabled. In May 2001, the Corps brought troops from Fort Bragg, North Carolina, and Fort Belvoir, Virginia, to New Orleans to map the electrical systems of hospitals, schools, and pumping stations so they could identify the generators needed to get essential services running quickly in the aftermath of a catastrophic storm.

But this burst of activity didn't last. FEMA was soon buffeted by political forces more powerful than a hurricane. Allbaugh had been awarded the job after losing a power struggle with fellow top Bush aides Karl Rove and Karen Hughes. FEMA was a consolation prize, but Allbaugh's appointment preserved the idea of presidential access and leverage that the agency depended on. But Bush and his aides had a completely different reason for maintaining that access and leverage. Their intent was to undo the Clinton-era changes to the agency. Part of this was political, a ground rule applied to everything from foreign policy to economics: if it had Clinton's imprimatur, it should be abandoned or reversed. Part of the reversal was philosophical or ideological: White House officials viewed emergency management as a job for the states and local governments. Allbaugh announced that the federal/state split on disaster prevention grants would go from 75-25 to 50-50, saying that being required to pony up would force states to be better prepared. Project Impact—the innovative disaster-proofing program started by James Lee Witt, Clinton's FEMA director—was canceled.

FEMA was once again on the outs. In an administration

where many top posts went to industry lobbyists, FEMA had no outside constituency that depended on it—other than the public, that is. Clinton-era officials began leaving, and FEMA once again became a political dumping ground, top-heavy with appointees who had little disaster experience. One of them was Michael D. Brown, Allbaugh's friend, general counsel, and eventual successor, who had been pushed out of his previous job as the judges and stewards commissioner of the International Arabian Horse Association.

On September 11, 2001, al-Qaeda terrorists hijacked airplanes and flew them into the World Trade Center towers and the Pentagon. A fourth plane crashed in a Pennsylvania field when passengers rebelled and attacked the hijackers. More than two thousand people died. In the space of a few hours, the country was at war, jolted out of its domestic reveries. Within weeks, Bush had launched attacks on Afghanistan that destroyed terrorist training camps and ousted the nation's fundamentalist Taliban leadership. Eighteen months later, American troops invaded Iraq, deposed Saddam Hussein, and began a long, grinding occupation that became the focus of Bush's presidency.

The 9/11 attacks wiped concerns about natural disasters from the national psyche and replaced them with anxiety about anthrax in envelopes, collapsing skyscrapers, and rush-hour subway attacks. City streets had suddenly become a front line in a global war, and first responders became national icons, heroes for the twenty-first century. Hundreds of New York City firefighters and other rescuers had died trying to rescue people from the Trade Center, and FDNY personnel, police, and rescue workers surrounded Bush when he stood in the rubble on September 14, speaking through a bullhorn.

"I want you all to know that America today, America today is on bended knee, in prayer for the people whose lives were lost here, for the workers who work here, for the families who mourn," Bush said. "The nation stands with the good people of New York City and New Jersey and Connecticut as we mourn the loss of thousands of our citizens."

"I can't hear you!" shouted one rescue worker.

"I can hear you!" Bush responded, and his audience burst into thunderous cheers that then got louder with each succeeding phrase. "I can hear you! The rest of the world hears you! And the people—and the people who knocked these buildings down will hear all of us soon!"

The president's grit and his promise to wield American power forged a spontaneous compact with the citizenry. In the space of a few moments, he had assuaged lingering doubts about the erratic course of his eight months in office. Bush was perfectly attuned to the national yearning for action: he offered a chance for redress of a horrible wrong, the restoration of a sense of security that seemed to have been forever lost.

As America went to war, politicians scrambled to do something more to respond, and the federal government shuddered and morphed. It had a new priority: security. And that would require, apparently, a giant bureaucracy. Big government was back, embodied by the new Department of Homeland Security.

DHS was a multiheaded monster. Besides FEMA, it absorbed the Customs Service, the Coast Guard, the Secret Service, most of the Immigration and Naturalization Service, the FBI's National Domestic Preparedness Office and National Communications System, the Department of Health and Human Service's National Disaster Medical System, the Commerce Department's Critical Infrastructure Assurance Office, the Energy Department's National Infrastructure Simulation and Analysis Center, and the Agriculture Department's Animal and Plant Inspection Service, among others—twenty-two agencies in all.

It was the latest burst of growth for a federal government whose size and reach had been expanding, in fits and starts, since the New Deal. Federal spending tended to rise no matter what party ruled. But generally speaking, Democrats had continued Franklin Roosevelt's tradition, pushing for new government services; while since Ronald Reagan's presidency, Republicans had won elections by attacking big government. The Bush White House tried to have it both ways. When it

backed a new agency or program, such as DHS or the new
Medicare prescription drug benefit passed in 2003, the White
House could claim the credit and dispense the accompanying
patronage and contracts. If new programs didn't work, Bush
went on portraying himself as an outsider suspicious of the government he headed. As a result, while Bush had no qualms
about creating sprawling bureaucracies, he didn't seem to pay
much attention to how they actually worked.

Yet with the exception of fighting a war, nothing depended
more on a well-organized, smooth-running bureaucracy than did
disaster response. But federal emergency management had always been something of an improvisation. Homeland Security's
ambitious aim was to end that uncertainty. Disaster response
would be tightly choreographed from the top down.

But as DHS was organized, and then reorganized, its own
employees became increasingly befuddled about its role in responding to natural disasters. An effective response during the
chaos of a disaster depended on a certain, elusive chemistry between agencies and individuals with established relationships.
When it kicked in, bureaucratic bottlenecks and obstacles disappeared; information flowed smoothly from local and state officials in the disaster zone to their federal counterparts, who
could target assistance with the vast resources at their disposal.
Witt's FEMA hadn't perfected this process, but it had won the
confidence of emergency managers around the country. But as
Homeland Security juggled FEMA's functions, those once-
robust relationships broke down. Agencies no longer had clear
mandates. Nor could they communicate effectively across bureaucratic boundaries. "They marginalized their capacity to get
accurate information and have it flow in a way that made sense,"
said George Haddow, who was Witt's deputy chief of staff. The
changes, he said, further demoralized the FEMA staff, and
more experienced employees departed. "If you are doing terrorism and not natural hazard stuff and you don't see a future, you
retire," he said. "There was a lot of talent and relationships lost."

FEMA ended up with the worst of all possible worlds. It
was no longer a freestanding agency but a tiny division of a huge

department that was still sorting out how all its constituent parts were going to work together. Allbaugh had no desire to be an undersecretary, and resigned.

Appointed to the top spot early in 2003, Mike Brown had no previous disaster management experience and an unremarkable resume. He was an Oklahoma lawyer who had worked in local government, lost a run for Congress, and represented a consortium of businesses in his home state, cultivating his political contacts along the way. At the International Arabian Horse Association, where he started work in 1991, some called Brown "the czar." In fact, he was more of a professional pain in the ass. His job was to police the judges of horse shows, investigating cheating and other irregularities, and he didn't hesitate to make waves in the insular world of champion horses. Brown launched several high-profile investigations: his biggest quarry was David Boggs, a prominent Scottsdale, Arizona, breeder and trainer who eventually received a five-year suspension for using plastic surgery on his horses. While the inquiry was still under way, Boggs filed a defamation lawsuit against the association for hurting his business. Defending against that suit and others ran up legal fees in excess of one million dollars, a lot for the small association. (It ultimately settled them.) Board members finally decided they'd had enough aggravation and pushed Brown out in 2001. Soon after, his old friend Allbaugh gave him a job as FEMA's general counsel and, later, deputy director.

Brown relished being at the helm of the agency; in his brief time there he had become passionate about emergency management. But his main mission became defending a rapidly shrinking piece of bureaucratic turf. FEMA and other agencies were being moved around like nuts in a shell game. Brown's first big battle was trying to keep the FEMA name, which was due to change to the less-catchy Directorate of Emergency Preparedness and Response. He won that battle. But he lost all the others.

"You have a department of a hundred and eighty-five thousand employees, and a hundred and eighty-two thousand are in jobs that have to do with prevention of terrorism—the border guys, the Coast Guard guys," Brown recalled. "You've got twenty-five hundred to three thousand that are FEMA guys. In this town, who do you think wins?"

The White House's original plan was to beef up FEMA by giving it the Justice Department's newly created Office for Domestic Preparedness—unifying the federal grants for both terrorism and natural disasters under one umbrella. But the ODP had powerful protectors in Congress who wanted to retain its law enforcement focus, and they vetoed the idea. And Brown's persistent kvetching about retaining FEMA's unique functions turned off Homeland Security Secretary Tom Ridge and other top officials, who wanted a single department managed from the top down. The talk turned to stripping out FEMA's preparedness programs altogether. Soon the ODP was handing out its own law enforcement grants—as well as the grants that had belonged to FEMA. Most of the grants were for terrorism first, natural disasters second—if at all. Terry Ebbert, a retired Marine colonel who ran the New Orleans Office of Homeland Security, applied for a federal grant to buy aluminum boats for city departments to use in flood rescues. He was turned down because the boats had no terrorism-related function (well, maybe if terrorists blew up a levee, but that was a reach).

A half dozen other problems were brewing inside FEMA as the Homeland Security honchos focused on other things. After 2002, funding was cut for FEMA's emergency response teams—groups of volunteers who were the first on the scene after a disaster. Their training exercises were suspended and their numbers fell. The National Disaster Medical System—teams of medical volunteers around the country who could mobilize and move equipment and expertise into an area—lost numerous key people as it was bobbled from one agency to the next. Volunteers complained that bureaucratic obstacles were making it harder to organize, train, and leap into action.

In September 2003 Brown wrote a blistering memo to Ridge saying that the changes "can result in an ineffective and uncoordinated response . . . shatter agency morale and would completely disconnect the Department's response functions from the responders and governments they are supposed to support."

But FEMA's authority continued to erode. The law that created DHS mandated the creation of a generic "National Response Plan" adaptable to any disaster. Brown had a logical idea: use FEMA's existing Federal Response Plan as the foundation for the new procedures. But Ridge wanted to start from scratch, so he gave the job to Coast Guard admiral James M. Loy, then running the Transportation Security Administration. Ridge didn't tell Brown or anyone at FEMA they'd been shut out. Nor did Loy or the other authors make a point of consulting state or local agencies.

The plan went through several drafts and was finally finished in 2004. It created a baffling two-tiered system that took away FEMA's ultimate authority but still expected the agency to do what it had always done: run the federal effort on the front lines. Homeland Security officials would execute the National Response Plan out of their own, brand-new emergency operations center on Nebraska Avenue in one of Washington's residential neighborhoods. There, computers, satellite communications, and flat-screen monitors would integrate information from more than a dozen federal agencies and local counterparts and allow top officials to obtain the "situational awareness" key to getting out ahead of events. But a few miles away, in its headquarters near the National Mall, FEMA would be running its own game plan out of its own emergency operations center, doing more or less the same thing—only in a more nuts-and-bolts way: delivering meals, directing medical and rescue teams. FEMA's "federal coordinating officer" would control things on the ground at or near the disaster's epicenter. But DHS's "principal federal official"—who ostensibly was superior—could come from any agency. With the benefit of the big picture, he was supposed to orchestrate the entire federal strategy.

Not surprisingly, Brown concluded that this was a bad idea. He believed that FEMA should retain the last word in disaster operations. His complaints were again dismissed.

The idea struck others versed in disaster management as peculiar, too. "We do not believe that we needed another layer of command. . . . Now all of a sudden you're going to have the federal coordinating officer respond and the principal federal officer, which in reality is going to be a political official who may or may not have command experience, who is going to be there to play the role of politician," John Buckman, a former International Association of Fire Chiefs president and a plan advisory panel member, complained to the *Federal Times* newsletter when it was announced.

Ironically, but somehow fittingly, Brown was the one assigned the job of introducing the completed plan to state and local officials on a nationwide tour, which he turned into an advertising campaign for the new department's dysfunction. "Look," he'd tell his audiences, "the National Response Plan was somehow developed in a vacuum. It's now back in the hands of FEMA. We want to review it with you and get you back as a part of it and see what needs to be fixed—we just don't have the resources to do that."

Comics had lampooned Ridge as affable but in over his head, mocking his color-coded terrorism alert system and his friendly advice, useless to most Americans, to stockpile duct tape to seal door seams during a poison gas attack. Not surprisingly, Bush had a hard time filling the job of DHS secretary when Ridge stepped down at the end of 2004. Bush's first choice to replace him, former New York City police commissioner Bernard Kerik, saw his nomination implode in a cascade of embarrassing revelations, among them an outstanding arrest warrant dating from his mismanagement of a condominium, and the revelation that he had carried on an affair with a prominent book editor in an apartment near the World Trade Center site used by police and rescue workers in the aftermath of 9/11.

Bush finally settled on a safer choice, Michael Chertoff. A federal judge, Chertoff was a different variety of Republican than Brown: a product of the GOP meritocratic establishment. During both Republican and Democratic presidencies, it was highly educated policy mavens like Chertoff who made the government run. They usually got the second-tier, deputy secretary jobs, hands-on positions charged with carrying out broad presidential directives. Chertoff had all the necessary credentials: he had attended an elite New Jersey prep school, Harvard College, and Harvard Law. He had made news in the 1980s while working for Rudolph Giuliani, then the U.S. attorney for Manhattan, winning convictions against key figures in New York's five Mafia families. Unlike many Republican officials of his generation, Chertoff was not part of the conservative movement; he was more of a pragmatist, and his intelligence and competence impressed Democrats as well. When Bill Clinton took office in 1993, Chertoff, then U.S. attorney for New Jersey, was the only top prosecutor from the George H. W. Bush administration asked to stay on. (Though he later earned both Bill and Hillary Clinton's enmity when he took a job running a Senate inquiry into their Whitewater land deal in Arkansas.) When George W. Bush took office, he appointed Chertoff to a top job in the Justice Department, where he became one of the chief architects of the war on terror, instrumental in the drafting of the USA PATRIOT Act, which expanded federal law enforcement powers after 9/11. Bush rewarded his efforts with a seat on the federal bench.

When Chertoff gave up his lifetime tenure there to take the Homeland Security job, political pundits said he had to be crazy. If there were a terror attack, he'd be blamed for whatever went wrong. Otherwise, like Ridge, he risked becoming a running joke for the late-night comics. But if anyone did, the intense and hard-driving Chertoff seemed to have the chops for the job. He had been tapped for his law enforcement expertise, and he set about reshaping DHS—again—to beef up its terrorism-related plans.

Like Brown, however, Chertoff had no emergency management experience or familiarity with policies relating to disaster preparation, response, or recovery. "I'm not a hurricane operator," he said later. But he was sensitive to the growing accusations from emergency managers that his department wasn't ready for a major catastrophe of any kind, so he proposed moving all preparedness efforts into a single unit—one that would not include FEMA. The proposal was controversial. Some praised it for its tight focus on getting ready. But many in the emergency management community worried that leaving FEMA out meant natural disasters would never get the attention they deserved. Brown wrote one last-ditch memo to Chertoff's office arguing that he should reverse Ridge, not build on what he'd done: "These recent organizational changes have divided what was intended to be one, all-hazards preparedness mission into two artificially separate preparedness categories of terrorism and natural disasters." But it was clear things were moving in the opposite direction. "It's a Hobson's choice," Brown e-mailed a colleague. "Take something that I don't believe in and that I don't think will work, or stay at FEMA and try to keep it from failing. Geez, what a life!"

Brown made plans to resign around Labor Day, 2005.

In New Orleans, meanwhile, things were looking up. Evacuation numbers had improved with Hurricane Ivan in 2004; surveys showed more than 60 percent of the metro area had left. After a long interruption caused by 9/11, the federal study of New Orleans's hurricane response and recovery began to move forward. FEMA, with some money finally freed up, agreed to cosponsor a five-day simulation. Beriwal's firm would run it, and LSU's Hurricane Center would design a realistic storm and flood. They dubbed the fictitious storm Hurricane Pam.

Hurricane Pam wasn't a worst-case, Category 5 monster, but a slow Category 3 preceded by twenty inches of rain. Nevertheless, it would put ten to twenty feet of water inside New Orleans and kill fifty thousand to one hundred thousand people who would be trapped when it struck. More than a million metro area residents would be left homeless, and 80 percent of the structures in thirteen parishes would be damaged or destroyed by flood or wind.

After months of preparation, more than three hundred people from every conceivable agency—federal, state, and local—and an assortment of voluntary organizations convened on the sprawling Baton Rouge campus of the state's new Emergency Operations Center and State Police Headquarters to hash out how to respond to Pam. After an introduction by FEMA's Brown, Beriwal and the LSU modelers kicked off the meeting with a hair-raising account of the imaginary disaster.

The storm was meant to give participants the greatest possible challenge and see how they'd deal with it. It was also meant to be a plausible challenge. Pam had been tailored to be just strong enough to exceed the stated capacities of the levee system. It played on the system's weaknesses—especially its network of canals connected to the Gulf of Mexico. The imaginary storm hadn't even overflowed the lakefront levees.

"Metropolitan New Orleans was under water. There were fifty thousand fatalities and a hundred thousand casualties. So what are you going to do?" said Maestri. He continued,

> The exercise begins and starts with search and rescue. How many people are you going to need? Where will you find the boats necessary to go in and get people on roofs and trapped in homes and out in the water? . . . The needs of the coroner were discussed, how to collect, transport, and store dead bodies. From there, we discussed special needs and medical needs, the evacuation of those with medical problems who might be trapped and their sheltering and so forth. Then we moved on to, as we get some of the water out, how do we turn the infrastructure back on? How do we operate the sewer systems, operate the drainage systems, get the pumps rebuilt?

In a dozen crowded rooms in the neighboring buildings, participants also looked at longer-term problems: where to put temporary housing, how to arrange schooling for evacuees, what to do with the millions of tons of debris, including thousands of pounds of hazardous waste, thousands of vehicles, and thousands of refrigerators, freezers, washing machines, and dryers.

Additional workshops continued up until July 2005. The final report wasn't exactly the Bible of emergency management, but it outlined the basic lines of responsibility in a way that had never been done before. "FEMA, the state, local officials are all meeting together and we're all agreeing on what will happen," Maestri said. "This is what I'm going to do and what you're going to do—what you will do for me and me for you. Everybody is signing off and saying this is what we can do, and that's what, in essence, the final report of the Pam exercise spells out. Who's responsible for what and when, and what time span." The plan assumed that state and local agencies would be completely overwhelmed, and that it would take forty-eight to sixty hours for federal help to arrive.

There was no chance, however, to test those relationships with more dry runs, or produce a true game plan. The project's funding ran out—again—amid Chertoff's second reorganization.

The language in Pam's workshops was dry, but its scenes suggested unimaginable pain and suffering. The most urgent challenge would be moving people out of the flood zone. The simulation envisioned five hundred thousand victims who have to be rescued or wade from rooftops and shelters. The saved would have to be left at drop-off points around the city, then transported to temporary medical clinics outside New Orleans in Baton Rouge, Thibodaux, and Hammond.

"A major limiting factor in executing this plan will be shortage of transportation facilities," a September 2004 report read. "The Louisiana National Guard will be tasked to numerous missions and will not be able to meet the need for transportation of victims. Sufficient transport to move personnel to [medical staging areas outside the flood zone] will not be available for 48 to 72 hours." The report went on to say that it would require four hundred buses per day to keep people moving. If everything went perfectly, 275,000 people would be moved out of the city—by the end of day three.

Hurricane Pam punctuated the advice that Maestri and others had been giving for years: get out. And it put attention back on the problem of the people who couldn't. A University of New Orleans study done by sociologist Shirley Laska estimated that

134,000 people in the city had no transportation of their own—more than a quarter of the population. Laska's study roughly tracked the 29 percent of the population living in poverty. To get around, they depended on relatives, friends, and the city buses run by the Regional Transit Authority. Evacuating these people before a storm was more than mere logistics—it was a social-policy problem of the first order.

To begin with, it was hard to recruit bus drivers to put their lives on the line by staying behind to work evacuation duty. But bus drivers were only one variable in a complex equation. Many of these residents rarely left their own neighborhoods. Some had never been out of the city. Even if there were an easy way to move them out, persuading them to leave for a storm that might end up missing the city wouldn't be easy.

Laska had studied the issue for years, and found that evacuations had a complex psychology. People were quirky, and they lived in quirky circumstances. Some didn't believe a disaster could happen to them. Some believed if they'd survived Betsy, then they could ride anything out. Some were young and believed they could survive no matter what. Some didn't have TVs or the Internet connections that the authorities depended on to get their message out. Some had been through one evacuation and that was quite enough, thank you.

Mayor Vic Schiro, elected without much black support, had started looking for a solution after Hurricane Betsy struck. Schiro was ubiquitous after the storm, but the devastation to the Ninth Ward mobilized the city's black community against him. Political opponents spread rumors that Schiro had "cut the Industrial Canal to drown the colored people so that they would not vote in the coming election," one caller to the mayor's office reported. Schiro staked the mayoral race on his ability to get aid and scored a victory when Congress passed a federal aid package with modest $1,800 grants. A few weeks after the storm, Schiro pulled out a narrow, 665-vote victory over his opponent, city council president Jimmy Fitzmorris. Four years later, his successor, Moon Landrieu—later Jimmy Carter's housing secretary—changed the political equation. Landrieu was a white liberal who, while on the city council, had pushed through an ordinance outlawing segregation in city accommodations. The election of the city's first black mayor, Dutch Morial, in 1978, continued the trend of consolidating black political clout. The city's black community had arrived, and it took hold of the levers of patronage. But there were many divisions within that community, and tensions began to manifest themselves before long. The city's Creole elite (largely light-skinned African Americans of mixed ancestry with local roots stretching back to the eighteenth century) had established its bourgeois bona fides generations earlier, and its leaders quickly rose to the top of the New Orleans political culture. Those with other bloodlines found themselves shunted aside. (White voters were a minority, but they voted more or less as a bloc and could sway an election.)

The incestuous culture of Louisiana politics bred corruption before blacks had power, and it bred corruption afterward. Black neighborhood political organizations, flush with federal funds, became effective patronage and vote-generating machines. Meanwhile, Edwin W. Edwards dominated state politics. Edwards, a famously droll and corrupt Democratic governor, also depended on New Orleans's network of black political organizations to get elected. The result, unfortunately, was often government as a spoils system. Most winning mayoral candidates ran on platforms promoting good government and competence. After they got elected, however, they fell back into business as usual.

During the 1980s and 1990s New Orleans grew poorer and blacker. As many residents left for the suburbs or to seek an education and opportunities elsewhere, the population shrank. Between 2000 and 2004 alone, it fell 4.6 percent. The city's police department endured a series of lurid scandals: one cop murdered three people, including a fellow officer, while robbing a restaurant; another, under federal surveillance for dealing drugs, was caught on tape ordering the killing of a woman who had filed a brutality complaint against him. (Authorities were too late to stop the murder.) The city's economy, anemic for generations, became more so. Port activity and tourism, the legs it stood on, could be wobbly. New Orleans depended more each year on its image as a quaint and unique American city. Hotels and conventions boomed, but not much else. The arrival of riverboat gambling and a single land-based casino near the waterfront—hyped by Edwards as a job-creating machine—accelerated the changes. The New Orleans that tourists encountered was a Disneyfied version of the real thing—a zone comprising the French Quarter (especially Bourbon Street) and the adjacent downtown hotel and restored warehouse districts, and the long tendril of the streetcar line along St. Charles Avenue that stretched through leafy Uptown districts. A visitor could tour these areas, feel he had done the city justice, and never see its much larger, seamier side—which in many spots lay right next to the tourist zone.

But those hidden neighborhoods were the city's cultural ballast. The Lower Ninth Ward, for example, was compact and isolated, across the Industrial Canal and miles away from the center of town. For most residents in other parts of town, it was easily forgotten, except during times like Mardi Gras, when neighborhood brass bands and "Indians"—men wearing elaborate feathered costumes sewn over the course of a year—emerged to march through black enclaves of Uptown, staging mock battles along the way. As late as the 1960s, many of the Lower Ninth's side streets were unpaved and had no covered drains. But its infrastructure of restaurants, small businesses, and family ties enfolded residents and drew gumbo aficionados from all over. The distinctive bluesy sounds of black New Orleans shaped jazz, rock, and Louisiana genres such as zydeco and nurtured the art of musicians such as Fats Domino.

The 2002 election of Mayor C. Ray Nagin looked like a decisive break with the past. Nagin was a classic good-government candidate—the vice president and general manager of the local outlet of Cox Cable, he was a businessman with no experience in politics. With his bald head and upbeat, technocratic attitude, he cut an unusual figure in a city used to backroom dealing.

Nagin pledged to clean up the city's corrupt political culture, make its institutions work, and continue pushing tourism and port activities. He launched corruption investigations of city agencies. On one astonishing Monday, he fired the city's entire auto inspection force when an investigation revealed many were taking bribes to wave faulty vehicles through.

But as happens with many reform attempts, Nagin's good-government efforts bogged down. They became more episodic. Nagin found it hard to push reforms through the city council. And on hurricanes, he lost his way.

As federal emergency-preparedness grant money flowed into the city after 9/11, city hall focused on terrorism, not hurricanes. Because it held the first major national event in the country following 9/11—the 2002 Super Bowl—New Orleans got more attention than most places. First FEMA, then DHS poured money out the terrorism spout and the city spent it on weapons-of-mass-destruction drills. Like FEMA at the federal level, the New Orleans Office of Emergency Preparedness was absorbed into a new Office of Homeland Security and Public Safety, headed by Terry Ebbert, the former director of the New Orleans Police Foundation. Neighboring parishes, such as Jefferson and Plaquemines, had professional staffs and sophisticated plans; the New Orleans OEP was a bureaucratic backwater whose staff consisted of a director and two clerks. Nagin's first emergency-preparedness director, Terry Tullier, was a former high-ranking New Orleans Fire Department official whose real talent was public relations. Nagin's predecessor, Marc Morial, had given him the job as an up-and-out move from the fire department before retirement. After Tullier stepped down in 2004, Nagin took months to appoint a successor. He ultimately followed Morial's example, choosing a senior fire official with no emergency-preparedness training, Deputy Chief Joseph Matthews.

As emergency professionals from the state and neighboring parishes gathered regularly for hurricane drills and planning, New

Orleans's participation was spotty. City officials seemed curiously uninterested in the most obviously urgent issue they faced. Hurricane Pam had dramatized the worst that could happen to New Orleans. But while the department had had a representative or two at Hurricane Pam exercises, it had no real leadership role and did little afterward on the recommendations. In early 2005, during the National Hurricane Conference—a gathering of meteorologists and emergency managers—participants from around the country gathered in knots in hallways discussing and debating among themselves how to get the people without transportation out of New Orleans; no city officials had bothered to attend.

Nor did Nagin take an active interest in the most pressing of the city's emergency issues, the fate of those without transportation. He rarely spoke with Tullier or Matthews. And with no clear mandate from the top, staffers' efforts to develop the last-ditch evacuation plan repeatedly faltered. Since 2000, officials had been negotiating on and off with the Regional Transit Authority and the school system for buses and drivers, and with Amtrak for trains, but nothing had come of it. Dr. Kevin Stephens, the director of New Orleans's health department, tried again in 2004 while the OEP was without a chief. It looked promising at first. "I called Amtrak and I called the school board and RTA and other guys . . . and asked them would they be willing to transport people out of the city, and they said sure, we'd be happy to," he recalled. Stephens drafted preliminary memos outlining how each would assist, then handed them off to Matthews when he took over the emergency office in March 2005. In June, the school board was still discussing it.

The city's newly drafted hurricane plan did call for a combination of transit and school buses to take people to safety. But that still depended on getting bus drivers to volunteer for hazardous duty. The city tried various recruiting approaches. The bus drivers' contract required them to help and granted them permission to bring their families along on the ride out. But the contract was not enforced, and only about a hundred RTA drivers volunteered for hurricane duty, a fraction of the number

needed. The Orleans Parish school system's troubles compounded the difficulties. It was bankrupt, and a private company had taken over its finances on the state's orders; even if
school board members were inclined to help, the financial problems made it less likely they'd pay drivers to risk their lives.

As the 2005 hurricane season got under way, Ebbert halted
the seemingly endless talks over buses and trains. "June starts
the hurricane season," he said later. "You can't go to war still
drafting your plan." At a Hurricane Pam meeting in July,
Matthews reiterated this potentially catastrophic omission in
the city's emergency plans to state and federal officials. But with
the hurricane season in progress, there wasn't much they could
do, either.

Officials threw up their hands. Ebbert and Matthews
agreed—as city officials had in the past—to urge local churches
and community groups to organize evacuation convoys for the
needy. And they tacitly decided that when a major storm approached, transit buses would carry people not out of town, but
to the Superdome. (Since Hurricane Georges, the Superdome
had been used one other time to shelter people: in 2004, Nagin
opened it to the general population as Hurricane Ivan approached. The opening came at the last minute, after the evacuation was essentially complete, so only 1,100 people, most of
them homeless, took him up on the offer.) The Dome was to be
a "refuge of last resort," and the term was literal. It meant no
perks would be provided: no cots, no comforts; minimal staffing,
food, and water. Anyone going was advised to bring everything
they'd need to live for two or three days. There were no other
shelters. After people nearly drowned in one of its shelters in
South Carolina in 1989, the Red Cross had declined to set up
shelters in potential flood zones. That meant most of south
Louisiana. For those with nowhere to go or no means to escape,
it would be the Superdome or the floodwaters.

Meanwhile, the Office of Management and Budget, intent on
reducing the Corps's attachment to pork-barrel projects, began
nickel-and-diming the New Orleans levees. They were, of

Soon after New Orleans mayor C. Ray Nagin announced that the Superdome would be opened as a "refuge of last resort" in advance of Hurricane Katrina, thousands of people lined up to gain entry. (U.S. Coast Guard photo)

A storm surge pouring through a variety of breaches in levee walls converged on central New Orleans, flooding homes and businesses and stranding thousands in attics and on rooftops. (U.S. Coast Guard photo)

The community of Yscloskey, an area outside the hurricane levee in St. Bernard Parish southeast of New Orleans, took the full brunt of a twenty-foot-high storm surge. (Photo by John McQuaid)

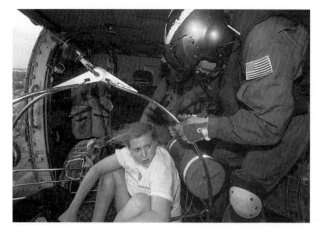

Coast Guard helicopters were instrumental in the rescue of more than thirty-five thousand people in New Orleans and St. Bernard Parish after the storm. (U.S. Coast Guard photo)

A Coast Guard rescue swimmer prepares two flood victims to be lifted into a helicopter. (U.S. Coast Guard photo)

A Coast Guard rescue swimmer helps a man off a rooftop in flooded New Orleans. (U.S. Coast Guard photo)

A section of flooded Interstate 10 in New Orleans that rose to cross the 17th Street Canal into suburban Jefferson Parish became the emergency ramp for dozens of rescue boats pulling survivors off rooftops in Lakeview. (U.S. Coast Guard photo)

Spray-painted warnings to would-be looters were hastily added to walls and doors in New Orleans following the storm. (U.S. Coast Guard photo)

A barge the length of a city block washed through a two-thousand-foot breach in a levee wall along the Industrial Canal and came to rest amid the wreckage of a Lower Ninth Ward home. (Photo by John McQuaid)

The weight of storm surge water in the 17th Street Canal shoved aside a flood-wall at 9:45 a.m. Monday as Katrina came ashore, heaving earth toward the adjacent Bellaire Drive in the Lakeview neighborhood in New Orleans. The torrent of brackish Lake Pontchartrain water released by the breach killed trees and bushes and flooded this schoolbus. (Photo by Mark Schleifstein)

Zephyr Field, west of New Orleans in suburban Metairie and the home of the AAA baseball farm team of the Washington Nationals, was used as a staging area for rescue and relief operations. (U.S. Coast Guard photo)

Federal Emergency Management Agency director Mike Brown briefs the media on August 29, after Katrina came ashore, at the Louisiana Emergency Operations Center in Baton Rouge. He is joined by Governor Kathleen Blanco (center) and U.S. Senator Mary Landrieu. (Photo by Jocelyn Augustino / FEMA)

A tug and barge bring about one thousand New Orleans residents to dry land near the Algiers Point ferry terminal on the west bank of the Mississippi River on September 1, three days after the storm. (Photo by Bobby Nash / U.S. Coast Guard)

Three days after Hurricane Katrina hit New Orleans, thousands of evacuees who had been bused to Houston found refuge at a Red Cross shelter set up on the floor of the Astrodome. (Photo by Andrea Booher / FEMA)

President George W. Bush is briefed on helicopter rescue operations by Captain Dave Callahan at the Coast Guard Aviation Training Center in Mobile, Alabama, on September 2. Listening in are FEMA director Mike Brown (behind Callahan), Homeland Security Secretary Michael Chertoff (right), and Alabama governor Bob Riley (left). (U.S. Coast Guard photo)

A line of dignitaries accompanied President George W. Bush on a whirlwind tour of flooded New Orleans on Friday, September 2. From left, Colonel Rich Wagenaar, commander of the Army Corps of Engineers' New Orleans District office; New Orleans mayor C. Ray Nagin; FEMA director Mike Brown; President Bush; and U.S. Senator David Vitter, R-La. (U.S. Coast Guard photo)

Louisiana governor Kathleen Blanco with Colonel Rich Wagenaar, left, commander of the Army Corps of Engineers' New Orleans District, and a Coast Guard official, on September 2. (U.S. Coast Guard photo)

Much of a Six Flags theme park in eastern New Orleans sat below water after the hurricane. (U.S. Coast Guard photo)

Almost a week after Katrina, floodwaters dropped slowly in New Orleans. Many abandoned pets, like this dog perched precariously on an air-conditioning unit, were eventually rescued by the Humane Society of the United States and other teams and were transported to shelters nationwide. (U.S. Coast Guard photo)

Vice President Dick Cheney talks with Coast Guard personnel, with Governor Kathleen Blanco in the background, during a September 8 tour of New Orleans flood damage. (U.S. Coast Guard photo)

Portable pumps were the mainstay of the Army Corps of Engineers' Task Force Unwatering, whose task was to pump more than one billion gallons of water out of the city. The job took six weeks. (U.S. Coast Guard photo)

Three weeks after Hurricane Katrina hit on August 29, much of the water in New Orleans had been pumped out, leaving behind prestorm debris, including this waterlogged *Times-Picayune* newspaper box with the Sunday, August 28, edition headlined KATRINA TAKES AIM. Its stories warned that storm surge would overtop levees and flood the city. (Photo by Walt Handelsman)

The future of flood control? Almost as long as the Eiffel Tower (but four times heavier), Holland's Maeslant Storm Barrier is one of the most advanced flood-control mechanisms in the world. Normally, the gates remain open until the water level rises. Then, they seal off Rotterdam and the surrounding area from storm surge. (Photo by John McQuaid)

One of the victims of flooding from the 17th Street Canal was this 2003 award presented to the *Times-Picayune* and reporters John McQuaid and Mark Schleifstein by the National Hurricane Conference, an annual gathering of meteorologists and emergency preparedness officials, for their series on increased hurricane risk in New Orleans, entitled "Washing Away." The award was on the first-floor wall of Schleifstein's home, which was flooded with twelve feet of water during Katrina. (Photo by Mark Schleifstein)

course, not a pork-barrel project but a piece of critical infra-structure. The OMB, however, was out to bring the Corps to heel and didn't make that distinction. In 2004, Al Naomi, the Corps project manager in charge of the system, told officials in Jefferson Parish he'd run out of money to continue work on sub-urban hurricane levees; he was two million dollars short. In the past, contractors assumed the money would eventually arrive and continued working on spec. But with the Office of Manage-ment and Budget cracking down, they were now more likely to just stop working. Jefferson officials put up barricades along the low points, raising the necessary money themselves through a property tax, but in other areas, construction ground to a halt. A preliminary study on building Category 5 levees was finished, but the Bush administration had declined to fund the next step—a more detailed look at the alternatives and their costs. All the while, the levees were sinking along with the entire delta, lowering the city's guard against a storm surge. The benchmarks it used to measure levee heights—markers embedded in the soil—had by now sunk as much as two feet. Yet the Corps still had not taken this into account for most of the system.

Wilson Shaffer, the National Weather Service's chief SLOSH modeler, had been refining his data to take account of the sinking, coastal erosion, and places where the levees were incomplete. In 2001, Shaffer had given a talk to emergency offi-cials at the Corps's New Orleans headquarters on the Missis-sippi River levee. His updated models showed for the first time that a Category 2 storm, coming in during a high tide at the right angle, could overtop levees on the east side of New Orleans and St. Bernard. When Shaffer returned in 2004, briefing an even larger audience at the Jefferson Parish Public Library, the latest models painted a far more dangerous picture: the levee system could be overtopped in multiple places by Category 2 storms and fast-moving Category 3s. That meant officials would have to plan for more frequent, and earlier, evacuations.

Some computer modelers had been noting such vulnerabil-ities for decades. H. Lee Butler had noticed some of the sys-tem's weaknesses not long after starting work at the Corps's

Waterways Experiment Station in Vicksburg in 1973. WES was one of the premier engineering institutions in the world, with an unmatched concentration of brainpower. Its main focus at its founding in the wake of the 1927 flood had, of course, been the river. But over the decades it had expanded its reach into environmental science, coastal issues, geotechnical (soil) engineering—and computer science, Butler's field.

Butler and a handful of colleagues were outsiders, one of a new breed of engineers who operated in a virtual realm rather than the Corps's traditional arena of water, mud, concrete, and steel. When he and his fellow computer scientists pushed virtual storm surges at the levees in the late 1970s, they identified a weak point. It lay to the east, between St. Bernard Parish and eastern New Orleans, where two levees came together like a giant *V* lying on its side, pointing west into the city like an arrowhead. That area was the most exposed of the entire system—it was open to the Gulf of Mexico across Lake Borgne and raggedy, decaying marshes. It was a likely target for storm surges propelled by counterclockwise east winds of a hurricane, and water flowing up the much-derided Mr. Go shipping channel. In dry rows of numbers on printouts, the model showed that such a storm surge would rise much higher than the Corps's original designs predicted. Indeed, it looked like water flowing into a funnel, and if the storm surge rose high enough in the V, it would overflow the levees. Worse, the outlet of this funnel was a canal—the Gulf Intracoastal Waterway—leading directly into New Orleans.

Butler and his colleagues put together a paper detailing their findings. By combining the model with the sketchy historical record, they got a pretty good reading of the likelihood of high water. That, too, was considerably higher than the Corps predicted.

The paper was never published. Corps engineers in New Orleans simply didn't believe the water could get that high. They contended there must be something screwy with the model. "The Corps district did not believe the results. That was the bottom line," Butler said. He shrugged it off and moved on to other projects.

By the 1990s, sophisticated storm surge models needed supercomputers, but they had grown incredibly accurate. Instead of Cartesian grids, the newer software used a mesh of triangular cells that could be molded to fit any geographical feature, predicting flood crests in the smallest nooks and crannies. With that power at their fingertips in 1996, Butler and his colleagues took another crack at a model, reevaluating the levee system's safety margins. The new model, called AdCirc, produced virtually the same result for the V.

Again, the Corps disagreed. A paper was published, but the results were never accepted by the Corps. Butler retired the next year.

The Corps took yet another shot in 2001 with computer scientists from Notre Dame and LSU running the show. The virtual water in the V again rose alarmingly high. At that point, the *Times-Picayune* hired Butler as a consultant for our series. He reran his old program and compared its results with newer AdCirc results. They lined up pretty well. His conclusion: the risk of a hurricane overflowing the levees into the Lower Ninth Ward, St. Bernard—and now suburbs in eastern New Orleans, an area that had been virtually empty when he did his first computer runs and was now populated thanks to the levee system— was approximately double what the Corps said it was. That meant people living there, the region's poorest and most fragile residents, were three times as likely as people in central New Orleans to have their homes wiped out by a hurricane. They were living in a spot where most people would never have built if they had known the real risk, where it should have been impossible to get flood insurance.

That conclusion put the Corps in an uncomfortable position. If the levees really weren't as safe as its engineers publicly maintained, that could mean going back to Congress for more money—even clear back to the drawing board. As they had when they first encountered evidence the levees were sinking with the delta in the 1980s, the traditionalists at the Corps resisted that idea, and not only because making such an appeal would be deeply embarrassing. The predictions just didn't make sense to them intuitively—the computer models had to be wrong. Jay Combe, then the director of coastal engineering for the New Orleans district, said he didn't buy it—the water shouldn't be rising that high. The model, he said, wasn't accounting for something, maybe the flow of water away from the levees at their base. (Joannes Westerink, the Notre Dame engineer working on the latest model, doubted that would make much difference.)

Butler looked with dismay at that V and other weak points in the system in 2002. The levee designs and their basic conceptual architecture had not been updated for more than two decades. In that period, the land under the levees had sunk. The marshes around them had all but disappeared. Storm surges could rise higher and reach farther inland. There were many low points a surge could penetrate before it reached the top of a levee—dips under bridges, joints, gaps. Yet all the original standards remained stubbornly in place. Corps officials said there was nothing that could be done unless Congress decided to take another look at it from the ground up, and Congress wasn't interested. And the city hadn't taken a hit from a big hurricane for a long time, so calm was the order of the day.

But not everyone was relaxed. "I think everyone familiar with this is sitting on pins and needles because nothing has happened in that lake for fifty to sixty years and you start to think, are we due?" Butler said in 2002. "And the answer I think is yes, statistically you're due. And that's scary. Based on my knowledge of hurricanes, I'd watch what happens very closely—and I'd get out of Dodge."

Chapter 8

KATRINA

I F THE EARTH WEREN'T spinning on its axis, the weather would be a dull affair: weak north-south breezes, zones of constant rain, gentle seasonal changes, and nothing more. Instead, as the globe revolves it drags its envelope of air along, exposing it to quick, intense flashes of sunshine and darkness, warmth and cold. As temperatures rise and fall across thousands of miles, lighter warm air rises over denser cold air. As warmth is wicked away, water molecules bouncing around in the air condense into rain or crystallize into snow. Wind blows from areas of high pressure to low in a constant, doomed effort to arrive at a peaceful equilibrium. And in two bands about 1,700 miles across, lying between latitudes five to thirty degrees north and south of the equator, where the ocean is warm and trade winds blow from the east, these ordinary motions of air and moisture can turn suddenly violent.

Near the coast of West Africa, hot, dry winds off the Sahara flow over moist ocean air currents. When the Saharan breezes are especially fast and dry, the weather is nice. But when they slow, they start to interact with ocean air and kick up tropical waves—groups of thunderstorms that ride the trade winds west. (Thunderstorms form where warm air rolls in over cold air, condensing water into rain and setting off quick updrafts, complete with electrical discharges and thunder.) Dozens of tropical waves form each year, and most last only a few days, dying out due to cool temperatures, an encounter with eastward-moving waves of high pressure, or some other obstacle in the upper atmosphere. But sometimes the low-pressure point at the system's center starts to focus like a slowly closing lens. As it does so, storms around it grow bigger. The tightening of the system's center has been compared to many things, but perhaps the most appropriate is a noose.

For the president, 2005 had begun on a high note. The previous fall, he had defeated his opponent in the 2004 election, Senator John Kerry of Massachusetts, by a scant 2.5 percentage points, the narrowest victory ever by an incumbent U.S. president. Bush had painted Kerry as a squishy vacillator on the Iraq war and other issues. "In Iraq, we saw a threat, and we realized that after September the eleventh, we must take threats seriously, before they fully materialize. Saddam Hussein now sits in a prison cell. America and the world are safer for it," Bush declared in his first debate with Kerry, on September 30, repeating what had become a standard distillation of his controversial strategy of preemption—attacking an enemy before he attacks you. "The biggest disaster that could happen is that we not succeed in Iraq," Bush said later in the debate. "We will succeed. We've got a plan to do so."

Security had been the source of Bush's bond with the public since September 11, 2001, and he made it the focus of the campaign, playing on fears of change and the unexpected. There had been no terror attacks on American soil since 9/11 and the unsolved anthrax attacks through the U.S. mail shortly afterward. That was a strong point in Bush's favor with a nervous public. In debates and campaign stops, Bush talked up safety and security, boasting of the money the White House poured into the Department of Homeland Security—its budget now tripled to thirty billion dollars. Meanwhile, the department itself issued more terror alerts using its color-coded system. One, announced in August, was set to last through election season, and some Democrats saw it as an attempt to stoke public fear of a change at the top.

Bush had interpreted his win over Kerry as a clear vote of

confidence in his presidency and his policies—the unalloyed affirmation that eluded him in 2000 when he'd lost the popular vote to Democrat Al Gore. As he kicked off his second term, the president set an ambitious agenda that would alter the basic compact between citizens and the government. "I earned capital in the campaign, political capital, and now I intend to spend it. It is my style," Bush declared to the media the day after the election. Again, the issue was security—Social Security. Bush wanted to alter the government's safety net. He proposed diverting some tax dollars from the Social Security program into individual, private investment accounts. Long-term benefit cuts would make the program fiscally sustainable. The privatization idea would reengineer the quintessential government social program, closely identified with the Democratic Party, along Republican, private-sector lines—and, Republicans hoped, speed an even more profound political realignment.

Bush barnstormed the nation to sell his reforms, which would affect almost every citizen by reshaping a familiar, seventy-year-old program. Such proposals usually rise or fall on a vigorous debate, but Bush didn't engage his opponents much at all. As in the fall campaign, he had dozens of question-and-answer sessions with handpicked supporters. Their questions were carefully screened to ensure the right message got across. But the more Bush barnstormed, the more unpopular his Social Security idea became. Public support plummeted. Members of Congress, lukewarm to the idea at first, fled from it. It had never drawn much buzz in polls—the public was satisfied with Social Security, and any fiscal Waterloo, if it came, was decades away—so this wasn't surprising.

What was surprising is that Bush seemed not to notice the PR campaign had crashed and burned, and that there was nothing left but smoldering ashes. He just went on plugging it in the same events. The tub-thumping and Q&A sessions hadn't moved the public, but they had shielded Bush from contrary views. The president's distaste for dissent was legendary. During his first debate with Kerry, he'd become irritated at being questioned and performed poorly. Critics and supporters wondered if he'd withdrawn too far into the presidential bubble and was losing the common touch, a sense of humility and awareness of the everyday concerns of American life. Bush's father had taken a hit when his curiosity about a supermarket scanner led to the widespread view—disputed by the White House—that he'd never seen one before. In a conscious contrast, the son prided himself on being a regular guy.

Meanwhile, despite Bush's optimism, the Iraq war was a mess and got messier. The original rationale for war, eliminating Hussein's nuclear, chemical, and biological weapons programs, was disproved when no weapons were found. The brewing Iraqi insurgency of Sunni Arabs (a minority thrown out of power with the fall of Hussein) and foreign fighters out to humiliate the United States had turned Iraq into a chronically violent and unstable country. An array of politicians—many of them Shiite Muslim clerics with a very different idea of democracy than Bush's—was struggling to put together a functioning government, with no end to the bombing and attacks, or the U.S. involvement, in sight.

As 2005 wore on, the White House staff found itself managing half a dozen bubbling problems that were also eroding the president's public support. A prosecutor was investigating White House staffers' leak of a CIA agent's identity, allegedly to punish her husband, who had attacked Bush's prewar assertions that Saddam Hussein had tried to buy uranium in Niger to advance a nuclear weapons program. The economy was finally healthy after a tepid phase, but polls showed the public was growing more anxious about it. Congressional scandals involving Bush allies occupied investigators. In July, suicide bombings in the London Underground briefly returned the focus to terrorism, but that didn't last.

Trying to reach past the national media, the president began a series of intermittent sit-downs with reporters from regional newspapers. The thinking was that anything the president said directly to a local reporter was automatically front-page news in that paper's community. As a result, the coverage tended to be more sympathetic. On August 2, Bush chatted with eight reporters in the Roosevelt Room, including Bill Walsh of the *Times-Picayune*. Sure enough, the president made front-page news in New Orleans, and it wasn't just for opening his mouth. Bush told Walsh he was throwing his support behind the ambitious, and thus far unfunded, plan to restore the disappearing delta.

"I strongly believe there needs to be a federal-state relationship in solving this problem of the disappearing lands, of Louisiana's coast," Bush said. "It's a big project, but it's a good start."

Those words were a surprising reversal. Coastal restoration had a fourteen-billion-dollar price tag, and the state's congressional delegation had been trying to create a consistent stream of federal money to get the project under way by claiming a share of the federal taxes on offshore drilling. But, as it had on levee funding, the Bush administration had worked hard to thwart them, arguing the proposal would cost too much in a time of federal deficits. (Instead, the White House pushed big tax breaks for the oil and gas industries.) Nevertheless, the proposal stood to benefit six states, and the committees kept it in a pending omnibus energy bill. The White House made a last-ditch effort to cut back on the amount, but when that also failed Bush decided there was no point in opposing a done deal.

"Maybe he's just hoping that people in Louisiana will forget, and thank him for the help he tried so hard not to offer," *Times-Picayune* columnist Stephanie Grace observed. "Still, it's pretty big news that Bush has finally pulled his chair up to the table. Hopefully, he'll stick around for a while."

The next day, Bush flew to Texas for his annual five-week vacation. It quickly took an absurdist turn.

On Saturday August 6, Cindy Sheehan, a California peace activist, showed up outside the president's Crawford, Texas, ranch and demanded a meeting with Bush. Sheehan's son, Army Specialist Casey Sheehan, had been killed a couple of weeks into his first tour in Iraq the previous year. His death had turned Sheehan into an outspoken critic of the war. Sheehan had met with Stephen Hadley, the national security advisor, and Deputy

Chief of Staff Joe Hagin, but not Bush, so she began a vigil under the blazing sun about three miles away, sleeping in a pup tent and setting up "Camp Casey," a temporary memorial to the dead complete with rows of white crosses. Within days, Sheehan's passionate pleas for a few minutes of the president's time became a media phenomenon. Reporters fed up with the unbroken tedium of the presidential vacation had a story. The beleaguered American left had a heroine with moral credibility. The right had a new target. Throughout August, Sheehan's standoff with Bush was a fixture on the nightly news and political blogs, her every hiccup dutifully accounted for, Bush's half responses noted. The president's quiet summer had turned into the summer of Sheehan.

Bush wasn't going to be pressured into meeting with anyone. And he was going to go on enjoying himself, thank you.

"I think it's important for me to be thoughtful and sensitive to those who have got something to say. But I think it's also important for me to go on with my life, to keep a balanced life," Bush told reporters before going on a bicycle ride on August 13. "I think the people want the president to be in a position to make good, crisp decisions and to stay healthy. And part of my being is to be outside exercising. So I'm mindful of what goes on around me. On the other hand, I'm also mindful that I've got a life to live and will do so."

There was another media frenzy under way as well, this one over hurricanes. Storms were a fixture of summer coverage, and many Americans regarded the sight of big-shot TV anchors clinging to lampposts, rain hats flapping, as a sign of the season.

But 2005 was proving far more dramatic. As summer approached, conditions were ripe for hurricanes. It had been a warm winter, the upper atmosphere was moist, and sea surface temperatures in the Atlantic and Gulf were at historic highs, about two degrees above average. A stubborn ridge of high pressure stretched across the Bahamas, Florida, and the eastern Gulf of Mexico, and often drifted northwest up the Mississippi Valley. The persistent sunshine and fair weather heated up the

Gulf and all but eliminated normal, cooling thunderstorms. Inland, a near drought starved the Mississippi for water. Its reduced flow meant less cool water mixed with the hot Gulf at the river's mouth. Satellite heat imagery of the Gulf there showed a deep orange, indicating temperatures over eighty-five degrees, well above the minimum seventy-nine to eighty degrees considered ideal for hurricanes.

Meanwhile, the cyclical warming of ocean temperatures in the eastern Pacific called El Niño did not take place, and its absence reverberated in the Atlantic. Normally, the Pacific warms and cools in cycles (the cold phase is called La Niña). Warm means stormy instability in the Pacific, but calm in the Atlantic. Usually the Pacific storms would spin off westerly winds at about thirty-five thousand feet over the Atlantic. These winds would create vertical shear: sharp changes in wind speed depending on height that can tear the tops off thunderstorms in a nascent hurricane. When the eastern Pacific cools, however, the wind shear over the Atlantic dies down and the thunderclouds reach to the heavens. In 2005, vertical wind shear over the Atlantic was 20 to 40 percent below average. There was nothing to stop hurricanes from forming and growing.

The season had begun early in June with the appearance of Tropical Storm Arlene—a full two months before any tropical storm had formed the year before. Then Tropical Storm Cindy tracked over New Orleans on July 6, its 70-mph gusts downing thousands of trees and snapping power lines, leaving more than 290,000 customers in the dark—the most since Hurricane Betsy. A few days later, Hurricane Dennis became the first Category 4 storm in history to appear before August. It thrashed Cuba and Haiti before striking the Florida panhandle on July 10. Less then a week after that, Hurricane Emily broke Dennis's record, reaching sustained wind speeds of 160 mph, a Category 5. It moved ashore over the resort island of Cozumel and the Mayan ruins of Tulum, crossed the Yucatán and the southwestern Gulf of Mexico before making its final landfall in Tamaulipas. Together, both storms caused billions of dollars in damage and killed more than one hundred people.

As August got under way, hurricane watchers everywhere felt a frisson of anticipation and fear. All the normal conditions that give rise to hurricanes—warm seas, unsettled air, the Bermuda high (the giant blob of high pressure that forms each summer over the Atlantic)—were acting symphonically. Tropical waves that usually flickered in and out of existence were growing into Category 4 hurricanes, and the clockwise winds around the Bermuda high were steering them toward the United States. As a result, the Atlantic had become a great engine of raging storms, one record-breaker after the next. The season had defied predictions issued months earlier by William Gray and assistant Philip Klotzbach at Colorado State University and by the National Weather Service, which had anticipated above-normal hurricane activity but fewer storms than there had been in 2004. Now meteorologists at NOAA and Colorado State struggled to keep their predictions current; Gray and Klotzbach upped the ante several times. In early August, both groups issued prognostications for the rest of the season: the number of expected storms had doubled.

On August 3, New Orleans was wrapped in a typically suffocating summer heat, still sometimes interrupted by fierce afternoon thunderstorms that would wet down the pavement and move off, leaving the city bathed in blue-orange, late-afternoon light. The news of the day was, as always, interesting. FBI agents had raided the Washington and New Orleans homes of the city's lone congressman, Democrat William Jefferson. Their investigation focused on Jefferson's role in helping set up broadband Internet businesses in Nigeria and elsewhere in Africa, allegedly in exchange for cash payments to a family business; FBI agents found ninety thousand dollars wrapped in aluminum foil and stowed in frozen food containers in a freezer in Jefferson's New Orleans home. It was unusual for a sitting congressman to feel such heat, but it caused only mild surprise in Louisiana, where public officials were investigated and indicted on a regular basis.

Governor Kathleen Blanco was trying to revive negotiations

with Saints owner Tom Benson, a local automobile-dealership tycoon, to keep the football team in the Superdome, part of a semiannual dance in which Benson would threaten to leave the state, then exact various concessions to stay put. Fishermen were complaining about the Gulf's "dead zone," a crescent-shaped area the size of Connecticut, devoid of all sea life, that developed each year around the mouth of the Mississippi as fertilizer-laced river runoff from the farm belt flowed down the river, contaminating the Gulf. The problem confounded Louisiana politicians, who had yet to find a way to make farmers in a dozen states upriver care about what was happening hundreds of miles downstream. A local shipbuilding firm was laying people off, but south Louisiana's oil and gas industry was making a killing on high oil prices. In the suburbs, animal control officials were fretting because alligators were making their way into canals and the neighborhoods.

When a hurricane formed in the Gulf, the years of doomsaying had trained New Orleans residents to snap to attention. For many, the appearance of a new tropical storm raised two possibilities: apocalyptic destruction and death (possible, but unlikely), or minor damage and massive inconvenience (likely). As a storm danced across the South Atlantic and Caribbean and then into the Gulf, people kept its progress constantly in the back of their minds. They began planning trips to Home Depot for plywood to board up windows and searched on the Internet for hotel reservations in distant places. Some made plans to stock up on food, fill their bathtubs in case the water supply got cut off, and hunker down. Most of the time, the storm would hit somewhere else and residents would be left with a bunch of excess wood, canned goods, and credit card balances. Every so often the computer models would spit out storm tracks that put New Orleans in the crosshairs, but even then, the eventual storm would only sideswipe the city, causing some flooding and wind damage, as Hurricane Georges had in 1998. Wolf had been cried.

Over the eastern Atlantic sometime around August 15, the stiff easterly trade winds began to ease up a little as they en-

countered the unstable air of a tropical wave moving west toward North America, approaching the Bahamas. Meteorologists
paid it little mind at first: in the stormy cauldrons of the Gulf
and South Atlantic, it was just another bubble. Three stronger
disturbances—including Hurricane Irene—were competing for
their attention.

August's tropical wave might have petered out if it hadn't
run into the last, sorry remnant of what meteorologists were
calling Tropical Depression 10, which had formed off the coast
of Africa a week earlier. The lonely patch of low pressure veered
north of the Virgin Islands, where it merged with the tropical
wave. The merger was like a shot of adrenaline: the wave suddenly strengthened as its pressure dropped. More warm air
vented upward and winds gusted faster toward the low, kicking
off new thunderstorms over the Bahamas. Drawing more
warmth from the sea, the tropical wave kept strengthening. As
bands of thunderstorms spun out on its edge, the pressure fell
further and its center grew more focused, with a definable edge
in the satellite photos. On August 23, the National Hurricane
Center dubbed the invigorated wave Tropical Depression 12
and noted it was moving west toward Florida.

As the globe spins, its lower latitudes move faster than higher
ones: someone sitting at the equator is traveling at a thousand
miles per hour; someone three feet from the North Pole takes an
entire day to move the ten feet of a complete circle. The varying
spin makes winds veer off a straight course, just as a ball rolled
across a twirling carousel will curve and roll off to one side. In
the same way, if a molecule of water vapor is pushed south over
New York along an apparently straight line, by the time it reaches
the latitude of New Jersey, immediately to the south, it will be
over a slightly fatter part of the globe, rotating faster beneath it;
that will displace it to the west, putting it over Pennsylvania.

This diverting is known as the Coriolis effect, named for
French engineer Gaspard-Gustave de Coriolis, who described
it in 1835. The Coriolis effect is so weak that it has barely any

influence on ordinary weather systems. But it provides exactly the right nudge to start winds spinning around the nascent vortex of a tropical depression. In the northern hemisphere, it pushes winds to the right—counterclockwise in a cyclone. In the southern hemisphere, cyclonic winds move clockwise. (Hurricanes cannot exist at or near the equator, where the Coriolis effect disappears.) And as TD 12 grew stronger, momentum from the rotating earth below began, gently at first, to spin the system like batter in a mixing bowl.

The National Hurricane Center occupies a gray concrete bunkerlike building, built after Hurricane Andrew and reinforced to withstand winds from a Category 5 hurricane, at the edge of Florida International University's south campus in Miami-Dade County, about twenty miles west of the Atlantic, well away from the danger of a storm surge. Its team of hurricane watchers soon turned a vast technological apparatus on Tropical Depression 12. A group of meteorologists sifted through mounds of data from dozens of sources, low- and high-tech: wind and pressure numbers from ships and planes; a kind of radar called a scatterometer that measured wind speed by bouncing high-frequency radio waves off the surface of the ocean; a satellite called TRMM that was probing rainfall, outlining the contour of the emerging storm's eyewall; computer models that estimated the storm's future track and intensity. There was art as well as science in this process. The data was sometimes contradictory—a plane showed wind speed at 70 mph, while a satellite showed 100 mph. Putting the pieces together into a whole required experience and intuition. Richard Franklin, one of the hurricane specialists following the storm, began every forecast track by eyeballing the data and then taking a pencil to a map, tracing his hypothetical track by hand.

"Everything's really done on the computer," he said, "but you don't really see and understand, you don't really know what you're doing until you plot it out by hand with paper and pencil."

At eleven p.m. EDT on Tuesday, August 23, meteorologist Richard Knabb projected that TD 12 would keep strengthening.

It was indeed destined to become a tropical storm and probably a hurricane, and it appeared headed toward Florida. He issued a tropical storm watch for the southeastern Florida coast, adding that a hurricane warning could be issued the next day. Forecasts were issued at six-hour intervals, and sure enough, overnight it began to look the part of a cyclone: a large band of heavy thunderstorms grew and wrapped itself around the north side of the storm. Early Wednesday, a Hurricane Hunter plane out of Keesler Air Force Base, in Biloxi, measured flight-level winds of forty-eight knots. Tropical Storm Katrina was born.

Katrina became the eleventh named tropical storm of the year. So far, with top winds of about 40 mph, it wasn't much. But it was obvious that it posed a threat—and not just to Florida but to the Gulf as well. The models showed Katrina would become a hurricane within hours. It would hit the Florida coast and then keep going across the peninsula, quickly regaining its strength once over the warm Gulf waters. Even so, it would probably be a manageable threat. Wednesday night's forecast predicted Katrina would probably hit the Florida panhandle late Sunday night, August 28, as a Category 1 storm.

As Katrina moved northwest through the Bahamas and then turned west toward Florida, its pressure kept falling. Updrafts of hot ocean air laden with water vapor fed thunderstorms clustering around the storm's core: a poorly formed column of warm, wet air welling six miles up through the top of the storm, where it cooled and spilled out in all directions. Winds drawn by the low pressure began to spin clouds, raindrops, and hail around the core at a steady 75 mph. Water vapor condensed into showers and thunderstorms whose clouds streamed out for hundreds of miles in a familiar, disarmingly beautiful spiral. Katrina was a now a hurricane.

On Thursday, the Bermuda high strengthened unexpectedly, pushing Katrina's course south, taking it exactly between Miami and Fort Lauderdale. As its outer edges moved in over south Florida's urban sprawl that afternoon, fifteen inches of rain fell in the space of a few hours, overwhelming storm drains and running through streets. Trees and power lines fell and a million homes went dark. Eleven people died, including two men crushed by falling branches. Katrina's eye crossed south of Hallandale Beach at 6:30 p.m., then moved west-southwest over Miami. Within an hour, it passed directly over the National Hurricane Center. The staff there had spent the day madly rushing back and forth, securing their homes and monitoring the storm's progress. As the eye passed, director Max Mayfield and a few others took a break and strolled outside (violating their standing advice to hunker down until a storm has passed). There, they stood on the sidewalk for a few moments, staring at an eerie, pale gray sky and ravaged greenery. The center's flag hung limp on the pole.

The storm weakened as it passed over the Everglades during the next six hours and the Hurricane Center downgraded Katrina to a tropical storm. (Meteorologists classified storms using the Saffir-Simpson scale, developed by engineer Herbert Saffir and then hurricane center director Bob Simpson in 1969. The scale ranked cyclones by their sustained wind speed: a tropical storm was defined as having winds of 39 to 73 mph; a Category 1 hurricane, 74 to 95 mph; Category 2, 96 to 110 mph; Category 3, 111 to 130 mph; Category 4, 131 to 155 mph. A Category 5 was anything above 155 mph.) Even though it had been downgraded, Katrina kept its distinctive shape: Doppler radar showed that just before Katrina made landfall, its core had shaped itself into a well-defined eye that had grown sharper as Katrina crossed onto land, and remained intact during the storm's trip across Florida.

Katrina moved out into the Gulf early Friday morning. Beneath it was a sea of warm, shallow water. Above the thunderheads seven miles up sat the Bermuda high. As Katrina maneuvered underneath it, the high became a kind of protective cap. Upper-level winds that would have broken up storm clouds calmed, and Katrina's heat engine roared to life as the high-pressure system's winds drew warm air up and out of the top. Within hours, Katrina had transformed from a tropical storm to a Category 3 hurricane. Its winds were now blowing at

115 mph—about one and a half times as strong as they'd been when it struck Florida.

As Friday wore on, Katrina kept strengthening. Each time a Hurricane Hunter plane went in, the pressure in the eye had reached a new low. Satellite images now showed Katrina's eye sharpening and growing more compact. The clouds capping the eye disappeared and the hole was suddenly visible from space: a dark, perfect circle at the center of a vast whorl covering most of the Gulf. Storm clouds rose higher, their temperature dropping, and bands of heavy rains thickened outward from the eye. Their curved tendrils stretched across Florida and south to Cuba.

The hurricane center busily ran at least six computer models simultaneously to predict where Katrina would make landfall. Most of the programs operated on the same general principles as storm surge computer models, subdividing the ocean surface and atmosphere above it into a three-dimensional grid. Using basic fluid dynamics equations and real-time data on atmospheric pressure, wind speed, water temperature, and other key variables, the model would create a virtual storm. By measuring and aggregating all the hourly changes going on over the sea in each tiny piece of the grid, a model would project where a storm was going and how strong it would get. One program was a metamodel—it took the output from the others, averaged it, and massaged it with data from past storms to get a kind of consensus view that was sometimes dead-on—but not always.

When the Bermuda high nudged Katrina south just as it made its Florida landfall, a lot of variables changed, and the models started spitting out wildly diverse storm tracks. Before then, the simulations had all shown Katrina moving due west out into the Gulf, then turning sharply northeast toward Apalachicola, on the Florida panhandle. But as Friday morning wore on and Katrina strengthened, three models—NOGAPS (for Naval Operational Global Atmospheric Prediction System), GFS (Global Forecast System), and GFDL (for the Geophysical Fluid Dynamics Laboratory that developed it)—showed this tight loop opening up and moved the projected landfall west into

Louisiana. But other models still showed a likely strike on the panhandle.

Nevertheless, this meant New Orleans had entered Katrina's potential strike zone, what Max Mayfield and his colleagues called the "cone of uncertainty." (On forecast maps it resembled an inverted cone with the storm at its point, widening out on either side of the projected track one, two, three days into the future as the uncertainty grew.)

When Mayfield joined the Hurricane Center in 1972 as a twenty-four-year-old satellite meteorologist, his coworkers sent out their forecasts using the hunt-and-peck method on surplus World War II Teletype machines. They mapped all data by hand. Computers housed in bulky black boxes were just being introduced. Now, the center had incomparable advantages. But uncertainty persisted more than a day or two beyond the present in hurricane forecasting. The weather was too complex, its rules too subtle. Hurricanes were mercurial, contrary. So there was no way to tell on Friday if Katrina would hit New Orleans on Monday. But it had just gone from unlikely to a distinct possibility, and Mayfield was worried.

He'd been the National Hurricane Center's director since 2000. In a classic nerd's tale, Mayfield's air force ROTC instructors at the University of Oklahoma told him he was too nearsighted to spot an airplane, much less fly one, so he'd taken a job as an air force weather forecaster instead. Within months after his stint ended, he'd gone straight to the hurricane center, where he began rising through the ranks. The director's job required an unusual mix of scientific, bureaucratic, and media talents. Earlier directors, including Neil Frank and Bob Sheets, had turned the position into a national platform, becoming familiar faces on TV during hurricane season as they updated concerned-looking anchors on the latest forecasts. Mayfield had continued the tradition. He detailed the latest tracking and satellite imagery for news and talk shows. He warned the public to evacuate. He briefed emergency officials along the coasts each spring about the upcoming hurricane season. When a storm approached, he worked the phones and kept officials in the most dangerous areas up on what the latest projections were saying.

As the day wore on, more computer models shifted Katrina's track west. Taken together, they showed it striking near Pascagoula, Mississippi, about a hundred miles east of New Orleans. But there were signs that the track wasn't done moving and that soon New Orleans would be dead center.

When Mayfield called him, Walter Maestri was at his own bunkerlike fortress, the Jefferson Parish Emergency Operations Center, in the suburb of Marrero, across the Mississippi south of New Orleans—an area more likely to stay dry than the more heavily populated Jefferson suburbs on the other side.

"This is what we've been talking about all these years," Mayfield told him. "It's a thirty-ninety storm." Thirty degrees latitude, ninety degrees longitude were the coordinates of New Orleans.

"Are you kidding me?" Maestri said.

"No, Walt, this is real," Mayfield replied. "I wanted to let you know that the next advisory is going to move the storm a hundred and fifty miles to the west."

"Okay," Maestri said, warily.

"Let me also tell you I think this storm, and my staff thinks this storm, will track right at you and it has definite potential to become a Category Four or Five. No, I'm not kidding."

Mayfield asked for the phone numbers for Mayor Nagin, Governor Blanco, and Colonel Jeff Smith, the new chief of Louisiana's Office of Homeland Security and Emergency Preparedness. Smith had only recently taken over after Colonel Michael Brown (no relation to the FEMA director) was suspended in connection with an investigation into contracts for raising and buying houses with FEMA grant money.

When Maestri called Smith a little later, Mayfield had already spoken with him. Given the storm's projected track at that point, Smith wasn't alarmed—yet. Maestri told him that he should be.

"You don't know Max," he said. "Let me tell you, when he calls you like that he's telling you to be ready, to be prepared."

In Baton Rouge, Blanco had met early Friday afternoon with Smith and officials from the state police, the National Guard, and other agencies, then declared an official state of emergency at four p.m. That activated the state's plan and put the National Guard on alert. State police made plans to activate Contraflow.

The hurricane center's five p.m. CDT advisory moved Katrina's forecast track west to a projected landfall near Pascagoula, around two p.m. Monday. A short while later, Smith led a conference call with emergency managers around Louisiana. A National Weather Service briefer cautioned that forecasting three days in advance was always going to be fuzzy. "But if you look at a Category Four storm surge," he said, "looking at the SLOSH models, you'd get into the fifteen- to twenty-foot range quite easily." That would be more than enough to top the New Orleans levees.

According to the state's evacuation plan, parishes were supposed to evacuate in a set order, coastal areas going first, starting fifty hours before gale-force winds were due to strike and driving became dangerous. New Orleans would go last—about thirty hours out—because its huge population could clog up the roads, possibly trapping people evacuating from more vulnerable outlying areas. But the plan was very much a work in progress.

As Hurricane Ivan menaced the Louisiana coast the previous September, the state police had waited several hours to begin Contraflow after Nagin and officials in surrounding parishes called evacuations. The result was another monumental traffic snarl all the way to Baton Rouge. Afterward, Blanco and Nagin had both pledged to do better. A few weeks before Katrina's appearance, with Hurricane Dennis in the Gulf, Jefferson Parish president Aaron Broussard called a press conference, announced the state was dragging its feet on revising its evacuation procedures, and said he didn't see any reason to follow its plan.

"If you have the means to evacuate, we recommend you do that now," he declared. "Now would be a great time to pack up the kids and head to Houston, to Dallas, to Branson, Missouri, to Nashville. . . . It's a pretty day. Pack up and leave!"

Dennis turned out to be a false alarm, but the damage was done. Blanco upbraided Broussard afterward, and he responded with even more defiance. If the state's plan required "an abrogation of my elected responsibilities," he wrote Blanco, "THEN I HEREBY NOTIFY YOU NOW THAT I WILL WITHDRAW MY SIGNATURE FROM YOUR PLAN BECAUSE I CAN NO LONGER IN GOOD FAITH SUPPORT IT."

Like Nagin, Mike Brown, Michael Chertoff, and a lot of others in key emergency positions, there was nothing in Blanco's background to indicate how she might perform in a real catastrophe. Before taking office in 2003 she'd been lieutenant governor, a mostly ceremonial position whose chief function was to promote tourism. By most accounts, she did a decent job hawking the state's funky charms (Blanco was a Cajun from New Iberia, in southwest Louisiana—her maiden name was Babineaux—and she had traveled to Nova Scotia to reach out to French Canadians). But in Louisiana's colorful political firmament, she was regarded by most as quite drab.

Blanco's two immediate predecessors in the governor's office had been a corrupt wheeler-dealer and a crusty straight-talker. With her pageboy haircut and tasteful, slightly dowdy suits and pearls, she looked more like the grandmother she was, embarking on a second career, than a canny Louisiana pol. But people tended to underestimate her. She had sharp instincts; she had leveraged her mild manner and cautious conservatism to take the political center, a particularly effective strategy in Louisiana. Conservative Democrats could still beat Republicans in Louisiana—unlike in most southern states—drawing support from the substantial black population and more moderate Cajun voters. In 2003, Blanco had stunned the political pros by beating Republican wunderkind Bobby Jindal, a former Bush administration policy maven, chief of the state's Department of Health and Hospitals, and university president. Jindal, then thirty-two, made his name as a policy genius who could discourse, rapid-fire, on every conceivable subject. He was an interesting personality as well, a Rhodes scholar and devout Catholic whose parents had immigrated from India, and he drew most of the national media attention during the campaign. But by stressing her own conservatism—like Jindal, she opposed abortion—and running some clever attack ads, Blanco prevailed, becoming the first woman governor in Louisiana history. She came in stressing continuity, inviting retiring Republican governor Mike Foster's chief of staff and executive counsel to stay on. (A year later, Jindal easily won a seat in Congress representing New Orleans's most affluent suburbs, including Jefferson Parish and Lake Pontchartrain's north shore.)

Late Friday, meteorologist Lixion Avila and his colleagues at the hurricane center were watching two systems: a ridge of high pressure moving over Florida and a trough of low pressure approaching the Gulf from the northwest. The large, lumbering masses of air—one peaceful, one stormy—were topographical features in the atmospheric landscape, and they were guiding the storm's course northwest, ever closer to New Orleans. "A hurricane simply moves with the flow around other weather features," Avila said. "If you have a high-pressure system to the north, the hurricane cannot move against that mountain."

Friday night, the models shifted west in unison. New Orleans was now at the center of Mayfield's cone of uncertainty—better known as the bull's-eye. Avila moved the official forecast path another hundred miles west in the ten p.m. forecast. Katrina was now definitely headed for southeast Louisiana. Worse, Katrina's path would take it near an offshoot of the loop current—warm water that enters the Gulf between Cuba and the Yucatán and moves in a tight circle. Normally a big hurricane will churn the ocean, bringing cooler water to the surface. This dampens the storm and keeps it from getting too strong. But over the warmer water of the loop current, an already strong hurricane just keeps strengthening. With that kind of high-octane boost, Katrina could turn into the season's second Category 5 storm.

The coming forecasts suddenly took on tremendous import—they would affect millions of lives, the disaster response, the ultimate impact of the storm. How strong would it get—and how long would it stay that way? Would its eye move inland to the west or east, or right over New Orleans? Given the strange dynamics of storm surges, slight ticks in one direction or the other, or a shift in the angle of approach, would mean the difference between a place staying dry or going under. In places that went under, many people could drown. The water would also cut off escape routes, trapping survivors.

At seven a.m. Saturday, Katrina was out over the center of the Gulf, moving straight toward the mouth of the Mississippi, 420 miles away. It was a Category 3, its top sustained wind speed 115 mph. The first official hurricane watches went up in southeastern Louisiana.

The mood at the hurricane center improved a bit that morning when data came in showing the swirling inner wall of Katrina's eye was starting to disintegrate—normally a sign of weakening. But in fact Katrina was merely redistributing its power, growing stronger. Soon a new outer eyewall began to form and the winds held steady. Wind speed then picked up around the central vortex and pressure fell again. Later in the day, Katrina's eye contracted quickly, like an iris reacting to a strong light, and the storm grew even more powerful. Masses of warm air rose higher and band after band of clouds and thunderstorms rippled to life.

Within a few hours, the storm doubled in size.

Katrina's clouds obscured most of the Gulf. Tropical-force winds were churning waves over an area 320 miles across. By late afternoon, the hurricane watch had been widened to include everything from western Louisiana to the Alabama-Florida border.

Chapter 9

"THIS IS THE BIG ONE"

WHILE LOUISIANA OFFICIALS STARTED gearing up Friday, the federal apparatus had been slow to focus on the threat to the Gulf Coast. FEMA had been running daily video conferences for federal and state agencies since before Katrina's Florida landfall, but aside from some discussion about the storm's future track, Friday's conference dealt exclusively with the response to damage in Florida.

But starting before dawn Saturday, federal emergency officials sent a blur of e-mails and paperwork flying between New Orleans, Baton Rouge, Washington, and Crawford. A team of FEMA emergency managers in Washington monitored the storm overnight and put together an e-mail memo sent out at five-thirty a.m. to agency bigwigs. They highlighted the text in bold type to drive the point home: New Orleans was in the crosshairs. Should the storm hit in the wrong spot the city would suffer the most dire consequences. A few hours later, FEMA officials distributed copies of the Hurricane Pam report to staffers and conducted an in-house briefing to prep for the storm. "Current projected path takes storm directly over New Orleans," read one PowerPoint slide. Another noted that the Hurricane Pam exercise had anticipated sixty-thousand dead and one million people homeless, numbers "exceeded by Hurricane Katrina real-life impacts."

A grand exodus away from south Louisiana and the Gulf Coast began. At nine a.m. St. Charles Parish, just upriver from New

Orleans, was the first local government to order a mandatory evacuation. Other area parishes quickly fell in line.

Some leaders abandoned the pretense of calm and started scaring people. "Residents of Kenner! I AM URGING, I AM BEGGING YOU TO LEAVE TOWN NOW! . . . THIS IS A KILLER STORM!" read an announcement by Kenner mayor Phil Capitano put on the suburb's Web site Saturday morning. If people insisted on staying, the announcement continued, ". . . one of the most important things to have is an ax, pick, hammer or some type of device that will allow you to break through your roof and get away from flood waters. And we do expect much of Kenner to be under water."

Though responsible for far more people, Nagin walked a more cautious—and strangely dissonant—line.

"Ladies and gentlemen, this is not a test. This is the real deal," he declared at a press conference with Blanco, who came down to New Orleans to oversee evacuation efforts. "Board up your homes, make sure you have enough medicine, make sure the car has enough gas. Do all the things you normally do for a hurricane but treat this one differently because it is pointed toward New Orleans."

Nagin held off until four p.m. that afternoon to formally declare a voluntary evacuation, waiting for the designated time in the state plan when New Orleans would go and Contraflow would be activated. Broussard's evacuation freelancing earlier that summer had convinced him to do things by the book. "I was worried about that, from the standpoint of the effect it had on the citizens' trust and confidence in government leaders," Nagin said later. "It was a pretty big event and a lot of people lost confidence in Aaron, and in our ability to make evacuation calls."

Nagin also announced the Superdome would be opened as a shelter for people with "special needs"—the elderly and the infirm. He did advise people in low-lying areas of the city, including the Lower Ninth Ward, to leave immediately. But it was more of a polite suggestion: "We want you to take this a little more seriously and start moving—right now, as a matter of fact."

As they strategized, Nagin and his aides had many things on their minds, too. Some were urging him to order the city emptied. But no New Orleans mayor had ever done that. (The only precedent offered little guidance: as Hurricane Georges approached in 1998, Mayor Marc Morial had declared a mandatory evacuation for one small eastern area outside the hurricane levee.) Nagin fretted about the legal issues a citywide order raised. Evacuations caused economic pain, and that went double for mandatory evacuations. Local businesses, especially the city's hotels, might sue for the lost business if the whole thing turned out to be a false alarm—which the odds still said could easily happen if the storm veered even slightly as it approached the coast.

FEMA's Saturday teleconference was a somber affair. "I would advise all the folks that are in the potential path of this storm to be looking at their maximum of the surge models . . . off of a Category Four or Five storm, and plan accordingly," Hurricane Center briefer Bill Reed told emergency officials tuning in. If that happened, the New Orleans levees would be overtopped.

All participants, including Jeff Smith and General Bennett Landreneau, superintendent of the Louisiana National Guard, reported they were ready. The state preparations were proceeding apace. Earlier that morning, Blanco had sent a letter to President Bush asking him to formally declare a state of emergency and stopped by the state Emergency Operations Center to set up a satellite office. The Louisiana Department of Wildlife and Fisheries was prepping two hundred boats for rescue operations.

As the briefing wound up, Mike Brown spoke for the first time: "I know I'm preaching to the choir on this one, but I've learned over the past four and a half, five years to go with my gut on a lot of things, and I've got to tell you my gut hurts on this one. It hurts. I've got cramps. So we need to take this one very, very seriously. . . . This is our chance to really show what we can do based on the catastrophic planning we've done, based on the teamwork that we've developed around here. This is our chance to really shine."

Mayfield had spent half his Saturday on TV, in briefings and speaking with reporters, advising everyone to get the hell out. The meteorologists had been meeting at intervals through the day with a FEMA liaison team, a series of terse encounters marked by ever-worsening news. Late in the day, forecasts indicated Katrina would come ashore as a Category 4 storm and strike New Orleans. That meant certain doom.

At four p.m. CDT, Mayfield called Mark Schleifstein at his desk in the *Times-Picayune* newsroom. Schleifstein had sent him an e-mail the day before, asking for an interview. But in this conversation, Mayfield asked the questions.

"Mark, how high is your newsroom? What's the wind strength of your building?" he asked.

"What are you telling me?"

"You know. This is the Big One."

Editor Jim Amoss, standing nearby, watched the color drain from Schleifstein's face as the call continued. Mayfield picked Schleifstein's brain about Nagin and Blanco. Did they understand the potential of the storm? Would Nagin call for a mandatory evacuation? Was the voluntary evacuation working? Would New Orleans residents listen?

After the call, Mayfield turned to others in the center for advice.

"Why don't you do what you did with Hurricane Lili?" Clay Stamp, an emergency director from Ocean City, Maryland, suggested during a chat with Mayfield. In 2002, another Category 4 storm named Hurricane Lili had been bearing down on New Orleans. Alarmed, Mayfield did something he'd never done before: he called then governor Mike Foster and told him New Orleans was facing the worst-case, fill-the-bowl scenario. Foster had been lucky—Mayfield's prediction that year was wrong. Lili weakened before coming ashore and caused only minor damage, knocking down sugarcane fields and trees.

"Okay, get the phone numbers together," Mayfield said. "You make the calls, and I'll get on the line."

At about 7:25 p.m., he called up Blanco in Baton Rouge and delivered the bad news, speaking with gravity and sorrow. Katrina was a "Camille-like storm," he said. It was impossible to say what New Orleans would look like after it struck. If people valued their lives, they should leave immediately. "I'm sorry, I'm sorry," Mayfield repeated several times. Blanco pondered what he was saying. Though the evacuation was under way and going well, Nagin had been hesitating on whether to go the extra mile, turning his voluntary evacuation into a mandatory one. There seemed no question what to do now. She told Mayfield she wasn't sure that Nagin fully appreciated what was happening, and asked him to give the mayor a call.

Blanco called Nagin and told him to expect the call, and also gave him Mayfield's number. When Mayfield called about a half hour later, after talking with Mississippi governor Haley Barbour, he got voice mail. But Nagin called back a few minutes later.

"I want to be able to walk out of the Hurricane Center tonight and go to sleep knowing I've done everything I can to make sure everybody knows the threat of Hurricane Katrina," Mayfield told him by way of explanation.

New Orleans, he went on, was in all likelihood going to see its levees overtopped and the bowl filled. Thousands of lives hung on how Nagin handled the evacuation in the coming hours. "This is the Big One. In my thirty-three-year history at the Hurricane Center, I've never seen a storm this powerful, nor with the conditions like this that will allow it to become stronger. I would do whatever it took to get people out of there."

Nagin called the city attorney. "Do whatever it takes," he said. "We've never done a mandatory evacuation, but we're doing one now."

The ten p.m. National Hurricane Center advisory changed the hurricane watch to a warning for the area between Morgan City,

Louisiana, and the Alabama-Florida border. It concluded: "PREPARATIONS TO PROTECT LIFE AND PROPERTY SHOULD BE RUSHED TO COMPLETION."

Cars had been streaming out of the city and suburbs all day, from the outer rim of the delta to the center of the city. Under the Contraflow plan, there was nowhere to go but straight ahead: on-ramps worked, exit ramps didn't. Traffic was moving slowly. By Saturday afternoon, a trip to Baton Rouge, seventy-five miles to the northwest, took several hours. State police measured the traffic flow at nine hundred vehicles per lane per hour; by early evening it had increased by 44 percent, to 1,300 per hour. Across the region, people made their decisions on whether to go and where. The Internet and phones lit up with hotel bookings from Houston to Jackson and beyond. But many decided they'd stay no matter what. In St. Bernard Parish, shrimper Ricky DeJean wanted to secure his trawlers—which were anchored down in Dulac—and keep watch over his house in Chalmette. In the Lower Ninth Ward, Robert Green, a fifty-year-old accountant, had no easy way to transport his mentally disabled cousin and his mother, who suffered from Parkinson's disease, out of the city. Even getting out of the neighborhood posed problems.

The disruption and price of leaving—and possibly never coming back—dissuaded many, especially the elderly. Under the law, nursing homes and hospitals were responsible for moving their residents and patients out. But nursing homes had always been loosely regulated in Louisiana, where lobbyists in Baton Rouge had been highly effective in watering down the government's oversight. Though state law required it, many nursing homes didn't have evacuation plans on file. Some administrators simply threw up their hands at the prospect of hiring buses and providing food and lodging on the fly—an expensive proposition that could run them up to a hundred thousand dollars, possibly for naught—so at dozens of nursing homes, administrators decided to tough it out.

Others improvised. A group home called the Abstract House, on Magazine Street—a funky area not far from downtown—

played host to a shifting roster of about forty mentally ill residents, mostly men, with every malady under the sun—manic depression, schizophrenia, severe depression. The manager, Bobbie Byrnes, was able to farm out some residents to their friends and family and put others on a bus to Baton Rouge on Sunday. But she still had seventeen men—the hard-core types, hard to manage—with no rides to safety. With no alternative, she dropped them off at the Superdome and told them to watch out for themselves.

Just after sunrise on Sunday, a Hurricane Hunter measured the storm's maximum sustained winds at 167 mph. Katrina was officially a Category 5 hurricane.

Mike Brown had called the president in Crawford early that morning. He had been peppering the White House staff with calls all weekend, talking mostly to Joe Hagin. He told Bush he thought the storm could be truly catastrophic. He and his FEMA colleagues had also been fretting about Nagin's hesitancy on ordering a mandatory evacuation. Brown asked Bush to push the issue. Bush seemed a bit reluctant to insert himself in what was, politically and legally, a local decision. But he called Blanco and put a word in for "mandatory." Bush later spoke briefly to reporters outside his ranch—the weather was beautiful and the president framed by a bright blue sky—and told people to get to "safe ground." He also took time to plug the new Iraqi draft constitution.

Eleven hours after his talk with Mayfield, Nagin met with his staff and leaders of the New Orleans police department and the state police to discuss how to bring off a mandatory evacuation. Suddenly the city was taking on more responsibility—and it was responsibility it really couldn't handle. Many of those without transportation didn't much want to go, and they certainly wouldn't like being ordered out of their homes. The New Orleans Police Department agreed to send cops out with bullhorns and sirens to spread the word. The Regional Transit Authority would send its buses around to designated pickup points to bring people back to the Superdome. Hotels were exempted: their guests could remain and gamble that the buildings would stay intact, or move to the Superdome. At 8:17 a.m., the state police issued a news release on its Web site saying that the city and some adjacent areas were now under a mandatory evacuation order. CNN put it on TV. At 9:30 a.m., joined by Blanco, Nagin went before the cameras, read the order, and laid out the details.

"The storm is intensifying and is still pointed towards New Orleans. And there's not a meteorologist or an expert that I have talked to that says that this storm will not impact New Orleans in a major way. As a result of that, I am, this morning, declaring that we will be doing a mandatory evacuation," he said, looking grim.

"This is an opportunity in New Orleans for us to come together in a way that we've never come together before," he said. "This is a threat that we've never faced before. And if we galvanize and rally around each other, I am sure that we will get through this. God bless us."

At 11:30 a.m., a local TV station pulled a video from its archives and put it on the air. It featured what was, under the circumstances, a surreal conversation between Marshall Truehill, the head of the local antipoverty group Total Community Action, and Allan Katz, a local political PR man and talk show host, about a DVD titled "Preparing for the Big One" that had been made months before. Truehill's message was stark: if you don't leave, you're on your own. The DVDs in question—seventy thousand in all—were sitting on warehouse shelves in Los Angeles waiting for free distribution among the city's low-income neighborhoods. That distribution was scheduled for sometime in September.

Katrina got another shot of energy Sunday morning, its top wind speed reaching 175 mph—as fast as a tornado. Also accelerating was the news cycle: cable talking heads commenced a continuous review of doomsday scenarios. The National Weather Service, FEMA, LSU, and dozens of other government offices put out warnings filled with muscular adjectives for mass death and destruction. One memo, by the National Infrastructure Simulation and Analysis Center in Los Alamos, New Mexico, focused on storm surge. "The potential for severe storm surge to overwhelm Lake Pontchartrain levees is the greatest concern for New Orleans," it said. "Any storm rated Category 4 on the Saffir-Simpson scale will likely lead to severe flooding and/or levee breaching. This could leave the New Orleans metro area submerged for weeks or months."

The Los Alamos memo bounced around DHS and up the chain of command. Finally, at 1:47 a.m. Monday morning, the Homeland Security Operations Center watch officer e-mailed it to the White House Situation Room.

Meanwhile, Robert Ricks, a meteorologist at the National Weather Service office in suburban Slidell, Louisiana, wrote an advisory that detailed the risks in minutely grim detail:

> MOST OF THE AREA WILL BE UNINHABITABLE FOR WEEKS . . . AT LEAST ONE HALF OF WELL CONSTRUCTED HOMES WILL HAVE ROOF AND WALL FAILURE . . . THE MAJORITY OF INDUSTRIAL BUILDINGS WILL BECOME NON-FUNCTIONAL . . . AIRBORNE DEBRIS WILL BE WIDESPREAD . . . AND MAY INCLUDE HEAVY ITEMS SUCH AS HOUSEHOLD APPLIANCES AND EVEN LIGHT VEHICLES . . . PER-SONS . . . PETS . . . AND LIVESTOCK EXPOSED TO THE WINDS WILL FACE CERTAIN DEATH IF STRUCK. WATER SHORTAGES WILL MAKE HUMAN SUFFERING INCREDIBLE BY MODERN STANDARDS.

All those "wills" were, of course, speculative. "This is a very, very complicated, very complex system of levees," Mayfield told that day's noon teleconference.

> On the forecast track if it maintains intensity, about twelve and a half feet of storm surge in the lake, the big question's going to be, will that top some of the levees? And the current track and the forecast we have now suggests that there will be minimal flooding in the city of New Orleans it-self. But we've always said the storm surge model is only ac-

curate to within about twenty percent. If that track were to be just a little bit to the west, it makes all the difference in the world. I do expect there will be some of the levees over-topped even out here in the western portions, here where the airport is. . . . I don't think any model can tell you with any confidence right now whether the levees will be topped or not, but that's obviously a very, very grave concern."

As he spoke, Mayfield pointed to a slide of the SLOSH model that showed most of New Orleans in blue, a color indi-cating flooding of a foot or more of water above sea level—something that would spare some areas but leave others under ten feet of water.

Mayfield couldn't see his audience, so after he wrapped up, he was surprised to hear Mike Brown introduce the president. Bush had joined the meeting, it seemed, primarily to buck up morale. He sat at the head of a conference table in a windowless room at the ranch, staring at images on a wide-screen TV, trading maps and briefing papers with Hagin, his hurricane point man.

"I want to assure the folks at the state level that we are fully prepared to not only help you during the storm, but we will move in whatever resources and assets we have at our disposal after the storm to help you deal with the loss of property and we pray for no loss of life, of course," Bush said.

A bit later, Brown tried to focus his troops. He said he was worried about sheltering people in the Superdome given the un-certainty over its structure. "The Superdome is twelve feet be-low sea level. . . . I am also concerned about that roof," he said. "I don't know whether that roof is designed to withstand a Cate-gory Five hurricane. So, not to be kind of gross here, but I'm worried about . . . the ability to respond to a catastrophe within a catastrophe."

Brown told people not to worry about the paperwork and bureaucratic snarls that were common pitfalls in disasters, and FEMA's Achilles' heel in the past. "If you feel like you need to, go ahead and do it," he said. "I'll figure out some way to justify it. Tell Congress or whoever else it is that wants to yell at me. Just let them yell at me. Don't worry about it—in fact, I don't want any of these processes in our way."

Chertoff had been focused on other things, working at home on Saturday, breaking away for briefings on the storm, but he chimed into Sunday's videoconference briefly, offering any help he could. He asked Brown if there were any Defense Department assets available, or if some arrangement for military assistance was in the works.

"We have DOD assets over here at the EOC," Brown said. "They are fully engaged, and we are having those discussions with them now." Brown meant military liaison officers. In fact, there was not yet any plan to send federal troops or other military assistance to supplement the National Guard.

"Good job," Chertoff said, and signed off.

The Superdome had opened at eight a.m. as a special-needs shelter. New Orleans health department chief Kevin Stephens had worked with city employees, police, and the National Guard to outfit the huge arena for a few thousand people. They'd brought cots, crackers, peanut butter, cereal, juice, and water, while the Orleans Parish sheriff's office promised to provide hot food. Organizers set up a ten-line telephone bank to take calls from potential evacuees. The organizers felt things were well in hand—enough so that on Saturday night, Stephens turned down an offer for help from the federal Department of Health and Human Services.

But with the danger mounting, the Superdome became the city's number one destination. Nagin and his aides scrambled to find buses and drivers to move people out of low-lying neighborhoods. With only a small pool of volunteer drivers, there were not enough people or time to drive the evacuees out of the city. The only choice at that late stage was the Superdome. Buses could loop through neighborhoods, pick people up, then repeat.

As the buses disgorged thousands of people onto Poydras Street through the day, the Superdome began to fill. By late afternoon, the line of those waiting for admittance snaked back hundreds of yards from the entrance ramp, inching forward slowly as National Guard soldiers checked everyone for weapons. Many got wet while waiting as showers and gusty winds kicked up. Numerous people had followed the mayor's instructions and brought their own bedding, beach chairs, and coolers packed with food for a day or two. They began filling the stands, the field, the gangways, setting up small makeshift camps, clumping together in groups of friends and neighbors. The crowd was overwhelmingly African American, with some white people—many of them tourists—mixed in. Problems began immediately. There wasn't much food. Hundreds of the special-needs patients needed dialysis, oxygen, or other special equipment unavailable at the Dome. That afternoon, state police commandeered buses and sent more than four hundred patients to hospitals in Baton Rouge, Lafayette, and elsewhere. This time, when Stephens talked with his contact at Health and Human Services, he accepted help—a federal Disaster Medical Assistance Team was ordered in, and FEMA sent Meals Ready to Eat (military rations) and water.

Nonetheless, FEMA's one representative at the Dome, Marty Bahamonde, was growing alarmed as the storm got closer. There were way too many people and not enough supervision or supplies. New Orleans homeland security director Terry Ebbert made an announcement in the EOC asking people to scrounge for supplies in City Hall and take them across the street to the Dome, and the doctors and nurses volunteering in the Dome complained they would soon run out of oxygen. By the middle of the evening, FEMA's Disaster Medical Assistance Team hadn't yet arrived from Oklahoma, nor had the trucks with MREs and water. Bahamonde sent off a series of anxious e-mails to his associates in Washington and Baton Rouge. "This is going to get ugly real fast," Bahamonde wrote in one e-mail to a coworker. "It will not be pretty," he wrote another. And when supplies finally arrived, Bahamonde estimated that the five trucks of water and forty-five thousand MREs were just a fraction of what was needed.

Bahamonde had arrived in New Orleans Saturday afternoon. Though experienced with disasters (he had spent weeks as a public affairs officer with a FEMA team tending to victims of an earthquake in Iran), he wasn't an emergency management expert or a medical professional. Brown had dispatched him from FEMA's Boston office to monitor the situation, reporting back on the FEMA teams and what Nagin and other city officials were saying and doing. Bahamonde would also be an advance man for any de rigueur postdisaster tour of the wreckage. He was FEMA's single point person on the ground in the city as the storm approached.

The possible destruction of a great American city had lured dozens of journalists, including teams of network correspondents. They were roving the emptying city, looking for human drama. But with the stress of the day, their sincere efforts sometimes turned absurd.

"You're live on Fox News Channel, what are you doing?" correspondent and anchor Shepard Smith asked a man on a Bourbon Street sidewalk Sunday afternoon whose dogs were lapping water from a glass. A bit strangely, Fox showed the line in front of the Superdome with Smith's encounter in voice-over.

"Walking my dogs," the man said.

"Why are you still here? I'm just curious."

"None of your fucking business."

"Oh, that was a good answer, wasn't it?" Smith said, taken aback. "That was live on international television. Thanks so much for that. You know we apologize."

By late Sunday, Katrina's tropical storm–force winds covered an area of the Gulf equal in size to California—double what it had been the day before. The vortex of winds and low pressure pushed and pulled surface waters up into a low bulge in the sea, about fifteen feet high, centered just northeast of Katrina's eye and moving before the storm. Tides rose along the coastline and pressed up the Mississippi, across Lake Borgne and through the open passes into Lake Pontchartrain. Already, Katrina was brushing against the outermost reaches of the levee system.

Mayfield could see where the storm was going, and his SLOSH model was predicting storm surges with a broad brush. But scientists at LSU's Hurricane Center in Baton Rouge had trained a lot more computing power on the problem and could anticipate what was going to happen much more clearly. They had been running simulations of Katrina's potential storm surge on SuperMike, a supercomputer that used an innovative—and cheap—parallel processing technique. For a mere two million dollars, LSU had gotten one of the most powerful computers in the world. In the space of a few years, storm surge modeling had gotten faster, cheaper, and more accurate. What once took days to compute now took hours. With enough information, Super-Mike could predict down to the city block what would be underwater and which routes out of town might be imperiled.

Modeler Hassan Mashriqui had been at the Hurricane Center three days straight, pausing only to drive home and grab some food and a fresh shirt while the computer took three hours to create its virtual flood. He was jazzed, operating on zero sleep. After Friday night's forecast had made New Orleans Katrina's likely target, Mashriqui had been e-mailing the flood maps to everyone he could think of. The maps showed levees being overtopped across the eastern side of the city. A sixteen- to twenty-foot storm surge would overtop levees to the city's east via the V-shaped "funnel." The resulting flood resembled Betsy's, though the water spread farther and was deeper: St. Bernard, Plaquemines, eastern New Orleans, and most of the Ninth Ward would flood. The storm could push water in Lake Pontchartrain as high as twelve feet—not quite enough to overtop the levees along the lakefront or in the canals, but dangerously close. For the moment, it looked like much of the city and suburbs to the west might be spared.

As computers ran, the bureaucratic machinery buzzed. Contingency plans were put into action. E-mails and paper flew. People and materiel moved. The White House okayed Blanco's second request, this time for a formal disaster declaration—only rarely granted before a storm struck—authorizing the federal government to immediately move aid and assistance into the area. Blanco mobilized the National Guard, calling up about four thousand men and women. Blanco's request was based on experience from past storms, but made with some anxiety: like its counterparts in other states, Louisiana National Guard units had been stretched thin. About 40 percent of them were deployed to Iraq, including the 3,700 members of the 256th Infantry Brigade, along with equipment such as satellite phones and amphibious vehicles that could prove useful in a disaster. No replacements had been left behind for the home front. Blanco also called around to other governors, asking them to prepare their own Guard troops to come in later, if necessary, under mutual assistance compacts.

FEMA moved people and supplies, including generators and satellite phones, water, ice, and food into staging areas in Pineville, in central Louisiana. Its search and rescue and medical volunteer teams assembled in Shreveport, Houston, Memphis, and Anniston, Alabama. Coordinators from the Defense Department and chemical and health experts from the EPA made ready. The Coast Guard announced it had moved its base of operations to Alexandria, Louisiana, about 170 miles northwest.

Brown and a small team of FEMA aides—his assistant, two media experts, a congressional liaison, and security detail—arrived in Baton Rouge Sunday evening. By that time, Brown was getting frustrated that nobody in the Blanco administration seemed to be asking him for much beyond what they had already. Blanco's people were equally peeved at Brown. Despite Brown's exhortation to ignore paperwork if necessary, the FEMA staff wanted requests for help drawn up into itemized lists and made formally, something that state officials didn't have time for. FEMA's bureaucratic procedures were getting in the way elsewhere, too. Hours later, as the storm came ashore, the air force's 920th Rescue Wing, operating out of Florida's Patrick Air Force Base, requested a green light to start search and rescue operations right after the storm subsided. But FEMA told the commander, Colonel Tim Tarchick, that it had no authority over military units—leaving him out of the game until he could get clear authority from somebody to proceed.

Traffic began to let up late Sunday afternoon, and by five p.m., the state police suspended Contraflow. About 80 percent of the metro population—one million people—had left, comfortably beating all past evacuations and the 65 percent result predicted by the Hurricane Pam exercise. By most measures, the evacuation was a spectacular success—an achievement of leadership and public policy, the result of a decade of practice, drills, and aggressive PR. But about a hundred thousand people remained in New Orleans proper, most of them in their homes, betting the storm would pass by—or hoping, perversely, to experience a real catastrophe firsthand. By nightfall, only a fraction of them—about ten thousand—had moved to the Dome. Meanwhile, Katrina came closer.

Chapter 10

THE FLOOD

AS KATRINA'S OUTER BANDS of clouds and rain enveloped the delta in the darkness just after midnight Monday, marsh grass fluttered then flattened in the wind, pointing west, then gradually southwest.

The wind shifted as Katrina slowly turned due north, on a track that would take it just east of New Orleans. That was a lucky break, meaning the city would be spared the worst: if the storm had tracked west of the city, its counterclockwise spin would have brought even more intense easterly winds, rain, and a bigger storm surge in off the Gulf. Instead, the city would be on the "drier" left-hand side of the storm and winds would come more from the north, off the land.

The course change had also brought Katrina over cooler waters, and it began to lose the terrifying strength it exhibited over the open Gulf. At the same time, a stream of dry air began to leach into its western rim, draining strength from bands of thunderstorms. The knot of winds around the eye lost speed, and the barometric pressure rose. The inner core of Katrina's eyewall—the continually regenerating heart of its convection engine—began to erode. The storm weakened like a deflating balloon, dropping from Category 5 to Category 3 in the space of twelve hours. But as it neared landfall it was still powerful, its winds keeping up a sustained speed of 127 mph. Showers pelted lakes and bayous as Katrina's eye moved closer to the coast. Nutria huddled in their mud burrows. Schools of redfish and black drum flitted to silty lake bottoms and stayed put.

Then, slowly at first, the storm surge wave began to rise over the delta.

Stormy winds over the Gulf had already pushed tides higher along the coast. Then, under the canopy of the storm, a great wave moved across the open marsh, filling lakes, bayous, and canals. (Rising water also moved up the Mississippi but was mostly contained by the levees.) The waterways soon overflowed their banks. Multiple streams and rivulets spread out through the grass, ponding at low spots, then rose higher and coalesced. Within minutes, vast swatches of marshland disappeared under water. Soon only trees, signs, pipelines, abandoned oil derricks, and buoys could be glimpsed above the waterline. The entire lower delta, its three river outlets splayed out into the Gulf like a bird's foot, disappeared some hours after midnight. Only the tips of the lower river levees remained above water, two thin lines in a dark, raging sea.

Among the small towns lining the bank of the Mississippi in lower Plaquemines Parish swallowed up by the wave were the fancifully named Venice, Empire, Triumph, and Hesperides (named for nymphs in Greek mythology who stand watch over a paradise at the end of the world). The towns were home to commercial fishermen and businesses catering to sportsmen: marinas and shops selling fishing rods, bait and tackle, and boating supplies. The river's most remote southern outposts, each of these now-lost places consisted of a few streets connected to Route 23, the main commercial artery paralleling the river. Those streets ended abruptly a few hundred feet away at the hurricane levee.

More accustomed than most to the hurricane drill, close to 99 percent of Plaquemines's twenty-seven thousand residents had evacuated. All that remained were a few stubborn fishermen and others without an easy way out. It was a long haul out of the area; Baton Rouge was 180 miles away.

At four a.m., the pressure difference between the inside and outside of Bobbie Moreau's house in the town of Nairn, about fifty miles southeast of New Orleans, was rattling the windows and creating a stifling stuffiness so bad it woke her up. Moreau went to her living room and slid a window open a crack. Shortly thereafter, the power went out; the electricity had failed hours earlier, but now Moreau's generator had stopped. She took a flashlight and went to her home office, about four steps down through a door. There was a pond where the floor had been.

Moreau wheeled around and sloshed back out, calling to her daughter Tasha to go to the den and get a trunk containing the family photos. There, one step down, the water was four inches deep, pouring in through some eroded grouting between marble tiles. Moreau told Tasha to go ahead and take her four-month-old daughter, Cassidy, upstairs. Moreau then went to collect five pets—a cat, two small dogs she kept inside, plus an "outside" dog she had put in the utility room, along with another one a neighbor had left behind. As she herded them all upstairs, the cat—an eighteen-year-old named Angle, with one eye—ran back down, and Moreau chased her. The rising water was heaving up the carpet in waves and she could barely walk, but she managed to grab the cat.

"Get the pistol—we don't know what we may be facing here!" Tasha yelled from upstairs, and Moreau grabbed it from a drawer and bounded up the stairs to the second floor, the water rising so fast it nearly brushed her heels.

The three crowded into a bedroom with the animals, and Moreau slammed the door, hoping it might keep the water out. The stuffiness was unbearable; the windows looked ready to explode out of their frames. Moreau held the baby on the foot of the bed, fanning her.

The pair got on their knees.

"Please, God, please save us," they prayed.

Through the vibrations underneath her legs, Moreau could feel the water was close to the ceiling on the first floor, and she got up and went to the window. The water had come up just underneath it. A pale gray light now illuminated the churning flood all around them. She staggered back, stunned.

"Mama, what's wrong?" Tasha screamed.

Moreau knew it: they were all going to die.

Then she decided that such an outcome was to be avoided, if possible. She tore the canopy from the bed and tied it in knots to make a rope she and Tasha could hold on to. She put the baby in a life jacket she had stowed for emergencies, securing it snugly with one of her belts. She grabbed a blanket for protection from the elements and ordered Tasha to make a bottle of formula. As the water rose past the foot of the bed, Tasha climbed out the window and pulled herself onto the roof. Moreau handed her the baby, then her three dogs, Snuggles, Tuppie, and Candy. The cat again escaped, and the neighbor's dog was big and fought her attempts to push it out the window, so Moreau gave up and climbed out herself, the blanket and a diaper bag dangling in her arms.

They positioned themselves precariously along the spine of the slick metal roof. It was just after six a.m., and the eye of the storm was making landfall over Buras, just to their south. The water around them was filled with dead dogs, cows, and other animals and fouled with oil and other debris.

Moreau spied a boat at a nearby house, partially submerged, its bow sticking out of the water.

"You have to swim and get that boat," she told Tasha. "I'd do it, but I'm too weak. You can do it!"

Tasha's eyes widened. "Mama, I'm too scared!"

"You have to do it. We will die if you don't."

Tasha handed her the baby, slid into the water, and swam for it.

The first boat was effectively sunk, so she swam on out of sight. Just then, the eye of the storm passed overhead. The wind stopped, and the sky cleared to a pale morning blue. Silence, broken only by the sound of water lapping at the sides of the house, enveloped Moreau and her granddaughter. Tasha was not responding to her shouts, and Moreau started to pray, tears streaming. Then she heard an outboard motor roar to life.

Then it stopped—and started again. After a few minutes, Tasha maneuvered a boat around the back of their house, pushing it as close as she could against the power lines blocking the

way. It was an aluminum johnboat—a flat-bottomed craft ubiquitous on the marshes—a big one with a cabin and two out-
boards, and in her haste Tasha had not only taken the boat but
the trailer it was attached to as well. The eye had passed and the
wind picked up, and she had to gun the motors to keep the boat
close to the house. Moreau had to dangle the baby between the
power lines into her daughter's arms, then hand over the dogs
before finally lowering herself.

Moreau picked up a pipe and tried to dislodge the clip holding the boat to its trailer. When that didn't work, Tasha handed
her a pair of baby scissors out of the diaper bag, and she cut the
clip's nylon bands. The trailer sank.

They were free, but a fierce wind had resumed, this time out
of the west, and it blew the boat almost as far as the river levee
before it came to rest against a small stand of trees. The three
slumped down on the floor of the cabin, under the steering
wheel, exhausted and terrified, the animals cowering around
them. The wind was whistling through a broken window. A powerful gust rocked the boat, nearly capsizing it, and they sang and
prayed to God for help.

Farther north, the surge wave was building up against the east
river levee. Along dozens of miles, whitecaps pounded the
earthen wall. It did not give way, though in some spots, water
rose more than twenty-five feet high and some flowed over the
levee crown, into the river, and then over the other side onto the
west bank.

As the storm moved north toward New Orleans, the levee
guided the great mass of water north. The wave molded itself to
the shape of the barrier as it moved alongside it, submerging all
obstacles, spreading out in the straightaways, rising higher in
the river's many crooks and bends.

Most of Plaquemines Parish was soon under water; thousands
of homes and all their contents, and everything from shrimp boats
to pickups, were tossed in a giant stew and stirred. Then high water reached the outermost limit of the Corps's Lake Pontchartrain
and Vicinity Hurricane Protection Project: Caernarvon, the same

spot dynamited in 1927. It jogged southeast for a mile or so, then ran due east for a dozen miles. The hurricane levee repelled the high water along that stretch, but the storm surge wave was already building up well north of Caernarvon. As Katrina had moved closer to New Orleans, it drove water over the Chandeleur Islands and the marshes due east of the city. Lake Borgne overflowed into the surrounding marshes, where it met water coming up the Mr. Go. The wind and steady westward current submerged and then splintered nearly everything standing in the outlying communities of St. Bernard Parish, including Yscloskey, Shell Beach, and Delacroix, their wreckage swept off. Shrimp boats and cars were hoisted onto rooftops. Torn bits of fishing nets clung forlornly to tree branches. Finally, as had been long predicted, the wave rose in the V-shaped funnel of levees between St. Bernard and eastern New Orleans, then into the Intracoastal canal, heading for the heart of New Orleans.

At 5:02 a.m., power went out in the Superdome and emergency generators kicked on, but they did not power the air-conditioning. Not long after, wind ripped giant white rubber sheets off the roof and sent huge shards of debris flying toward Uptown. Rivulets of rainwater began finding their way down through the ceiling, dripping and pouring into the stands, mezzanine, and football field. Without ventilation, the air began to get gamy with the smell of sweat and garbage. The bathrooms stopped working. Many people slept; others waited, mostly in silence.

Katrina's eye was still hours away, but parts of New Orleans were already flooding. An eighteen-foot storm surge moved against the city's eastern hurricane levees, the ones that Lee Butler had warned about. They were only sixteen feet high, and water poured over them. The steady flow peeled off the grassy covering on the barriers and ate away at the earth underneath; miles of levee disappeared in an hour. As they did so, water gushed over floodwalls protecting eastern New Orleans, eroding the supporting earthen berms on their dry sides. The walls keeled over in multiple spots.

Meanwhile, seawater flowing in from the east had been filling the Industrial Canal for hours, along with a more modest influx from Lake Pontchartrain. As it rose, the water put mounting pressure on the canal's concrete I-walls and flowed through various gaps. Sections on both sides began breaking around four thirty a.m., sending water streaming into eastern New Orleans and into the Gentilly neighborhood on the west side. Two hours later, the canal was overflowing into neighborhoods. Wall sections began to collapse. Soon, a big chunk of wall fronting the Lower Ninth Ward began shuddering under the water's weight. Its sheet pile foundation bent, and the wall slowly tipped toward the homes it was supposed to protect. Water roared over it. Amid the wind and waves, a two-hundred-foot barge broke loose of its moorings and, drawn like a toy boat from an overflowing bathtub, floated clear over the collapsing wall, scraping its bottom on the concrete on the way.

The wall broke with an explosive bang and collapsed. Water thundered through the two-hundred-yard gash, taking chunks of concrete with it and widening the breach.

The wall of water tossed the barge against homes on Jourdan Avenue at the foot of the levee. The double blow pushed some buildings off their foundations and into streets, then ripped them apart from the inside out. Splintered wood, cars, and personal belongings—teddy bears, T-shirts, necklaces, and wedding albums—flowed through the streets in the torrent. From the air, the neighborhood looked like someone had picked it up, shaken it to pieces, and dropped it on the ground.

Robert Green and five family members were sitting in the candlelight in his house at 1826 Tennessee Street, two blocks from the breach. Green, a fifty-year-old tax accountant, had grown up in the Lower Ninth Ward and knew that water was always flowing just a few blocks away on three sides—the river, the Intracoastal Waterway, and the Industrial Canal. But he believed he was safe. He was an experienced hurricane veteran, having lived through Betsy and a half dozen other storms.

Not that he hadn't considered leaving. The family had attempted to drive out of town, but they'd gotten stuck in traffic and turned back because Green's seventy-year-old mother, Joyce, had Parkinson's disease and could not abide sitting in a car for hours. He'd thought of taking her to the Superdome, but from what he'd heard on the radio it was getting crowded, so that wasn't a good option either. They had opted to ride out the storm instead.

Of the family members in the one-story house, only Green and his brother, Jonathan, a forty-six-year-old teacher and basketball coach at a local school, were able-bodied adults. The others were Hyman Sheppard, known as Herman, a sixty-year-old cousin who was mentally challenged, and Green's granddaughters, Shemiya, two, nicknamed Muffin; Shenae, three, known as Nae Nae; and Sheniya, four. Green had been babysitting them while their parents—his son, Everidge, and his wife, Deanna Thomas— were working; the plan had been to take the girls to visit relatives in Tennessee.

Jonathan had awakened around four a.m. and seen water in the street. He waded out, investigated the empty two-story house next door, then returned and picked up his mother. But the water was rising too quickly.

Then a wave washed up against the side of the house with a dull roar. Robert looked out the window and sized things up. The Claiborne Avenue bridge over the Industrial Canal was only a few blocks away—could they make it on foot? He looked at his mother and figured it was impossible. As they made for the attic, water coursed under and around the house, up through the floor and in through the windows. Lifted off its concrete slab, the house spun and began to bob in the water. Bringing up the rear as they clambered up into the attic over a floating wardrobe, Robert fell back into the water in his living room. Thrashing momentarily amid the floating furniture, lamps, and detritus, he slammed his hand into something sharp and got a puncture wound. Then he pulled himself up.

Jonathan punched a hole in the roof, and they moved outside one by one. Pushed and pounded by the current, the house started to creak loudly underneath them, then broke in two. The main part of the house began to float away from its foundation, leaving a small addition behind. It joined a bizarre procession of floating houses, jostling for position in the current. Two homes on either side nudged the Greens' house into the middle of Tennessee Street, where the current was flowing south toward the main road, Claiborne Avenue. For five minutes, the family home floated lazily down two blocks, ending up next to 1617 Tennessee Street near the corner of Claiborne. Green frantically scanned the floodwaters and remaining structures, desperately trying to come up with a plan.

Then the rest of the house began to disintegrate.

As they positioned themselves to jump into the water, Green was jerked back—his sweatshirt was caught on a nail. He tore the clothing off. Jonathan had a life vest on and tried to keep Joyce and Herman afloat, pulling them over to the top of a U-Haul truck bobbing in an adjacent driveway, its rear end floating upward, then onto the roof of the neighboring house.

Robert had the girls, but as he pulled them, Shenae slipped from his grasp. The current sucked her away and she disappeared.

"Oh, JESUS! JESUS!" he shouted, frantically brushing the water with his hands in the darkness. She was gone. In the confusion, he lost Sheniya, too. But the four-year-old was a good swimmer and managed to get to the truck by treading water close to the side of the house.

Meanwhile, Joyce slipped under the water as Jonathan tried to pull her to safety. He managed to drag her partway up onto the rooftop, but she was having tremors and slipped back down again and again. The third time they pulled her out she was unconscious. They worked to revive her, pushing on her chest to expel water from her lungs. She coughed. She was alive.

Jackson Barracks, the local headquarters of the Louisiana National Guard, had been designated a staging area for rescue operations, with forty boats and twenty-four amphibious vehicles. More than a thousand guardsmen were riding out the storm there, on a hundred-acre base stretching over twenty-five city blocks, sandwiched between the Lower Ninth Ward and the St.

Bernard community of Arabi. The white-columned headquarters building dated to the barracks' founding in the 1830s as a fort overseeing U.S. coastal installations in the wake of the War of 1812. Named for Andrew Jackson, hero of the Battle of New Orleans, Jackson Barracks was built to be impervious to attack. But its brick walls had not been built to repel water, and many guardsmen did not know how to swim.

Water had been seeping onto the grounds for hours and was no higher than the top of a guardsman's boot. But sometime after seven a.m., water coursed across the lawn, carrying chunks of earth, garbage, and shards of wood along with it. A section of wall at the western edge of the base crumbled and collapsed. A house rose clear off its foundation. Hundreds of guardsman ran upstairs to the base's second floors.

Lieutenant Colonel Jacques Thibodaux radioed the military's Joint Operations Center in Baton Rouge, officially relinquishing command of the guard's New Orleans effort.

Three men from the 61st Troop Command (a maintenance and support unit), Colonel Thomas Beron, Sergeant Jeremiah Thompson, and Lieutenant Chris Black, left their unit waiting in a barracks' second floor as they made their way to a nearby garage where Black had stowed his fishing boat. Chest-deep in the water, they strained to push the garage door high enough to get the boat out. Then, Black at the tiller, they piloted the boat around the base past headquarters. Rain blinded them and stung their faces, and debris whipped by. They aimed for Building 35, which sat on high ground. Seven more boats were stored there—some belonged to the Guard, some to the state Wildlife and Fisheries Department. They found the guard command had taken refuge there.

"You can't go. You made it through once already," Gary Jones, a brigadier general, told Beron as they checked in.

"No, I need to go back. It'll be a calming influence on the men. I've been in boats all my life," he said.

The three took a total of four boats back to the barracks, putt-putting against wind and the current. The water had risen to the bottom of the second floor and stopped, and Beron briefly considered waiting out the storm there. But then it started going up again, so forty-odd soldiers climbed out windows and into the boats, pushing most of them dangerously low in the water. Together, they motored back to Building 35 and waited for the winds to die down.

Nearby in Arabi, Craig and Cindy Ratliff were sitting on a second-floor balcony above the rising water, inflating a kiddie pool to use as a raft.

Craig Ratliff—an earnest student minister at the First Baptist Church two blocks away—had grown up in coastal North Carolina, Cindy Ratliff in West Palm Beach, Florida. Both had ridden out hurricanes in the past, and they decided to stay and see what would happen. They had remained behind while urging most everyone they knew to leave.

Craig had been able to sleep only an hour or two—he wanted to be awake to see and remember. As it got light outside, things began to change. The firehouse across the street, where firefighters had been hanging out all night, was now abandoned. Then, just after eight a.m., water had started seeping up through the floorboards of their first-floor apartment. When Craig went outside he saw water flowing from the east down Judge Perez Drive, rising along the sidewalk. Soon it was a foot deep around the apartment building. He sent Cindy up to the second-floor balcony—attached to a neighbor's abandoned apartment—and ran inside, throwing some granola bars and bottles of water into a book bag, then going up himself. Then he ran back down into the water again, taking a couple of packs of water bottles, the kiddie pool, and a hand pump. He went down one last time and grabbed keepsakes—diplomas, photos—that were now floating in four feet of water. They had put them in a container on top of the refrigerator in hopes the water wouldn't get that high, but— Craig belatedly realized as he sloshed through water and debris—refrigerators float.

Above, Cindy sat in a folding chair, watching the contents of their church floating by: hymnals, Bibles, toys, children's chairs, toys, puzzles, office chairs, and supplies.

The water rose about six feet, then slowed, then started rising again. Soon it was approaching the balcony. They inflated the pool and tossed it into the water, then climbed in and took out some bungee cords, wrapped them around the railing, and held on. But as water poured from the roof into the makeshift raft, they realized they couldn't stay afloat much longer. They began to push themselves around the building's corner, then hand-paddled to the next apartment building over. The plan was to get to the church, which had a roof and spire twenty feet or more above ground. The water was now about ten feet and still rising.

About ten miles to the southeast, where the St. Bernard suburbs gave way to fishing villages, the sixty residents of St. Rita's Nursing Home believed, at least for a short while, that the storm had passed them by without incident. The wind had subsided a bit, and Sal Magano, one of the owners, had gone outside with a couple of other men to inspect the exterior of low-slung brick structure for wind damage.

As state law required, St. Rita's had a two-step evacuation plan on file with the parish: the residents in most fragile health would be bused out first, forty-eight to seventy-two hours before a storm hit, to Baton Rouge or Lafayette; those remaining would all be out a day in advance of landfall. Yet despite St. Bernard's mandatory evacuation order, Magano and his wife and co-owner, Mabel, had opted not to evacuate; St. Rita's was the only one of the parish's five nursing homes not to transport its occupants out as Katrina drew near. The Maganos had been confident they'd ride it out without incident; they were even hosting two dozen friends and neighbors along with their patients and had declined an offer of buses relayed by Bryan Bertucci, the parish coroner.

As Magano and his friends looked around outside, they heard a dull rumble. In a minute, water coursed around the building, quickly rising over their ankles. Yet another distinct flood had begun, this one water from Lake Borgne that had earlier washed away the hurricane levees along the Mr. Go. Now the flood had topped the last line of defense, a parish levee dividing settled areas from marsh.

The men rushed inside and tried to secure every opening against the floodwater. They slid a couch against a door and flipped a table against a window and hammered nails around its edges. Of course it did no good. Within minutes, the water was bursting through the windows, doors, and seams of the building. In twenty minutes, it had risen more than eight feet. Residents, trapped in their rooms, found themselves gasping for breath in narrow spaces between the waterline and the ceiling. For many there would be no escape: thirty-five quickly drowned. The rest, assisted by the Maganos, staff, and their guests, managed to crawl onto the roof. Rescuers—already out in force—found them not long afterward and began taking them away.

In the Hyatt Regency Hotel near the Superdome and city hall, Police Chief Eddie Compass was eating Oreos for breakfast. It was his birthday, and they were a present from his aide and spokesman, Marlon Defillo. It was a brief, happy moment amid mounting chaos. The New Orleans Police Department was falling apart. Only 82 of 120 officers called to duty at two a.m. had shown. As the floodwaters rose, calls poured into the NOPD's 911 system—six hundred in the first twenty-three minutes after the major breaches. There wasn't much they could do. The winds were too high to mount any rescues—and the police force for this city of 450,000, surrounded by a river, a lake, and the sea, had only five boats.

Meanwhile, police stations began going under water, too, their skeleton crews pinned down and fruitlessly calling for help. Katrina was slicing up the communications webs that Compass, Nagin, and political leaders and emergency managers in Baton Rouge and Washington relied on to "see" what was going on around the city. Electricity was out. Landlines and telephone switching stations were being submerged. Some cell phone towers had lost power; others had been knocked over. After the brief burst of activity, the 911 system was going down. One by one, police, city, state, and federal agencies were going blind. As thousands of people clambered onto rooftops, most of the people who could help them were paralyzed.

Even the Hyatt, where officials had set up a temporary command post on the fourth floor, did not appear safe. (They had moved operations there because the city EOC was too small; Nagin had joined them there overnight after aides suggested staying in his second-floor city hall office would be too dangerous.) Now the hotel began to vibrate as high winds rattled its hundreds of tinted windowpanes. Suddenly the wind and pressure differences started ripping panes out of their housings. Windows began cracking and exploding, showering glass onto the street and rooftop below. Rain—by this time riding horizontally on the wind—blew into hundreds of rooms.

Across the eastern half of the United States, millions awoke, grabbed their remotes, or flipped on their computers, curious about the fate of the city. The morning shows had booked Nagin and Blanco. At 7:15 a.m., Nagin spoke with NBC's Matt Lauer by telephone from the Hyatt. Based on sketchy initial reports, the media consensus of that hour was that Katrina had largely spared New Orleans.

"It's still going to be kind of hairy for the next few days, but you have to be optimistic based on what you're hearing this morning," Lauer said.

"We're still not out of the woods as it relates to that worst-case scenario," Nagin cautioned. "As a matter of fact I've gotten reports this morning that there's already water coming over some of the levee systems. In the Lower Ninth Ward, we've had one of our pumping stations stop operating. So we will have some significant flooding, it's just a matter of how much."

Katrina's eye moved past New Orleans at about nine a.m., approximately twelve miles east of the center of town, over the shallows of Chandeleur Sound and back into the Gulf, on its way to a second landfall in Mississippi. As the fiercest winds—now mercifully less than one hundred mph—moved over the metro area, what made the most searing impression on many people wasn't water but noise: rain pounding glass and roof shingles, wind screeching as it ripped through man-made structures, windows shattering and timber cracking, strange crashes and groaning as buildings strained under extraordinary forces and came apart.

As water poured into the city's east side, the storm surge was also flowing into Lake Pontchartrain. Along the rim of the eye, the strongest winds pumped seawater through the Chef Menteur and Rigolets passes and over the shallower, marshy areas around them. The level in the lake's wide, shallow basin slowly rose. Early on, as Katrina made landfall, water lapped against the concrete steps along the lake's southern shore. It soon rose over Lakeshore Drive and against the fourteen-foot-high earthen hurricane levee that snaked for miles along the shore. Water seeped behind Lakefront Airport—a man-made peninsula—and began splashing, then pouring over the levee on its backside, which was only eleven feet high. The rising water also flowed through three existing openings in the lakefront levee: the 17th Street, Orleans, and London Avenue canals, each reaching like delicate fingers miles south into the city's neighborhoods.

At Pumping Station Seven at the southern end of the Orleans canal, water began pouring through the large gaps in the never-completed floodwalls. The water ran over the grass in adjacent City Park, flowed under the Interstate 610 overpass nearby and into Mid-City neighborhoods beyond. It kept pouring, but because the gaps allowed the water to drain out and into the city, the level in the canal remained modest.

But water was still rising in the 17th Street and London Avenue canals, and as Katrina's eye passed the city, the water peaked—thankfully, just short of the eleven-and-a-half-foot level that the canals' concrete floodwalls were designed to withstand. But even if their walls were high enough, the canals had never held so much water, and the I-walls and their earthen foundations strained to contain the immense weight and water pressure. A cubic foot of water weighs about sixty-two pounds. Ten feet of water in an eighteen-and-a-half-foot-deep canal meant the pressure at the bottom approached one ton per square foot.

The 17th Street canal divided New Orleans from the Jefferson Parish suburb of Metairie. A few hours earlier, canal walls on both sides had begun to lean outward under the water's weight. Unusual stresses rippled through concrete, steel, and soil. Already, a small crack had opened up, causing street flooding in the adjacent Lakeview neighborhood. As the water rose higher, the wall on the New Orleans side tipped faster and farther. Along one section about a half mile south of the lakefront near the Hammond Highway Bridge, a gap suddenly opened between the concrete-and-steel wall and its earthen base, like a garden edging tool opening a trench between lawn and flowerbed. Water gushed into it and it quickly widened. Meanwhile, pressurized water percolated through the earth below. It pushed on the wall's sheet pile foundation and seeped through the squishy soil underneath it. The seepage was slow at first, but as the pressure doubled, then tripled, it sped up. Like a jet from a fire hose blasting through a box of Ping-Pong balls, the water began to dislodge soil particles, seeking a faster and more direct exit.

It soon found one.

It might have been an especially soft point in the soil, or a rotting tree root, or the decaying remnants of a century-old railroad trestle, or a nest of Formosan termites, the ferocious underground species that had colonized vast areas of town. Whatever it was, when the water found a weak point, it pushed and shoved, and the earth began to move en masse. The floodwall's factor of safety, in engineering parlance, dropped below 1.0. At about ten a.m., a great mass of particularly weak, soft clay under the floodwall's foundation, about eighteen feet down, slid away from the canal. Eight fifty-foot concrete panels, joined together with flexible gaskets, broke away with a crack and slid with it.

The floodwaters exploded through, taking down more wall sections and slamming into homes on Bellaire Drive, pushing some off their concrete slabs, shooting through living rooms and kitchens and knocking walls down on its way east. A four-hundred-foot breach had opened. A new flood—this one flowing in from the west side into the center of New Orleans—had begun.

An hour later, two more breaches opened up, these two and a half miles east in the London Avenue canal. One was on the canal's west side, not far from Lake Pontchartrain, the other on the east side, near Mirabeau Street, about a mile from the lakefront. In both spots, pressurized water bubbled up on the dry side of the wall in small eruptions called sand boils, the telltale sign of an imminent collapse. At the first site, soil heaved upward out from under the levee, leaving an eight-foot mound in adjacent backyards and sections of the upended floodwall violently accordioned. At the other, an I-wall section leaned over, then broke, the resulting torrent scouring a hole thirty-two feet deep on the other side. As the walls and soil gave way, tons of silty gray sand spewed up and out into the light for the first time since it lay on a marshy lagoon beach five thousand years before, depositing itself on homes and streets only a few decades old. The earth was the sea, and the geologic ghosts of New Orleans had risen.

As it had earlier in St. Bernard and the city's eastern wards, now water coursed through the more prosperous upper-middle-class neighborhoods around the canals. A block away from the first London Avenue breach, Harvey and Renee Miller looked out the window at 10:30 a.m. and saw Charlotte Drive turned into a raging river, churning white and kicking up spray as it surged around tree trunks, lampposts, and utility poles. A Cadillac parked across the street rose, gently bobbing and turning like a toy boat, then was carried off. They couldn't see the top of their own car. The Millers sat down and looked at each other.

"You know, we may not come through this," Harvey said.

They were both a bit fragile: he was seventy-three, she seventy-two. Renee had undergone surgery to repair a heart valve earlier in August and was still recuperating—the reason they'd chanced it and not evacuated—and Harvey, a professor at LSU Medical Center, had been through a double knee replacement a couple of years earlier. They had decamped from their own one-story ranch house down the street earlier that morning when they saw water in the street and moved into an empty two-story home owned by a friend. As they took a pause and sat down in the lawn chairs they'd brought into the living room, Renee looked down.

"What's that brown spot on the floor?" she said. "There's another one! Another!"

Within a few seconds the spots multiplied and grew together.

"My God, there's water coming through the floor," Harvey said. He opened the front door. The water whipping past the house had risen to the top of the steps, about five feet off the ground. He shut the door, and they took the lawn furniture, their cot, and the food and water they'd brought along—as well as their dog, Monet—to the second floor. When they looked out the window, the water had submerged a six-foot-high fence around the school next door. A few minutes later, it rose past the classroom air conditioners mounted about eight feet up. They had no clue what was happening, or why it was happening so fast. Harvey had heard a brief mention of a possible levee breach at the 17th Street Canal—but that was miles away.

The water continued to rise.

Jaime Cooper—Loco to his friends—had been adopted as a boy from a Panama orphanage, and he had thoroughly embraced his new home, New Orleans. Cooper joined a group of Mardi Gras Indians and, in his job as a carpenter, worked on the grand and sometimes decrepit houses in his Eighth Ward neighborhood. As his neighbors had evacuated, he had decided he was game to ride out a hurricane. He was small but built like a bantamweight boxer, and he believed he could handle it. He wanted to see Katrina, to live through a movie.

Cooper waited out the storm in his mother's house on North Miro Street in Gentilly, a middle-class, mostly African American neighborhood. The house was located a few miles west of the Industrial Canal and southeast of the London Avenue canal. On Sunday evening, he had made a mental note of who had stayed behind on his block—an elderly couple across the street, a single mother with a couple of teenagers, young couples—in case they needed help or needed to band together later on. He stayed up all night, listening to a portable waterproof radio that a friend had given to him. As the wind picked up, it blew away one of the plywood boards he'd put on the windows. Early in the morning, he pushed open the front door against the wind and peered out. There was water running through the street. It wasn't very high, but the worst of the storm was obviously approaching and he decided to execute his hurricane plan. He climbed into the bathtub with his radio and a telephone, pulled a mattress over himself, and waited.

It was not much of a plan. Soon Cooper dozed off. He awoke to the sound of the telephone falling and hitting something. The house had a hardwood floor. But the sound he heard wasn't a *clunk*. It was more of a *floop*. The bathroom was filling with water.

Cooper grabbed a bag with some basic supplies and climbed up the stairs to the attic. The house had a gabled roof with old-fashioned slate siding. The wind had blown the slate away on both ends, turning the attic into a wind tunnel, but that also meant there wouldn't be any of the odd pressure buildups that could cause buildings to disintegrate or explode. The roof probably wasn't going to blow off, but he wasn't taking a chance. Some time before, he'd left a hammer up there. Now Cooper found some nails and started hammering where the roof beams met the rafters at the peak of the house, fortifying it. He hammered like mad as the wind and rain whipped through the attic and chilled his skin. He drove dozens of nails within minutes.

Satisfied, he hollered over to the neighbors to make sure they were awake and aware, then moved partway down the steps, out of the rain but above the flood in the living room, and waited, listening to the radio.

Daylight came, and as the wind died down he went out on the roof to put up an orange reflectorized vest on a stick to signal for help. He was thinking of going out into the street—the water was four or five feet deep and receding.

But only for a moment. "Then all of a sudden it rose up fast, real fast, like somebody unplugged something," he said later. "It started coming up fast and high."

The flood from the 17th Street and London Avenue breaches had coursed south and east and finally reached Cooper's neighborhood, mixing with the water that had entered from the Industrial Canal. The two floods had joined into a single deluge.

The waters raced to the roofline. Cooper thought of swimming for it. There was a broken wooden gate nearby—maybe he could use it as a raft. As he scanned the water, lying flat on the roof and peering over the edge, he looked into the eyes of a dead man. The body was floating next to his house, staring faceup.

Cooper was tempted to pull the man out, but he decided not to risk it. He would stay put for the moment. He called to his elderly neighbors and told them they should hang a flag or something bright out their second-story window, which they did.

A few miles farther east in the Lower Ninth Ward, the Greens had been joined on top of their perch by some similarly dispossessed neighbors, including a man who'd been stuck in a tree and a couple with a tiny white poodle, now turned black by its swim through muddy water laced with gasoline, garbage, and household waste.

They waited, but no help arrived.

Jonathan decided to see if they could find a better place to bide their time. By jumping from house to house, hopping across debris, and swimming, he made it to the second floor of a tie shop across Claiborne Avenue. But he couldn't open the door, and the others figured rescuers would be able to spot them where they were. Robert, feeling as if his entire body was about to break, managed to doze off a couple of times, awakened by rain and wind across his face. He was in shock, blaming himself for the disappearance and almost certain death of his granddaughter. But he resolved not to break down—at least not until he and the remaining family members were safe.

But now his mother was failing. She drifted in and out of awareness, having occasional tremors, not speaking. Finally she fell into unconsciousness. A few hours after they had pulled her up out of the water, Joyce Green stopped breathing. They barely uttered a word, shedding a few silent tears as they sat there huddled together, shielded only by a big piece of foam insulation, waiting.

Across the city, a thousand others were also dead—or about to be. Hundreds had drowned when the initial surge of water came through the Ninth Ward and St. Bernard Parish. Now the second flood from the canals was trapping and drowning hundreds more in their homes and attics. Some slipped off rooftops or were swallowed up by water as they tried to make their way to safety. Some were struck by floating or flying tree limbs, or shards of utility poles. In many places, bodies floated in the streets, dead tissue beginning to bloat in the dirty flow.

At the *Times-Picayune* building about a mile north of the Superdome, photographer Ted Jackson jumped into his pickup and drove east toward the high water at about eleven a.m. The 1996 Toyota had 332,000 miles on it and probably wouldn't last much longer, so Jackson was willing to take some chances with it. A twenty-one-year veteran of the paper, he was one of the most talented and insightful photographers on the staff, the one editors turned to most often for ambitious projects and to plunge into extreme situations.

Since the night before, about 230 staffers and family members had been camped out at the newspaper's headquarters, about a mile north of the Superdome. They'd slept on air mattresses and crawled into sleeping bags on office floors. As the storm passed that morning, the news staff had remained mostly indoors, under the eye of longtime editor Jim Amoss (though Jackson had ventured out to the French Quarter and the Superdome, then driven back through ninety-mph winds). They had managed to keep gathering information by phone from sources around the region and from reporters placed in strategic locations, as well as by listening to local radio and watching television, and they were posting a stream of information on the newspaper's hurricane blog.

The newspaper building, constructed in the 1970s, was a

gray-and-white brick box with a distinctive lighthouselike tower with the paper's name wrapped around the crown. It had survived the hurricane with only minor damage. The third-floor editorial and executive offices were protected by bulletproof glass, but at four a.m. one of the panes in the executive suite had blown out of its aluminum frame, allowing rain to pour in. The roof had been damaged, too, and water sprinkled down through the ceiling and soaked some carpets and furniture. Power had gone out overnight, but the two generators on the roof had kicked in. A big tree in the front lawn had fallen toward the building entrance, crushing a parked car. Otherwise, it appeared the newspaper was in good shape. The first floor, where the presses were, was raised about four feet off the ground. Still, the paper's leadership had in essence taken a gamble. There was only about two days' worth of generator fuel. If the building flooded and the presses were damaged, there was no contingency plan to keep publishing. And, of course, those inside the building had taken their own gamble in staying.

But, for the moment, the storm had passed and there was a huge flood to the east, and it was time to document it. Jackson drove east on St. Claude Avenue to Poland Avenue, parallel to the Industrial Canal. The water there was nearly hip-deep, and it was impossible to drive any farther, so he got out, camera bags slung over his shoulder, and waded to the St. Claude bridge. He climbed to the crest and scanned the Lower Ninth Ward laid out in front of him. The view was virtually identical to the one President Johnson and his party had seen from the same vantage point forty years earlier: hundreds of houses sat in a vast lake with water up to their eaves, the current flowing slowly east around them. Hundreds of people clustered on rooftops. Some were hanging off the sides, contemplating swimming for it.

Jackson walked down toward the water. The St. Claude bridge descended gradually between homes into the neighborhood, and he soon drew even with a house to his right—he made a mental note of the address, 4702 St. Claude—where seven people were clinging to posts on the front porch. Several children were among them; the water was up to their necks. It appeared the flood was still rising, and the parents were clutching the children, desperately trying to keep their heads above the waterline. They started screaming at Jackson for help. There wasn't much he could do: a torrent ran between the bridge and the house, about fifty feet away, and the wind was still howling at hurricane force. Another man was also standing on the St. Claude span, and he and Jackson looked at each other quizzically, each trying to figure out how to help. Jackson screamed out to the stranded family in the wind. They hollered back that they had been standing on the porch railing since eight a.m.— about four hours.

"Please do something!" they shouted.

"There's nothing we can do!" he yelled. "It's too deep! Can you go into the attic?"

"We can't—it won't hold us!"

As he was puzzling over what they meant by that, they began to maneuver a piece of wood in front of the porch so they could put one of the children, a little girl, on it and then push her across. They had taken an empty ice chest and were planning to send another little girl over in that.

"Please, please stop!" Jackson shouted. "They'll drown. You've just got to hold on—someone will come!"

They stopped, looking utterly defeated and afraid.

Then Jackson began pondering a dilemma. He was an intense and reflective man, a Christian known for his moral rectitude. His job dictated he shoot a photo of the shocking drama in front of him. But he wondered, "If I can't help them, is it okay to shoot their picture?"

Adding to the quandary, the man on the bridge had objected when he took out a camera. But Jackson made a compromise with himself. He would shoot only a few frames. He hoped the family wouldn't notice.

"Listen," he told the man on the bridge, "I have to do my job, and that means showing what is happening here. I'm going to shoot some pictures."

"I am not going to let you take that picture!" the man yelled.

Jackson walked away from him, back up the span, trying to find an angle to shoot discreetly.

"I can see you trying to sneak a picture!" the man said.

"I'm not sneaking anything," Jackson replied evenly. "I'm telling you I'm going to shoot this picture."

He shot three or four frames, walked back to his truck, and drove back to the newspaper.

None of it made sense. Katrina was gone—on its way to the Gulf Coast, where it would bring a record thirty-foot storm surge over the seaside towns, their neighborhoods, tourist strips, and casinos. By early afternoon, the wind and rain were letting up and the sky brightening. But like the dead hand bursting out of the ground after the false ending in a teen horror film, terrible things were still happening in New Orleans. The city continued taking on water like a great sinking ship. Its flood defenses had been all but destroyed. Earthen barriers protecting the east side had been overtopped and breached in dozens of locations. For all intents and purposes, that side of town was open to the Gulf of Mexico. Canal levees within the city proper were breached at dozens of points. The swollen lake could take another two days to drain out, and as it did, most of the city would flood.

It could have been far worse. The lakefront levees had mostly held, overtopped only near the airport and in a few areas where waves had splashed over. The flood from the drainage canal breaches was flowing through gaps, not over the tops of walls. It was a slower-moving, shallower flood than the fill-the-bowl scenario. But the complex pattern of flooding—a quick inundation from the east, joining up with a more gradual one from the drainage canals farther west—confused people unfamiliar with the city's peculiar geography. The flood's slow spread gave some people time to escape. It could have given rescuers a bit of breathing room as well, a little time to assess the situation and launch what would have to be one of the largest rescue operations in American history. But so far, nobody in a position to do anything about it knew Katrina's deadly flood was on its way to covering most of the city.

The dire situation in the eastern areas had been communicated quickly. Dozens of reports had come in via landline, cell phone, and radio shortly after the flooding began. The whole country knew part of the city had been hit. At 11:13 a.m. Monday, the Homeland Security Department had issued a general advisory clearly laying out the situation in those areas: "Flooding is significant throughout the region, and a levee in New Orleans has reportedly been breached, sending six to eight feet of water throughout the Ninth Ward area of the city. The Homeland Security's Operation Center reports that due to rising water in the Ninth Ward, residents are in their attics and on their roofs."

Emergency officials thought it was a manageable situation. During that morning's eleven a.m. videoconference—which included FEMA director Brown, Governor Blanco, and Joe Hagin, but no one actually in New Orleans—they were sounding notes of confidence.

"I think a lot of the planning that FEMA has done with us over the last year has really paid off in this particular operation," Jeff Smith, Louisiana's emergency preparedness director, told participants.

But without much hard information, Blanco was much less upbeat or coherent. "We keep getting reports in some places that maybe water is coming over the levees," she said. "We heard a report unconfirmed—I think we have not breached the levee. We have not breached the levee at this point in time. That could change, but in some places we have floodwaters coming in New Orleans."

After the initial burst of information about St. Bernard and the Lower Ninth, reliable communications had all but shut down, and there was nothing available to fill that void. Though fallen cellular towers and crashing 911 systems were the logical consequences of a long-predicted event, neither the federal, state, or local governments had an emergency plan. FEMA had mobile communications units that operated out of SUVs, trucks, and campers, typically used by its employees after a storm. FEMA had positioned some in Shreveport, a seven-hour drive away—but none in New Orleans or in Baton Rouge. Nor had the state asked that any be brought in. The National Communications System (an interagency panel dating to the aftermath of the Cuban Missile Crisis, lately absorbed into DHS) was charged with reestablishing communications in a disaster. But it usually let telephone companies do the heavy lifting, and local emergency radio systems were not part of its responsibility. Its director, Peter Fonash, had never heard of the "New Orleans scenario" before Sunday.

A haze descended. Most officials outside of New Orleans stuck with the idea that only the city's east side had flooded—it was, after all, the only concrete information they had. The only thing that would convey the big picture would be flying over the city. But with the winds still gusting at hurricane force, flying would not be possible for a few more hours.

In fact, as Blanco was speaking, the 17th Street breach had just been confirmed. A group of firefighters from New Orleans Fire Engine Company Number 18 had spent the night in their station at 778 Harrison Avenue, located in the northwest of the city in the Lakeview neighborhood. As the storm raged that morning at about eight a.m., they decided to go outside on patrol to see if anyone needed help. As they trudged through the streets, looking at downed power lines and trees, roof piles, and shattered windows—garden-variety hurricane damage—water began running around their feet. Soon it was up to their ankles, then their shins. There was no obvious source.

"Water has risen eighteen inches over the past half hour in Lakeview," Captain Paul Hellmers radioed the New Orleans Emergency Operations Center at 8:26 a.m. "A levee may have broken. Or water may be pouring over the levee."

At about 10:50 a.m., Hellmers and several other firefighters trudged a mile and a half from the station and up to the top floors of the Lake Marina Towers condo building. The condos were perched near the edge of the lake, next to the New Orleans Yacht Club and several marinas holding pleasure craft from sloops to speedboats, all of which Katrina had tossed around like pool toys. It was also near the mouth of the 17th Street canal.

They stepped into a stairway landing on the eighteenth floor and waited a few minutes for the rain to clear, squinting down through the mist.

A quarter mile away, they spied water rushing through a large breach. At first, it looked like a gap about twenty feet wide. But as Hellmers stared, the rain eased and the scene became clear: the breach was closer to a football field in width. Water was pouring through it into the Lakeview and Bucktown neighborhoods, churning a wake of white froth at the edges of the gap. Trees were listing in the light-brown current, which carried shards of timber and siding through the leafy, curving streets of the prosperous neighborhood. Car roofs peaked above its surface.

Hellmers felt sick.

"We knew it was all over," he later told the *Times-Picayune*. "The entire city was going to flood."

The firefighters went up on the roof to get a clearer look at the scene and radioed the news to the city EOC at the Hyatt just before eleven a.m. They videotaped the breach for good measure. "You can . . . see the water pouring through the wall," Hellmers said on the tape. "You can see that the wall is gone— you can see the water pouring through, it looks like about a two-hundred-foot section of wall that's gone! The water is continuing to rise—very slowly."

At the Hyatt, Nagin, New Orleans Homeland Security director Ebbert, and FEMA's Bahamonde listened in shock as they heard the description from an aide. Water was flowing freely into the city, and the flood would continue until someone found a way to stop it. (It wasn't immediately clear whose responsibility it was, the Corps's or the Levee Board's.) The city officials methodically identified the breached area on a city map. They notified the Levee Board and the officials at the state EOC, where Blanco, Brown, and their underlings were monitoring things. Bahamonde shot off e-mails to associates in Washington and Baton Rouge informing them of the break.

The information took a circuitous route. In Washington,

Mike Lowder, FEMA's deputy director of response—who had been involved with planning for the New Orleans scenario for years—forwarded Bahamonde's information back to Brown in Louisiana.

"He has been trying to reach [FEMA Louisiana coordinating officer Bill] Lokey," the message said. "New Orleans FD is reporting a 20-foot-wide breech [sic] in the lake pontchartrain side levy. The area is lakeshore Blvd and 17th street."

"I'm being told here water over [the levee] not a breach," Brown BlackBerried back. (Brown typed as the videoconference was already under way.)

"Ok," Lowder replied a few minutes later. "You probably have better info there. Just wanted to pass you what we hear."

At two p.m., the city publicly announced the breach. The news went out over the radio and into the *Times-Picayune* hurricane blog, which announced, almost as an aside to reports of rescuers having trouble reaching stranded people, "Meanwhile, City Hall confirmed a breach of the levee along the 17th Street canal at Bellaire Drive, allowing water to spill into Lakeview."

As New Orleans was going under, George Bush stuck to his preplanned schedule, which was taking him away from his vacation—and Cindy Sheehan—for a couple of days. Brown had called him twice on Monday morning to update him on the latest, the second time as Bush jetted to Arizona on Air Force One. He arrived at Luke Air Force Base at around noon New Orleans time. Under a blazing sun, he cut a melting cake to mark Senator John McCain's sixty-ninth birthday. (The Arizona senator had been a bitter rival of Bush's in the past but was one of the president's firmest supporters on Iraq. He was also planning a possible presidential run and doing his best to mend fences.)

Bush then moved on to an RV resort and country club in nearby El Mirage for a question-and-answer session on the Medicare drug benefit program, set to begin in a few months, during which he threw in a pledge to improve border security—an issue that had begun heating up and could spell trouble for him. Then he departed for Southern California for another Q&A on Medicare. Bush made passing reassurances about Katrina at each stop, but nothing that betrayed an awareness of the extraordinary nature of what was unfolding in New Orleans.

"This was a terrible storm. It's a storm that hit with a lot of ferocity. It's a storm now that is moving through, and now it's the time for governments to help people get their feet on the ground," Bush told his audience in Rancho Cucamonga, California. "For those of you who prayed for the folks in that area, I want to thank you for your prayers. For those of you who are concerned about whether or not we're prepared to help, don't be. We are. We're in place. We've got equipment in place, supplies in place. And once the—once we're able to assess the damage, we'll be able to move in and help those good folks in the affected areas." He then changed the subject to Iraq.

From their vantage point in the condo tower, the firefighters near the 17th Street breach spotted several boats in the neighborhood below that looked salvageable. Leaving Captain Fincher behind to monitor the breach, Hellmers and the others went downstairs, stood for a moment on the exterior steps, then plunged into the flood, swimming through floating debris to retrieve the boats. Hellmers swam to one of them and pulled himself up—slashing his foot on some sheet metal and broken glass under the surface. He fired up the engine and brought the boat back to the condo. There, they decided he'd better not risk infection or further injury. Instead, using the Lake Marina Towers building as his headquarters, Hellmers would coordinate their fledgling rescue operation.

The firefighters began making sorties in their fleet of commandeered boats, responding to cries for help from inside homes and off rooftops. They inched through debris-strewn water, dodging sunken cars and toppled trees and limbs and electric, cable, and telephone wires. For a few hours, a city dispatcher relayed 911 calls from their vicinity, until the system crashed. The first one came from an elderly man in Lakeview. They found him standing on the edge of his first-floor bathtub with water up to his neck. A few minutes more, and he would have drowned.

Across town at Jackson Barracks, most guardsmen had no

orders other than to await an airlift somewhere else. Unwilling to just sit around, they took the boats they had commandeered and began making forays into the surrounding Lower Ninth Ward and St. Bernard neighborhoods, plucking people from roofs and dropping them at a staging area being set up near the west side of the St. Claude bridge, close to where Jackson had parked his truck. Only Captain Beron got another assignment— security at the Superdome. As he was airlifted by helicopter that afternoon, for the first time he could see the full scope of the flooding. It was stunning: the city had joined with Lake Pontchartrain, Lake Borgne, and the Gulf. What had once been a mighty city was now an archipelago of rooftops, its pathetic denizens clinging to desperate hopes.

At one p.m., a neighbor in a bass boat came by and rescued the Greens from their roof in the Lower Ninth Ward. There was only so much room in the craft; they were forced to leave Joyce's body behind. They were dropped at the Claiborne Avenue bridge (a mile south of the St. Claude bridge), and as they trudged over the Industrial Canal they could see two things clearly: Joyce splayed out pitiably on the rooftop below and the red-hulled grain barge that had floated through the breach bobbing incongruously near the splintered frames of some houses a block or two away.

On the west side, some men in a pickup truck ran them up to the National Guard staging area near St. Claude Avenue. Helicopters had begun airlifting people out.

Green was desperate. "My mother's body is on the roof of 1617 Tennessee Street!" he told a National Guardsman, then another, and another—anyone with a uniform on. But there were bodies everywhere. Rescuing the living was the top priority. No one was going to help him.

Miles to the south, Bobbie Moreau, Tasha, Cassidy, and their pets had bobbed for hours in the heat near the Plaquemines Parish river levee. Bobbie had been fiddling with the radio, flipping the channels, calling for help. She raised one man, on a boat up north of her in Empire. He couldn't help them. "Everything is gone," he remarked.

But, the man added, they were speaking over a Coast Guard channel; if she stayed on it, sooner or later, help would come. Bobbie kept at it. Sometime after two p.m., her plea was picked up and relayed to the Coast Guard headquarters in Alexandria: "a Mayday from a frantic woman saying that her and her daughter . . . and her grandchild were stuck on a small boat in the middle of the city of Port Sulphur."

Soon, a voice rattled back at her:

"This is the United States Coast Guard. What is your location?"

Not long afterward, a helicopter was hovering above them. It was 2:50 p.m., and it would be the Coast Guard's first rescue. Blocked by the trees the boat was resting against, the rescuers could not drop directly onto the deck. Instead, they lowered rescue swimmer Laurence Nettles into the water nearby. He climbed on board and guided tethered baskets over the deck. He helped the boat's occupants, one by one, into them.

"You want me to come to the right?" the pilot asked via radio.

"No, hold position," Nettles ordered. "On deck, picking up slack, waiting for the survivor to get in basket. Hold position. Woman and baby are getting in the basket. Ready for pickup. Picking up slack. Start taking the load. . . . Clear vessel, clear back to the left."

"Okay, I can move it to the right, if I can," the pilot said.

"Roger, that's fine. . . . Basket's coming up . . . basket's halfway up. . . . Roger, she's got a dog with her, too."

"That's fine. Let her bring the dog, it's fine."

All three animals made it all right. Cheers erupted at the temporary Coast Guard offices in Alexandria and St. Louis. The game was on.

Meanwhile, rescuees in military trucks, commandeered buses, and even a U-Haul trailer began to arrive at the Dome—as many as forty people at a time would get off and tromp up the, ramp into the facility. Later, helicopters from the National

Guard and Coast Guard began dropping people there, too. Finally, people began arriving on foot. The Dome had become the default rendezvous point.

On Monday, it would have been possible to transport at least some of those people out of the city. There were conflicting reports about the safety of the two causeways heading east and north over Lake Pontchartrain, but most other routes were clear, among them the bridge over the Mississippi to Algiers (named the Crescent City Connection), Interstate 10, and several other roads that led west into Jefferson Parish and then upriver to higher ground. Sending a vehicle out of the city to shelters in Baton Rouge would guarantee the passengers' safety but tie up the vehicle for hours; sending it back and forth to pull people out of immediate danger was, in most cases, deemed a higher priority.

Then, as communications links had done earlier, the remaining escape routes from New Orleans began to disappear. The first—on Monday afternoon—had been a point under a railroad bridge where the interstate dipped ten feet below sea level. An elaborate pumping system had been only recently completed there, but it failed during the day and the dip filled up with water from the 17th Street canal breach. With that, the main route out of the city was cut.

Early in the afternoon, as the sky brightened and the rain let up, reporters and photographers at the *Times-Picayune* clambered into their cars and SUVs and struck out to see what was happening around New Orleans.

Several of them took bicycles and headed north toward the lake to investigate the reports of the breach. Just a couple of blocks from the newspaper, they found looters—surprisingly orderly ones—lined up outside Coleman's, a clothing warehouse and retail outlet adjacent to the B. W. Cooper housing development, one of the city's 1950s-era brick enclaves for the poor. Some were exiting the store toting large green garbage bags stuffed with clothing. Others carried boxes on their heads. A pickup truck pulled up and honked its horn, the bed filled with cheering onlookers, while other spectators gathered and watched from a distance away, at the edge of a big pond that had formed on Earhart Avenue.

Ted Jackson, meanwhile, was on his way back to the Ninth Ward, along with Brian Thevenot, an experienced reporter who had recently spent a month in Iraq embedded with National Guard and army troops.

This time, Jackson had borrowed an inflatable boat and a fifty-foot length of rope from fellow photographer Elliott Kamenitz. He threw them in the back of the truck.

"If we have to make a choice between getting a story or saving lives, are you okay with saving lives first?" he asked his companion. Thevenot said yes.

They headed for the St. Claude bridge. The family Jackson had seen before was gone. The pair spied a couple of boats pulling people out of an attic up the street, and they called out to them to see if they'd rescued the family at the other end. The answer was no.

Jackson felt a hollow in the pit of his stomach. He assumed they had been so desperate to get off that porch, they had swum for it and drowned.

The St. Claude bridge had been turned into a makeshift launch, used by a dozen rescue boats or more, most of them privately owned except for those of a couple of SWAT teams. Jackson and Thevenot hitched a ride with Jerry Rayes, a forty-eight-year-old St. Bernard locksmith. Rayes had spent the night in a downtown hotel, then launched his boat and joined the flotilla. Accompanied by his son and nephew, he'd already rescued about fifty people off rooftops near Elysian Fields Avenue, not far away.

Rayes was on his way to St. Bernard to rescue a friend, and he ignored pleas for help from dozens of trapped flood victims along the way.

"Hey! Damn! Hey!" one woman yelled as they went by.

"You can't save everybody," Rayes told them. "That's all we heard for hours this morning." Soon they were gliding past a pink-and-yellow-trimmed house, a local landmark belonging to legendary rocker Fats Domino. Domino was still inside, and group of men stood on the balcony, yelling and waving wildly at them. Rayes ignored them, too.

"What am I going to do? I got to go to the parish," he said. "There's way too many people out there and too few boats."

When they got to the designated spot, though, he found his friend had already been picked up. So he reversed course and started checking the rooftops and second stories for other people to evacuate. They soon had a full boat. Some people declined their help.

"You all right?" his son Ian Rayes, twenty, asked one man.

"Yeah," he said. "I'm just here with the dogs. The family's out."

They dropped their passengers at a bank building that sat on a rise, then went back out for more.

On the opposite side of town, two staffers from the *Times-Picayune* Living section—editor James O'Byrne and art critic Doug MacCash—rode bicycles out toward Lakeview, first heading west and then riding along the top of the 17th Street canal levee. The farther north they went, the deeper the water got. Finally, as they approached the breach itself, they were forced to stop. Around them, the Lakeview neighborhood (which included O'Byrne's house) was itself a lake, its prosperous streets under as much as twenty feet of water. Nearby, the Southern Yacht Club was on fire. Sailboats had been tossed and smashed against concrete walls. Cars had been flipped, one on top of the other. Water was still flowing from the lake into the canal and then into the city, now a gentle but steady current. By the time reporters began returning to the *Times-Picayune* late in the afternoon, a few inches of water covered the parking lot.

At about three p.m., Colonel Richard Wagenaar, the commander of the Corps's New Orleans district, and some aides tried to drive out to the 17th Street breach to confirm it with their own eyes. (Most helicopters had been taken out of the hurricane strike zone before the storm, and as they returned they were immediately tasked with search and rescue.) Wagenaar had been in his job only six weeks. His previous assignment had been heading an engineering division of the Combined Forces Command in South Korea, where he'd worked on war contingencies. Now he was in for a war of an entirely different sort.

The route—a relatively straight shot four miles north—was blocked by fallen power lines, debris, and flooded streets. They left from their headquarters, a shimmering steel-and-glass structure sitting on the Mississippi River levee, and first drove west, aiming to approach the canal from the dry side. Obstacles forced them to turn east onto Interstate 10, but they soon ran into spreading floodwaters. Wagenaar looked down from the freeway overpass and saw only roofs and treetops. He didn't know the city well, but he knew that rain could never produce such a flood.

By five p.m., the breaches in the Industrial Canal and 17th Street—though not the ones along the London Avenue canal— had been noted and publicized by the city. The local Corps office had also sent some initial observations to Washington. But the Homeland Security Operations Center—a movie set of a control room built to manage the worst terrorists could dish out—had not been able to sort fact from rumor in the reports it was getting— some from officials, some from the media. It issued a report saying: "Preliminary reports indicate the levees in New Orleans have not been breached; however, an assessment is still pending." Chertoff's massive security apparatus was not just mildly off in its perceptions—it was in its own reality, one that bore no relationship to what was actually happening in New Orleans.

At around six p.m., President Bush called Governor Blanco, reaching her at her office at the EOC in Baton Rouge. It was a courtesy call, part of the standard presidential choreography after any disaster, in which assistance is offered, then accepted, and usually little of substance is discussed. But this time the circumstances were quite different. Blanco had been up since before dawn and been barraged all day with ever-worsening reports about the catastrophe. She knew it was bad, worse than Betsy, certainly, probably the worst natural disaster a Louisiana governor had ever faced. But the information was still sketchy; some TV reports were saying the city had been spared a direct hit, and a complete picture of the storm damage had not yet taken shape in her mind or in those of the other state and federal officials in Baton Rouge. Between the two of them, they commanded vast resources—Blanco her National Guard troops, Bush the entire federal government—but at that point, neither had a clue what to do with them.

Bush asked her for the latest on the situation, and Blanco filled him in on the details she knew—levees overtopped, some breached, large areas flooded, tens of thousands of victims. "This is serious. It's very big," she said.

Bush assured her he was ready to provide assistance.

"We need your help," she declared. "We need everything you've got."

The courtesy call was complete. Blanco felt she'd done all she could in conveying the magnitude of the challenge ahead to the president. The details would be left to others.

Blanco sat down with Mike Brown a short while later. Despite the fact that the disaster was still unfolding and would pose exceptional problems, Brown went down the standard checklist of FEMA postdisaster assistance—food, water, and medical supplies, Small Business Association loans, and grants for damaged homes. Then something caught Blanco's attention: Brown had mentioned that FEMA had five hundred buses on standby. Unlike a low-interest loan, buses could be immediately useful. Thousands were being rescued and dropped on levees and overpasses. Some were being trucked to the Dome. All of them—perhaps one hundred thousand people in all—would likely have to be transported out of New Orleans to shelter somewhere else—where, she wasn't sure. But she told him she wanted those buses.

"Then I promise you we will get you those buses," he said. Displaying his hobbyist's fascination with emergency management minutiae, Brown warned Blanco the drivers could only work for twelve hours at a stretch, after which regulations required they rest. Perhaps they could double-team, Blanco suggested, and switch off at the wheel to keep the buses moving. "Some do that," he said, "but others don't."

Brown told Bill Lokey and FEMA staffers in Washington to get the buses rolling.

Unfortunately, Brown's buses were entirely hypothetical. Under the National Response Plan, it would be up to the federal Department of Transportation to provide them at FEMA's request. Over the weekend, Jules Hurst, a FEMA transportation official familiar with the city's predicament from the recent Pam workshop, had given his DOT counterparts a heads-up, telling them to locate between one thousand and two thousand buses for the entire Gulf Coast. The DOT officials had then called the DOT bus contractor, Landstar, to check on availability. But lacking an explicit request, they had done nothing more.

Earlier in the day, Marty Bahamonde had requested a Coast Guard flyover to confirm the extent of the flooding. At five p.m., he finally got it, after a Coast Guard pilot figured that Bahamonde might be able to more quickly communicate the city's plight to the White House than if the information traveled, much more circuitously, via the Coast Guard chain of command. The helicopter lifted off from the Superdome for a ten-minute swing out to the lakefront and back. The sight was a shock. Nearly 80 percent of the city was flooded. He saw the clean break in the 17th Street canal wall and the water still flowing in. Thousands of people were perched on rooftops. Others had climbed up onto overpasses and bridges. Dozens of rescue boats could be seen plying the waters as well. The Coast Guard and Wildlife and Fisheries Department had already rescued hundreds of people by boat and helicopter.

A few minutes after he was dropped back at the Dome, Bahamonde went up with the Coast Guard again, this time for a forty-five-minute trip. Now he could take in the full sweep of the disaster. To the southeast, there was no longer any demarcation between Gulf, marshland, and neighborhoods. Due north from there, the Interstate 10 causeway over the lake into suburban Slidell was impassable, the concrete slabs of its eastbound lanes kicked off like loose slats on a rope bridge. New Orleans itself was a sea, and the only sure route out of town lay to the immediate east of downtown, across the Crescent City Connection. When Bahamonde got back around seven p.m., Nagin was on the helipad and was the first to get the grim news. Bahamonde then ran into the Hyatt and burst into the command center, his FEMA Windbreaker rustling, and asked if there was a way to set up a conference call so that local officials could consult with FEMA and Homeland Security. But there weren't any speakerphones, and the phone system wasn't set up for such calls.

Bahamonde sat down and, with some difficulty because of spotty service, called his bosses individually, starting with Brown. He outlined the scale of the damage and the problems—ground transportation shut down; thousands trapped; thousands more gathering in the Dome; food, water, and medical care all in short supply.

"Thank you. I'm going to call the White House," Brown said.

Brown dialed Crawford and got Joe Hagin, his usual contact point. Though he believed Bahamonde had a tendency to veer into hyperbole, Brown did not mince words. "We're realizing our worst nightmare," Brown told Hagin. "Everything we've planned about, worried about, that FEMA has worried about for ten years is coming true." He described the unimaginable scene unfolding in New Orleans.

Hagin asked if there was anything he needed.

Brown did not ask for anything. He didn't think it would do much good.

In previous disasters, Brown had a free hand, and calling the White House—as past directors did in the days FEMA was a freestanding agency—enabled him to reach out easily to other agencies, especially the military, for assistance.

But that kind of end run wasn't built into the National Response Plan, not to mention the new architecture of Homeland Security. In a call earlier that morning, chief of staff Andy Card had somewhat awkwardly told Brown it would be better to go through Homeland Security than to try to get help directly from the White House. Brown felt caught, uncertain of his exact role. Did the buck stop with him or with Chertoff or with someone else? Now, it appeared he was obligated to follow the chain of command through several layers of bureaucracy and up to Chertoff. Yet Chertoff and other agency honchos seemed to him to be disengaged from the disaster, relying on him to handle things. They'd never been much help, and he doubted they'd start now. Brown didn't even bother calling Chertoff during the day, figuring it wouldn't help. But as he was reaching out that night, they chatted briefly, and Chertoff offered him whatever he needed. Brown also sent an e-mail to Card reiterating that New Orleans was under water, a catastrophe. Brown didn't state it outright, though the message was clear: direction from the White House was needed ASAP.

But no one in the Bush administration seemed to be overseeing the federal government's response. Chertoff had left it in Brown's hands, but Brown had been bureaucratically marginalized two years earlier. He was also in Baton Rouge, close to the action but not to the bureaucratic levers that can get coordinated action across the federal government. The Homeland Security Operations Center was processing information, not making command decisions.

Theoretically speaking, this was surprising. By any objective measure, Katrina was a textbook case of the disaster that the federal government's shiny new emergency machinery had been engineered to address. The National Response Plan had already created contingencies for the worst national disasters: the Catastrophic Incident Annex and the Inter-Agency Incident Management Group, the latter a panel of agency representatives with disaster experience who could cut through red tape; the former authorizing the Secretary of Homeland Security to mobilize federal resources immediately, without waiting for the state to make requests through bureaucratic channels. A "catastrophic incident" was defined as

> Any natural or man-made incident, including terrorism, that results in extraordinary levels of mass casualties, damage, or disruption severely affecting the population, infrastructure, environment, economy, national morale, and/or government functions. A catastrophic incident could result in sustained national impacts over a prolonged period of time; almost immediately exceeds resources normally available to State, local, tribal, and private-sector authorities in the impacted area; and significantly interrupts governmental operations and emergency services to such an extent that national security could be threatened. All catastrophic incidents are Incidents of National Significance. These factors drive the urgency for coordinated national planning to ensure accelerated Federal/national assistance.

But no one in the upper levels of the government had seriously discussed invoking the Catastrophic Incident Annex. Some—including Chertoff—were unsure exactly what it was, or how it differed from an Incident of National Significance (a general term applying any time a presidential disaster declaration was made). On Saturday, Janet Benini, a White House staffer who had been involved in drafting the nation's catastrophic disaster plans, had sent an e-mail to FEMA official David Garratt asking if there was "any talk of implementing the Catastrophic Plan . . . with a Cat 4 heading directly into New Orleans this might be the time." His answer was no. Most of the top Homeland Security officials had spent the previous two years, and some their entire careers, girding the nation against terrorists and criminals. As far as they were concerned, hurricanes were still FEMA's business, and they expected the FEMA they had systematically dismantled would go ahead and do what it always did.

So instead of getting action from the top, Bahamonde continued down through the lower rings of bureaucratic hell to

FEMA's Regional Response Center in Denton, Texas, and the EOC in Baton Rouge, trying to round people up for his conference call. A few minutes after he began, a colleague called him back. There was some resistance to a conference call—was he sure things were that bad? After all, cable TV had been reporting all afternoon that the city had been spared the big hit.

"I've never been surer of anything in my life," Bahamonde replied testily.

Soon Bahamonde's new information was being BlackBerried around among FEMA and Homeland Security officials. It wasn't treated as cold fact, however, but as just one more among dozens of conflicting accounts. The public relations staffs—of which, of course, Bahamonde was a member—found it the most useful. At 8:27 p.m., Homeland Security public affairs official Brian Besanceney e-mailed a group of colleagues in Washington, including Chertoff's chief of staff, John Wood, saying, "the first (unconfirmed) reports they are getting from aerial surveys in New Orleans are far more serious than media reports are currently reflecting. Finding more extensive flooding and stranded people than they had originally thought—also a number of fires. FYI in case tomorrow's [situation reports] seem more 'severe.'"

A short while after Bahamonde began putting the word out, Nagin and about twenty-five staffers met to discuss options. The mood was somber, but businesslike. No one knew what was coming, what would become of the city—not to mention their careers, possessions, and even their lives. They agreed to request help from whoever could provide it and to focus on plugging the 17th Street breach. Bahamonde told Ebbert afterward that they should put together a plan, listing what they needed, and send it through channels—the governor's office on up to FEMA and Homeland Security. It was standard protocol: their plea might take longer to make its way to the top, but once it did Homeland Security could send in the cavalry quicker if they had a formal request. So Nagin signed off on a hastily assembled but comprehensive five-page list. It addressed dozens of topics—including the possibility of opening the Ernest N. Morial Convention Center on the waterfront to house some of the tens of thousands then being rescued. But the situation at the Superdome was at the top. In addition to food, water, and people from FEMA, city officials requested generators, portable lights, and an audiovisual system that could broadcast news and entertainment to the Dome, which now had nearly twenty thousand occupants.

The Coast Guard dropped Bobbie Moreau and her daughter, granddaughter, and three dogs at West Jefferson Medical Center in Marrero, south of New Orleans across the Mississippi River, at her request. Cassidy had been a preemie and was on a heart monitor. She seemed OK, but they wanted to have her checked out. They were left on the sidewalk outside the hospital, barefoot, with no money, credit cards, or ID.

Once Tasha took the baby inside, Bobbie collapsed on the sidewalk, holding the dogs. A woman approached and asked if she'd like to put her dogs in her grandmother's yard. It was across an elevated expressway, and the two of them carried the dogs underneath to the other side. Moreau walked back to the hospital. A guard barred her at the door. She waited until he wasn't looking, then snuck inside. Tasha and Cassidy were waiting for her. A hospital administrator told Bobbie that a bus would take them to a shelter. When they arrived, it was dark. The building had no power and no water. The toilets weren't working. A hundred people were crammed into a small room. But they stayed inside, not wanting the mosquitoes to get Cassidy. They settled down on the floor and tried to sleep.

As night fell, the Ratliffs were sitting on wooden seats in the bleachers of Chalmette High School, St. Bernard's principal emergency shelter. At ten a.m., they had been rescued by a guy in a fishing boat and taken over to the high school. Over the course of the day, more than three hundred people ended up there.

The high school was on high ground and the gym floor was raised even higher, so it was mostly dry. But conditions were bad. The air was wet and stifling. Evacuees had brought more than a hundred pets—dogs, cats, parrots, and other animals— and they were making a terrific racket, pissing and shitting on the floor because there was nowhere to go outside, the water being too high. The bathrooms had stopped working, and a closet and trash bucket were being used as a makeshift john. Once one bucket filled up, it was moved to a nearby room and replaced. As the evening wore on, things got increasingly surreal. A group of politicians led by local state senator Walter Boasso showed up and began making speeches.

"St. Bernard has been abandoned, but we'll help you," Boasso said, evoking the 1927 sellout. Then, as if they were at a political rally or an Elks Club gathering, he introduced all the other pols and officials with him to the crowd.

In the Eighth Ward, Loco Cooper and his neighbors began hearing boats buzzing on nearby streets around midafternoon. He tried flagging down the first one he saw with his orange vest, but it moved off. Then he spied some police and National Guardsmen at the edge of Interstate 10, only a block from his mother's house. They saw him and yelled for him to sit tight. A couple of hours later, as the sun was going down, a Coast Guard boat picked him up. He tossed his bag and stepped gingerly down into the boat, and it took him to a nearby freeway ramp. From there, he was trucked to the Superdome as night fell.

Cooper waited on line. His bag was searched and he was admitted. He was parched and hungry, and saw stacks upon stacks of bottled water.

"No, you can't have one," a guardsman told him. To get one, he had to stand in another line. After waiting for two hours, he finally got a water bottle and an MRE. He opened the packets and the smell disgusted him, so he ate only the crackers and cookies inside. Then he roamed around, looking for anyone he knew.

The Dome was quiet but scary, the crowd's discussions and murmuring making for a dull white noise. More and more people were milling around on the field, in the stands, in the hallways. The searches hadn't gotten all the weapons; Cooper saw guys carrying knives. He ducked into a bathroom, where he saw a guy shooting heroin into another man's vein. Cooper nodded matter-of-factly, then moved over to the sink and stripped off his clothes. He took an old shirt and a bar of soap out of his bag and washed the grime from the flood off. He felt better as he walked back out, and soon he ran into some of his neighbors. They were all frightened—there were so many people and so little law enforcement.

"Right now, there are all kinds of criminals around here," he told a friend. "We don't know what they are going to do, of if anybody can stop them. We got to keep an eye out for ourselves."

He made a pact with a bunch of acquaintances to stick together if things got bad. He laid a cardboard box on the floor of the hallway outside the stands and tried to get some sleep, though it wasn't easy. There were lots of conversations, the noise of thousands of footfalls, sometimes screaming.

The Greens, meanwhile, had been granted special treatment. It wasn't clear to them why—whether it was because two family members were dead, or if they had simply lucked out. When their truck pulled up at the Superdome, they were ushered past the masses and up to a skybox, where the National Guard had set up a special area for rescuees. They had a kitchen going, so there was hot food—fried shrimp, fried fish, fettucine. There were cots to sleep on. They were impressed and a little guilty, knowing that the great majority of people were making do with MREs below them. They felt like the house slaves lording it over the field slaves.

When Harvey Miller looked out the window in Lakeview late in the day, he saw what must have been an optical illusion: there was a flat pond of water stretching in all directions. Only the peaks and second floors of nearby houses were visible, and some trees and utility poles. The London Avenue canal, the source of all that water, looked to have disappeared under the surface somehow. There was no visible sign of a breach. Miller was mystified.

The mystery kept the gravity of the Millers' situation from sinking in. After all, the important thing was they were alive—albeit trapped. When they heard someone on their two-inch TV talking about having escaped to Baton Rouge, Harvey laughed. "Why did they leave?" he chuckled darkly. But as night fell, the neighborhood sank into pitch darkness. The only noise was the water lapping against the walls outside and mosquitoes buzzing in their ears. They put one of their three fluorescent lanterns on the windowsill, hoping someone would see it. Then, with the odd boredom that comes with waiting, they lay down on their cots and fell asleep.

When Jackson and Thevenot returned to the *Times-Picayune* building that night, they couldn't park in the garage because floodwaters had crept into it. The garage was the lowest spot in the paper's property and often flooded in rainstorms. They drove up onto a nearby overpass and parked there, then descended along a pedestrian walkway. The water at the bottom was waist-deep. That was also the occasional result of heavy rain, so they didn't think much about it and went into the building. Jackson went to sleep early in his corner of the photo lab, hoping to get a fresh start in the morning covering the beginning of the big cleanup.

Appearing on CNN's *Larry King Live* at eight o'clock central time, Brown painted a grim portrait of a ruined city, based largely on Bahamonde's eyewitness account. Yet he hedged on the question of levee breaches. "We've got some storm surges that have come across the levees," he said. "We have some—I'm not going call them breaches, but we have some areas where the lake and the rivers are continuing to spill over. The floodwaters are continuing to spill into those neighborhoods, so it's frankly going to get worse before it gets better."

Around nine p.m., Bahamonde finally got his conference call, briefing colleagues in Baton Rouge, Denton, and Washington. They seemed curiously unimpressed.

"Thanks, Marty—we already knew most of this information, but thanks for providing it," said Scott Wells, FEMA's deputy coordinating officer in Baton Rouge. This struck Bahamonde as peculiar, since as far as he knew, only a few Coast Guard 'copters had been up over the city to see the full scale of the disaster, and he'd been on one of them.

Ever since the first Gulf War, politicians, bureaucrats, and most people had relied heavily on cable news to bring them an accurate, instantaneous account of what was happening. But Katrina defied this strategy. The networks themselves were still trying to piece together a picture based on a kaleidoscope of water, mysterious geography, and fragmentary reports from the field. When they saw flooding, editors often didn't know what part of the city they were looking at.

At the Homeland Security Operations Center, Matthew Broderick, the marine brigadier general in command, arrived early in the evening and watched a TV report of people toasting their survival in the French Quarter. New Orleans's original high ground was one of the areas that did not flood.

"It led us to believe that the flooding may have been just in isolated incidents," Broderick said later. "It was being handled and it was being properly addressed because we were not seeing it."

Some of the reports Broderick was getting appeared to conflict—levees were breaching, levees were overtopped, the whole city was going under, only parts of it were submerged. Of course, all of these things were true—they were coming from different areas of the city. But, like the TV reporters, Broderick and his staff had limited knowledge of the complex topography of New Orleans. Anyone passingly familiar with it knew that the French Quarter was the area least likely to flood.

Broderick had been hoping for a clear, fact-based report from Brown. But Brown was ignoring Homeland Security and didn't contact Broderick's office. (Though if Broderick had been watching Larry King, he could have gotten Brown's input easily enough.) At one point, he called someone at FEMA and complained—but he was told that all he could expect were situation reports at twelve-hour intervals—once in the morning, once in the evening. Nevertheless, facts from Bahamonde's reports began filtering in later that night, and Broderick realized there were indeed serious problems, but he could not make a conclusion about how bad it was. He went home for the night.

Chapter 11

TUESDAY

AT ABOUT TWO A.M. Tuesday morning, a convoy of SUVs and trucks transporting a FEMA Disaster Medical Assistance Team pulled up in front of the Superdome. The Dome sat at the northern edge of downtown New Orleans, and over the previous few hours, floodwater had crept down Poydras Street and was pooling around the base of the enormous stadium, seeping into its basement. The water in the streets was about a foot deep, and the convoy's wheels kicked up a wake as it approached in the darkness. It had taken the team (made up of two dozen doctors, nurses, and paramedics from Albuquerque, New Mexico) four hours to travel from the city's border with Jefferson Parish, less than five miles away. That border was marked by the 17th Street canal, and Katrina had transformed it into the dividing line between a modest disaster and a world-class catastrophe.

On one side, the suburbs of Jefferson Parish looked ragged, with fallen trees, downed power lines, ripped billboards, and damaged roofs. Water had inundated part of Old Metairie, the parish's wealthy enclave. On the New Orleans side, the flood continued to spread and deepen. Seen from the air and in satellite images, the two sides were literally light and dark: the Jefferson side had the green, black, and gray signature of leafy subdivisions and strip malls; the New Orleans side a soupy brownish-black with flecks of color here and there. Crossing the

17th Street canal meant entering a nightmare landscape where normal routes were blocked, ordinary means of transport and communications did not work, institutions were falling apart, and, for most people, there was no escape.

Like most of the outside world, the medical team was only dimly aware of the deteriorating conditions in the city. Its medical director, Mark Shah, an assistant professor of emergency medicine at the University of New Mexico, sat in the front seat of an SUV, surreal scenes flashing by him in a dark blur. Shah had disaster experience, having served on emergency teams in several hurricanes, but he'd never seen anything like this. As they arrived at the New Orleans border, rendezvousing with a state police escort, he could just make out the tall buildings of downtown hulking ominously in the dark, only a few generator-powered lights dotting the void. Shah's team began to move painstakingly across the map, block by block. Before they could advance, the police truck in the lead would inch forward down a street. If it reached the end of the block and the next block looked clear, the entire convoy would move forward. If deep water, branches, or a fallen power line blocked the way, they'd try another route. All they could see was a confusing montage of wreckage and flood straight ahead of them, illuminated in the headlight beams. They zigzagged for hours across the broken cityscape, encountering nary a soul except for a solitary man struggling to wade out of town.

FEMA had called them up on Saturday, along with seven other DMATs, as they were known. Six trucks carrying the implements of a mobile emergency room, along with food and water for the team members, departed Albuquerque immediately. The rest of the team flew to Houston, where they waited out the storm at a hotel, then caravanned to Baton Rouge. After receiving Bahamonde's e-mails about deteriorating conditions, FEMA at least knew the Dome was a trouble spot. (Normally, after a formal request from local officials, assessment teams were sent in first to size up the situation and advise the DMATs on how to deploy. But FEMA never received a request out of New Orleans or Baton Rouge, so no advance assessments had been made, and the thwarted advance team was actually traveling with the New Mexico group.)

The medical workers had been dispatched to the Superdome to supplement another team from Oklahoma. When they finally reached their destination at around four a.m., they cooled their heels outside for a while as the National Guard officers inside tried to figure out exactly what to do with them. Eventually, they were directed to the basketball arena adjacent to the Dome.

The Dome was a brewing public health disaster. The number of patients with chronic health problems had exceeded expectations from the beginning, and the number of people inside had doubled in twenty-four hours, becoming a virtual city of twenty-thousand, overwhelmingly poor and African American. Some flood victims had picked up skin and eye irritations and were wheezing after soaking for hours in water laced with gasoline, oil, and a stew of household chemicals and garbage. Hundreds had lost their medication in the flood—blood pressure and asthma medicine, antiseizure and antipsychotic drugs, insulin—or simply run out, and were starting to suffer the consequences—breathing problems, fainting, heart trouble, seizures.

The New Mexico team staked out a hallway in the arena near the aerial walkway connecting it to the Superdome. Shah and about half of his crew went to sleep on cots—they'd been up almost twenty-four hours—while the rest began setting up equipment so they could start treating patients in earnest once morning arrived.

At five a.m., the Homeland Security Operations Center finally put out a memo confirming the 17th Street canal levee had, indeed, been breached and that most of the city was flooding.

When Marty Bahamonde—who had sent in his report and photo of the breach eleven hours earlier—woke up from his spot on the Superdome floor and went outside an hour later, the water was four to six feet deep in some places and continuing to rise. Some vehicles were floating around, nudging each other like bumper cars. Bahamonde recognized what the medical team had not: the throng inside would soon effectively be trapped, if they weren't already. There would be no easy transport out. Meanwhile, conditions would deteriorate further as the floodwater penetrated the Dome. Bahamonde messaged Bill Lokey in Baton Rouge and sent an e-mail to another colleague inquiring as to when Brown and Louisiana VIPs would be coming for a planned survey. "There will be no ground tour," he noted.

At six thirty a.m., Bill Quigley was sitting on a mattress pad on the floor of Memorial Medical Center, a hospital in the center of New Orleans, when his cell phone rang. It was a call from some friends in Haiti. A professor at New Orleans's Loyola University Law School and director of its legal clinic, Quigley was active in human rights causes and had recently represented a jailed dissident in Port-au-Prince.

"You're in our prayers—we're thinking of you," his friend signed off.

Quigley thought it a bit odd that the Haitians would be praying for Americans rather than the other way around, but he didn't give it too much thought. He figured the worst was over.

Quigley and his wife, Debbie Dupre, had spent two days at Memorial, where Dupre worked as a nurse in the oncology department. The hospital was a small campus of interconnected buildings, located smack in the middle of the New Orleans bowl near the intersection of two principal thoroughfares: Napoleon Avenue, which ran north–south, bisecting the city's crescent, and Claiborne Avenue, which followed the river's curve east–west. Dupre was on a volunteer emergency crew tending to patients who couldn't be easily moved, and as a spouse Quigley had been invited to ride out the storm with her. All told, the hospital held about two hundred patients and a thousand more staff and family members, spread out on different floors. (Some patients had gone out in a helicopter airlift Sunday. Those who remained included cancer patients, elderly people, and pregnant women.)

The pair bunked down along with a shifting crew of two or

three others on foam pads on the floor of a standard hospital room on the third floor. As the storm came through early Monday, the walls shuddered, rattling the blood pressure monitor and ear scope in their housings. At 5:10 a.m. Monday, the city had gone dark, and the hospital's emergency generators kicked on after a minute. Quigley arose and walked downstairs to the lobby. Before his eyes, windows along the crosswalk to the adjoining building began exploding out of their casings, one after the next. He'd been hearing booms and crashes during the night, but now the commotion reached a crescendo. As it did so, broken glass skimmed across the wet floor. Water blew into the lobby and the wind whistled. As he climbed back upstairs, he could hear the sound of a waterfall in the elevator shaft.

Tuesday morning, Quigley decided it was time to head home. He packed up his duffel bag and prepared to walk home, about two miles away. His wife would stay on duty at the hospital. But at the last minute, hospital staffers asked him to stay and help out. There was water in the street—not a huge amount yet—and it wasn't clear when they'd be able to evacuate the patients. Quigley moved to the lobby to take phone calls and help guard the front doors.

Shortly after Quigley began his new duties, the hospital's principal emergency generators—which were supposed to last a week of continuous operation—suddenly died. Computers and medical equipment continued to function on backups, but the air-conditioning and most lights went off.

There had been water in the streets on and off since the day before, but it rose higher as the morning wore on and soon the hospital buildings were surrounded. The basement—where everyone kept their pets—started to fill up. Quigley ran up and down the stairs in the darkness, helping to evacuate dogs and cats to the parking garage.

Midmorning, Mike Brown and a delegation of Louisiana politicians—Governor Blanco and senators Mary Landrieu (a Democrat) and David Vitter (a Republican)—took a National Guard Black Hawk helicopter up over the city to gauge the situ-

238 / JOHN MCQUAID AND MARK SCHLEIFSTEIN

ation with their own eyes. The rising summer sun cast light over a huge man-made lake, with levee walls, rooftops, trees, utility poles, and highways peaking above the surface. The quickest way in and out—the interstate—was flooded on the west side, wrecked on the east. Water extended almost to downtown. From the Black Hawk, the politicians could see people using axes to chop their way out of attics, mothers cradling babies on rooftops, thousands clustered along elevated roadways, waiting, bodies floating. Only the French Quarter, the central business district, and areas extending out from the river's crescent were still dry.

In outlying areas, things were worse. The Lower Ninth Ward and all of St. Bernard were submerged. Beleaguered survivors were gathering on the river levee and at the St. Bernard port facility, the Chalmette slip. Farther south, past Violet, Katrina had obliterated entire towns, leaving nothing but shards of lumber and piles of debris.

When the helicopter circled downtown and landed on the helipad outside the Superdome, Blanco looked across at the tarmac next to the stadium. The National Guard had let some people out for air, and they were milling around in the heat. There was no way she could easily reach them—the helipad was separated from the Dome, and there was water below. They didn't look happy, and she wasn't sure what the prospects were for getting them out quickly. Blanco figured she better come back later for a visit.

Brown, Blanco, Vitter, and Landrieu met with Nagin, Ebbert, and Compass in the conference room of the small cinder-block-and-steel office next to the helipad. Nagin went back over the list he and his aides had drawn up the night before. Nagin appeared tired but clearheaded as he led the meeting, ticking off the prepared list of things the city needed. Under the circumstances, Brown and Blanco were both impressed with the sometimes mercurial mayor's composure. The main goal, everyone agreed, should be getting people out of the city. But there was no clear plan for doing that. Not only were most escape routes cut off, but the pool of rescued people was growing exponentially. The Coast Guard and state agencies had just launched rescue boat flotillas, but Coast Guard and National Guard helicopters had continued to pick people up during the night, dropping them on levees and along highway overpasses and ramps—anywhere above the waterline, basically. At the Superdome, the rescue helicopters were landing every few minutes, disgorging additional people, adding to the problems inside. Meanwhile, the Dome's emergency generators—providing limited light and ventilation—had nearly busted when water poured into the basement. Guardsmen had gone down into the underground flood and sandbagged the generators, but nobody knew if that would hold. If it didn't, there was no telling how the massive crowd would react.

In Washington, Michael Chertoff was boarding a plane for Atlanta, where he was due to meet with Michael Leavitt, the Secretary of Health and Human Services. The topic: the threat of avian flu. (A deadly influenza strain had been spreading steadily through the world's bird populations, and scientists feared it could mutate, begin spreading from human to human, and turn into a catastrophic global pandemic. But only fifty-four people, infected through direct contact with birds, had died so far.)

At about seven a.m. Washington time, an aide had printed out and handed Chertoff the memo from the Homeland Security Operations Center describing the 17th Street canal levee breach. (The Secretary of Homeland Security generally avoided using e-mail.) But the significance of the breach still wasn't clear to Chertoff, and he saw no reason to interrupt his trip, which had been planned for months with the staff at the Centers for Disease Control. Brown and FEMA were in charge in Louisiana, he figured; there was nothing much he could do that was not being done already.

When the avian flu briefing concluded around midday, Chertoff made a point of heading to FEMA's Atlanta regional office for a Katrina update, where staffers filled him in on the latest. He was dismayed to hear that things were, apparently, spinning out of control. At last, he realized something was going

on in New Orleans that demanded his full attention. On his return flight to Washington that afternoon, Chertoff began drafting
language for a letter officially invoking the National Response
Plan.

At the *Times-Picayune* building Tuesday morning, Schleifstein
got out of his sleeping bag and stumbled down the hall to the
room where a bunch of computers were running off the generator. He looked at electronic images of the day's newspaper.

CATASTROPHIC, a big headline read, STORM SURGE SWAMPS
9TH WARD, ST. BERNARD; LAKEVIEW LEVEE BREACH THREATENS TO
INUNDATE CITY.

The paper had not seen print—the presses could not run on
generator power, and in any case there was no way to distribute
the paper. But the *Times-Picayune* Web site, nola.com (actually
a separate entity run by Advance.net, the Internet branch of the
paper's parent company, Advance Publications) did run on generator power, and it had been getting upwards of thirty million
hits per day. Around the country, evacuees and anyone interested were calling up the site and particularly the hurricane
blog, where reporters continued to post stories, press releases,
announcements, and stray observations.

"Come down to the cafeteria *now!*" someone yelled. But before he could get down the escalator, people began streaming
back up. Ashton Phelps, the publisher, normally crisply composed and a bit rumpled, was running from room to room.

"Get out now! You cannot stay in the building!" he shouted.

The flood from the breaches was rising. It was about three
or four feet deep, approaching the top of the steps to the first
floor where the presses were housed. It was just over the tires of
the paper's big delivery trucks. If they waited any longer, the
staff, in all probability, would be trapped in a useless facility and
have to wait for rescue from the rooftop like tens of thousands
of others. And then the newsroom picked up rumors of unrest at
the flooded Orleans Parish Prison, only three blocks away.

Phelps and editor Jim Amoss had ginned up a plan. The
newspaper's interrupted publication would continue for at least

another day. That was a grievous blow to any newspaper, which—somewhat quaintly in an era of continuously updated Internet news—still prided itself on printing hard copies every day, year in and year out. The plan called for the staff to disperse to locations in Baton Rouge, eighty-five miles northwest, and Houma, sixty miles southwest.

A few minutes later, as Phelps was ordering the photo staff to get downstairs, photographer Alex Brandon strode into the newsroom. He was soaking wet, having just swum over from the NOPD headquarters, adjacent to the prison, across Interstate 10 from the paper. There, he was embedded with a SWAT team and had spent the previous day on search and rescue missions. Like many photographers who love to court danger in search of the perfect image, Brandon was a bit of a cowboy. He had shot the Tuesday paper's searing image, run across six columns, of police officers clad in black body armor, chest-deep in water, pulling an elderly man out of his house.

"Where's my cards?" he asked Ted Jackson. He wanted a bunch of digital photo cards he'd left with Jackson so he could keep shooting rescues.

"Everybody to the trucks!" Phelps hollered. "Go! Go! Go!"

"The trucks are useless. The water's too deep. I swam here!" Brandon yelled back at him.

Flustered, Phelps said: "We're getting out of here. We're going to leave right now!"

Jackson pulled Brandon aside and told him to shut up, that Phelps was thinking of everyone in the building, from babies to elderly parents of staffers. Staying was not an option.

As the *Times-Picayune* delivery trucks that could escape crossed the Crescent City Connection from downtown New Orleans to the dry west bank of the Mississippi River, Schleifstein looked over the city out of the open rear of the truck. He saw a strange panorama of water and rooftops shimmering in the heat. Smoke rose from scattered fires. Hundreds, maybe thousands, of people were gathering on the high ground along the river and highway on-ramps, some starting to congregate at the convention center, a sprawling, mile-long structure abutting the base of the bridge at the southern end of downtown's warehouse district.

The trucks stopped at the paper's West Bank bureau and staffers raided it for supplies—laptops, notebooks, sodas, and snacks in its refrigerator. At that point, David Meeks, the sports editor, was struck by the incongruity: there were thousands of people in New Orleans, and there was still some dry land. It was still possible to report, and it was each reporter's duty. So why were they leaving?

(Jackson, in fact, had already decided to tough it out. He had found a small rowboat in the hallway just before the last truck departed the newspaper building, hopped into it, and managed to hand-paddle his way over to the ramp where his car was—passing Brandon along the way, wading neck-deep through the water, the bag of photo cards between his clenched teeth. Jackson took the plastic oars from the raft in the bed of his truck, then set off across the urban sea.)

Meeks was known for his drive and easy self-assurance, and he made a pitch to his bosses to go back into the city. Editor Jim Amoss was skeptical at first. "How are you going to eat?" he asked. "How are you going to file?"

Though he didn't know the answers, Meeks told him the situation was not as insurmountable as it seemed: people would help them; journalists in war zones had faced worse obstacles to reporting and filing and managed to come through.

"I'm a resourceful guy," he declared.

"I know you are," Amoss said, a half smile creeping across his face. "Do it. Who do you need?"

The newly deputized *Times-Picayune* New Orleans bureau team—including Meeks, Thevenot, reporters Mike Perlstein, Bruce Nolan, and Doug MacCash, music critic Keith Spera, photographer John McCusker, and editorial page editor Terry Troncale and her deputy Dante Ramos—took a truck and went back over the river, while Schleifstein and the rest of the staff headed west. (Others who were stationed elsewhere during the previous day, including reporters Trymaine Lee and Jim Varney, later joined up with the New Orleans crew.) As they tallied up their supplies, they better understood the gamble they were taking: they had water to last only a few days, some snacks raided from vending machines, a few reporter's notebooks, and one laptop.

Meeks and company turned first down Tchoupitoulas Street, next to the river levee, and drove into the parking lot of a Wal-Mart. The doors had been opened, apparently by police and firefighters, whose vehicles filled the parking lot. Expecting to see an organized giveaway of essential supplies, they found chaos instead. Hundreds of people were looting the store. Some had formed lines and were passing iPods and TVs out the door to waiting vans outside—though it was not clear if they'd ever be of use if there was no electricity and no way out of the city.

"Free samples! Free samples!" a man hollered after smashing a jewelry case. Some cops and firefighters were loading up their own shopping carts. One had a twenty-seven-inch flat-screen TV and a Compaq computer. Some cops stood looking on, not participating, bemused. Radio communications had gone out. They couldn't summon backup or consult higher-ups. There seemed some risk the scene might tip from bedlam into a full-scale riot if they intervened.

The newspaper group took some basic items out to the truck: food, clothing, a camping stove. But they immediately recognized that if they kept the stuff, they'd be looters, too. "We toyed with taking inventory of the goods later and sending Wal-Mart a check but ultimately took a unanimous vote to immediately return every item, even if it only meant someone else would take it," Thevenot wrote.

As they were concluding the ethics debate, McCusker shot a photo of a cop carrying a pile of DVDs. *"Times-Picayune's over there taking pictures!"* one man yelled. "Let's go take care of business!" The journalists hopped into the truck and drove—they weren't sure where.

At the northwestern entrance to New Orleans from suburban Metairie, where Interstate 10 and I-610 split, officials from the Coast Guard, the state Wildlife and Fisheries Department, state police, the state health department, and other agencies set up a rescue boat launch. By midmorning, dozens of small craft were making sorties off the north side of the highway. They were operating on the fly, but their movements were choreographed according to the model developed in the Hurricane Pam exercise: rescue people, move them to an intermediate high ground where they could receive emergency medical care, then evacuate them.

Kimberly Foster, a petty officer with the Coast Guard station in New Orleans, was one of three people doing rescues in a small johnboat. They ran north, toward Lakeview, floating over cemeteries.

"You'd go down one street, you could see people in every roof," Foster later recalled. "At West End [near the mouth of the 17th Street canal], we picked up people off of each and every house. In some areas, we'd go off on one road, and there would be nobody there. One house we went by, there was a guy hanging out of the second-story window, and three guys had a barbecue grill up on the roof. They were fine, they didn't want to be rescued.

"We went to a church, and there were a few people that needed medical assistance. One guy in his eighties had diabetes and had had no medication for two days. We had a guy who was in a wheelchair and was so dehydrated that the texture of your fingers would rip his skin."

As the day wore on, more and more of the rescued walked the mile along I-10 from the split into Metairie to the Causeway Boulevard cloverleaf—something like seven thousand people by the end of the day. The boats were bringing them back faster than they could be trucked out of there, and the modest stores of food and water that FEMA and other agencies had brought were exhausted. The crowd, under the stifling summer sun, was getting restive and had no immediate hope of escape.

Bobbie Moreau and Tasha wanted out of the shelter they'd been dropped at on the west bank of Jefferson Parish. Cassidy was wheezing and coughing, and they needed to get her to some-place quiet and cool—if possible. "I am not going to let my baby die," Tasha declared, and they tried to leave. But the Jefferson Parish sheriff's deputies guarding them told them that would be impossible: no one was allowed to leave. The conversation turned tense. Soon the cops were yelling at them, telling them if they tried to go, they'd be arrested.

"Do what you want to do—I have nothing left anyway," Moreau told them.

Just then, a scuffle broke out behind them, and Bobbie and Tasha took the opportunity to slip out past the distracted cops. They kept walking without looking back. On and on they trod in the stifling heat, unsure of where to go next. They were a pathetic sight: shoeless, dirty, and suppressing sobs as they trudged along. Bobbie asked a woman unloading furniture off a truck if she might give them a lift somewhere. She said no. Bobbie asked if they could go inside the woman's house so Cassidy could cool off. She said no. They walked on. After a while longer, they finally managed to hitch a ride to a friend's house nearby, riding in the back of a pickup truck.

The friend had evacuated, but Bobbie broke a window and let them all into the house, where they comforted Cassidy, took showers, and raided his cupboard for some canned food. Bobbie scooped some quarters out of a drawer, then went out and called her nephew in Arkansas on a nearby pay phone. He broke down when he heard her voice.

"I tried to come down there to see you, but I could not get into New Orleans," he said. If they could get out, he could come get them.

Fortuitously, their absent host had left the keys to his pickup on the bar. The truck's tank was empty, but Bobbie managed to siphon some gasoline from his boat in the driveway. After she wrote him a note explaining the break-in, they donned some of his boxers and T-shirts, the only clothes that fit them. They got into the truck and drove away, over the Sunshine Bridge upriver. Her nephew picked them up in Prairieville, outside of Baton Rouge, and they drove north—far away from the Gulf of Mexico.

Katrina had reduced much of the Corps's sprawling levee system to ruins. Forty years of work had been undone in a mere six hours. Miles of the massive earthen levees protecting St. Bernard and the Lower Ninth Ward were simply gone. Floodwalls were breached in dozens of places, their concrete and steel components bent, broken, and scattered into the backyards they had once protected. Floodgates had been ripped from their hinges. The city was once again open to the sea, now more exposed than at any point in its history.

Out near the lakefront, engineers from the Corps, the Orleans Levee District, and the state Department of Transportation and Development had met at the 17th Street canal breach at 7:15 a.m. to take stock of the most urgent problem they faced. Lake water was still gushing through the breach, churning white. The flood level was just a couple of feet short of the top of the floodwall—they estimated it was twelve feet above sea level—meaning the water in Lakeview might be twenty-five feet deep in some places. Mike Stack, an engineer with the Transportation Department, lived only a few blocks away. He knew instantly his house had been destroyed.

Later that morning, their bosses helicoptered over the site. "What struck me were the twin obstacles of fixing the breach: lack of communication and extreme flooding, which made transportation of equipment to and from the breach nearly impossible," said Johnny Bradberry, Louisiana's transportation secretary.

The agencies began discussing what to do. Incredibly, none had an emergency contingency for sealing levee breaches. Such an absence of planning was the custom with river levee crevasses, where all efforts went into prevention; once that battle was lost and a breach occurred, it was almost always too large and too dangerous to repair before the water level subsided. That scenario applied, more or less, to the massive breaches along the Industrial Canal and in St. Bernard; there was no way to fix them quickly. But at 17th Street, the breach might be small enough to repair in a tight time frame; if the flow could be stanched, entire neighborhoods might be saved.

Colonel Wagenaar and his engineers from the Corps concluded the best approach was to block off the canal with sheet piling driven easily enough across a stretch north of the breach. Doing so would protect the entire canal with a minimum of effort—important if other floodwall sections along the canal's five-mile length were also close to collapse. But the local agencies, which also included the West Jefferson Levee District across the river, tapped for help and supplies, opposed Wagenaar's plan, fearing they'd lose the ability to pump water out. Instead, they wanted to seal the breach itself. The decades-old interagency dispute over flood-control strategy—gates vs. levees—had begun again.

Exasperated, Wagenaar and Major General Don Riley, the Corps's director of civil works, yielded to the state and local agencies. (Legally, the responsibility for such repairs did belong to the local levee district in whose territory the break had occurred, though the Orleans District's equipment and supplies were under water at its Lakefront Airport base.) It wasn't long before they realized that sealing the gap would be a significant engineering challenge. It was not yet clear how deep a hole had been scoured at the breach, or how long it would take to block it off. (Its bottom was later determined to lie thirty-six feet below sea level.) Levee patches also had a tendency to leak.

The Orleans Levee District did have some extra-large sandbags in a nearby maintenance yard. When filled, they weighed three thousand pounds. But getting them into the breach was terribly cumbersome. Prisoners were conscripted to start filling them, and a single helicopter obtained from the Texas Air National Guard to drop them. The 'copter would hover over the breach, the wash from its rotors kicking up whitecaps and spray, while its crew released the sling holding the sandbag. Each time, the bag hit the water with a loud crash—then disappeared beneath the surface. Meanwhile, coordinating the effort was exceedingly difficult. Phone service was spotty, and state Transportation Department engineer Mike Stack and his colleagues resorted to using a functioning landline at a house in nearby Metairie to call his wife's cell phone. She would then call his bosses at the EOC in Baton Rouge and relay their messages back to him. By late in the day, only twelve sandbags had been dumped into the breach, to no visible effect. All the while, the city continued to flood.

In Baton Rouge, meanwhile, FEMA was foundering at its core mission: delivering aid and support to disaster victims. The bureaucratic minuets it had once excelled at were not happening. "In every disaster, you go where the state has established its hub of operations and you put your [Federal Coordinating Officer] on the ground there, and the FCO works with the state emergency manager. And they among themselves decide what they need, who's going to do it, and how are we going to get it done," Mike Brown recalled. "We were never able to do that. . . . I don't know if it was a cultural thing, or if they hadn't been hit in so long [in Louisiana], they just weren't ready for it; but you just couldn't get anybody to sit down in the conference rooms to say 'Where are we, what's happening, what do we do next?' It was just surreal. I felt like I was grasping at straws."

Budget cuts had decimated FEMA's Emergency Response Teams, which set up offices and coordinated aid dispersals. In the Clinton era, each team had more than one hundred members; now most had twenty-five. Speed was essential to emergency response, but half of the FEMA team assigned to Baton Rouge had not even arrived before Katrina did. The rest arrived later, but there still weren't enough people to staff the office round the clock. One employee assigned to process requests worked twenty-hour days. All were crammed into a tight space with state employees, who were working double shifts themselves.

Though they were literally side by side, the two groups inhabited different bureaucratic universes. The state had one outmoded computerized system for processing requests for help from state and local officials; FEMA had another equally balky one, and the two systems were incompatible. (Brown's bosses at Homeland Security had turned down his request for a new logistics computer system.)

Countless absurdities resulted. State workers didn't bother to sort out the frivolous requests from the life-or-death ones; as a result, FEMA ended up with a mountain of unprioritized requests and frequently got bogged down figuring out how—or whether—to respond. The New Orleans police department wanted four hundred M-4 rifles, twenty-five thousand rounds of ammunition, fifteen hundred pairs of black military boots in various sizes, and two hundred Crown Victoria police cruisers. The city fire department asked for ten golf carts for firefighters to use at Zephyr Field (home of the Zephyrs, the AAA farm team for the Washington Nationals), where FEMA was staging supplies. Mayor Nagin's office requested a single bus to go to Shreveport (the reason unclear) and portable air conditioners, and the Louisiana Department of Social Services wanted the federal government to call a cab to transport somebody from a hospital to a shelter.

Snafus like those turned the EOC into a frantic, stressful, maddening place, churning and going nowhere. Even the most basic and important organizational efforts, like getting all the principals sitting around a table to share information and agree on a common course of action, weren't happening. The cramped conditions compounded the problem. Meetings were held mostly on the fly, in corridors, the only place where there was enough room.

That's not to say nothing was happening. Just enough forward motion was under way to provide some glimmers of hope. Though the different agencies were not coordinating their activities, search and rescue was proceeding apace. Louisiana officials had sent out a blizzard of requests for help to other states, invoking Emergency Management Assistance Compacts— agreements providing for supplementary National Guard troops and other assistance—and that help had begun to arrive. Texas, for example, had sent a thirty-five-member water rescue team with five boats on Monday; on Tuesday, six Black Hawk helicopters with their own trained rescue crews arrived. And FEMA had managed to resupply the Superdome with MREs and water the previous night, banishing, at least momentarily, the specter of twenty thousand starving, thirsty, dying residents.

But the biggest problem—evacuating approximately one hundred thousand people from the city—was still nobody's responsibility and beyond everybody's capabilities. There were plenty of plans for prestorm evacuations. But nobody in any agency had ever wrestled with a *poststorm* evacuation, let alone one to be staged in the middle of a flood. Brown's promised buses had not arrived. In fact, FEMA still hadn't routed the request to the U.S. Department of Transportation. Blanco asked Brown again, and was again told they were coming. Aware of the worsening conditions at the Superdome and receiving more reports of growing crowds at the Interstate cloverleaf and other drop-off points, Blanco ordered her own staff to look into how to procure buses. It didn't look promising. Nagin had told them the city buses were under water. In fact, there were two hundred Regional Transit Authority buses sitting on high ground on the riverfront at the Poland Street Wharf, but RTA officials had not informed the city.

Around noon, a FEMA team led by Phil Parr helicoptered into the Dome. Parr was another one of Brown's trusted utility guys—he'd tried to get into the city before the storm but had only gotten as far as Houston. He had long experience as a firefighter and administrator with the New York City fire department and was the sort of man who came in, took over, and knocked heads together. He had been given the job to create a key node in the federal response effort, setting up a makeshift headquarters for running operations to outlying parishes.

He hit trouble immediately. Parr had expected to operate out of Red October, a high-tech mobile communications center with thirty computer workstations that traveled on the back of a tractor-trailer. With satellite phones and Internet capability, it would enable him to knit together a makeshift network and let people reliably communicate. But Red October was still at Barksdale Air Force Base in Shreveport in northern Louisiana—a six-hour drive away. FEMA officials had tried ordering the vehicle to Baton Rouge and then to New Orleans—but the request was countermanded by FEMA headquarters because Brown had reserved it. Now, there was no way to get it to the Dome. It might be able to get through the water, but it wouldn't be able to maneuver around all the debris. And FEMA's smaller communications vehicles would likely end up swamped.

As a result, the communications failure proved almost insurmountable, rendering Parr's job momentarily irrelevant. E-mail and text messaging worked sporadically. The National Guard's four telephone lines at the Superdome worked sometimes but were only available after the guard got through with them. Even when officials in New Orleans got a phone, they couldn't call out easily. It was impossible to reach Washington. It was just as difficult to reach Baton Rouge, where Brown and Blanco were. The entire state disaster apparatus was a communications black hole.

They had some luck reaching the FEMA regional office in Denton, Texas, so they routed their calls through there. Through that route, Parr managed to contact people in Baton Rouge exactly once Tuesday. In a meeting with Nagin and his people at the Hyatt, city Homeland Security Director Terry Ebbert told him that they were having trouble closing the 17th Street breach. They had suspended operations as they tried to figure out what to do. It also appeared that the water in the Dome basement was close to overflowing the sandbags around the generators. In fact, Ebbert said, it was about an inch from the top.

Parr miraculously raised the state EOC on a telephone at the Dome and relayed the city's requests for help to his bosses. He said the Dome might be dark soon—very troubling news— and the city was continuing to go under.

Dr. Louis Trachtman, sixty-six, an official with the state's Department of Health and Hospitals, had reported to the Dome Sunday evening after failing to get out of New Orleans on time. He was working triage with special-needs patients. By Tuesday morning, the heat and odor problems in the Superdome were so bad that officials decided to move the special-needs group to the arena, where the FEMA teams had set up and were treating those with more urgent medical problems.

A growing sense of paranoia had gripped those guarding the Dome population. They had heard reports of looting and snipers outside, and rumors of rape and murder inside were beginning to spread.

"The guardsmen told us it won't be any safer over there because there were so many entrances to the building on different levels that they couldn't promise us security," Trachtman said. "But the air was better and there was more light, more windows. So we got all the patients out." To get to the arena, a third of the four hundred special-needs patients had to be carried, a third were taken in wheelchairs, and a third walked on their own. One of the helpers was a nine-year-old boy. The patients' conditions and needs were jotted down on scraps of paper.

Someone opened one of the emergency doors, setting off a piercing alarm. The alarms operated on twelve-hour batteries, and after some discussion they agreed to try to disarm it. Nearby, Shah's FEMA team had unloaded its trucks and set up generators for its own equipment, including heaters for people with hypothermia. Trachtman asked one of the medical teams for a screwdriver for the alarm and was given a multiblade utility knife. He and some others went to work to silence it. It took two hours.

Outside, James Seaberry, a forty-six-year-old New Orleans police officer, was starting to get scared. In a twenty-year career, Seaberry had been an instructor at the police academy on community relations and worked in the Sixth District, which included the infamous Desire Housing Project, since torn down. Since he'd awakened early Tuesday and discovered a huge moat around the Dome, he'd heard the rumors, seen the strain in people's faces. As he patrolled outside, he did the math.

"I know we've got thirty thousand to forty thousand [in fact, it was closer to twenty thousand] people evacuated here from their homes and all we've got are sixty police officers and not that many military personnel," he recalled. "And the police officers had to find some sort of refuge to protect themselves. So we all made a little camp between Macy's and the Dome, and we wouldn't let civilians in that area." Inside that private zone—on an elevated walkway between the two buildings—they'd be safe from the anarchy they believed was about to erupt.

President Bush, meanwhile, continued with scheduled, artfully choreographed events that had nothing to do with the expanding crisis. Tuesday morning, in front of a group of veterans in San Diego, with navy ships crisscrossing behind him in the mist, Bush noted the relief efforts, then awkwardly segued into his theme for the day:

"As we deliver relief to our citizens to the south, our troops are defending all our citizens from threats abroad."

His speech marked the sixtieth anniversary of V-J Day, drawing parallels between American efforts to rebuild Japan and the struggle in Iraq.

After the speech, press secretary Scott McClellan told reporters that after flying back to Crawford later that day, Bush would depart for Washington the following morning, where he would chair a meeting of Cabinet officers on the storm. Despite the history-making drama of a president cutting short his vacation to manage a national crisis, McClellan's responses to reporters' questions were as obtuse and nonresponsive as they always were. Asked if the federal response to Katrina was bigger or different from previous ones, he didn't answer directly, saying only that it was "one of the most devastating storms in our nation's history" and that the White House was focused on saving lives. Asked if the president would designate a single point person to be in charge of relief, as Coolidge had done with Hoover in 1927, McClellan noted that "Joe Hagin has been very involved in it."

The White House aides were hoping the announcement would convey the image of Bush in action, but this impression was quickly undone by what was happening backstage. There, country singer Mark Wills gave Bush a guitar emblazoned with the presidential seal, and Bush made a show of playing it. A reporter snapped a photo that moved on newswires and then spawned multiple copies across the Internet.

Bush's jocularity in the face of a dire emergency on American soil struck many as bizarre. It earned an instantaneous backlash, as liberal bloggers began denouncing him for strumming away while New Orleans burned. TV pundits followed suit soon afterward, wondering why he was so far away and apparently disengaged. The president's role in any national crisis is part operational, part inspirational, and Bush seemed to be flunking at both. The striking image of Bush speaking out from the rubble of 9/11 was being supplanted by images of Bush on vacation, reading rotelike statements of reassurance as people died in New Orleans attics.

At a midafternoon press conference at the Baton Rouge EOC, Blanco and her colleagues—including the two senators and FEMA officials Bill Lokey and Scott Wells—tried to put a brave face on the response. But at times they misstepped, as when David Vitter attempted to put minds at ease about the flooding.

"In the metropolitan area in general, in the huge majority of areas, it's not rising at all," Vitter said. "It's the same or it may be lowering slightly. In some parts of New Orleans, because of the 17th Street breach, it may be rising and that seemed to be the case in parts of downtown. I don't want to alarm everybody that, you know, New Orleans is filling up like a bowl. That's just not happening." While technically true—the city was not filling up to the rim of the levees—it only added to the flood of contradictory information.

As the day wore on at Memorial Medical Center, the water pressure dropped suddenly, and the toilets on the uppermost three floors stopped working. People arriving at the hospital in boats, seeking shelter, were turned away. The hospital corridors, which had seemed at least seminormal just a few hours earlier with the sounds of brisk footfalls and chats, got very quiet. As lunch was served, people took turns crying—nurses, doctors, patients, and children. As doctors talked to each patient one on one to triage them for an evacuation that no one was sure was coming, a voice announced via loudspeaker that the water was getting so high it would soon wipe out all backup generators and electrical equipment—including ventilators, incubators, and other life-sustaining machines.

Memorial did not have helicopters at its disposal. It would

have to rely on the Coast Guard, National Guard, and army, and administrators had been frantically calling, trying to evacuate the sickest people. But it wasn't clear what would happen with everybody else. Coast Guard protocol, for example, dictated that only people in immediate danger—that is, people exposed to the elements—were candidates for rescue. There was no contingency for people trapped in appalling circumstances— but still relatively safe.

The doctors separated people from their families, directing the sickest patients up to the helipad on the roof to await evacuation. Doctors and nurses carried babies, many in incubators, downstairs; one doctor held two infants in his arms. The ordinary route into the parking garage was blocked, so the staff passed the incubators and patients—some being hand-ventilated, others accompanied by IVs and heavy oxygen tanks— on stretchers and in sheet slings through a hole that had been knocked in a wall on the second floor to volunteers on the other side. There, patients were put in the back of a truck or an SUV and run up to the eighth floor of the garage, near the helipad.

Starting that evening, help finally did arrive. Helicopters started carrying off the intensive-care patients—with the exception of three ill people who had signed DNR (Do Not Resuscitate) forms. As the evening wore on, several code blues sounded over the still-working PA system. A couple and their two children paddled up to the hospital in a boat, and a man acting as a guard— with a weapon—told them to move along. The man grew angry. He started pleading for shelter.

"You can leave your children here, but you can't stay," the guard told him.

Speechless, the man paddled off, taking his family with him.

Blanco helicoptered back to the Superdome late that afternoon with her husband, Raymond, a genial college administrator known as "Coach" from his days coaching high school football in Texas and then NCAA football in Louisiana. She wanted to talk to the people there, see how they were, give them some hope—though she still didn't know how to get them out. There were no media accompanying them, and the Blancos waded into the crowd on the walkway near the helipad.

People started telling them their stories. They complained of long lines, the heat, the stink inside. One woman complained she had been separated from her husband and children; during her rescue, they had run out of room in the boat. A father held his child up to the governor's face. "I want to bathe my baby," he said, "but there's no fresh water in here."

Inside, Loco Cooper was ending his day as it began: with a two-hour wait on a line to get an MRE and water. In between, he'd fought growing fear and boredom, occasionally wandering outside. (At first, the guardsmen opened the doors only reluctantly, but they soon realized they had to release their charges from their confinement to get fresh air. Any remaining hesitation disappeared when a toxic odor, bad as tear gas, wafted through the Dome, making thousands gag.) Inside the Dome, many people lay sprawled on the concrete floors, sleeping or unconscious, some obviously needing medical attention. As Cooper was walking along the gangway on one of his sojourns, he accidentally kicked the foot of one of these prone figures.

"Sorry!" he said. "Are you all right?" No response. He nudged the guy's leg again. No response. He knelt down and tried shaking the legs. Nothing: the guy appeared to be dead. Cooper got up and quickly moved on.

Cooper carried his radio with him and let people listen to the news. It didn't sound good. The mayor, governor, and other top officials had finally realized they didn't have a way to get people out of the Dome. And people wanted out.

Craig and Cindy Ratliff, meanwhile, were on a ferry to nowhere, out in the middle of the Mississippi in the darkness.

Hours before, some National Guardsmen had come to Chalmette High School, in St. Bernard Parish southeast of New Orleans, and asked for volunteers to go to the levee to help set up a shelter. Craig was turned down at first for being too old— he was twenty-nine, and they were looking only for people eighteen to twenty-five—but they took him on the next round. Once there, he helped move pallets around in a warehouse at the Chalmette slip, the main port facility in St. Bernard, to clear space for people to sleep.

Eventually, the National Guardsmen announced that a ferry would be leaving soon and asked for volunteers. After praying, Craig figured he couldn't take the chance, and he started walking back into Chalmette. It was dry for a while, but soon he was wading chest-deep.

It was dark when he reached the back door of the gym. Most of the crowd had already left. Others were packing up.

"If you're going to the Chalmette slip, you're going to have to walk. If you're going to go, you better go tonight," a woman who'd been sitting near them told him. He sighed. He would have to turn around and march back.

Cindy was gone, but he knew she had maybe the only working flashlight in the place, so he followed the line of people slogging slowly through the water and made his way to the front as they came onto dry land—sure enough, she was leading the way. They embraced and kept going.

From the courthouse, they made their way to a ferry terminal where they were guided onto a boat and told it was going across the river to Algiers, opposite the French Quarter. This was the first they'd heard of Algiers as a destination, but it was dry, so they weren't going to argue.

A ferry ride from St. Bernard to Algiers usually takes about fifteen minutes. But this one took more than twice that long. Told upon arrival to keep the St. Bernard people in St. Bernard—Algiers couldn't handle them—the people in the boat turned around and made for the Chalmette slip instead. Waving their flashlights, the Ratliffs led the evacuees tentatively forward in the darkness, through a hole in the wall where the boat's gangplank had been wedged, up some steps, and onto the pier.

A warehouse sat a short walk down the dock. It was dry, and someone had placed a generator and some lights inside. There was a shipment of wood beams and a stack of unused pallets, but otherwise the warehouse was empty. The evacuees started pulling down the pallets to use as beds. A fine black dust in the air settled quickly on their skin and clothes and made it hard to breathe. They were still damp, the air was stifling, and they tried to sleep atop the plywood.

Tuesday afternoon, the U.S. Northern Command—which has jurisdiction over domestic military operations—appointed Lieutenant General Russel Honoré, commander of the U.S. First Army based in Atlanta, to command what was to be called "Joint Task Force—Katrina." Honoré, native of Lakeland in Pointe Coupee Parish northwest of Baton Rouge, had worked on hurricane relief in the wake of Florida storms the previous year. A cigar-chomping, commanding figure, Honoré represented a great hope to Blanco and other officials in Louisiana, the vanguard of the massive federal response they hoped was coming. Over the course of the day, there had been confusion over exactly what the federal response should be. Blanco and other locals nevertheless wanted a big influx of federal troops to help with the evacuation and free up more National Guardsmen to tamp down on looting and restore order.

Chertoff, by his own account, had tried to reach Mike Brown all day, left a number of messages, but still not gotten through. After the morning meeting with Blanco and Nagin at the Superdome, Brown had spent much of the day touring the devastated areas of the Mississippi and Alabama Gulf Coast. Still, it was depressing and annoying: the head of Homeland Security completely unable to reach the head of FEMA. Chertoff had yelled at Brown's staffers without much effect. He and Brown finally spoke just before seven p.m. New Orleans time, via cell phone. Brown gave him a rundown of the situation.

"You better get yourself into that operations center in Baton Rouge," Chertoff snapped. "You have to be in a position where you can be reached—immediately." He ordered Brown to cancel a helicopter tour planned for the next day.

That night, Bill Quigley and some friends discussed what to do. Rescue helicopters had been few and far between, and it wasn't clear that anyone in the hospital beyond the sickest patients would be evacuated. "No one knows what's supposed to happen. We're just sitting here like sitting ducks, and there is no realistic evacuation plan," a friend said. "We do know you know how to raise a certain amount of hell—can you get the word out?"

Quigley composed an e-mail describing the hospital's predicament and sent it out to his network of activist friends and acquaintances:

Dear Friends:
There are about 1,300 people here who need help. I would appreciate it if you could forward this information to federal and state authorities and press in the US and in Louisiana to make sure these sick people are cared for. I am in Memorial Hospital in New Orleans. We have nearly 200 very sick people, hundreds of staff and hundreds more families.

The hospital has some basic electricity but many rooms have no electricity and many stairwells have no electricity. There is no a/c and no external windows. We cannot phone out and can receive few incoming calls. The water is rising and the hospital is already surrounded by water. Once the water hits the first floor, the computers, the email, all intercoms, and all internal communication inside the hospital will cease.

Our phones do not work so this is the only way I can reach out. This is not official but what I have been able to find out from listening to many, many people here.

The City of New Orleans is completely overwhelmed. No electricity. Incredible wind damage and now a broken levee that is flooding the city even further. Please make sure that someone is working to make sure these sick people and their families are helped.

They need care. For hours they have been announcing that patients are going to be medivaced (is this a word?) to other hospitals and shelters. But little real action so far. I know there is much, much to do out there, but these sick people need attention asap.

Please reach out in whatever way you can to make sure these folks are cared for.

Peace and love,
Bill Quigley

The message rocketed its way around the Internet in minutes and soon appeared on left-wing Web sites that were already abuzz. The city was still full of people, most of them poor and African American, and the Bush administration was fumbling around, seemingly at a loss to help them—or anybody else. Quigley's e-mail was picked up by *Democracy Now,* a talk show hosted by Amy Goodman, who managed to reach Quigley by cell phone. Among other things, she asked him about Haiti.

"Well, you know, I had always hoped that Haiti would become more like New Orleans, but what's happened is New Orleans has become more like Haiti here recently," he said. "You know, we don't have power. We don't have transportation. At this point, I think, at least the people in the hospital have some fresh water, but they're telling people you can't drink the water out of the taps. So there's people wandering around the city without water, without transportation, without medical care. So in many senses, we have about a million people in the New Orleans area who are experiencing, you know, what Haiti is like."

Quigley went to bed at 12:41 a.m. At 12:58 the last emergency generators failed.

Late into the night, FEMA's Phil Parr worked with National Guard officers at the Superdome on a plan to get people out, consulting by phone with FEMA's Denton office and Washington headquarters—but not with anyone in Baton Rouge. It was still unreachable by telephone: downed cellular towers and flooded landlines had severely limited communications in the New Orleans area, and the influx of evacuees had doubled Baton Rouge's population and overloaded its communications circuits with calls.

At the Homeland Security Operations Center in Washington, they were tossing around every evacuation option—could they build a dike out of sandbags that people could walk over to safety? Bring in military amphibious landing craft?

The best option was helicopters, Parr concluded, though there were apparently only three readily available from the National Guard. The emerging plan would take twelve. They knew there were two dry airports just a short hop away—Louis Armstrong International, fifteen miles to the west, and Belle Chasse Naval Air Station, south and across the river. With enough 'copters, they could rotate them in every fifteen to twenty minutes round the clock, and move anywhere from three hundred to five hundred people an hour. If there were fifteen thousand people in the Dome—their estimate at the time—it would take a minimum of thirty hours to get them all out. After that, buses would take them—somewhere. It wasn't quite clear to where, or, for that matter, where the buses would come from. But at least those inside the Superdome would no longer be trapped.

Parr got an initial go-ahead from Denton and thought the evacuation could begin early Wednesday. But it wasn't to be. Unbeknownst to him, there had been a parallel discussion going on in Baton Rouge. They'd decided they couldn't take helicopters off of search and rescue, and that using them for a mass evacuation could pose safety risks. Before dawn on Wednesday, Honoré and Landreneau pulled rank, and Parr's plan was canceled. Landreneau called Parr between five and six a.m. and thanked him for his efforts, but said that Honoré would be in charge of the evacuation. (In fact, Honoré had not yet accepted that responsibility.) Whether Parr's plan would have worked was debatable; regardless, as officials sorted out their responsibilities and tried to figure out what to do, any evacuation would take at least another day to begin.

Chapter 12

WEDNESDAY, AUGUST 31

A S HE DOZED CURLED up on his cardboard in the darkness of the Superdome early Wednesday, Loco Cooper felt a sharp jab in his gut. His eyes flicked open with the pain. He'd been kicked in the stomach. A man had grabbed his duffel bag and was walking away. Cooper lay there for a few seconds and felt his breathing resume, then got up, ran to a cot nearby, ripped a hollow aluminum bar off it, and sprinted after the thief, swinging the bar over his head. Cooper reached him easily and smacked him in the back of the skull. The bag dropped. The man dropped to the ground, arms over his head. Eyes blazing, Cooper jumped him and brought the bar down on his head and upper body again and again, but it was hollow and didn't do much damage. People converged on them, and a couple of men grabbed him and pulled him off.

"He's trying to rob me," Cooper said.

"No—it's my bag!" the man said. "He jumped me—get him away from me!"

Cooper grabbed the bag off the floor, pulling his passport and his clothes out. He was only 5'6" and 130 pounds—nothing like the heavyset would-be thief. He flashed the passport and gestured to his slender frame.

"See?!" he said. "This guy is too big for these clothes. He's trying to rob me. I was just trying to hold on to what's mine!"

Satisfied, the crowd dispersed, leaving Cooper and the at-tempted robber standing there, not sure what to do next. The rod was still in Cooper's hand. He felt his fingers tighten around it, and he swung and smacked the guy again. The man tried to grab the rod, and they started punching and kicking each other. Once again, a group of men converged and pulled them apart. Cooper and the thief were forced to go their separate ways.

Near the London Avenue breach, Harvey and Renee Miller were still awaiting rescue as Wednesday dawned, nearly forty-eight hours after the flood stranded them on the second floor of their neighbor's house. At intervals through the day Tuesday, they heard the *thwop-thwop* of helicopters passing low overhead. Harvey took his undershirt, put it on Renee's cane, and waved it out the window as high as he could reach. They stayed by the window all day, waving the shirt, but no one came. Their cell phone no longer worked, and their modest stores of snacks and water were running low. They were able to work the toilet by dumping buckets of water into the tank. The muggy heat was nearly unbearable, and at times they each felt close to fainting.

Soon after they woke from a restless sleep Wednesday morning, the Millers heard a neighbor calling them and looked out the window. At first, they couldn't see where she was. Then they saw a woman and her father standing on the roof of an adjacent house.

"Somebody's coming by with a boat," she said, "and we're going to send them back to you to take you out of here."

But the boat turned out to be a tiny canoe, and the would-be rescuer was paddling with a broken broom. He seemed pretty confident, though. "Slide down the roof and I'll catch you!" he said. "I'll take you over to UNO—it's dry there!"

That wasn't going to work: Harvey weighed 250 pounds, and Renee wasn't strong enough to swim.

"Come around the front door," Harvey said, figuring the water was just low enough he could get it open. "I'll go back and get a regular boat," the guy said, and paddled off. He did not return.

On Memorial Medical Center's parking garage ramps that morning, the sickest people lay on stretchers, some being sustained by nurses or doctors with hand ventilators, trading off on the work. They'd stopped dispensing all but the most urgent medication—with the computers down, nobody knew what the patients should be taking. Nearby was a menagerie of pets, mostly dogs and cats, making a racket and defecating on the concrete, entertaining visits from their owners.

It wasn't clear why, but the helicopters had stopped coming. Some pilots told them that Women's Hospital in Baton Rouge, the first destination, was now full and that the next option might be Alexandria, Louisiana, still farther away. There was also talk that rescue operations were switching away from hospitals and back to people on rooftops.

The hospital had used up most of its food. The previous night Quigley and Dupre had dined on Cheetos and warm Hawaiian Punch from busted vending machines. Now the supply of fresh water was starting to dwindle. Inside the hospital, it got miserably hot, and people started smashing the windows out, which, unfortunately, didn't help much.

Quigley jotted down observations:

> 7:15 a.m. All phones now dead.
>
> 8. Hoping that there are boats to take people away, but there are boats trying to get in. . . . Batteries on walkie-talkies dead. No way to communicate out. Hospital announcing people will not get out today.
>
> 9:30. One patient in bone marrow unit just left. People are starting to say, I have never felt so alone.
>
> 10:30. People reporting looting at Walgreens, within sight of the parking garage. People swimming back and forth to Salvation Army.

On Wednesday morning, Coast Guard chief warrant officer David Lewald docked his ship, the 160-foot construction tender *Pamlico,* at the Algiers ferry terminal across the Mississippi from downtown New Orleans. Lewald had a plan, cooked up on the fly, to evacuate St. Bernard Parish. Thousands of people were at the Chalmette slip and the ferry terminal nearby. It would be easy enough to transport them across using the two ferries and the tug and barge that Lewald had already commandeered. The only question was what would happen after they were dropped off, but he figured he'd worry about that later. Algiers, at least, was dry and accessible. Lewald strode ashore and inspected the parking lot. It was mostly empty. He ordered his men to clear the debris. It would be a landing zone for helicopters—if he could get them.

The *Pamlico,* with a crew of fourteen, had withdrawn upriver to Baton Rouge during the storm, then returned the day after with no specific assignment. The ship was based out of the Industrial Canal, and Lewald lived in Diamond Head, Mississippi, just over the Louisiana state line on the Gulf. He didn't know what shape his home was in, but at this point it didn't matter. He'd evacuated his family to stay with relatives in Maryland. There wasn't anything else to do but address the matter at hand.

Blunt-ended and black-hulled, with a large crane mounted in the middle of its main deck, the *Pamlico* was neither pretty nor graceful. Its usual mission was installing and maintaining about twelve hundred buoys, signs, and other navigational markers along south Louisiana's waterways, including the Mississippi. That meant pulling old wood pilings and driving new ones, sinking anchors—a lot of mud and grease. "It's a pretty big endeavor, but somebody's got to do it," read a Coast Guard Web site featuring the *Pamlico*'s crew.

Lewald and his crew had experienced a rocky return to New Orleans the day before. As the ship chugged downriver, the crew saw folks waving from broken windows in the Hilton hotel and an adjacent riverfront condominium building. Many looked to be partying through the storm, but Lewald heard radio reports of the widespread flooding and people trapped. The *Pamlico* responded to a U.S. Navy request, ferrying about forty officers, employees, and their families from a New Orleans wharf to the Naval Support Activity campus on the west bank. Sixty other people also climbed on board for the ride, but after they'd all disembarked and tried to enter the navy facility, guards marched the civilians to the gate and shut it behind them.

"What the hell are they doing?" Lewald said out loud, to no-body in particular. "They're just cutting those people loose?"

Then a call was routed to him from a company next to the base.

"Those people are walking on private property," a man said. "They are trespassing. What are you going to do about it?"

"Uh, yeah, I'll get on it first thing in the morning," Lewald said, and hung up, disgusted. The civilians walked off to find their own way to a more hospitable welcome. Lewald then ra-dioed the base, seeking permission to tie up and use the dock there as an evacuation staging area. The lieutenant he got said that was not going to happen.

"Okay, fuck it," Lewald said to himself. It was eleven p.m., too late to do anything more.

On Wednesday, Lewald went about a mile downriver to the Algiers ferry terminal to set it up as his command post. Back across the river in St. Bernard, he talked with Tony Fernandez, the deputy chief of the St. Bernard parish sheriff's office, and agreed to use the Chalmette slip as the launch point. Deputies were dispatched to tell people to leave the St. Bernard ferry ter-minal and wade the half mile to the slip. Lewald arranged trans-port for Fernandez upriver to Zephyr Field, where FEMA had set up its local base of operations for search and rescue missions. There, he was able to run down another boat—the *Creole Queen*, a sightseeing riverboat—to use as a floating command post.

Meanwhile, Lewald's ferries began bringing people over. Two days after Katrina struck, this still-unfolding evacuation ef-fort was the only large-scale attempt under way to take stranded victims out of the flood zone.

While it didn't seem that way, the initial search and rescue operations had been a success—the Coast Guard alone had al-ready pulled more than ten thousand people off rooftops. But moving people in small groups over short distances was one thing. Moving crowds of dehydrated, sick, miserable people out of the area required a large and systematic effort. There were now more than twenty thousand people at the Superdome, and about seven thousand people at the cloverleaf a mile from where the interstates met. There was a token presence of authority in those places, some food and medical professionals. But since Tuesday, another ten thousand people had now gathered at the convention center, where there were no police, National Guard, or medical teams. Adding to the problem, hotels were running short of food and water, and some had begun to kick guests out into the street—if there was a street left to kick them out onto. And as the helicopters and boats kept rescuing people, and others swam or waded to safety, the numbers of the rescued-but-in-need-of-rescue were mushrooming.

Blanco, Nagin, and FEMA all had high hopes for Honoré. He could lead a massive influx of federal troops. He could take over the evacuation. Whatever he ended up doing, they hoped and believed he was the guy with the chops and the bureaucratic authority to cut through the paralysis. The general flew into New Orleans Wednesday morning and visited the Superdome. He didn't have troops with him, just a handful of aides. Scott Wells, FEMA's deputy coordinating officer in Louisiana, took Honoré aside during the tour and asked if he would take charge of the evacuation responsibilities. Honoré seemed a bit nonplussed.

"Whoa—wait a minute," he said. "I need to get my people here. Then we'll talk later." For New Orleans, the clock continued to tick.

Meanwhile, with the New Orleans police department decimated and National Guard troops yet to arrive in force, the looting of the city's supermarkets, convenience stores, appliance and department stores—at least the ones on high ground—spread. Overnight a trickle, then a flood of disturbing reports of violence began flowing into the city and state EOCs, and then out into the media. At the Superdome, a man had plunged to his death from the stands—apparently a suicide. Across the river, a looter had shot at a police deputy, grazing him in the head. Word spread that armed gangs were roving the city—and the Superdome and convention center—not just stealing, but terrorizing, raping, and killing. Late Tuesday night, Denise Bottcher, Blanco's chief spokeswoman, described a scene of terror unfolding at Children's Hospital in the Uptown area near the riverfront: a gang of looters was at the front door, trying to break in and ransack the place. A hundred children were defenseless inside. No police or National Guard units had responded despite desperate pleas for help.

In fact, there was no gang of looters, and hospital administrators had to spend much of Wednesday trying to knock down the rumor, reassuring callers and the media that everything was okay. (A bunch of people had shown up during the day— apparently believing a mob had already broken in and the hospital was fair game—but officials merely locked the doors and they went away. There was a bright spot in broadcasting the rumor, however: Children's Hospitals around the country began ringing up their New Orleans affiliate, and administrators were able to secure spots for all their patients elsewhere.) As the flow of alarming reports continued, it was impossible to determine what was true, what was false, and what was exaggerated. But inevitably, the sense of rising anarchy set the tone for the day's national media coverage and fed a growing sense of panic among government officials and among those trapped in New Orleans who had even fewer sources of information. Only four years earlier, the United States endured an unthinkable terrorist attack that had stripped away some of the fabled American innocence. The nation seemed suddenly vulnerable again, this time to the terrors of nature and our own incompetence and greed.

All agreed that the best way to restore order to New Orleans would be a massive show of force. But the logical candidates—the National Guard, NOPD, and the state police—were focused on search and rescue and the mounting troubles of managing stranded crowds numbering in the tens of thousands. On the talk shows and in the meeting rooms of

Baton Rouge and Washington, officials spoke of deploying the U.S. military. But as before, the lack of leadership from above meant little actually got done. On Wednesday morning, Nagin and Blanco made another round of television appearances. Yesterday it had been all about shock, but today the full scope of the problem—and their helplessness—was revealed to the nation. Speaking from the state EOC, Blanco outlined the seemingly insurmountable challenges to Matt Lauer on the *Today* show.

"We are going to try to bring law and order back into the streets of New Orleans, but first of all we've got to continue our search and rescue mission. We've got to try to stop the breach. It's been an engineering nightmare to try to control the water situation in New Orleans, and we need to evacuate the people in the Superdome and in other shelters and in the hospitals in New Orleans," she said. "So those are our—our basic missions today."

Dressed in a blue suit, Blanco looked exhausted and a little spooked. Changing microphones between interviews, she confided to Denise Bottcher, her press secretary, that she had misgivings about bringing in soldiers to keep the peace, but then concluded, "I really need to call for the military."

"Yes, you do; yes, you do," Bottcher replied.

"And I should have started that in the first call," Blanco said wearily, referring to her Monday evening discussion with the president. She'd asked for "everything you've got," but put no numbers on it, and the result had been less than zero.

These inevitable interviews worried Blanco. She was afraid the media's sudden focus on the breakdown of order, coupled with the growing calls to bring in the military, could divert attention from what she saw as the most urgent issue—evacuation. More National Guard troops were on the way; right then, they needed buses more than they needed extra boots on the ground. She called the White House but was told Bush was unavailable. She asked for Andrew Card. He was also unavailable. She continued down the chain of command and spoke briefly with Maggie Grant, an aide to Karl Rove.

Finally, White House Homeland Security Advisor Frances Townsend (who had finally returned to Washington from her Maine vacation) called Blanco back.

"We're desperate, Fran," Blanco said. "The situation is so bad. We've got to have boats, helicopters, and especially buses. We've got to have those buses to get people out of there. Nobody really understands the magnitude of the problem."

Card called Blanco back a short while later. She asked for buses again, saying the original number Brown had tossed out— five hundred—wouldn't work.

"How about five thousand?" she said, only half-joking. Card said he'd do what he could.

At the Dome, meanwhile, the situation was deteriorating. Frustrated at the lack of action, Bahamonde sent Brown an e-mail late that morning.

> Sir, I know that you know the situation is past critical. Here are some things you might not know.
>
> Hotels are kicking people out, thousands are gathering in the streets with no food or water. Hundreds still being rescued from homes.
>
> The dying patients at the DMAT tent [are] being medivac[ced]. Estimates are many will die within hours. Evacuation in process. Plans developing for dome evacuation but hotel situation adding to problem. We are out of food and running out of water at the dome, plans in works to address critical need.
>
> FEMA staff is OK and holding own. DMAT staff working in deplorable conditions. The sooner we can get the medical patients out, the sooner we can get them out.
>
> Phone connectivity impossible.

A few hours later, Bahamonde was forwarded an e-mail noting that Brown wanted some extra time before a TV appearance to go out to eat. A colleague dryly asked how much time

Bahamonde needed to go "to the restaurant of your choice." He responded:

> OH MY GOD !!!!!!!! No won't go any further, too easy of a
> target. Just tell her that I just ate an MRE and crapped in
> the hallway of the Superdome along with 30,000 other close
> friends so I understand her concern about busy restaurants.
> Maybe tonight I will have time to move the pebbles on the
> parking garage floor so they don't stab me in the back while I
> try to sleep, but instead I will hope her wait at Ruth Christ
> [Ruth's Chris, a steakhouse] is short.

After his would-be rescuer failed to come back, Harvey Miller decided to swim down the street from their temporary abode and check out what had happened to their own single-story house.

"I'm not sure I remember how to swim," he said to his wife, Renee, as he stripped down to his jockey shorts. But there was nothing else to do, so he pushed the front door open and eased his way into the floodwaters. Renee ran to the uppermost window and watched him make his way down the street. Harvey scanned the water but couldn't see his car under the murky, slightly oily surface. Just as he reached the house, a large school of fish appeared around him, then flitted off.

The water was six inches below the roofline—the house was a total loss. Bemused, he paddled out to the middle of the street and began splashing. A helicopter hovering nearby moved over him to see what the splashing was. Filthy waves churned up by the propeller washed into Harvey's face and he nearly went under. He swam over to a live oak and estimated the depth, based on how high the branches now were from the top of the water. He put the depth at twelve feet. "I can't believe it," he muttered.

The 'copter dropped a rescuer on the roof of an adjacent house.

"Hey! My wife and dog are staying next door!" Harvey shouted.

"I can pull you out of the upstairs window," the guy responded. "You better get back in there!"

Harvey swam back into the house. A couple of recreational fishing boats came down the street, their skippers waving the helicopter off. Two burly guys got off one, and one of the men hoisted himself up through the second-floor window.

"How are y'all?" he asked. "Everyone all right? Have you eaten? Had enough water?" Gingerly, he lifted Renee up and out of the window and lowered her to another rescuer on the bow of the boat. The dog slid and dropped right onto the deck. Harvey announced he was too fat to go out the window, so he went out through the front door and they hauled him on board. The Millers took their battery-powered lanterns, leaving only the tiny TV.

It was eleven a.m. as the boats moved out. They went up to Robert E. Lee Boulevard and then headed west, passing by the ruined school, women stranded on the top of an apartment, and a Greek Orthodox church, water halfway up its stained-glass windows. At the bridge over St. Bernard Avenue, the boat hit shallow water, and the Millers and others in the rescue boat scrambled out and walked across. On the other side, they got back in and continued on. They heard abandoned dogs howling all along. At one point, a big Weimaraner swam up to the boat and they tried to bring it on board, but the dog was so excited and upset it bit the hand of the man pulling it up, and they let it slip back into the water. The boats turned south onto Canal Boulevard. Dozens of cars had been left on the median by owners who hoped the slightly higher ground would be enough to keep them dry. It wasn't.

The boats arrived at rescue central, the point where the interstates split, and dropped the Millers and everyone else off at a ramp leading to dry land on the other side of the 17th Street canal and the cloverleaf in Metairie.

Not long after Air Force One left Waco for Washington, Bush took a call from King Abdullah of Saudi Arabia, who expressed his condolences for the loss of life in the disaster and made promises of support. Though the king offered nothing specific, help from a major oil producer might soon come in handy. Katrina's economic fallout had started to spread. Gulf oil and gas production had virtually shut down before the storm, and some platforms and pipelines had been heavily damaged. That was something that Bush, a former oilman, understood intimately. (Aides to Vice President Cheney, another ex–oil executive, had already taken the unusual step of calling up a Mississippi utility and ordering it to fix two electrical substations powering the Colonial Pipeline, which supplied petroleum to much of the Northeast. Repair crews were diverted from nearby hospitals to do it.) With supplies already tight, oil prices briefly spiked above seventy dollars per barrel that day. (A year before, they had been averaging forty dollars per barrel.) Soon the price of gasoline would follow, hitting consumers' pocketbooks.

Air Force One soon diverted off its usual course and flew toward New Orleans and the Gulf Coast to give the president a look at the damage from the air. Bush and his aides considered an on-the-ground visit but thought it would disrupt an already-disrupted situation. But doing a flyover also meant that the president would forgo the important gesture of reaching out directly, showing rather than telling people he cared, as Johnson had done forty years earlier and as Bush himself had done in the World Trade Center rubble. He wouldn't see the appalling damage and human suffering up close with his own eyes— something that might have jolted him out of the double insulation of the presidential bubble and his vacation, which some aides believed had contributed to his halting public performance so far. As Air Force One approached New Orleans, Bush and his aides could see the flood stretching for miles, the land and sea intermingled over neighborhoods and roads. The plane dropped down to 2,500 feet and circled the city, briefly dipping to 1,700 feet. Bush saw the surreal scene of the flooded Six Flags theme park in eastern New Orleans, its rides broken like toys, pieces strewn over bridges and roads. Then Air Force One continued eastward over the wreckage dotting the Mississippi and Alabama beaches. Clad in a blue flight jacket, Bush spent thirty-five minutes sitting on a couch near the front of the plane, staring out the window, gazing pensively at the distant scenes of terrible strife. "It's devastating," press secretary Scott McClellan later quoted Bush as saying. "It's got to be doubly devastating on the ground." The White House released a distinctly unremarkable photo of this supposedly history-making scene: a man staring out of a tiny window.

Bush's staff was trying to figure out a way to get on top of the situation, both operationally and politically. Besides criticism from blogs and interest groups, they were taking hits from TV pundits and Democratic politicians for being slow to react to the storm. The previous December, critics around the world had chided Bush for his slow reaction to the tsunami that had killed hundreds of thousands in south Asia. The tsunami hit on December 26, and Bush had remained cloistered at his ranch, clearing brush and bicycling, while the death toll grew exponentially. Bush spoke out every time there was a terrorist attack somewhere in the world, but it appeared that he didn't assign much importance to natural disasters. The White House explained it as self-conscious restraint, contrasting it with Bill Clinton's public empathy. ("He didn't want to make a symbolic statement about 'We feel your pain,'" an aide told the *Washington Post*.) But the Bush compound had remained a stubbornly impervious place, and now an almost identical dynamic was playing out again, this time with the fate of an American city hanging in the balance. One obvious path to getting the upper hand was the idea of federalizing the response, giving Bush direct control over the National Guard and the military, and putting boots on the ground forthwith.

David Vitter had been speaking with the White House staffers on and off since before the storm had hit. Vitter was a loyal Republican and popular among Louisiana voters, who had elected him in 2004 to fill the seat once held by Senator Russell Long. But Vitter, a forty-four-year-old Harvard graduate and Rhodes scholar, was viewed with some suspicion by his fellow Louisiana politicians. Many saw him as a habitual freelancer, less interested in teamwork than in advancing his own political fortunes.

Now Vitter was in a peculiar position, with conflicting loyalties to the White House, Louisiana Democrats, and his own beleaguered constituents.

Vitter walked into the EOC in Baton Rouge and up to Blanco's executive counsel, Terry Ryder. That morning, Vitter had spoken with Karl Rove about getting troops into the city to supplement the National Guard, and whether the entire effort should be federalized. Rove, he said, had told him that Blanco was thinking of federalizing—apparently misinterpreting some comments she had made earlier. Blanco's staff was alarmed. First, the governor wasn't thinking any such thing; Blanco wanted Washington's help, not its harness. But more than anything else, it was Rove's name that raised hackles. Rove was officially Bush's chief policy advisor, so it wasn't surprising to hear he was involved. But his primary role was Bush's chief *political* advisor and sometime hatchet man, the scourge of Democrats everywhere. Did his involvement mean the president was more worried about electoral advantage than saving lives?

Federalizing the Louisiana operation was one way for the president to get back on top of things, but it presented legal and political problems of its own. The president could send federal troops into a disaster zone at the request of a governor—indeed, that's exactly what Blanco wanted. But legally, they could only engage in relief operations; federal troops were barred from engaging in law enforcement on American soil under the Posse Comitatus (Latin for "force of the country") Act of 1878. Police powers remained in the hands of the local and state authorities, the National Guard, and ultimately the governor.

But if order was to be restored quickly in New Orleans, the U.S. military might have to assume police powers. Under another law, the Insurrection Act, the president was allowed leeway to suspend Posse Comitatus in times of emergency (to put down "any insurrection, domestic violence, unlawful combination, or conspiracy" beyond the resources of an individual state to control). The White House and Justice Department had already reinterpreted some laws to expand federal police powers in the pursuit of terrorists on U.S. soil. But Posse Comitatus had never been suspended before for a natural disaster, and doing so would be a matter of the utmost delicacy. It would strip Blanco of her control of the National Guard and make it appear the White House was stepping in to save her hide. That touched more hot buttons than even Rove's political operation was accustomed to.

"Can you imagine how it would have been perceived if a president of the United States of one party had pre-emptively taken from the female governor of another party the command and control of her forces, unless the security situation made it completely clear that she was unable to effectively execute her command authority and that lawlessness was the inevitable result?" one anonymous White House aide later told the *New York Times*.

Asserting presidential power at the expense of a governor would also infringe upon states' rights, a concept revered by conservatives, especially in the South, the region where Bush's core political support resided.

Blanco was having none of it. Just after two p.m., she tried calling Bush again. The president had arrived back in Washington and was preparing for a cabinet meeting, and this time she got through.

"Mr. President, I do not want to federalize the National Guard," she began, repeating the phrase more than once. Then she told him what she did want: forty thousand troops. "I don't care where they come from, National Guard or regular army, but I want troops that will actually be on the ground," she said. The number one need, she said, was transportation out—buses, airplanes, and personnel to operate them. The furious improvisation of the past few days, Blanco told the president, was beginning to get some results. Some real help could make a substantial difference.

Things were indeed looking a little bit brighter. More National Guard troops were on the way. Overnight, FEMA had at last officially tasked the Department of Transportation to procure the buses that Brown had promised, though for some reason,

FEMA had cut the number of buses from five hundred to 455. "Some bean counter looked at it and figured that, you know, we didn't need this," Jeff Smith said later. Still, once the paperwork was done, things started to move. The order went to DOT at 1:45 a.m., and fewer than five hours later, the first buses arrived at a truck stop in LaPlace, about twenty-five miles northwest of New Orleans. By later that day, two hundred buses were in place. On Tuesday, Blanco had also asked Leonard Kleinpeter, the head of the state's Office of Community Programs, to reach out to parishes for school buses. Initially, Kleinpeter got a lot of commitments, but on Wednesday, he started running into resistance because administrators were hearing the reports of violence and didn't want to send their buses or drivers somewhere from which they might never return. On Wednesday, Blanco issued an executive order to commandeer school and tour buses. Meanwhile, Texas governor Rick Perry agreed to open the Houston Astrodome to evacuees. FEMA medical teams from Oregon, Texas, and California began arriving at the New Orleans airport and set up a temporary emergency room and triage center.

But this scattershot approach—a little help here, a little there—was also a symptom of the larger problem. Louisiana might just as well have been firing requests for military assistance with a blunderbuss. The governor was asking Bush, Honoré, other states, and the National Guard Bureau, which coordinates Guard activities, to send troops. FEMA was asking for various forms of military assistance through its own channels. The requests were not coordinated in any way, and some were vague to the point of meaninglessness. As a result, nobody really knew the total amount of federal help that had been requested or how much of it was actually on the way.

Chertoff's official declaration of an Incident of National Significance had made little difference; there was still nothing resembling the "unified command" envisioned by the National Response Plan. It wasn't even clear who was in charge at the Superdome—the NOPD was nominally running things, but it appeared that the National Guard was calling the shots. When

FEMA official Scott Wells arrived Wednesday morning, no one could tell him who, per the unified command plan, was in charge.

Worse, Mike Brown was Chertoff's choice as "Principal Federal Official"— the top position in the new disaster response structure. Brown had opposed creating that position two years earlier, believing it added an unnecessary layer of bureaucracy. First Chertoff had immobilized Brown; now he had saddled him with an amorphous job he didn't want (and hadn't trained for, either). Chertoff seemed not even to know what a Principal Federal Official did. He later said he was deputizing Brown as his "battlefield commander." But, theoretically anyway, the FEMA director already had such authority. At least as the National Response Plan vaguely defined it, a PFO's role was not to command but to stand back, act as the secretary's eyes and ears, and kibbitz: iron out conflicts, tighten up the overall effort.

Nor was Honoré going to be the one to ride to New Orleans's rescue. To the last of them, everyone who met Honoré that day, including the governor and her staff, and Brown, Lokey, Wells, and Parr of FEMA, thought the tough-talking general would be leading a huge influx of regular army troops. They were crestfallen to find he had brought no troops at all, just a few dozen officers and aides.

And despite their hopes—not to mention the White House talk of federalizing military operations—Honoré had no intention of bringing in army troops, nor did his bosses at the Defense Department. They were sticking to the established policy of deferring to the National Guard before activating their own soldiers.

"This was not a classic military operation," Honoré later told congressional investigators. "In a classic military operation, I would have sat here in Atlanta and put a brigadier or a major general in Camp Shelby and maybe send a brigadier to New Orleans and to Biloxi. . . . In this case, I reversed a paradigm. I left my staff at home and went forward on the battlefield, which may have given a perception to people when they saw me that all the federal troops were there, which was not the case. And I never [pretended] that that was the fact when I got there, but people come up with their own assumptions."

As if to drive that point home, as Honoré was meeting with Blanco later that day, an e-mail came in from Major General Richard Rowe, director of operations for the U.S. Northern Command, the joint military organization overseeing American homeland security:

> There should be calls coming your way. There is a desire to concentrate National Guardsmen into [New Orleans] for [law enforcement]/security tasks. Governor has asked that federal troops pick up rest of the tasks being uncovered by Guard in state. Thoughts? What does this mean in terms of scale? Type [of] capabilities?

Colonel James Hickey, Honoré's executive officer, responded:

> [We] think there are enough ARNG [Army National Guard] Soldiers and volunteers to perform all these missions.

Paradigm shift or not, it seemed obvious that New Orleans desperately needed a lot of troops, fast. Ignoring that was at best a bad decision, at worst a conscious bias in favor of procedure over people in need. The one person who could easily overrule the Defense Department on the matter was the president. But he and his staff were caught up in the legalities and politics of who controlled the troops—not the human suffering those troops could alleviate.

In the meantime, the folks in Louisiana, now including Honoré, would have to keep improvising. "The burden was not alleviated when he [Honoré] arrived," Blanco said. "I just had yet another person in the mix who was working hard to try to get everything going. But he was working handicapped."

Now there was a new wrinkle. Blanco had never been on the friendliest of terms with the White House. After all, she was a Democrat, and her surprise 2003 victory had been a black eye for the Republican Party. Now the relationship began to turn noticeably chilly. On Wednesday afternoon, Bottcher was fielding calls from the media, and she began to get whiffs of accusation in their questions.

"'Why didn't you all do this and that?' And I'm saying, 'We did that!'" Bottcher said. "I started feeling that something was remiss. We're in the midst of this huge search and rescue mission. Why are they asking these questions? And none of those questions are coming from the local media." Perhaps she was being a bit paranoid, as the blame game was a perennial Washington sport from which no one was exempt, but Bottcher figured the White House, or some arm of the Republican Party, was subtly trying to direct blame their way.

That afternoon, Bill Lokey, FEMA's Federal Coordinating Officer for Louisiana, also started pondering the value of federalization. "This is beyond FEMA, it's beyond the state," he told Brown. "We need a massive influx of the military here."

"Well, let me check with OGC [Office of the General Counsel] and Homeland Security," said Brown. (Neither had been privy to White House discussions on the topic.)

Word reached Blanco's staff quickly. Soon Brown and Lokey were asked to pay a visit to the governor's office at the EOC, where they found Blanco sitting at her desk, surrounded by several aides. General Bennett Landreneau, the chief of the Louisiana National Guard, was there, too. The discussion was tense, curt. Blanco asked why they were pushing to federalize the effort.

"Ma'am, we would never do this without coordinating with you," Brown said. "It's similar to what we did with 9/11. We were doing the what-ifs in case, you know, it got that bad." (Actually, New York Mayor Rudolph Guiliani and Governor George Pataki had not ceded authority of National Guard troops to the federal government during the aftermath of 9/11.)

Lokey began to add something, but an aide interrupted him.

"Mr. Lokey, the state of Louisiana is still sovereign."

"We can still handle this," Landreneau said.

That was the end of the conversation. Shortly thereafter, Brown called headquarters and set the wheels in motion for a standard FEMA request for military assistance—one that would bring in the military for support, but not put it in charge.

Later that afternoon, Brown gave a press conference—the first time he had given a solo briefing. No Louisiana officials had been notified or invited. Blanco didn't know what to make of that, but she emerged from her office and joined him at the podium. He wrapped things up without inviting her to speak. Blanco took center stage and spoke anyway, delivering a brief update and answering questions from reporters. Brown quickly left.

"You've just broken White House protocol," Nicole Andrews, a spokeswoman with Homeland Security, told Bottcher. "You're going to hear from the White House."

"Well, just tell me what I did wrong, because no one gave me the playbook on White House protocol," Bottcher replied. It appeared to them that the White House was, subtly or not, pushing Blanco to the margins.

Bush met with cabinet members, and a little after three p.m. New Orleans time, he spoke on the storm in the Rose Garden.

"The vast majority of New Orleans, Louisiana, is under water," Bush said. "Tens of thousands of homes and businesses are beyond repair. A lot of the Mississippi Gulf Coast has been completely destroyed. Mobile is flooded. We are dealing with one of the worst natural disasters in our nation's history." Bush went on to outline the efforts the federal government was making. It seemed less like a rallying cry than a pledge drive. "You can call 1-800-HELPNOW, or you can get on the Red Cross Web page, RedCross.org," he said.

By Wednesday evening, even die-hard Bush supporters were sounding alarms. "The minute that he'd heard that the levees had given way and the flooding was beginning, he should have hopped on a plane, canceled his schedule, and showed up here [in Washington], even if only to make a speech on national television to say that he was going to mobilize all his resources and, secondly, to say that he was not going to visit the area until the last person was rescued," conservative columnist Charles Krauthammer said Wednesday night on Fox News.

Cut off from its presses and computer system, and with only a skeleton staff on the scene of the biggest story in its 168-year history, the *Times-Picayune* had, somehow, reconstituted itself. Some staffers were at the *Houma Courier*, putting together electronic editions. In Baton Rouge, others had decamped to student space at LSU's Manship School of Mass Communications, the rest to an office park where the Baton Rouge *Advocate* had lent some space. In the early morning hours of Wednesday, James O'Byrne, the Living section editor, dispatched IT staffer Chris Ruppert to obtain the components of a newsroom. "He went out in the Baton Rouge night and came back in a couple of hours with twenty-two thousand dollars of computer equipment," O'Byrne said—twenty-two laptops, along with software and the makings of a network. Manuel Torres, another editor, went to a Baton Rouge office of Avis Rental Car, flashed the publisher's American Express card, and dropped the name of Advance Publications, the paper's parent company, owned by the billionaire Newhouse family. Avis rented him thirty cars.

The *Times-Picayune* prided itself on its rich local coverage, but for the journalists in New Orleans, this was local reportage of another order: familiar places had been utterly transformed; their fellow citizens were caught in desperate straits. They visited the Lower Ninth Ward and paddled into St. Bernard. They talked with refugees huddled on the interstate under the sun, in the stifling heat of the Superdome, and at the convention center. Their days were a fugue: report, file, then sleep (crashing in staffers' homes in dry areas), then repeat.

Ted Jackson had spent the night in the suburban LaPlace home of Brett Duke, a fellow *Times-Picayune* photographer he'd met up with late Tuesday. The pair had driven back to Jackson's boat and paddled back into the center of town, where they took some photos of rescuers pulling people into helicopters. Then, with some other photographers, they made their way past checkpoints into the Superdome. Blocked by a guardsman at one entrance, they managed to talk their way onto the floor at another, and spent fifteen minutes taking pictures. Then they decided they were pushing their luck and started to leave.

On the way out, while pausing to talk with a few people on the floor, they heard one woman from the Ninth Ward mutter over and over: "Can you believe they dynamited the levee?"

She told them she'd heard that the loud bang residents had heard when the Industrial Canal floodwall collapsed was really the sound of dynamite. The levee had been blown up, the story went, to redirect the flood to spare the richer, whiter parts of town. The false rumor recalled the 1927 dynamiting of the levee at St. Bernard. (Setting the ugly politics of such an act aside, a hurricane flood is simply too unpredictable to "manage" by blowing up levees, nor is it a simple task to set off charges at exactly the right moment in the middle of a massive hurricane—in fact, Corps engineers had been shut in a bunker during the storm.)

"Do you really believe that?" Jackson asked her.

"Yeah," she said. "They've done it before and now they've done it again."

"Do you realize that [mostly white] Lakeview has flooded, too? Their levees failed, too?"

"Well," she said, "I really feel better now."

Meanwhile, bedraggled refugees continued to migrate west across the city by boat and on foot, looking for a way out—or failing that, food, water, and a place to rest. (Heading east was not an option; that would mean traveling no fewer than twenty-five miles across Lake Pontchartrain, part of the way via a damaged causeway, only to reach more devastated areas on the other side.) The journey out of the flood zone was long, hot, and harrowing: some eastern New Orleans neighborhoods lay ten miles or more away from downtown, across a vast urban sea whose brown water rose fell with the tide. Once they reached terra firma, the police presence was spotty and looters roamed. Upon reaching downtown, unfortunate travelers soon found there was no way out of New Orleans, nor was any shelter available. The Superdome was, understandably, turning people away. Traveling farther would do no good; in adjacent Metairie and across the Mississippi in Algiers, crowds were also congregating on highways and under overpasses waiting for someone to take them away.

As a result, the sprawling convention center complex and the sidewalk in front of it had become the default destinations for thousands. The crowd grew steadily throughout Wednesday; with no authorities present, the scene soon became even more chaotic than the Superdome. People were gathered inside the building on its staircases, in meeting rooms, kitchens, and exhibition spaces. Some sat on the sidewalk in lawn chairs, fanning themselves, others lay sprawled in the street. The same kinds of rumors that were plaguing the Dome (rapes, murders, mayhem—most of them baseless) spread like viruses, breeding anxiety and anger.

Once there, however, people had some reason to believe help would be provided: after all, authorities had opened the building and the crowd's predicament was obvious. But hours, then days went by and no help arrived. Somehow, fifteen thousand people fell through the cracks: though the city had opened up the convention center on Nagin's orders the day before, Terry Ebbert had never bothered to inform FEMA of the decision; as far as the federal government knew, the convention center was not a shelter; there was no crowd, and no need for food, water, security, or medical care.

Earlier Wednesday, Nagin had ordered the beleaguered police force off search and rescue; instead they were trying to restore order. "They are starting to get closer to the heavily populated areas—hotels, hospitals— and we're going to stop it right now," he declared. But the convention center needed an organized force on the scene—a handful of cops and soldiers rolling by wouldn't do.

On the median in front of the convention center for most of Wednesday afternoon, the body of a ninety-one-year-old man named Booker Harris sat, propped up in a lawn chair. Harris had been evacuated from eastern New Orleans with his wife, Allie, but he had died in the back of the Ryder truck on the way out. The driver had dropped Allie and her husband's body and left. Allie sat next to him under a street sign, eating crackers. A group of guardsmen came later on and took her and some other elderly evacuees. The body remained, covered by a yellow blanket.

About a mile away at the Superdome, meanwhile, rumors continued to feed a panic. Petty crimes were common, but soon stories of terrible crimes began spreading—though it was unclear exactly how bad the problem really was, as few serious crimes were confirmed. Some believed a girl had been raped and stabbed to death in a bathroom. There were other reports of serial child molesters. People began wading out into the street to get away. "There's people getting raped and killed in there," Lisa Washington, who had come to the Dome from Algiers, across the river, told a *Times-Picayune* reporter. "People are getting diseases. It's like we're in Afghanistan. We're fighting for our lives right now." A relative added that there had been fourteen rapes in the Dome.

When he heard that a man had raped and killed a little girl, and that the authorities had caught him but then let him go, Loco Cooper became outraged. He and some friends got together and discussed it heatedly.

"We were going to take the law into our own hands," he said. "He was going to be the example for anyone else to not do this. Nobody else was enforcing any laws."

They drew a bead on the guy in question. They heard he had been identified by a child witness who'd seen him trying to drag another kid away from her mother. With word spreading fast, soon everybody knew who he was. Cooper and his friends found him in a hallway outside the stands. They grabbed him, pushed the guy into a corner, and started beating on him. He fell, and they kicked him in the gut. He was quiet; he didn't shout or protest. They left him on the floor, nearly unconscious.

Cooper was angry. He was basically a prisoner, and there was no one, seemingly, advocating for him and his fellow inmates. Guardsmen were tossing water bottles at old people, who had to duck to avoid taking one in the face. A guardswoman brandished her weapon at him and almost dared him to bump into her. He took issue with another soldier singing a mocking song and told him to can it.

"If you were in this situation, you wouldn't be singing that," Cooper said.

"Shut the fuck up," the soldier replied.

"If I see you in the street I will beat you down to the ground till you are beyond recognition," Cooper said, and walked away.

Quigley continued his jottings throughout the long day at Memorial Medical Center.

11:49. Two guys pushing floater with trash bags with possessions, to try to get out of chest-high water.

1:40. Two middle-aged white guys, canoeing down street with black woman clutching paper bag with clothes.

1:46. Babies crying, kids . . . they could pick up on tension.

2:20. Satellite phones not working. Carried up bottles of oxygen (to parking garage).

3:08. People panicking. Rumors of looters seeking narcotics. No food, little water, on entire floors going down to first floor.

3:34. People breaking glass in hospital. Glass showering down to atrium on third floor. Kids on our floor start screaming and crying.

Around five p.m., Quigley went up to the roof with a National Guardsman to try to flag down a helicopter. They unfurled a sheet that said HELP: PEOPLE DYING.

One helicopter buzzed by without stopping, but then the ploy worked— three 'copters landed. Unfortunately, evacuation wasn't their top priority. One was privately hired—it picked up a man and a woman and left. Another was looking for some ambulance technicians who were needed elsewhere. One marine helicopter left two boxes of canned Vienna sausages and a case of water. After days of junk food, the sausages made Quigley sick to his stomach. The hospital denizens were stranded for another night.

Quigley and Dupre were on the second floor now, along with about sixty people of all ages, hunkered down on a walkway going between the two buildings—a bit cooler than other spots. After hearing more than a dozen code blues a bit earlier and realizing that most of those people were probably dead, they decided to take some quiet time and went to the hospital chapel. They opened the door and went in, and the beam of their flashlight fell on two bodies. The chapel was now a morgue. They shuddered and left quickly.

People had padlocked the hospital doors and organized security teams to keep watch. But some people had made it inside—he could tell because they were covered in mud. What they were up to, he had no idea.

In the hours after the storm, the radio had been the best link to the world outside. The phones were working, but you couldn't call out, and the cable didn't work. But the longer the radios were on, the more anxiety they caused. Rumors started circulating, smushing tidbits of information from inside the hospital with radio reports and things people had seen outside. By Tuesday afternoon, most people just stopped listening.

Other means of communication were out, but cell phone text messaging still worked. Before he tried to go to sleep, Quigley sent a message to a friend: "No water, sick, no heat, call somebody for help."

After being dropped off at the interstate cloverleaf, the Millers walked up to the medical station, then waited in line for a spot in the back of one of a line of pickup trucks and vans waiting to take evacuees to the staging area about a mile west in Metairie. When they got there, the sight was horrific. Thousands of people were waiting, crowding around a handful of buses. There was no organization, no toilets, just chaos. Helicopters were landing every few minutes, disgorging more people into the mob. Every half hour or so, a few buses would leave and a few more would take their place. People would crush in around them, pushing to get on. The Millers tried repeatedly to get on, but when they reached the front they were turned away because of the dog. At one point, a National Guardsman offered to shoot Monet for them—humanely—if it would get them on a bus. They declined.

Renee, meanwhile, hadn't taken any heart medication for

two days and began to get sick, feeling weak and woozy, so they moved to the medical area and sat her on a cot next to an unconscious man. It was so crowded Harvey and Monet walked across the highway and sat down on a curb. There, someone gave them water. Someone else gave Monet some dog food. Renee motioned that they should try to get on a bus if they could. So they tried again—and failed again. A couple of teenaged girls with babies screamed at them to get the dog away.

"Don't mind them," an elderly black man told Harvey. "They have nothing. All they have are those babies, and they want to take care of them. So don't mind them."

It was dark, and Harvey chatted with the man. Both were afraid they'd never get on a bus, being older and weaker than the young people muscling their way on. They got some MREs from a National Guardsman. Harvey drew red beans and rice with sausage. It was dreck, so he ate only the crackers. He fell asleep by the side of the road.

That night, Cooper came upon some people busting down a door in the Superdome. Behind it, they found a big kitchen. They threw open the cabinets and freezers and found alcohol, and some food that hadn't rotted yet—some canned red beans and rice, some chicken. They got the gas grills working and cooked it up, passing it out to anyone who came in. Smoke filled up the room and people started choking, so they rotated in and out. One man would watch the food while another ran out and caught his breath. Some were swigging beer. Cooper grabbed a big bottle of Hennessy cognac and started swigging it. After the food was used up, he shut down the grills, then left with his bottle. He was falling-down drunk and forgot for a few hours where he was. He staggered around, then fell asleep on the floor.

"When I woke up," he said, "I was still there." So were thousands of New Orleanians, still on the floor and in the stands of the Superdome.

Chapter 13

THURSDAY, SEPTEMBER 1

AT 12:31 A.M. THURSDAY, the first bus from New Orleans pulled up to the Astrodome, soon to be the shelter for twenty-thousand-plus refugees. Its appearance took organizers by surprise, since it wasn't part of the official evacuation at all; it was an Orleans Parish school bus that a young man had commandeered, loaded up—mostly with children—and driven to Houston. FEMA officials called them "renegade buses," and at that point, no renegade was getting into the Astrodome.

The bus remained parked outside the entrance to the arena, its driver uncertain what to do. "At this point, our plan, our agreement, is to take the Superdome buses," declared Robert Eckels, a county judge overseeing Houston's homeland security and emergency management agency, who then departed shortly afterward. Once Eckels was gone, Margaret O'Brien-Molina, a spokeswoman for the American Red Cross, spotted the solitary school bus and told the National Guard to let its occupants into the shelter. The passengers went inside.

Hurricane Katrina had hit days before, but the start of the official evacuation was still hours away.

Around six p.m. Wednesday evening, Blanco had formally tasked General Honoré with running the evacuation. Landreneau, the Louisiana Guard chief, would focus on restoring order. As they met, Brigadier General Mark Graham walked into the EOC with a bunch of aides, fresh from a seven-hour drive from the 5th Army headquarters he commanded in San Antonio. The Defense Department had assigned Graham to back up Honoré, who immediately assigned him to run the evacuation.

That night, Graham organized a staging area at the Texaco truck stop in LaPlace, about thirty miles west of New Orleans on Interstate 10. As the night wore on, hundreds of commercial buses converged there, got their tanks filled, and awaited orders. Running convoys in and out of the city would not be a simple task. Officials eventually settled on a route through the city's dry zones that ended on the south side of the Hyatt hotel, where there was only about a foot of water in the street. At the Superdome, meanwhile, buses began to evacuate remaining special-needs patients. Some went by helicopter to Louis Armstrong International Airport, where another crowd in the tens of thousands was gathering.

At the Superdome at four a.m. Thursday, Robert Green and his brother, cousin, and grandchildren were awakened by guardsmen hollering at them through bullhorns: "Attention! Please gather your belongings and prepare to depart!"

Over Tuesday and Wednesday, Green and the others had lived in a kind of dream. They were sequestered from the great mass of humanity below and eating well. Green felt grateful but guilty, and the searing memories of Monday gave him the jitters. He felt like something big was trying to swallow him up. The thought of Shenae slipping out of his grasp and disappearing kept flashing through his mind, despite his attempts to tune it out. (The sad news of his granddaughter's death had been communicated to her parents: the Greens had met up with the girls' aunt in the Dome, and she had managed to reach Deanna to tell her that her children were safe—but only two of the three.)

Green had no idea what he was now going to do with his life. But he considered himself a problem solver, someone who would do what was necessary to get a job done without self-doubt or distractions, and he focused on the one task he knew he had to perform: retrieving his mother's body off that roof. He had told the guardsmen running the place about it, but they'd told him there was nothing they could do. He had tried to get word to somebody outside, somebody in charge, but nothing worked.

Now their stay in limbo was finally ending. The guardsmen described the drill. Their departure would be secret—otherwise, the whole restless, angry Superdome population might erupt. (It didn't help matters that, overnight, a guardsman had accidentally shot himself in the leg while on patrol, and rumors were spreading that he'd been attacked.)

Then, as Green and his family were gathering their stuff together, word spread that a shot had been fired outside the Dome, where a helicopter was dropping supplies. Nobody knew exactly where the shot came from—or even if it was a gunshot. Across the city, some people were trying to attract helicopters by firing guns in the air—not, of course, the best way to go about it—but the noise could have been a vehicle backfiring or even driving over a plastic bottle, or another rumor. "Psychic gunfire," Honoré later called it.

They left the skybox, ten at a time, descending via back staircases to the lower levels of the Dome, wading through sludge. Green was barefoot—he couldn't see what he was stepping on, and he nearly slipped several times. Eventually they emerged into the street near the south edge of the Dome, close to the mall and Hyatt complex.

It was about five a.m., but the crowd on the plaza around the Dome was stirring. Somebody spotted Green and his group, and suddenly hundreds of people rumbled over to the edge of the concrete plaza above them. The guardsmen shoved Green and the others back out of sight and waited about ten minutes. Once the crowd lost interest, they waded over to the New Orleans Plaza, the mall between the Hyatt Regency hotel and the Superdome. As they did so, Green sliced up the bottoms of his feet walking on broken glass. Finally, they trudged into the first-floor food court and were told to sit down and wait.

After the shooting reports, Richard Zuschlag, the owner and CEO of Acadian Ambulance, which had been evacuating the special-needs patients, said he'd had enough. It was too dangerous for his pilots, Zuschlag told reporters, and he was suspending the flights "until they gain control of the Superdome." Meanwhile, more rumors filtered up through the guardsmen on the floor to the commanders. Something, the story went, was going to happen. It wasn't clear what—an organized riot, an attempt to seize control and commandeer the buses that were set to begin taking people out, possibly at ten a.m. As the sun was coming up, Phil Parr was outside on the concrete deck when General Gary Jones, the commander of the Guard troops at the Dome, came up to him with a melodramatic message.

"I don't believe I can protect you or your people any longer," Jones said. "We're going to be making our last stand."

Jones pointed to a nearby parking lot, the planned escape route.

"When it's time, get behind us and we'll do what we can."

With the evacuation struggling to get off the ground, Parr didn't want to leave. But if the Guard was panicking, if the vague rumors had any substance, the choice might not be his. He checked to make sure the medical team would be able to continue to do its job as long as possible. A California team had arrived only hours earlier, around midnight, to replace the exhausted New Mexicans. The team members told him that the Guard had pulled security from their space in the basketball arena—apparently because the soldiers were needed to help the evacuation. They no longer felt safe and were leaving on their own—along with the city medical personnel. Parr was irritated, but he couldn't stop them.

There were still five hundred sick patients waiting to depart, and without anyone to oversee them, more fatalities were likely. Dr. Ralph Lupin, a Guard general overseeing the Dome, angrily broke the news to Jones.

"You know, how do you expect me to deal with all of these critical-care patients here?" said Lupin, irate.

"What are you talking about?" Jones replied.

"All the patients over there on that ramp."

"Why are you dealing with them?"

"FEMA left. They left!" he said. "They didn't leave any supplies, I don't have charts, I don't know what's wrong with these people, I don't know—they've got IVs in their arms, I don't even know really what's supposed to happen, what the plan is or anything else!"

No riots erupted, and FEMA personnel returned to the Dome that afternoon, some feeling a bit sheepish. Meanwhile, though, the agency also pulled its search and rescue teams out of the city for security reasons, suspending operations for the balance of the day.

In Washington, Diane Sawyer interviewed Bush on ABC's *Good Morning America*. Sitting in the Roosevelt Room—a conference room equipped with a large video screen that flashed images of the devastation—she asked the president what images stuck in his mind, then reeled off some images of her own as Bush sat stoically, nodding.

"People still in the attic waving. Nurses are phoning in saying the situation in hospitals is getting ever more dire—"

"Yeah," Bush said.

"—that the nurses are getting sick now because of no clean water. And some of the things they have asked our correspondents to ask you is, they expected, they say to us, that the day after this hurricane that there would be a massive and visible armada of federal support. There would be boats coming in, there would be food, there would be water, and it would be there within hours."

"Yeah."

"They wondered, what's taking so long?"

"Well, there's a lot of food on its way. A lot of water on the way. And there's a lot of boats and choppers headed that way. It just takes a while to float them," Bush said. "I mean, for example, the [amphibious assault ship] *Iwo Jima* is coming from the east coast of the United States toward New Orleans. And people have got to know that there is a massive—one of the, the, most massive federal relief effort ever, in combination with state and local authorities. And there is a lot of help coming."

"But given the fact that everyone anticipated a hurricane

five, a possible hurricane five hitting shore, are you satisfied with the pace at which this is arriving and which it was planned to arrive?" Sawyer asked.

"Well, I fully understand people wanting things to have happened yesterday. I mean, I, I understand the anxiety of people on the ground. I can—I just can't imagine what it's like to be waving a sign that said, come and get me now. So, there is, there, there is frustration, but I want people to know there's a lot of help coming. I don't think anybody anticipated the breach of the levees. They did anticipate a serious storm. These levees got breached, and as a result, much of New Orleans is flooded and now we're having to deal with it and will."

Bush's levee comment instantly became fodder for the growing ranks of critics, shorthand for fumbling cluelessness. It wasn't clear exactly what he meant. After copious prelandfall briefings, everybody from Bush on down was aware that levees might fail in the storm. True, the focus had been on levees being overtopped, not breached. But they had breached early Monday, and Bush's own people had then bobbled the ball, not recognizing the dire nature of the problem until sometime the next day. It was one thing to say the government had been surprised by the levee failures. Yet what had been done since then?

After five hours of waiting quietly in the food court, the Greens were ushered through the Hyatt and placed onto a bus that took them across the river and on to Houston.

Behind them, the Guard and police, using bullhorns and little else, had tried to push people into a single line. But the crowd had a mind of its own. It fanned out around the entrance to the mall, pressing to get in. Scuffles and fights were breaking out. As the morning wore on, it got worse: thousands of people began wading to the Dome and convention center from hotels and from homes around the city, hoping to hop on a bus out of town. The crowd swelled well past twenty thousand.

Elsewhere, things were also starting to move, albeit haltingly. The sound of a National Guardsman shouting had awakened

Harvey Miller from his restless sleep by the side of the interstate at about five a.m.: "Everybody up! The buses are coming
and they're going to load on the south side of the road!"

Groggy, Miller looked back across the road, where he'd left
Renee. She wasn't there. He assumed she'd been evacuated.
(She had been bused to Lafayette overnight, where she had
ended up in a hospital, her heart racing uncontrollably. The doctor gave her a prescription—but the overloaded hospital phar-
macy couldn't fill it. Thursday morning she was able to call their
daughter Beth in Little Rock, who hadn't heard from them and
was wild with worry. Beth's in-laws came from Lake Charles,
about thirty miles away, and picked Renee up.)

Hours went by, and Miller still hadn't gotten on a bus. He
was carrying Monet, and several drivers rejected him for that
reason. He tried to bribe ambulance drivers, who rejected his
offers. Then a kid came up and asked him if he was having trouble getting out because of his dog. Soon he found himself in the
people-with-pets area. The kid's family had three cat carriers
and a golden retriever. Three or four others came over with dogs.
A lady with an SPCA truck pulled up and offered to take the animals to a shelter northwest of there. Figuring it was the best solution, he signed over Monet. When he started walking away,
she began wailing and howling. It felt like a knife in his chest.

When he returned to the staging area, things were finally
starting to get organized. A state police officer was marking out
lines on the pavement and walking forty people at a time from
the mass of people to each line. After Harvey gave a brief interview to a reporter, another state police officer came over, asked
Harvey if he was alone, and then put him on a bus bound for
Houston.

At about 9:30 a.m., a stream of helicopters had begun arriving at Memorial Medical Center to pull the remaining patients
out. Fed up, the hospital's parent company, the Tenet Health-
care Corporation, had contracted a private transport company to
do the job. They were lucky to get there at all—many privately
run helicopters had been diverted and conscripted to other jobs,
some by FEMA, others by the National Guard.

At the same time, rescue boats began evacuating the rest of the hospital's occupants. Like the helicopters, it wasn't anything official, just boat owners running their own rescue missions. A little after noon, Quigley and Dupre climbed on board a johnboat piloted by a construction worker and a real estate agent and headed south, toward the "beach" at the intersection of Napoleon Avenue and Dryades Street. Every so often they'd run over the roof of a car, the passage accompanied with a clunk.

At the intersection they got out and walked a few more blocks through the mud to St. Charles Avenue, where a crowd had gathered. Buses were now running them out of town. Cops were jamming some old and infirm people onto a container truck. Most of the officers were just standing around, unable or unwilling to organize the crowd. When a bus came, the crowd pressed in around it, and only the most aggressive managed to get on.

After an hour, Quigley and Dupre managed to climb on the back of a flatbed garden truck. They stood next to a young, pregnant African American woman who said she'd tried to get into the Superdome but been turned away twice. All she had to her name was a Ziploc bag containing a half-empty bottle of antibiotics and thirty dollars in change. The truck motored out fast, and people started banging on the sides, afraid they'd fall out or hit a dangling power line.

"If you don't like it, get the hell out!" hollered the driver.

They were dropped in the crowd at Interstate 10 and Causeway Boulevard. There were thousands of people—most of them black—milling around on the mud, on the highways, on the cloverleaf. Helicopters, army trucks, and ambulances were everywhere—it looked like the end of a Hollywood action flick. There were no toilets they could see.

Dupre and Quigley waited underneath the Causeway bridge over the freeway. Again, there was no system to get people onto the ragtag fleet of school and tour buses that had finally materialized. After ninety minutes, they considered walking the seventy-five miles to Baton Rouge, as they had done once during a protest against the death penalty. But they were in no shape to do that. Then they figured they'd join in the medical re-lief effort. Quigley and Dupre approached a couple of guys in stethoscopes, who turned out to be nursing student volunteers. They were on their way back home to Lafayette and offered to take Quigley and Dupre to her mom's house in Opelousas, not far away.

With each passing hour, the convention center had become a more appalling and at times bizarre spectacle, playing out in real time on television and the Internet. The crowd there ap-proached twenty thousand people. Food and water were scarce. There were still no authorities there save roving black-clad state and city SWAT teams riding around the site on their urban as-sault vehicles, stopping only to respond to calls for help from a group of employees sequestered inside. Thieves had hotwired seventy-five forklifts and electric carts and gone on a looting rampage, rifling the building's caches of food and liquor. Some were armed, and from time to time people reported hearing shots. More rumors spread—none true—that dozens were dy-ing, that baby killers and gang rapists were on the loose.

The body of Ethel Freeman, a ninety-one-year-old woman from eastern New Orleans, sat slumped in a wheelchair under a convention center entrance. On Wednesday, Freeman's son Herbert Freeman Jr. had loaded her, her wheelchair, and some food into a small canoe and paddled his way to dry ground. Then he'd pushed her for miles to the convention center.

Ethel, a former custodial worker, took nourishment by feed-ing tube and wore diapers. She'd begun to feel sick on their trek across town, and as the day wore on, she begged her son for a doctor or a nurse. He told her a bus would come, but he felt help-less. They prayed. Early Thursday, she passed on. Her son cov-ered her body with a plaid poncho and sat in a folding chair a few feet away in a spontaneous vigil. Photographers and television cameras soon captured the image of Freeman's body, the bright red doors of the convention center behind it, and beamed it out to the world. It joined a stream of other images of American citizens starving, desperately thirsty, fainting and dying in the stifling heat.

Earlier in the week at the EOC, Colonel Jeff Smith had alerted Bill Lokey that thousands were starting to congregate at the convention center, and on Wednesday, Lokey had dispatched trucks with food and water there from one of FEMA's staging areas, Camp Beauregard in central Louisiana, a 220-mile-drive from New Orleans. But on Thursday, as rumors of anarchy spread, Lokey was told that the National Guard had blocked the trucks from entering the city because there weren't enough soldiers to protect the drivers.

Otherwise, two days after flood victims colonized it, the convention center remained off the bureaucratic map. Wednesday night, Guard reconnaissance patrols had reported back to their commanders at the Superdome, noting, almost offhandedly, that "you've got another group of about fifteen thousand sitting over there." Mike Brown, working side by side with Lokey, didn't realize there was a problem until Thursday morning, when he saw the television reports. At that point, FEMA finally arranged a quick delivery of MREs and water, though not nearly enough. The helicopter was unable to land as people converged beneath it, so soldiers had tossed the supplies from ten feet up.)

A few blocks away at the Hyatt, Nagin and Ebbert decided they had to get people out of the convention center any way they could—on foot if necessary. Early in the afternoon they wrote up a statement and gave it to CNN.

"We have just received this statement in from the mayor, Ray Nagin," Wolf Blitzer announced on air. "'This is a desperate SOS,' he says. 'Right now, we're out of resources at the convention center and don't anticipate enough buses.' He goes on to say, 'We need buses. Currently, the convention center is unsanitary and unsafe, and we're running out of supplies for fifteen thousand to twenty thousand people. We are now allowing people to march. They will be marching up the Crescent City Connection to the West Bank Expressway to find relief wherever, wherever they can.'"

Meanwhile, National Public Radio's Robert Siegel was interviewing Secretary Chertoff and asked him about the crowd at the convention center. Chertoff responded that help was on its way to the Superdome and other "staging areas"—which the convention center most decidedly was not.

"We are hearing from our reporter—and he's on another line right now—thousands of people at the convention center in New Orleans with no food, zero," Siegel said.

"As I say, I'm telling you that we are getting food and water to areas where people are staging," Chertoff said. "And, you know, the one thing about an episode like this is if you talk to someone and you get a rumor or you get someone's anecdotal version of something, I think it's dangerous to extrapolate it all over the place. The limitation here on getting food and water to people is the condition on the ground. And as soon as we can physically move through the ground with these assets, we're going to do that. So—"

"But, Mr. Secretary, when you say that there is—we shouldn't listen to rumors, these are things coming from reporters who have not only covered many, many other hurricanes; they've covered wars and refugee camps. These aren't rumors. They're seeing thousands of people there."

"Well, I would be—actually I have not heard a report of thousands of people in the convention center who don't have food and water," Chertoff replied. "I can tell you that I know specifically the Superdome, which was the designated staging area for a large number of evacuees, does have food and water. I know we have teams putting food and water out at other designated evacuation areas."

In fact, Brown had not communicated his discovery of the convention center crowd up the chain of command. That, he said later, was the Homeland Security Operations Center's job. But with all its high-tech capabilities, the Operations Center had seemingly not bothered to make use of a basic street map; it had gone on operating under its mistaken impression that the convention center and Superdome—about a mile apart—were in the same complex. Later Thursday, the Operations Center director, Admiral Matthew Broderick, sent Wendell Shingler to investigate. Shingler, who headed the Federal Protective Services, the agency that oversaw security at U.S.-owned facilities, was coordinating the department's law enforcement activities. That evening, Shingler reported back that there were about a thousand people at the convention center, that food and water were available, and that the NOPD had secured the place. But Shingler had, it seemed, visited only one part of the building, which stretched on for nearly a mile.

Since Monday afternoon, it had been clear to anyone watching television that the majority of people trapped in New Orleans were African Americans, most from the low end of the income scale. In fact, the flood had not discriminated, hitting white and black and rich and poor neighborhoods, and later reviews of death records showed nearly as many whites as blacks had died. St. Bernard, where most of the trapped were white, was inaccessible except by air or by boat, so reporting from there had been sparse.

But the truth was that much of New Orleans's white population had departed before the storm hit, while the remainder lived in areas closer to dry land and found it easier to escape.

For the first few days, reporters mostly avoided mentioning the obvious. In a column posted Wednesday night, Jack Shafer, the media critic for the online magazine *Slate*, attributed this to a fear of appearing racist and suggested that not mentioning it was an abdication of journalistic responsibility: "By ignoring race and class, they boot the journalistic opportunity to bring attention to the disenfranchisement of a whole definable segment of the population. What I wouldn't pay to hear a Fox anchor ask, 'Say, Bob, why are these African-Americans so poor to begin with?'"

On CNN, commentator Jack Cafferty noted Shafer's column and asked viewers to send in their comments on race, class, and Katrina. "If those congressmen saw their rich, white constituents in trouble, they would have called a special session of Congress the next day. Why the hesitation?" one e-mailed.

On his popular radio show, conservative commentator Rush Limbaugh ascribed a different cause to the plight of New Orleans residents:

"Why can't they afford [cars]? What is it about New Orleans that doesn't pay? It's a sixty-seven percent black population," he noted. "Socialism to one degree or another has failed everywhere it's been tried. New Orleans has been run by liberal Democrat governments, people, for as long as I can remember, and there's an entitlement mentality there. You are never going to have a thriving city relying on handouts, or on welfare payments, whatever you want to call them. It's just not going to happen."

Out at the 17th Street canal, Corps engineers continued to bicker with their counterparts from the Orleans Levee District about who, exactly, was in charge. Finally, Major General Don Riley, the Corps's director of civil works, and Johnny Bradberry, the state transportation secretary, visited the breach site, conferred, and decided that the Corps would oversee the operation. The breach-closing would continue, but the canal would also be sealed off with sheet piling. Both sides would get what they wanted—and it had only taken several days of catastrophic flooding to work out the compromise.

The seat-of-the-pants operation, with its helicopters, slings, and giant sandbags (filled by prisoners from the Jefferson Parish jail), was still moving forward slowly. Several helicopters were now dropping bags into the hole, but they were still days away from sealing it.

Through the afternoon, a huge, mostly unchoreographed dance unfolded across the high ground of New Orleans. Under the burning sun, clouds, and then rain, tens of thousands of people escaped their watery perches and trudged along the high ground, making for the Dome, the convention center, or hoping to flag down a bus, 'copter, or SUV that could get them out. Many hadn't eaten or drunk anything in days.

With supplies running out and emergency workers looking for lodging, downtown hotels had been turning people out since Wednesday and locking the doors behind them. Nagin had ordered everyone out of the city the night before. He had also told people to cross the river if they could, but earlier that day, authorities had blocked foot traffic over the Crescent City Connection, one of the best routes out of the city. Thousands had walked across the bridge since Monday afternoon, and officials in Gretna (a nearby suburb) and the Jefferson Parish sheriff's office had ginned up a modest convoy with three school buses and two transit buses to pick them up and take them to the staging area at Interstate 10 and Causeway. On Wednesday, they made dozens of trips and ferried thousands. But they'd started to run low on food and supplies.

Thursday morning, Gretna police chief Arthur Lawson, Craig Taffaro of the Jefferson sheriff's office, and Mike Helmstetter, the chief of the bridge police force, met at the bridge office in Algiers and decided to mount a blockade. They had nothing more to offer people crossing over, and they believed that a large-scale evacuation of New Orleans would begin soon. If people kept coming, it might get ugly.

Officers from all three police forces took up positions on the bridge.

While the bridge blockade cut off the route from New Orleans, the Coast Guard's evacuation from predominantly white St. Bernard to Algiers—at the foot of the bridge—continued all day Thursday. Lawson, Taffaro, and Helmstetter denied any racial motivation, but the decision to blockade the Crescent City Connection became a symbol of a stark divide. Gretna and the West Bank were predominantly white. Viewed through the racial prism, it appeared the police thought the black people trapped in New Orleans had already trashed one town and couldn't be trusted anywhere else. They would have to remain in the Hobbesian prison that they, the hurricane, and their leaders had created.

David Lewald had been running his three ferries, tug, and barge back and forth for a day and a half from the Chalmette slip. At night he slept on the *Pamlico*. There was now a crowd of about 2,500 people milling around the edge of the parking lot at the Algiers ferry landing, waiting for rides out. In the heat, old people were fainting. Diabetics were begging for insulin. One man, apparently a drug addict, collapsed and could not be revived. The nurses propped his body up against a tree and left it there.

Still, Lewald's evacuation was working. Sometimes it wasn't exactly clear why, but things got done without anyone asking. A nurse who lived nearby showed up each morning to tend to the sick, the dehydrated, the diabetics, then disappeared around nightfall, when it got dangerous, declining offers of an escort.

"There was a guy, a janitor at Algiers," Lewald said. "There's trash everywhere, and this guy would walk around all day long, muttering to himself, sweeping up. That landing was always clean."

And then there was Lewald himself, refusing to give up.

To all the world, it appeared New Orleans was descending into anarchy, an incredible fate for an American city. There were bodies in the streets; the scenes of suffering were like something out of the Third World. Thugs were breaking into stores and looting at will around the city. Rapists and murderers were preying on the dispossessed. But the city wasn't quite the portrait of the apocalypse that the media was broadcasting to the world. The bodies were, for the most part, drowning victims who had been dead for days, except for a few poor souls who had died for lack of medical attention. Looting was widespread, fights broke out at the Superdome, and groups of armed young men roved menacingly around the convention center. But at both places, the vast majority of people were, if a bit disorderly in the absence of food, water, and authority, largely peaceful.

As of Thursday, only 5,804 Louisiana National Guard troops had been deployed in the state—the number had not increased in several days. They were reservists; nearly half of the state's National Guard troops were in Iraq. There were also 2,555 Guard troops from other states—a modest influx of about 1,300 since the day before. It was nowhere near what was needed, but more were on the way. On Wednesday morning, responding to requests from Blanco and Landreneau, General Stephen Blum, the chief of the National Guard Bureau, had ordered the Army National Guard to get more people. E-mails went out to adjutants general around the nation, and soon more troops were motoring toward New Orleans from around the country.

Thursday morning, Honoré again stressed that in his view a ramped-up National Guard could do the job and that federal troops were not needed. "PUSH BACK. I WILL SEE GOV TODAY. WILL SHOW HER FLOW OF NG TROOPS. NG HAS GROUND FIGHT IN HAND WITH [24,000] IN NEXT R6 HOURS," he wrote in an e-mail to General Rowe, his boss at Northcom. Blanco, though, still wanted those troops. Honoré was technically correct: make enough requests to governors and the National Guard Bureau, and the Guard would come through—eventually—making federal troops irrelevant.

Still, the response so far was a disaster for Bush, Blanco, and Nagin. First Iraq had slipped the American grasp, now a city on American soil was doing the same. In the style of cold war debates about communism, people were asking, "Who lost New Orleans?"

The politicians tried to coordinate a response to the criticism. Blanco's communications director, Bob Mann, who had written a biography of Russell Long and was intimately familiar with national politics, spoke with aides to Senate Minority Leader Harry Reid Thursday afternoon to coordinate the strategy. "Bush's numbers are low, and they are getting pummeled by the media for their inept response to Katrina and are actively working to make us the scapegoats," Mann wrote in an e-mail that afternoon. "By the weekend, the Bush administration will have a full-blown PR disaster/scandal on their hands because of the late response to needs in New Orleans." The corollary was that the White House and its Republican Party apparatus were likely to try to pin the blame on Blanco for the lack of response.

Mayor Nagin, meanwhile, had also reached the boiling point. After handing over his list of requests on Monday, there wasn't much he could actually do to provision aid to his embattled citizenry; most of that was being done through Baton Rouge. And where some politicians sought the spotlight and contact with constituents in a crisis, Nagin had maintained an unusual degree of isolation at the Hyatt. Concerned about his own safety, he chose not to visit the Dome or the convention center. He communicated sporadically with Baton Rouge and Washington, and departed the Hyatt to give press conferences and make forays to view repair operations at the 17th Street canal.

Meanwhile, the disconnect between what he knew to be going on in the city and the reassurances he saw on television had grown greater with each passing hour, as had the stress and uncertainty. "It was a buildup of things," Nagin said later. "Keep in mind that from Monday right after the event we had been promised that buses were coming. More food and water were coming. We were promised that there were forty thousand National Guard troops on the way. And you know, I just kind of had enough of it. There were all these press conferences I kept hearing about. I was listening to WWL [a local radio station] and they were doing another press conference, and I was totally upset about what I was hearing. It wasn't the truth. It wasn't reality."

Nagin vented in an interview later that night with stentorian local radio host Garland Robinette.

"They don't have a clue what's going on down here," the mayor declared. "They flew down here one time, two days after the doggone event was over, with TV cameras, AP reporters, all kinds of goddamn—excuse my French, everybody in America, but I am *pissed*."

Robinette asked him about the formal rules of disasters: "Apparently there's a section of our citizenry out there that thinks because of a law that says the federal government can't come in unless requested by the proper people, that everything that's going on to this point has been done as good as it can possibly be."

"Really?" Nagin said.

"I know you don't feel that way."

Nagin responded,

Well . . . did the tsunami victims request? Did they go through a formal process to request? Did Iraq—did the Iraqi people request that we go in there? Did they ask us to go in there? We authorized eight billion dollars to go to Iraq, lickety-quick. After 9/11, we gave the president unprecedented powers, lickety-quick, to take care of New York and other places. Now you mean to tell me that a place where most of the oil is coming through . . . a place that is so unique, when you mention New Orleans anywhere around the world, everybody's eyes light up . . . you mean to tell me that a place where you probably have thousands of people that have died, and thousands more that are dying every day, that we can't figure out a way to authorize the resources that we need? Come on, man.

Nagin's tirade captured the frustrations of many, but it was a bit peculiar for someone privy to the relief effort. By then the Superdome evacuation was well under way, and more troops—if not yet the hoped-for forty thousand—were due the next morning.

Harvey Miller walked into the Astrodome around eleven p.m. His bus had pulled into the parking lot at sunset, then stopped in a queue for four hours. People were allowed out to stretch their legs, but otherwise they sat and waited. After finally getting into the stadium, they went through a medical area, then into a registration zone where it took another thirty minutes to get processed and get an ID wristband. The floor of the Astrodome was full of cots. There were many people sitting in the stands. Most of the cots were already filled, but Harvey found a vacant one and sat down. A Red Cross volunteer brought him some fruit and cheese, as well as a comb and toothbrush. Then he found a phone bank and called his daughter in Little Rock.

"Dad! Where are you?" she asked.

"I'm in the Astrodome in Houston, and I have no idea where your mother is. I know where Monet is but not where your mother is."

She brought him up to date, and they arranged for her brother-in-law, who lived in Houston, to come pick him up. He went and sat on the curb. No one came. Finally, he borrowed a bus driver's cell phone and found his ride was on the opposite side of the Astrodome. Harvey walked back around and got in the car. It was well after midnight. Back at his in-law's house, he fell asleep immediately, then woke up at three a.m. and took a shower. At five, he got up again and took another shower. He couldn't shake the smell, the grimy feeling on his skin, but he was safe.

Chapter 14

FRIDAY AND SATURDAY, SEPTEMBER 2–3

A T FOUR A.M. FRIDAY morning, Loco Cooper had inched his way close to the front of the Superdome's evacuation queues. Like everything else since Monday morning, waiting to get out was an ordeal demanding both physical endurance and a high tolerance for tedium, and Cooper had plenty of the first, none of the second. He had been in line for sixteen hours. As day, then night dragged on with seemingly incremental progress, the anxious crowd repeatedly pressed forward. Each time, soldiers policing the edges ordered people up and down the ranks to take three steps back. Around midnight, someone shoved Cooper forward.

"Take a step back!" a guardsman growled at him.

"I can't do it! Look at this!" he complained, gesturing over his shoulder.

"Shut up and get the fuck back!"

Cooper did what he could.

Shortly after four a.m., the line halted again. Exhausted and angry, Cooper gave up, returned to the Superdome, found a piece of cardboard, and collapsed.

Mike Brown had spent a lot of time that week on TV, trying to look and sound the part of the earnest, knowledgeable commander directing the movements of people and materiel over a vast area. Now, fairly or not, as the public face of the government's Katrina debacle, Brown had been labeled an incompetent bumbler of historic proportions. Friday morning, he was lambasted by a gauntlet of outraged anchors on ABC, CBS, NBC, and CNN.

"FEMA has been on the ground for four days, going into the fifth day. Why no massive airdrop of food and water?" CNN's Soledad O'Brien asked him. "In Banda Aceh, in Indonesia, they got food dropped two days after the tsunami struck."

"That's what we're going to do here, too," Brown said. "And I think—"

"But, sir, forgive me—"

"Soledad, just a moment, please. We're feeding those people in the convention center. We have fed over one hundred and fifty thousand people as of last night. That is happening."

"I understand that you're feeding people and trying to get in there now, but it's Friday. It's Friday," she said after more back-and-forth, then lit into him again.

"Do you look at the pictures that are coming out of New Orleans?" O'Brien said. "And do you say, 'I'm proud of the job that FEMA is doing on the ground there in a tough situation'?"

"Soledad—"

"Or do you look at these pictures and you say, 'This is a mess and we've dropped the ball; we didn't do what we should have done'?"

"Soledad, I look at these pictures and my heart breaks," Brown said. "My heart breaks just like the rest of the country's heart breaks."

Brown added that he had "mission-assigned" the military to deliver supplies, and he hoped that would solve some of the problems. In fact, he was trying to persuade the Defense Department to take over FEMA's core function: directing supplies into the disaster zone. After a week of breakdowns, Brown was punting.

"FEMA's logistics capability has been overwhelmed," operations director Ken Burris had told Colonel Richard Chavez, a senior advisor in the Defense Department's Homeland Defense office, on Thursday. "We want DOD to take over logistics operations in Louisiana and Mississippi."

"Is that really what you want us to do?" an incredulous Chavez replied. There was no precedent for such a request; Burris might just as well have told him to immediately start supplying somebody else's army in the midst of a raging battle. He told Burris that such a move would require a formal agreement between secretaries Chertoff and Rumsfeld. But the wheels were set in motion, and on Friday Rumsfeld approved the request. Defense Department logistics experts immediately began studying how FEMA moved supplies around and were amazed to see just how primitive its system was. Once something was in transit, it could not be tracked—one reason why a lot of things were simply getting lost.

Cooper woke after a few hours, brushed his teeth and washed his face with water from the bottles he'd saved, then returned to the Superdome line. It looked the same. He watched as helicopters thundered overhead. A short while later, General Honoré's retinue appeared near the front of the line.

Honoré had not brought troops. But he had brought something New Orleans, its beleaguered residents and their exhausted police, guardsmen, and public officials desperately needed: a little dose of self-confidence. Unlike Bush, Blanco, and Nagin, Honoré projected command and self-assurance. If he didn't know what he was doing, he didn't let on. People listened to what he said and did what he told them to do.

From his place in line, exhausted, angry, and grimy, Cooper saw things the same way: "He had a red hat. He had a big ol' cigar. And I said, that man, that man is the man we've been waiting for. We are getting out of there. He told them what to do. At first we had six lines, then they turned six lines into four. And then everybody started to move. Once I jumped in that line, we were gone. It didn't take but twenty minutes."

Nearby, a force of a thousand National Guard troops from Louisiana and Arkansas was rolling into the city on a convoy of fifty vehicles, including more than a dozen trucks laden with food and water. Guardsmen sat on the roofs and hung off the sides of Humvees and amphibious vehicles, children splashing through the water alongside them. Their objective: take control of the convention center.

Earlier that morning, at the request of the city, Colonel Jacques Thibodeaux of the Louisiana National Guard had planned out the mission with the precision of a surprise attack. His intelligence from the site, just a few blocks away—anecdotal reports making their way back to the Guard commanders and the mayor's office—indicated the convention center had been transformed into a lower rung of hell. Criminal gangs were preying at will on the crowd, robbing, raping, and killing. Tourists who wandered too close were ambushed. Bodies lay scattered on the floor in pools of blood. The oppressed crowd was seething, ready to erupt. There was no telling how they'd react when authorities showed up. So, Thibodeaux decided, the Guard would make a show of overwhelming force. But a delicate balance was required. After all, the takeover was not an attack but a rescue mission; it would have to be orderly and peaceful. If shots were fired and innocent people injured or killed, the effort would be yet another disaster on the week's long, dark list.

The Guard vehicles rolled down Loyola Avenue past the Hyatt and stopped at Poydras Street, a major intersection twelve blocks away from Convention Center Boulevard. Guardsmen hopped off and lined up. Honoré left the Superdome and walked the half block from the Hyatt to the impromptu staging area, talking to Guard commanders on his cell phone. Though the troops were not under his command, he looked them over.

"Keep your weapons lowered at all times," he instructed the soldiers. "This is not a military operation. This is not Iraq."

Brandishing his cigar, Honoré hopped into the lead vehicle, and the convoy headed toward the river. It arrived at the edge of the convention center at 12:25 p.m. As they rolled down the wide boulevard, past hotels and the Riverwalk Mall, the first thing they saw was smoke and flames rising from makeshift grills. It wasn't clear where the food had come from, but it was an encouraging sign. Then people started applauding, jumping up and down, shouting out welcomes and hallelu-jahs. They came up to the soldiers, arms spread, wanting to touch them.

"We need food, water. . . . How are we going to get out of here? . . . Please just help us! . . . What is going on? . . . Thank you, Jesus! Thank you so much for coming here!"

"It reminded me of the liberation of France in World War II. There were people cheering; one boy even saluted," Lieutenant Colonel John Edwards of the Arkansas Guard told the *Times-Picayune*. "We never—never once—encountered any hostility."

It took only twenty minutes to establish control and begin setting up six food distribution stations along the length of the building.

A team of Arkansas guardsmen was assigned to sweep the building. When they entered, they were dismayed to see people splayed out on the floor, apparently dead, nearly everywhere they went. About a hundred altogether were scattered through the building. The guardsmen continued on, exploring the building's vast interior space (about fifty-three football fields in area). They found no gangs, no thugs. When they surveyed the interior again a few hours later, almost all of the one hundred bodies were gone. The guardsmen concluded they had merely been passed out from heat, dehydration, and starvation. In the end, only four bodies—including those of Booker Harris and Ethel Freeman—were found.

Friday morning, the first paper editions of the *Times-Picayune* rolled off the presses of the *Houma Courier*, fifty thousand copies altogether—a fifth of the normal press run. "**HELP US, PLEASE**" read the headline bannered across the front page in heavy type. Beneath that was Brett Duke's photo of a young woman named Angela Perkins screaming those words, kneeling on the sidewalk in front of the convention center, her hands coming together in a gesture of prayer.

Later, New Orleans bureau staffers David Meeks, Trymaine Lee, and Mike Perlstein drove up to the convention center, not knowing what to expect. Meeks pulled a stack of *Times-*

Picayunes out and began waving them around like a newsboy hawking an extra. People ran up. Hands reached out from all directions, grabbing for the papers. They were gone within minutes. Images of the convention center crowd had been beamed around the world, but the people there didn't know that. For days, they had been trapped in an information vacuum as well as a city sidewalk, subsisting on rumors of death and atrocity, uncertain who, if anyone, knew or cared about them. They hungered for news. Now, suddenly, they had something palpable between their fingers that told them the world was indeed watching.

Even as the focus shifted from search and rescue to evacuation, thousands of people were still roughing it in flooded houses across the flood zone. Some didn't want to leave; when rescuers came, they declined to answer the door or refused to depart, whether through pigheadedness, a mistrust of authority, or knowing that it meant a kind of surrender. Others wanted out, but days went by with no sign of help. Most of the stranded lived in eastern New Orleans, the Lower Ninth Ward, and St. Bernard, which were farther from dry land and from rescuers' staging areas than central New Orleans. When rescuers did come, the chaos and stress made it hard to be systematic— some streets got multiple sweeps; others were completely missed.

Fisherman Ricky DeJean and seven other people had spent the balance of the week roughing it on the second floor of his flooded house in Chalmette. Before the storm, DeJean had secured his shrimp boat in Dulac, about seventy miles southwest of New Orleans, then returned home to be near his father and stepmother, who lived close by and did not want to evacuate. They all had been through Betsy and Camille, so they figured they'd seen the worst.

DeJean's house sat on a gentle slope, making it relatively safe compared to the surrounding dwellings. When the floodwaters rose, he had crossed the street and fetched his dad and stepmother, escorting them through waist-deep water that soon reached a height of seven feet at his house. On Tuesday, he had swum a block and a half to where he knew a neighbor kept a motorboat. As he was trying to get the outboard to start, he heard cries for help from a nearby house. Stranded inside were an eighty-three-year-old man and his mentally disabled daughter. DeJean couldn't get the motor to start, so he pulled each of them through water back to his house.

Soon, word got out to others in the vicinity that the DeJean house had both dry rooms and food, and by Wednesday eight people were encamped on the second floor. Still no help came. They slept on the floor and waded downstairs to cook when necessary. (On Monday afternoon, a strange tableau had unfolded in the kitchen: DeJean's dad cooked fish on the gas stove as water rose past his waist; he'd stopped only when the floodwaters burst through the windows, dousing the burner. Then, as the week wore on, the water level dropped to about waist-high and they were able to light the pilots again.) Each morning, DeJean made forays out to the homes of his houseguests. He raided everything in their freezers that hadn't rotted or been submerged, and they fried it on the stove and ate it.

Friday morning, salvation finally arrived. It wasn't U.S. troops, but Canadians—the medical unit of an urban search and rescue team from Vancouver that had offered help to Louisiana. Doctors checked out DeJean and his houseguests. The team didn't have enough space in their boat to transport them all, but agreed to send help. An hour later, two big road excavators commandeered by the St. Bernard sheriff's office rolled through the water and up to the house. They took everyone away except DeJean, who decided to stick around for another day to secure his remaining belongings from looters.

Craig and Cindy Ratliff had spent three days sitting and sleeping on plywood in the warehouse at the Chalmette slip. It had filled up fast after they got there, and on Friday there were two thousand people in it and hundreds of pets. But unlike other spots, there was a semblance of order—proof that with manpower and competence, the crisis could be managed. St. Bernard police and guardsmen had established a constant presence. They managed petty disputes and meal distribution—MREs and water had arrived by helicopter on Wednesday—and they told people to take their pets outside if the animals needed to go. The cops instructed the group to be ready to leave at any time.

The Ratliffs ended up camped out near some people from their church, so they had someone to chat with. But the wait went on forever, and after a day Cindy felt ill and spent most of the time lying on the pallet, trying to sleep. Craig relieved his boredom by wandering. At night he'd walk the dock, and during the days he'd stroll down the levee to get some privacy and wash off the sweat and black dust from the warehouse with floodwater. Then he'd walk north into the flood to assess whether the water was receding. On Tuesday, at Chalmette High, it went down steadily—first six, then eight, then twelve inches—then stopped. After that it dropped more slowly, but it was receding.

On Friday morning, after a couple of hours, they were told to line up outside to get on a ferry to Algiers. Dozens of school buses were lined up at David Lewald's staging area at the Algiers ferry landing. "Somebody's got a gun!" a man shouted as the Ratliffs got into a line, and the loading stopped for about ten minutes. Then, finally, at about two o'clock they got on a bus, men in back, women in front. They were handed an MRE and a bottle of water each. The bus—part of a convoy of twenty—took them through the West Bank suburbs and back over the Huey P. Long Bridge upriver from New Orleans, then to the airport so the passengers could make a pit stop before continuing on to a Dallas shelter.

Almost proudly, President Bush had once noted in an interview that he rarely read newspapers or watched news reports; instead, he relied on his aides to keep him updated. "The most objective sources I have are people on my staff who tell me what's happening in the world," he had told Brit Hume of Fox News. Bush's estrangement from the media went beyond that: over the previous four years, the White House had sought to marginalize the mainstream media, believing it could get its message across via direct appeals, sympathetic conservative media outlets, and the local press. "I'm mindful of the filter through which some news travels, and somehow you just got to go over the heads of the filter and speak directly to the people," he told a group of local broadcasters in one such attempt. But like the troubles in Iraq, Katrina was a hard reality that did not yield to the famous Bush message discipline, and by Thursday, the White House staff decided that the media had its uses. A little news might focus the president, who still seemed not to have fully absorbed the enormity of the task at hand or its likely political fallout.

On Friday, the president jetted down to the Gulf Coast to see the damage for himself (with the Guard beginning to get a handle on security and the evacuation proceeding, a presidential visit had been deemed manageable). On the way, Bush watched a DVD of news reports on Katrina's toll compiled by his communications director, Dan Bartlett. Terrible images of neighborhoods under water, people stranded and pleading for help flashed before his eyes.

Meanwhile, the White House worked on a way to assert more control over the military effort. If urgent danger was the principal reason for asserting control, the White House was a little late. Order was slowly returning as more troops entered New Orleans and MPs began patrolling through the floodwaters and taking up positions at intersections.

But given the continuing news reports of horrific conditions and widespread mayhem, officials at all levels were still fuzzy on what was going on, and a chorus including Nagin, Blanco, senators, congressmen, pundits, and outraged TV reporters was screaming for action from the top and raising broader questions about Bush's whole Homeland Security apparatus. The criticism was not just from Democrats. "If we can't respond faster than this to an event we saw coming across the Gulf for days, then why do we think we're prepared to respond to a nuclear or biological attack?" Newt Gingrich, the former Speaker of the House, told the Associated Press.

At a hangar in Mobile, Bush was briefed by Coast Guard and National Guard rescuers, then delivered a few off-the-cuff remarks, again alternately grave and upbeat.

"We've got a lot of rebuilding to do. First, we're going to save lives and stabilize the situation. And then we're going to help these communities rebuild," Bush declared. "The good news is—and it's hard for some to see it now—that out of this chaos is going to come a fantastic Gulf Coast, like it was before. Out of the rubbles of [Mississippi Senator] Trent Lott's house—he's lost his entire house—there's going to be a fantastic house. And I'm looking forward to sitting on the porch." Lott, standing nearby, chuckled.

"I want to thank you all for—and, Brownie, you're doing a heck of a job," Bush told Mike Brown, standing immediately to his left, looking a bit awkward in a spotless button-down shirt. "The FEMA director is working twenty-four, they're working twenty-four hours a day," Bush continued to scattered applause. "Again, my attitude is, if it's not going exactly right, we're going to make it go exactly right. If there's problems, we're going to address the problems. And that's what I've come down to assure people of. And again, I want to thank everybody."

Asked why America couldn't get food and water to its own people during a brief walking tour of Biloxi a bit later, Bush repeated the administration's emerging—and incorrect— explanation for the slow response.

"The levees broke on Tuesday in New Orleans," he said. "On Wednesday, we—and Thursday we started evacuating people. A lot of people have left that city. A lot of people have been pulled out on buses. It's—I am satisfied with the response. I'm not satisfied with all the results. I am satisfied with the response." A bit later, he elaborated on his dissatisfaction: "I'm talking about the fact that we don't have enough security in New Orleans yet." Bush was at least conceding that the reality of the catastrophe in New Orleans existed, and that it was causing some problems; but not, apparently, any serious failings by the federal government.

Air Force One flew to New Orleans that afternoon (though not with the president on board; he arrived via helicopter after touring the damage from the air). A luncheon powwow was set with local officials. As everyone else had at various points during the week, the White House staff had trouble reaching Nagin due to technical problems. After failing to get through to the mayor in New Orleans, Bush aides had ended up contacting his press secretary, who had evacuated to Houston. She, in turn, got through to his communications director, Sally Forman, at the Hyatt, who gave Nagin the word on the lunch. The mayor told Foreman he hadn't had time to shower or shave and had had only two hours of sleep. Word came back he could take a shower and eat on the plane.

As Nagin helicoptered out to the airport in the early afternoon, he tried to gather his thoughts as he viewed the city below him. Supposedly, the president liked it when people cut through the BS, and Nagin had a simple message: he wanted someone in charge.

"At the time, there was no one at the top of the heap who had full authority over everything going on," Nagin said. "The state police had pretty much left, and we only had a small number of National Guard. There were supposed to be forty thousand National Guardsmen on the sideline, but they weren't there." On the other hand, Nagin knew his venting of the previous night might have rubbed Bush and others the wrong way. He wasn't sure how to say what he wanted to say.

Air Force One landed shortly after Nagin arrived at the airport, and he was escorted to a bathroom on the presidential plane and took his shower and shaved his head and face. White House aides finally took him to the dining room, where most of the congressional delegation, Blanco, Brown, Chertoff, Card, Hagin, and the National Guard Bureau chief, Lieutenant General Stephen Blum, had already gathered. After they began eating their meal of grilled chicken and vegetables, the president arrived and prompted them to start talking.

It wasn't a pleasant discussion. As they went around the table, the Louisiana officials listed snafu after snafu with the federal government. Bobby Jindal, the suburban congressman Blanco had defeated in the 2003 governor's race, described how FEMA had instructed a local sheriff to send his pleas for assistance via e-mail. "The guy was sitting in a district underwater and with no electricity," Jindal told *Newsweek*. "How does that make any sense? . . . The president just shook his head, as if he couldn't believe what he was hearing."

Nagin was the last to speak. His emotions got the better of him again, and his voice rose close to a bellow as made his plea.

"Mr. President, I don't mean to be too presumptive or pushy, but there's still a lot of people left in our city and if you and the governor don't get together and determine who has the final authority on how to fix this disaster, we're all going to be in trouble," Nagin said. "I see this incredible dance going on and nobody has the final say. If you don't want to give me the full authority, give it to General Honoré. If the two of you don't get together on this issue, more people are going to die in this city, and you need to resolve this immediately!"

With that, he slammed his hand down on the table.

"Okay, everybody in this room, let's go in another room so they can settle this," Nagin added. Everyone else looked on, stunned. Nobody yelled at the president—especially this one—much less gave orders for him.

"No, you guys can stay," Bush said, looking surprised but unruffled. "There's an office where the governor and I can talk in private."

Blanco was taken aback. She thought Nagin had gone off the deep end and wondered if she was being sandbagged, maneuvered into accepting some kind of federal control, though she believed any need for it was by then superfluous. "At that moment, it was obvious Ray Nagin didn't even know what was going on in his own city," she said later. "The National Guard had been moving people out of the Dome since the day before. They were closing down the convention center even as we were getting on the plane. . . . I don't know if it was all staged, looking back on it. It was just bizarre."

On the other hand, she was delighted to get a private meeting with the president. Bush and Blanco, along with Hagin, conferred for almost forty minutes in an office close to the front of the plane. It was a polite, careful dance by both. Bush strongly suggested that Blanco back an idea agreed to that morning by the Pentagon. It was a "dual hat" structure: there would be one commander, presumably Honoré, in charge of the Guard and the regular military troops. The commander would have two bosses—Blanco for the National Guard troops, Bush for the federal troops. In 2004, that structure had been used at both the Democratic and Republican political conventions and at the annual G8 summit with the world's economic powers. To the generals, this had the advantage of unifying the chain of command—sort of—while finessing any infringement on states' rights. On a practical level, though, it wasn't clear what difference, if any, it would make.

"If we send more military forces in, how do you think it can be managed without a single voice?" Bush asked Blanco.

"Well, I believe it can be managed like it's being managed now," Blanco said, pointing out that the number of guardsmen in New Orleans was now, finally, rising steadily—another five thousand guardsmen arrived that day, bringing the total to between twelve thousand and thirteen thousand—but it was still well short of the forty thousand total troops she wanted, and active-duty military troops would help make up that difference. Honoré could command them, while she retained control of the National Guard.

"You sent Honoré in, the mayor likes Honoré," she said. "Give Honoré soldiers."

Blanco felt she couldn't turn the president down cold, so she agreed to discuss his proposal with her staff and with General Landreneau. Blanco thought she had been unambiguous about her position, and left with the impression that Bush would be dispatching federal troops immediately. Nagin was then summoned to the room, and Blanco walked out as he walked in.

"I'm ready to move today," Bush told the mayor. "We had a good conversation, and there are a couple of possible solutions." But he said he was waiting for Blanco to decide on the command structure within the next day. Nagin didn't know what to say. He found it astonishing that no agreement had been reached.

"It would have been great if we could have left Air Force One, walked outside, and told the world that we had this all worked out," Nagin told CNN afterward. "It didn't happen, and more people died."

After the meeting, the group helicoptered out for a tour of the area, concluding at the 17th Street canal breach, where they watched prisoners shovel sand into the giant sandbags. Nearby, a barge and a pile driver had nearly completed the job of sealing off the canal with sheet pilings.

"Here's what I believe. I believe that the great city of New Orleans will rise again and be a greater city of New Orleans," Bush declared on the tarmac before he departed for Washington, again sounding an oddly jocular tone. "I believe the town where I used to come from Houston, Texas, to enjoy myself—occasionally too much—will be that very same town, that it will be a better place to come to. That's what I believe."

There would be no quick comeback, however. Many city landmarks, including Tulane University and the Saenger Theater, were flooded, along with most of the region's housing stock, a total of two hundred thousand units. The storm surge deposited countless tons of sediment through living rooms, kitchens, and family dens. It was sometimes mixed with sewage or crude oil, forming a gooey paste as the waters subsided. In the hot, humid days that followed the hurricane, mold began migrating up walls and across ceilings, turning homes and businesses into giant petri dishes.

Across the city, floodwaters were also penetrating the viscera of modern life—electrical and telephone wires, copper and fiber-optic cables, natural gas lines, sewer pipes, and storage tanks. As the city's technological systems crashed, that secondary disaster soon rivaled the initial natural one in cost and complexity.

Damaged natural gas lines burst, and small fires had erupted around the city. New Orleans firefighters found to their frustration that the floodwater all around them was not only useless, but setting back their efforts: it had taken out the power to the city's water treatment plant, so there was no pressure to the hydrants. The fire department had to rely on water drops from helicopters.

Nearly all of the city's pumping stations, including those containing forty-eight of A. B. Wood's original pumps, were also damaged. Some pumps would require months to repair. Entergy, the owner of the local electric utility, had so many broken power poles, transmission lines, and flooded transformers that it placed its New Orleans subsidiary into bankruptcy.

Thankfully, the "toxic soup" anticipated by emergency managers turned out not to be as hazardous to human health as predicted. But the storm still spread countless tons of unwanted waste through neighborhoods. After floodwaters inundated a sewage treatment plant in eastern New Orleans, its contents fouled surrounding homes. In St. Bernard Parish, debris apparently busted open a major crude oil storage tank during the storm, and the accompanying surge wave carried almost two million gallons of oil through an adjacent neighborhood. That was just a tiny fraction of the petroleum products Katrina sent sloshing over the Mississippi delta: all told, more oil spilled during and after the storm than from the Exxon *Valdez* tanker in Alaska sixteen years earlier.

The storm also spread around tons of hazardous wastes, byproducts of the region's oil and gas production. Large kerosene and fuel oil tanks floated free, along with acetylene torch canisters and barrels of oil field waste and drilling by-products. So many hazardous waste containers—some still intact, but many broken open and emptied—ended up dotting levee slopes in St. Bernard and Plaquemines that emergency disposal teams later had to inspect all levee stretches and guarantee them safe before contractors would begin work on repairs.

Louis Armstrong International Airport had never been a great transit hub, but it was now. It had become the latest temporary home of the displaced and the desperate. Since Tuesday, a crowd now totaling more than fifteen thousand people had moved in, colonizing the concourses, the main hall, the baggage areas, and the sidewalks outside. Many were sick people from hospitals and nursing homes who'd been airlifted out of the Superdome.

Helen Miller, an emergency trauma doctor in charge of an Oregon medical team, had arrived only the day before, a day and a half late, without supplies and with only the most basic equipment. It was FEMA's fault. Since the beleaguered agency had taken control of the National Disaster Medical System from the Department of Health and Human Services—one of the few expansions in FEMA's portfolio as Homeland Security reorganized—the bureaucracy had grown and support had shrunk.

Miller's team had gotten its marching orders on Tuesday, told to get the next flight out and to put their vehicles and equipment on a FedEx cargo plane—as they'd done when responding to Hurricane Ivan in 2004. Miller was packing when word came back that their flights would have to be booked through a FEMA-approved travel agent. It would take a day for the paperwork to go through. And the medical equipment, FEMA now declared, couldn't go by plane. Miller tapped six team members to drive the trucks from Portland to New Orleans. That would result in an additional two-day delay—if they drove round the clock.

The remaining team members, about twenty in all, arrived in Houston around midnight Wednesday, got rental cars, and drove three hours to Baton Rouge. They checked in with FEMA and then headed to New Orleans, arriving at the airport around dawn on Thursday.

Miller was stunned at the scene—people were walking around on the pavement, lying on the floors, sprawled on every available surface. There was no power and the place stank. The toilets were piled high with human waste. The National Guard was there but was focused on medical evacuations rather than providing security. And her supplies were still a day away.

"Usually we come in with seventy-two hours of MREs for our own team," she said. "But our team didn't have its stuff. We didn't have anything to sleep on, anything to eat, and we don't do mass care and feeding for fifteen thousand storm victims."

So they improvised. Helicopters were landing on the tarmac, sometimes a dozen an hour, bringing sick people in. The team members ran out, *MASH*-style, examined the patients as they came off, and pinned a piece of paper with their condition and a priority number on each one. They'd carry them inside and upstairs to the concourse "field hospital"—a treatment area with hundreds of stretchers, some on the floor, some on airport benches. If a patient got too sick, he'd be tagged for medevac, carried back out, and helicoptered to a real field hospital at the Pete Maravich Arena in Baton Rouge. Many didn't make it that far. Over the course of the week, twenty people died at the airport. By Friday morning, their hospital had about a thousand patients sprawled on stretchers, and they were treating people from the crowd who were swooning from heat, dehydration, and hunger. There were heart attacks, asthma attacks, seizures.

The National Guard was planning to airlift people out, and FEMA and other agencies had worked with the Air Transport Association to get fifteen private passenger planes in. But by Friday afternoon they—and the staff necessary to get evacuees on them—had only begun to arrive.

When the Ratliffs's school bus pulled up outside the airport, people eyed it almost hungrily.

"The folks at the airport had an extreme dislike for us," Craig said. "They wanted to know why we were on the buses and they weren't."

They sat in a bus queue for two hours in front of the airport, moving six feet every ten minutes or so, enduring the continued stares of the crowd. As they waited, their National Guard escort took the remaining MREs and water bottles and dumped them on the curb as a peace offering.

After the passengers had finally used the bathrooms, the guardsman told them the evacuation plan was still being worked out.

"We're not leaving yet," he told them. "We've had some discussion of whether you're going to stay here, but it looks like the airport is full, so we have to take you someplace else—probably Baton Rouge."

The escort consulted with someone on his radio. Baton Rouge was now full, too.

"Well, we're not sure where we're going to take you, but we're leaving now," he said. "Thank you."

The bus convoy pulled out of the airport drop-off zone and turned right onto Airline Highway, a honky-tonk strip of hotels, truck stops, and daiquiri shops. They drove for no more than a minute when they met a police barricade at the border between Jefferson and St. Charles parishes. After a minute, more cops pulled up and one parked a car in front of the bus.

Their escort, a sergeant, got off and joined a scrum of men in uniform arguing heatedly. Police from Kenner—the suburban town surrounding the airport—had set up the cordon. The cops, it seemed, wanted those buses to evacuate their own local residents. Though Kenner had seen only some street flooding, the buses had entered the cops' jurisdiction without permission or safe conduct, so they were to be expropriated on the spot, their passengers left at the airport to fend for themselves. The cops had no legal right to the buses, but in a situation of de facto martial law, with federal, state, and local authorities all trying to maintain order and evacuate people, anything could happen. Soon, police cars were parked in front of the caravan and behind it, and local SWAT teams toting submachine guns were walking up and down the highway around the buses, apparently making mental notes on how many people they could hold.

The standoff at the parish line had been under way for half an hour when the passengers got off to stretch their legs. Their National Guard chaperones worried this was an invitation for the cops to seize the buses, and they were told to get back on.

After an hour, the passengers saw thirty or forty school buses from the Kenner school system drive past, heading west.

"Why are they getting to leave, and we're stuck here?!" someone asked.

"They're Kenner people. They're headed for Baton Rouge," the sergeant said wearily.

"Why is Baton Rouge full to us, but not them?"

"People, please try to remain calm," he said. "It's not going to do any good getting upset about this situation—it's only going to make it worse for everyone. Trust me, this will be worked out, but it will go smoother if you can stay calm."

Three hours passed. The sun set, darkness fell. Around the middle of the evening, the cops gave up and pulled back, and the convoy began to move again. The sergeant told them that a high-ranking Guard commander had helicoptered out and pulled rank on the police. They were soon heading west on Interstate 10. At around midnight, partway to Baton Rouge, they stopped and switched to air-conditioned commercial coaches and headed for Dallas.

After a fifteen-hour drive, Loco Cooper's bus ended up in Bonham, a town in northeast Texas near the Oklahoma border, where a shelter was waiting. He called his girlfriend and mother to tell them he was alive. Then he fell asleep.

Friday night, NBC had put on a benefit program for storm victims featuring well-known singers and actors. One appeal paired actor Mike Myers and rapper Kanye West.

"The landscape of the city has changed dramatically, tragically, and perhaps irreversibly. There is now over twenty-five feet of water where there was once city streets and thriving neighborhoods," Myers read woodenly.

"I hate the way they portray us in the media," West said, extemporizing.

> You see a black family, it says, "They're looting." You see a white family, it says, "They're looking for food." And, you know, it's been five days because most of the people are black. And even for me to complain about it, I would be a hypocrite because I've tried to turn away from the TV because it's too hard to watch. I've even been shopping before even giving a donation, so now I'm calling my business manager right now to see what is the biggest amount I can give, and just to imagine if I was down there, and those are my people down there. So anybody out there that wants to do anything that we can help—with the way America is set up to help the poor, the black people, the less well-off, as slow as possible. I mean, the Red Cross is doing everything they can. We already realize a lot of people that could help are at war right now, fighting another way—and they've given them permission to go down and shoot us!

Myers stubbornly stuck to the script, no doubt realizing this was headed down an unfamiliar and dangerous road: "And subtle, but in many ways even more profoundly devastating, is the lasting damage to the survivors' will to rebuild and remain in the area. The destruction of the spirit of the people of southern Louisiana and Mississippi may end up being the most tragic loss of all."

"George Bush doesn't care about black people!" shouted West.

At about 11:15 p.m., General Blum of the National Guard Bureau called Blanco at the governor's mansion.

"I'm sending you a letter for your signature," he said. "You should fax it back to me in five minutes."

"What?" she said. "What's it about? I never sign a letter and send it back without our lawyers looking at it."

"It's about the hybrid command arrangement."

"Well, we'll look at it," she said, dismayed. The night before, Blum had laid out all the reasons against federalizing the troops. Now he was the vanguard of the White House effort to persuade her to do just that.

A few minutes later the letter came over the fax. Terry Ryder, Blanco's executive counsel, picked it up and read it over.

Blanco's name was at the bottom, along with a space for her signature. As expected, it was a request to federalize all Katrina military operations with a "dual-hatted" command. "Mr. President, these actions are essential to ensure unity of effort and a fully coordinated state and Federal response to this extraordinary disaster," the letter read. It outlined the proposed command structure: Honoré would be placed over all troops in Louisiana, including the National Guard. He would answer to Blanco on the Guard's actions and to Bush on the actions of the regular military. In the event of a conflict, Blanco would defer to the president. If she wanted to dispute a decision, she'd have to go to court.

Ryder called around, waking up several exhausted staffers, and told them to meet him at the EOC as soon as possible.

Within a half an hour, a group including Ryder, Landreneau, and Clinton-era FEMA director James Lee Witt (now a private consultant whom Blanco had retained earlier in the week to advise her) were parsing the letter's legal and political subtleties. Since the immediate security crisis appeared to be passing, they doubted a dual command would make much difference on the most mundane level: what troops did on the ground. But signing the letter would not only create a political liability for Blanco, it could set an unsavory precedent for other governors. Bush had pushed the boundaries of presidential power in various ways during his nearly five years in office. He had informally sanctioned the torture of terrorist suspects, expanded the government's investigative reach, and attached "signing statements" to laws passed by Congress that indicated that he would ignore provisions he disagreed with. Blanco's staff worried that legally, they would be signing away the sovereignty of Louisiana—and perhaps the other states. They called Blanco and went over the arguments, including the ones Blum had made the night before.

A bit later, Andy Kopplin, Blanco's chief of staff, talked with Andy Card. If Blanco signed the letter, Kopplin later told congressional investigators, Card "indicated that it would improve coordination and speed the delivery of federal assets."

Blum called Blanco back.

"They need it by six a.m.," he told her.

"Why do you need it then? I certainly don't want to make any midnight decisions."

"I'm at the White House," he said. "They're not going to let me leave until they get this."

"Well, then, you might as well go home, because I'm not signing it."

Andy Card came on the line and insisted she sign. She refused again, and they argued. "Thanks," she told Card. "You've destroyed yet another night of potential rest for a group of people who desperately need it."

She asked him why it couldn't wait until the morning, so they could discuss it without pressure. Card sighed. The president, he explained, was going to make a televised address on the troop deployment at nine a.m. Saturday, Washington time, and that the issue had to be resolved by then.

"Well, why don't you fax me a copy of his statement?" Blanco said.

Card seemed taken aback. "I can't do that," he said. "It hasn't been vetted."

"If you can't fax it to me, then read it to me."

He read it.

"It was not something I wanted to go along with. It was very presumptuous," Blanco said. "We had come to the end of the most trying week in Louisiana history. We had successfully evacuated those two facilities and all the highways, the interstates, and all of a sudden on Saturday morning the president's saying federal troops are coming in to save us? That didn't make a lick of sense to me."

At 8:56 a.m. Saturday morning, Blanco called Card back and told him she was not signing the letter. A short while later, staffers faxed the White House their own letter, which not-so-subtly rearranged the language of the original to render it meaningless. The White House's "single commander" would be in charge of federal forces only.

"I . . . agree with your idea that—given the unprecedented requests for federal military assistance that I, and my fellow Governors in Mississippi and Alabama have made—a 'single military commander' of 'Federal Joint Task Force Katrina' be named for federal forces. . . . This could also enhance the contribution of over 25 National Guard states currently being commanded by the Louisiana Adjutant General."

An hour later, Bush appeared in the Rose Garden to announce he was sending 7,200 active-duty troops to the region under Honoré's command. They would come from the 82nd Airborne, the 1st Cavalry, and the 1st and 2nd Marine Expeditionary Forces. Friday's chummy glad-handing was gone. The president, Rumsfeld, Chertoff, and General Richard Myers, chairman of the Joint Chiefs of Staff, made a somber, dark-suited tableau. Bush spoke slowly and gravely, acknowledging the rage that many felt.

"I know that those of you who have been hit hard by Katrina are suffering. Many are angry and desperate for help," he said.

> The tasks before us are enormous, but so is the heart of America. In America, we do not abandon our fellow citizens in their hour of need. And the federal government will do its part. Where our response is not working, we'll make it right. Where our response is working, we will duplicate it. We have a responsibility to our brothers and sisters all along the Gulf Coast, and we will not rest until we get this right and the job is done.

By late Saturday, the Superdome and convention center had been emptied by bus, helicopter, and ferry. Many thousands of people were still scattered around town, some still awaiting rescue, some on the freeways. But help was coming, soldiers were in the streets, and there wasn't much left to loot.

With the first wave of the crisis subsiding, Katrina was turning into an open wound, a monstrous tragedy, an absurd comedy. Bush began trying to turn aside the rising tide of criticism and displace blame from the White House. "We will not let criminals prey on the vulnerable, and we will not allow bureaucracy to get in the way of saving lives," he said, linking the looting of New Orleans with the faulty government apparatus he himself had created—but now, seemingly, stood apart from and condemned.

Or maybe it was Blanco's bureaucracy he was condemning. An anonymous "senior administration official" told the *Washington Post* that the governor had not yet declared a state of emergency. That wasn't true, and the *Post* later published a correction. In the next sentence, Bush communications director Dan Bartlett echoed the "bureaucracy" line: "The president will not let any form of bureaucracy get in the way of protecting the citizens of Louisiana." In the same article, Brown opened up on

Nagin. "The mayor can order an evacuation and try to evacuate the city," he said. "But if the mayor does not have the resources to get the poor, elderly, the disabled, those who cannot, out, or if he does not even have police capacity to enforce the mandatory evacuation, to make people leave, then you end up with the kind of situation we have right now in New Orleans."

Saturday evening, Blum spoke with Ryder by telephone to explain his reversal on the federalization issue, explaining that he was "under political duress."

"I apologize for an absolute goat screwing," he said.

In a sense, the shift was predictable. Anyone who had paid attention to the Bush administration could have anticipated that blame would be shifted, authority tardily asserted. The White House might have failed miserably when it came to saving New Orleans, but it would not be so casual about saving its own skin.

Chapter 15

AFTERMATH

AFTER THREE HUNDRED YEARS, New Orleans's struggle to keep out the sea had finally been lost. A great American city had been brought to, if not over, the brink of ruin. Indeed, in the days after the last evacuees left the Superdome, New Orleans was no longer a city at all in the ordinary sense of the word. It was a mostly empty, sodden hulk, large sections slowly rotting in the late summer sun. As the days wore on, the floodwater turned black and gummy in spots, a sink for bacteria, and the wreckage of what had once been began to exude a ripe odor that hung in the air for weeks. The infrastructure that made ordinary day-to-day life possible—clear roadways, gas, electricity, telephone service, hospitals, police, stores—was obliterated across a vast area. On September 7, Mayor Nagin ordered the city completely emptied. Cops and guardsmen went door to door trying to get people out. Hundreds of holdouts resisted the decree, some out of fear that if they left, they might never return. For these few, it was preferable to go on living waist-deep in floodwater. Their hearts could not stand further breaking.

Little by little, authorities began the slow, agonizing work of restoring what was left of the city. The Corps undertook the task of draining the city, something it had long planned for. The engineers called it "unwatering," and it involved breaking levees with backhoes in strategic locations around eastern New Orleans and St. Bernard. Central New Orleans would have to wait longer; as breaches were filled in, dozens of temporary pumps were set up to lift water over levees while Corps contractors and workers from the city's Sewerage and Water Board restored power to the permanent pumping stations.

The Monday after the storm, the breach in the 17th Street canal was finally sealed. It had taken seven thousand sandbags, ten thousand pounds each—a total of thirty-five thousand tons of sand, gravel, rocks, and mashed-up concrete. The sheet pile dam across the entrance to the canal was partially dismantled, and the pumping began, though at nowhere near full capacity. Meanwhile, contractors began repairing the London Avenue canal breaches.

Early estimates predicted it would take months to drain the city, but once under way the unwatering went much faster. The weather worked in the operation's favor: much of the month of September was dry, so a significant fraction of the floodwater simply evaporated. After a couple of weeks, much of it was gone.

But nature's cooperation was short-lived. In late September, a tropical disturbance formed in the Caribbean, then strengthened into Hurricane Rita. As Rita entered the Gulf it crossed the loop current, the same giant swirl of warm water that had pumped up Katrina's strength. Within a day, Rita had become the season's latest Category 5 storm, its maximum winds topping out at 180 mph. Around the nation, people watched weather reports with renewed horror. The broken and washed-out levees could not survive a direct hit even by a minor storm; if Rita so much as sideswiped New Orleans, it would be the coup de grâce for the devastated city.

Chastened government agencies took Katrina's lessons to heart. FEMA and the Department of Homeland Security scrambled to position food, water, National Guard units, and emergency response teams proximate to Rita's likely targets. Local governments ordered mandatory evacuations over hundreds of miles. In New Orleans, meanwhile, Nagin was aggressively proceeding with plans to reopen certain zip codes, fearing that if residents did not return quickly, they might get on with their lives elsewhere. As Rita approached, Algiers had already been reopened. (The only section of New Orleans on the west bank of the river, it had never flooded.) But on September 19, alarmed by the strengthening storm and prodded by President Bush, the mayor declared a "reevacuation," the fourth time he had ordered people out of the city since the approach of Katrina.

Meanwhile, Corps contractors worked feverishly to patch up the levee system before Rita struck. They hammered sheet piling deep along the entrances of the 17th Street and London Avenue canals to keep out any storm surge. Trucks dumped tons of rock and gravel into the long breaches along the Industrial Canal in an attempt to provide at least ten feet of protection there.

Rita made landfall on the Louisiana coast near the Texas border, too far to the west to do much damage to New Orleans, but coastal towns across southwestern Louisiana were left under water—including the Indian community of Isle de Jean Charles. The houses lining the marshy ridge had taken mostly wind damage during Katrina, but Rita raised the water level nine feet, inundating most of them. The water subsided quickly—the only saving grace of their location outside the hurricane levee. Chief Albert Naquin and two of his relatives, Father Roch Naquin and Chris Brunet, solicited donations and supplies from other Indian tribes, then dispensed them from a ginned-up emergency relief operation in Brunet's garage.

Rita did not completely spare New Orleans. Its modest storm surge was still enough to wash out the gravel levee patches along the Industrial Canal, and soon floodwater was once again flowing through the Lower Ninth Ward and into St. Bernard. But it was a temporary setback. On October 14, the Corps declared it had pumped clear virtually all of the water contained within the levee system: 225 billion gallons in all.

New Orleans soon became an odd, attenuated version of its former self. The places that remained dry—the original high ground of the French Quarter and areas along the river—slowly stirred to life as electricity was restored and debris cleared. Restaurants and bars in this area were filled night after night with weary returnees and relief workers letting off steam in the months after the storm. Suburbs that had sustained little or no flooding, such as the Jefferson Parish towns of Metairie and

Kenner, quickly regained residents. But much of the New Orleans area remained completely uninhabitable. The devastation stretched on for dozens of miles, across once-busy city streets, out to the fishing towns in the outer reaches of St. Bernard and Plaquemines parishes, where nothing but shards and splinters of houses remained. But there were signs of life sprinkled here and there: storefronts opening, FEMA trailers in driveways and yards, workers tinkering with the electrical grid. Ubiquitous sights—refrigerators decorated with anti-FEMA messages and left on curbsides, and the blue tarps used to patch rooftops, for example—became symbols of the city's daily struggles.

With the possible exceptions of Galveston in 1900 and the San Francisco earthquake of 1906, such wholesale destruction had never been visited on an American city. More than two hundred thousand people were scattered around the country, a diaspora not seen since the Depression-era Dust Bowl, when a half million people fled failing Midwestern farms. Many of New Orleans's dispossessed were poor African Americans with few resources. They were the least likely to benefit from any postdisaster reconstruction; historically, cities rebuilt after catastrophes became smaller, richer, and whiter.

New Orleans's unique culture, the product of three centuries of brutal history, was suddenly in flux, as was its latter-day identity as an overwhelmingly African American city. In a speech in January, Nagin made an impassioned—and somewhat weird-sounding—declaration on the subject: "I don't care what people are saying in Uptown or wherever they are. This city will be chocolate at the end of the day. This city will be a majority African American city. It's the way God wants it to be." Critics blasted him for a unique achievement: being racially insensitive toward blacks and whites simultaneously. But Nagin was reelected in May 2006, drawing an overwhelming black vote—and some conservative white votes as well—to defeat Lieutenant Governor Mitch Landrieu, the liberal son of the former mayor.

But race issues aside, for many people an immediate return wasn't feasible. Millions of household dollars were locked up in mortgages on properties whose worth was unknown, dependent on reconstruction decisions not yet made. The Bush administration and Congress hesitated at first, but eventually agreed to front billions of dollars to fund a grant program with options to rebuild or be bought out. The other burning question was where people would live. Some argued it would be better to try to manage reconstruction, guiding development away from areas that were likely to flood again. But Nagin backed a laissez-faire approach: people could return wherever they wanted to and give it a go. If some areas did not come back, the city would deal with that down the road.

Over the fall and winter of 2005, devastated neighborhoods became sites for urban homesteaders. Byron LaFrance decided to return before any of his neighbors to his home at 1612 Lizardi Street in the Lower Ninth Ward. There, he and his brother started refurbishing two houses with no power or city services available, in a neighborhood that might ultimately not survive. LaFrance drove a truck to make ends meet. Every night he'd return to a motel room in Algiers and collapse. "Me and my brother did something nobody thought we could ever do," he said some months after the flood. "Ain't nobody going to tell me when can I rebuild my property. The levees failed me. The government failed me. But I can't fail my family or my kids. I'm the leader."

Robert Green, whose Lower Ninth Ward house had broken up and floated away, ended up staying with his brother David in Nashville for weeks after the storm. For a while, he toyed with the idea of restarting his accounting business there. But he couldn't bring himself to abandon Louisiana. He returned in mid-October, moving in with his son Sheppard, who had found an apartment in Baton Rouge. Soon after, he got word from FEMA's temporary morgue in St. Gabriel that his granddaughter Shenae's body had been identified. He volunteered to collect the remains, which were in a tiny body bag. They had not, it appeared, been refrigerated. Trembling, he unzipped the bag to see if she was recognizable. "She looked like a dried dog in the street," he said. She was buried on November 19.

More time passed, but there was still no word on his mother's body, left on the roof of the Ninth Ward house where they had ridden out the storm. Governor Blanco had suspended searches in early October, but people were still encountering corpses on a regular basis. Tired of waiting for government action, on December 29, the Green family decided to go find their matriarch. Led by David, who was visiting from Nashville, they first went to a Wal-Mart and bought picks, shovels, and gloves. But when they arrived at the house, there was no need to dig. "She had fallen off the roof on top of some tumbleweeds," Robert said afterward. "She was in plain sight." They collected her skeletal remains, still clad in a housedress, and took them away. Joyce Green was buried on January 14, 2006, in the same suburban cemetery as her great-granddaughter.

Katrina had a way of sending lives on strange and unfortunate trajectories. Loco Cooper, evacuated from the Superdome to northeast Texas, went to Baton Rouge, where his girlfriend had gotten an apartment. A few months later, he took his FEMA housing money, bought a car, and returned to New Orleans. In February, he was living out of the car and gutting his mother's house, where he'd ridden out the storm. A friend got him a job working at the port, loading and unloading cargo. It was close to quitting time on his third day when a stack of pallets holding several tons of coiled brown rope tipped over on top of him. His coworkers had to dig him out. When they uncovered him, he couldn't move. His back was broken, and he was paralyzed from the waist down. Cooper convalesced at West Jefferson Medical Center in Marrero, where as spring arrived he was preparing to enter a rehab program. He was not bitter. He had lucked out before: when his mother had adopted him from a Panamanian orphanage, and when he'd survived Katrina, and various other times he could not even count. He was alive.

After his week guarding the denizens of the Superdome, NOPD officer James Seaberry was granted two days off. A fellow officer drove him to Houston. There, he was supposed to catch a flight to Greensboro, North Carolina, where his wife had evacuated. Unfortunately, she had mistakenly booked him to Greenville, South Carolina, so their reunion was delayed by a day. Shortly after arriving, he began to have bouts of intense anxiety and flashbacks to his week at the Dome. He went to see a psychiatrist, who diagnosed him with bipolar disorder. Feeling as if he was coming apart, he flew to Atlanta, rented a car, and drove to a family house in Mississippi. After he'd been there a few days and his wife had joined him, he had too much to drink and got into a fight with her in a hotel parking lot. He ended up in the backseat of a police cruiser. "They took me to jail and I cried like a baby and I knew my career and life was over," he said. "I never felt so embarrassed in my life. But my wife told the police what had happened, that I'd been in the Dome, the stress. The judge understood it." Seaberry was released.

Eventually, he forced himself to return to New Orleans. But by then the police department had declared him AWOL. He was one of about two hundred officers terminated after the storm, most for disappearing. Seaberry and his wife moved into a FEMA trailer in Mississippi, where he did odd jobs and saw a therapist regularly. Memories of the Superdome remained constantly on his mind. "You're trying to help somebody," he recalled, "and you couldn't do nothing for them."

The hurricane and its aftermath continued to reverberate in the national psyche as well. President Bush struggled to overcome the enormous political damage done by his hesitancy in the days after Katrina hit, his appointees' fumbling, and the confusion of the federal response. Mocked by the late-night comics and scapegoated by the media and White House, Mike Brown resigned not long after the storm hit and became an emergency management consultant. But his boss, Michael Chertoff, whose performance before and after the storm was arguably far more clueless, remained in place. Along with the chronic chaos in Iraq, Hurricane Katrina buried the reputation Bush once enjoyed as a decisive, no-nonsense manager. The storm became an icon of administration incompetence and indifference to the workings of government. In some ways, it was all a bit unfair; the government failures that led to Katrina stretched back decades. But Bush had done nothing to change those trends and much to accelerate them. At the peak of its technological versatility and military strength, the U.S. government had failed to protect one of its own cities, then stumbled all over itself trying to rescue the victims of its neglect and incompetence. And for many around the world, the question of whether the Bush administration's profound failure was the result of incompetence or indifference only added to increasing doubts about American leadership at home and abroad.

In early October, Gus and Daniel Cantrell, father and son engineers, returned to the family home at 6119 Pratt Drive. The modest brick ranch house had been next to the breach on the west side of the London Avenue canal. A layer of gray sand, churned up from fifteen feet underground, ran through the backyard, the living room, the front yard, and out into the street. Judging from the damage, water had roared from the busted floodwall into the kitchen, knocked the refrigerator over, and set the ceiling fan spinning. In the living room, it lifted the sofa and hurled it against a wall. The neighboring wall had exploded clear off the side of the house and into the yard, leaving the electrical box dangling in midair. Once the flow had equalized, the house and its contents were left under water for weeks.

But nearby was the most surprising sight of all. Daniel's childhood clubhouse had been sitting flush against the toe of the levee, where the earth rose slightly off the lawn at the base of the floodwall. Miraculously, the clubhouse was still there. And unlike most every other structure for miles around, it was completely intact.

Gus had built the clubhouse himself twenty-five years earlier, girding it with sturdy wood-frame construction. But that was hardly strong enough to withstand a thundering wall of water.

Gus had recently retired from the University of New Orleans, where he had overseen the entire physical plant. Daniel was a civil engineer with a Houston firm. They realized that as the water rose in the canal, the soil deep underneath the floodwall had suddenly erupted out and up with a great *whump,* spewing water and sand, lifting the clubhouse. The clubhouse's base was now at about the same level as the eaves of the Cantrell house. Tufts of healthy grass decorated the top of this peculiar hillock, the only living greenery around. The heave had also upended the floodwall panels, of course, letting the flood-water rush through.

The Cantrells both knew what the strange scene in the backyard meant, and they were outraged. The flood had never reached the top of the wall, which should have stayed upright, but the earthen foundation had failed anyway. Their home and neighborhoods for miles around were flooded because of some kind of structural flaw: in other words, human error.

In the weeks immediately after Katrina struck, the Corps of Engineers had struggled to explain what had gone wrong with the London Avenue and 17th Street canal floodwalls. Else-where, it was obvious that levees and floodwalls had simply been overwhelmed by the storm surge, which had flowed right over them. Where breaches had opened up, most appeared to have been caused by flowing water scouring out earthen foun-dations. At first, Corps engineers suggested that same thing had happened to the floodwalls in the two drainage canals. "They were designed to withstand a surge for a Category Three or less storm," Al Naomi, the levee system project manager, told the *Times-Picayune* three days after the storm. "You might have had one or two feet of water pouring away over the top of the wall, cutting away at the earth below it, and as that happened, the walls began to collapse."

But after viewing the breaches by boat within a week of the storm, Ivor van Heerden, the deputy director of the LSU Hurri-cane Center, could find no evidence of overtopping. Visible wa-ter and debris lines stopped short of the peaks of the walls, fourteen feet above sea level. At the edge of Lake Pontchartrain, near the 17th Street canal outlet, it appeared the water had risen to only about ten feet. The water had been slightly higher at London Avenue, but still short of the top near the Cantrell house. Van Heerden was not a civil engineer, but he recognized something was seriously amiss. He began calling the breaches "catastrophic structural failures." Joseph Suhaya, the LSU scientist who had also worked on hurricane preparation, drew a similar conclusion after touring the damage.

There was something comforting to those in power who had failed to help New Orleans that the storm's damage could be explained away as an "act of God" beyond any fruitful intervention. But the suggestion that breaches were caused by human error would change every assessment of the Katrina disaster. If borne out, it would mean that individuals and institutions, most prominently the Corps—which had ultimate authority over the design and construction of the system—were complicit in much of the damage, deaths, and mayhem that had occurred on August 29 and in the days immediately afterward. The breaches at the London Avenue and 17th Street canals had been responsible for flooding fully 88 percent of the central New Orleans bowl, according to calculations by the LSU Hurricane Center. And an analysis by Knight-Ridder newspapers showed that at least 588 bodies were recovered from areas flooded by the two breaches, compared with 286 in other areas including the Lower Ninth Ward, eastern New Orleans, and St. Bernard.

Whatever the Corps's faults—its addiction to congressional pork, its flawed economic analyses, the glacial pace of its projects—the things it built usually remained standing. Now, suddenly, its two-hundred-year legacy of competency was called into question. Politicians and outside engineers began calling for a shake-up and outside peer reviews of Corps's designs. The Corps launched an investigation. Some questioned whether an agency could credibly investigate itself, but the Corps's chief engineer, Lieutenant General Carl Strock, disagreed. "If it does develop that we have a design or construction problem in there, then we will accept accountability for that," he told the *Times-Picayune*. "I don't know what form it takes—shoot me at sunrise or whatever. But we will own up to that because we have to. If there's any problem there, we need to know because we cannot afford to put back a system that's flawed."

But for Gus Cantrell and many others, the Corps might be able to repair the levees, but never its credibility. "There's no way I want to ever live in a place where I have to depend for my safety and the safety of my property on the actions and activities of the Corps of Engineers," Cantrell concluded. "I know a lot of those guys on the Corps. I am a member of the ASCE [American Society of Civil Engineers] and serve on many committees with them. They have some responsibility here. They destroyed the city."

The mystery of the broken levees drew the rapt attention of engineers around the country, including a couple of geotechnical engineers at the University of California at Berkeley, Raymond Seed and Robert Bea. A former Corps employee and avuncular former New Orleans resident whose house had flooded during Hurricane Betsy, Bea was a bit of a provocateur. Unlike many scientists, he enjoyed mixing it up with the press and had a gift for the pithy quote. Seed was more media-shy, but intense and passionate, with a tendency to sometimes go overboard in expressing his outrage at the Corps's bureaucratic foolishness. With a grant from the National Science Foundation and pro bono help from other academics, they began an independent investigation. Joined by J. David Rogers, an engineering professor at the University of Missouri and former navy intelligence officer who specialized in the study of levee and dam failures, they began bombarding the Corps with requests for information. They spoke to Congress and the FBI. They made noise.

As they gathered data, an appalling picture emerged of sloppy design work, from small details like the soil boring work on up to the architecture of the entire system. To them, New Orleans was not just the victim of a few bad calculations. It was a latter-day version of the *Titanic*'s sinking or NASA's two space shuttle disasters, where a cascade of bad decisions had tragically doomed ambitious technology. They concluded that the Corps, abetted by its junior partners, the local agencies, had failed as an institution long before the levees actually collapsed.

In March 2006, investigators with the Corps issued a preliminary report that included a theory of why the 17th Street canal wall had failed. It was a two-step process: rising water had pushed the wall, opening a gap between the soil and the sheet pile foundation. Water poured into the gap, weakening the entire structure, then a layer of soft clay underneath it suddenly slid forward. That combination of forces, they said, was something totally new—the designers could not have anticipated it. "I would not say right now that it's never happened or it's never been documented. But we've never seen it yet," said the panel's cochair Ed Link, a University of Maryland professor and former Corps engineer. "We're still looking."

But in fact, the Corps had foreseen exactly this, years before. In 1985, Corps engineers had run a field test in Louisiana, flooding a sheet pile wall embedded in soft soil to see what would happen. The wall had bent away from its earthen base, and small fractures had formed. When Seed, Bea, and Rogers pointed this out, the Corps admitted the results of the test had indeed been well known—just not taken into account by the designers of the 17th Street canal wall.

The Corps's misleading statements had the appearance of spin—a potential credibility destroyer for a scientific investigation—and were the last straw for the normally staid American Society of Civil Engineers, which had its own panel peer-reviewing the Corps's investigation. Historically, the ASCE's scientific credibility rivaled the Corps's. But it had remained silent while evidence piled up of levee engineering errors and while Corps officials refused to admit anything was amiss. A week after the Corps's press conference, the ASCE's peer review committee wrote Strock a remarkable letter. For all its dry engineering lingo, its message was unmistakable: you screwed up.

"Taken collectively, decisions made during the original design phase appear to reflect an overall pattern of engineering judgment inconsistent with that required for critical structures," the letter said. "We conclude that a determination of the overall safety of the hurricane protection system cannot be made." In other words, nobody knew what other flaws might be lurking out there—even a weak hurricane might bust up the levees and flood the city again. The ASCE also rained contempt on the Corps's outdated Standard Project Hurricane, which even after

Katrina remained the basis for Corps repairs and upgrades. "This approach is inconsistent with the logic used in design of structures to resist earthquake loadings and floods. . . . Without a statistically valid approach to determining the standard project hurricane, no rational hurricane protection system can result."

Two weeks later, Strock finally conceded the obvious while testifying before a congressional committee. "We have now concluded we had problems with the design of the structure. We had hoped that wasn't the case, but we recognize it is the reality."

Nevertheless, the Corps announced it would rebuild the levees to their former level of protection, something that would still leave New Orleans nearly as exposed as it was before. Contractors embarked on the work at a breakneck pace, trying to finish much of the work by the start of the 2006 hurricane season.

The improvements did address some of the most glaring weak spots: the 17th Street, London, and Orleans canals would finally get floodgates, and the city's pumping stations would be moved to the lakefront, out of the low-lying residential areas they'd occupied for a century. Some levees would be armored with rocks. But it wouldn't come cheap: the price tag for the repairs and improvements was about six billion dollars, far more than the original cost of building the system from the ground up. The Corps also announced that some areas of Plaquemines Parish would be prohibitively expensive to enclose, and short of a political miracle, it looked like it wouldn't get the protection it needed. They'd be outside the federal levee system, exposed. Some wondered whether it was only the beginning of a final retreat. And incredibly, given the risks, at one point Seed, Bea, and Rogers discovered Corps contractors dredging up weak soil and incorporating it into a new levee. It was not a good sign. New Orleans had staggered to its feet as the referee neared the ten count. Another punch could end its fight to survive. But the pressure to brag that New Orleans was back in business exceeded the concern over what might happen next time. It had happened before. But Katrina had been unlike its predecessors. And the storms on the horizon promised to be as bad—and probably worse.

Chapter 16

SUPERSTORMS

VEN AFTER HURRICANES KATRINA and Rita had left New Orleans a soggy wreck, devastated the Mississippi Gulf Coast, and put southwest Louisiana under water, nature wasn't finished. The astounding 2005 Atlantic hurricane season went on. And on.

In mid-October, a tropical depression near Jamaica quickly gathered force and was dubbed Tropical Storm Wilma, the last name available on the National Weather Service's alphabetical list for the year, and the first "W" storm since authorities had begun naming hurricanes in 1950. A day later, Wilma underwent a startling transformation. Moving over warm water and with weak winds above it offering little resistance, its heat engine roared into overdrive. Warm, wet air riffled skyward, releasing waves of heat as the moisture condensed into raindrops. Storm clouds fluffed high into the atmosphere. As the pressure in the eye began dropping, more waves of warm air were sucked into the whirling vortex. Hurricane Hunters flew through the maelstrom, releasing dropsondes to measure the wind and pressure. Their data showed Wilma was undergoing "rapid deepening," a sudden muscling up that could turn the weak tropical storm into a furious giant in the space of a few hours. Sure enough, over ten hours, the air pressure in the eye plunged by 8 percent, then kept going, ultimately reaching 882 millibars—a new record low, equal to the average air pressure on a mountainside three quarters of a mile up, enough to cause some people shortness of breath. It was like someone pressed an accelerator: Wilma's winds, a relatively anemic 70 mph, revved to 185 mph. Wilma had become the year's fourth Category 5, and the most powerful hurricane in history in the Atlantic basin.

The storm pummeled Cancún and other resort towns on Mexico's Yucatán peninsula, then turned northeast and strafed the Florida Keys before cutting diagonally across south Florida and Miami with one-hundred-mph winds, killing five people and causing the largest power outage in Florida history and a total of twelve billion dollars in damage. Finally, it barged out over the North Atlantic on its way toward Nova Scotia.

Even as Wilma was thrashing the Yucatán coast, another tropical storm coalesced in the Atlantic. Out of names, the National Weather Service was obliged to go to its fallback, the Greek alphabet. Tropical Storm Alpha went on to strike Haiti and the Dominican Republic. Then, unaccountably, the storms kept coming through the fall, past the official November 30 conclusion to hurricane season and on into winter, getting the names Beta, Gamma, Delta, and Epsilon. The last, Tropical Storm Zeta, did not peter out until the first days of 2006.

With Zeta, the busiest hurricane season in history had finally ended. Its twenty-eight storms shattered the previous record of twenty-one. The fifteen hurricanes and four Category 5s set new records as well. The level of damage was unprecedented, far exceeding one hundred billion dollars. More than 2,200 people died.

The profusion of giant hurricanes was just one symptom of a global climate that seemed to be going haywire. The year 2005 was also the hottest on record, capping a distinct uptick in global temperatures. The added warmth's most immediate impact was felt at the ends of the earth. A satellite study showed the Antarctic ice sheet was melting at a rate of thirty-six miles per year at a time when scientists had expected it to be growing. At the opposite pole, the Arctic ice was disappearing, too, shrinking to its smallest recorded area, putting polar bears and other wildlife in danger of extinction. Bewildered Inuit communities, warm for the first time in memory, watched generations-old icy pathways and hunting grounds disappear before their eyes. Greenland's glaciers—which contained enough water to raise sea levels by twenty-one feet—were speeding southward at twice the rate they had a decade before, shedding their outermost layers, which broke away and fell into the sea with a crash, "calving" new icebergs. A steady drumbeat of scientific studies tied these events to global warming—the gradual heating of the earth's atmosphere due to carbon dioxide and other greenhouse gases generated by modern industrial activity: power plants, factories, vehicles.

Even before Katrina, the scientific community and the media had been abuzz about possible links between global warming and hurricanes. Afterward, with a major American city in ruins, the theoretical abstractions seemed terrifyingly real. What if the 2005 hurricane season was only the beginning?

For generations, hurricane activity had fluctuated within certain limits. Some seasons were bad, others relatively quiet. Scientists agreed that the Atlantic was clearly in a strong "up" cycle that would likely last for decades, posing frightening new threats for the nation's newly developed, eroding coastlines. Then, many believed, the trend would eventually run its course, ushering in a new era of quiet in the tropics.

But to some scientists, it appeared those already-pessimistic expectations might be wrong and that nobody knew the upper limit of the destructive power of hurricanes—or even if there was one. If modern society heated up the planet, it might fuel storms of biblical proportion—a literal blowback of cosmic dimensions, the ultimate "Wexelblat disaster" described by the MIT computer scientist, where the unpredictable entanglements of civilization and nature go awry, sending disaster cascading through man-made systems—in this case, coastal cities and towns around the globe.

In January 2006, in a darkened conference room in a Miami research center, atmospheric scientist Kerry Emanuel flashed a series of PowerPoint slides and explained to fellow hurricane experts that he had come to a startling conclusion: global warming was indeed one likely cause of a new and frightening generation of superstorms.

Emanuel had recently published two scientific papers on the topic. "My results suggest that future warming may lead to an upward trend in tropical cyclone destructive potential, and—taking into account an increasing coastal population—a substantial increase in hurricane-related losses in the twenty-first century," he had written a few months before in the prestigious journal *Nature*. The small group of scientists who specialize in hurricanes and climate was divided on the issue, and Emanuel's audience at the U.S. Atmospheric and Oceanographic Meteorological Laboratory included several colleagues who sharply disagreed with him.

Emanuel, a professor of atmospheric sciences at MIT, didn't view himself as an academic bomb thrower. He had studied the possible links between global warming and hurricanes for two decades. In 1987, he had been among the first scientists to demonstrate that the rising carbon emissions in the air that lead to warmer temperatures could also heat the oceans, fueling destructive storms. But over the years, like most scientists, he had been circumspect about any direct cause-and-effect links that might exist between global warming and hurricanes. For a long time, the problem was simply beyond the capacity of the available computer models and data sets. There was, for instance, the problem of scale. Computer models of global warming's effects on the atmosphere typically covered the whole world. Such programs often did a poor job with hurricanes, especially during formation, when cyclones occupy very small regions of the sea.

But both technology and insights were continuing to evolve, and so was a strong scientific consensus on global warming. One thing was indisputable: since 1900, the average global temperature had risen by about one degree Fahrenheit, most of that in the second half of the twentieth century. Climatologists began correlating the increase with concentrations of greenhouse gases, which had begun increasing around the start of the industrial revolution in the nineteenth century, then accelerated in tandem with global prosperity after World War II. The gases trapped infrared radiation, energy from the sun that would otherwise reflect off the earth back into space, which heated the atmosphere (thus the greenhouse analogy).

The Intergovernmental Panel on Global Climate Change, an international group convened to assess the evidence and be the voice of authority on the subject, summed up the consensus in 2001, declaring that "there is new and stronger evidence that most of the warming observed over the last 50 years is attributable to human activities." The report predicted this warming would only quicken, citing studies that showed temperature rising by 2.5 to as much as 10.4 degrees between 1990 and 2100. The general scientific agreement did not resolve the political debate in the United States, where business interests and conservatives leery of environmental regulation—including President Bush—fiercely resisted the idea that the government should take proactive steps to tamp down greenhouse gas emissions.

The link between global warming and hurricane activity sounds commonsensical: if the air warms up, so will the ocean. And tropical sea surface temperatures had indeed risen, by 0.9 degrees between 1970 and 2004, setting new records.

But it wasn't that simple.

The atmosphere and the ocean are enormously complex systems, each with currents flowing and layers rising and falling over thousands of miles. The two are in a constant dance with each other: winds drive ocean currents; water evaporates off warm seas, then falls as rain or snow somewhere else; heat flows from one point to another through water and the air. The birth of a tropical storm depends on a certain set of conditions, including updrafts from the warm ocean surface to cooler levels of the atmosphere; if the ocean and the air are *both* warmer, that dynamic may be disrupted.

In addition, to speak of global warming as a single phenomenon can be misleading. As a whole, the globe is indeed getting hotter. But temperature changes vary dramatically depending where you are on that globe; at a given time, some areas are cooling and others are warming. And while the extra heat in the atmosphere does predictable things like melt ice, it also does unpredictable things, nudging ocean currents and atmospheric oscillations around into new configurations that cause surprising weather patterns.

Even after years of study, scientists did not have a clear picture of what such large-scale changes did to hurricanes. Some studies indicated it should pump them up. But others showed it could just as easily snuff them out, for instance, by directing cooler ocean currents into hurricane breeding grounds. And since both hurricane mechanics and global warming were still only sketchily understood, discerning how one affected the other was a highly theoretical exercise. With the computer models and data available, scientists could just begin to tease out some large-scale trends.

Emanuel's early computer modeling indicated warmer temperatures would provide fuel for more powerful storms. Now that the temperature had actually risen, he found himself in an unusual and felicitous position for a scientist: he could test his theories in the real world.

There are many ways to gauge hurricane activity, each with its uses: overall frequency, the number of powerful storms, the atmospheric pressure in the eye, wind speed. But by itself, none of these metrics had what Emanuel was looking for—a more general measure of a storm's destructive power, the total energy it vents as it crosses the sea, releasing heat and driving winds—so he seized on something he called power dissipation. In physics, power is the amount of work (that is, energy used to move things around—in this case, wind and water vapor) as a function of time. Calculating power dissipation would yield the overall energy a hurricane expended during its brief lifetime, usually a week or two. By adding together an entire season's worth of storms, he would get a single number showing how much hurricane power was out there—and how it was evolving year to year.

Emanuel calculated the total power dissipation of every North Atlantic hurricane and tropical storm since 1949, when reliable data from Hurricane Hunter planes became regularly available, then summed each year's total. He plotted the numbers along with sea surface temperatures. The results were shocking: from 1949 to 1995, both quantities fluctuated up and down like a sine curve. But after 1995, both had shot upward: as sea surface temperature rose by about one degree, total hurricane power had more than doubled.

"The near doubling of power dissipation over the period of record should be a matter of some concern, as it is a measure of the destructive potential of tropical cyclones," he wrote. Other data buttressed the finding. Emanuel found that over thirty years, maximum wind speeds of big storms had gone up an average of 15 percent, and those storms were lasting 60 percent longer.

The implication was clear: as temperatures rose further, so would the "destructive potential" of hurricanes. If the findings were borne out, that would mean more Katrinas—a lot more.

"It's the water vapor, the potential evaporation," Emanuel said, that was the driving force for increasing intensity. "The relative humidity of the air next to the ocean doesn't change a whole lot from one season to the next without climate change. So it's the rate of evaporation of sea water, which really controls hurricane intensity, that goes up." More heat and evaporation means more clouds, instability, rain—all fuel for the hurricane furnace.

Other studies lent credence to Emanuel's ideas. One, by a pair of scientists at Purdue University, and published in the *Geophysical Research Letters* in June 2006, used a slightly different measure of hurricane power and closely tracked Emanuel's results.

In another, led by atmospheric scientist Peter Webster, a team had scoured a large data set of every tropical cyclone everywhere in the world over the previous thirty-five years, looking for patterns in hurricane strength and duration as ocean temperatures rose. In an article published in the September 2005 issue of *Science,* the Georgia Institute of Technology researchers reported finding that in nearly every ocean basin, the number of storms each year had remained more or less flat. The exception was the North Atlantic, where there had been a sharp uptick in the number. Webster's results argued against the idea that warmer temperatures were incubating more hurricanes since the total had remained more or less constant, about ninety per year. But the data revealed another, more alarming trend: more storms were growing into powerful Category 4 and 5 hurricanes. During the 1970s, there had been an average of about ten such storms per year. Between 1995 and 2004, that number climbed 80 percent: the world was now averaging close to eighteen major storms per year. "We conclude that global data indicate a 30-year trend toward more frequent and intense hurricanes," the authors wrote. "This trend is not inconsistent with recent climate model simulations that a doubling of CO_2 may increase the frequency of the most intense cyclones."

As Emanuel wrapped up his Miami presentation about growing hurricane power, he opened the floor to questions. Not surprisingly, there were a lot, and an hour-long free-for-all ensued. Christopher Landsea, the Hurricane Research Center's chief scientist, pointedly questioned some of Emanuel's methods, particularly whether he had overcorrected on some wind data, ending up with more dramatic results than were warranted for the North Atlantic. Emanuel ventured that he could be right.

Landsea was a protégé of William Gray, the legendary Colorado State University atmospheric science professor known nationally for his annual forecasts of the coming hurricane season, and also for his fierce skepticism on global warming. In his work at NOAA, Landsea had been instrumental in updating the nation's historical records of hurricane activity, using information gleaned from old ships' logs and newspaper archives to add storms and revise storm paths and intensities from the years before satellites allowed reliable tracking of all cyclones.

He saw the underlying dynamics behind the superstorms quite differently than did Emanuel. Where Emanuel saw the curve of hurricane activity arching ever upward due to warming seas, Landsea believed that global warming would affect hurricane strength only marginally. His research, based on extensive study of ocean currents and atmospheric disturbances, showed that hurricane activity would likely continue its historic cyclical pattern. In a 2001 paper, Landsea and Gray, along with NOAA scientists Stanley Goldenberg and Alberto Mestas-Nuñez, had tied this cycle to a pattern of shifting ocean temperatures called the Atlantic Multidecadal Oscillation. The paper was the most comprehensive explanation of why Atlantic hurricane activity waxed and waned.

Though the 2005 season was indisputably a high point, Landsea believed it was still part of that cycle, and that what goes up must come down. "The greater activity results from simultaneous increases in North Atlantic sea-surface temperatures and decreases in vertical wind shear," he and his colleagues wrote in 2001. "Because these changes exhibit a multidecadal time scale, the present high level of hurricane activity is likely to persist for an additional 10 to 40 years."

The Atlantic Multidecadal Oscillation was a little-understood fifty- to seventy-year cyclic combination of fluctuating sea surface temperatures and coinciding wind patterns. In down cycles, the water was cooler, and westerly winds tended to be strong a few miles up, near the peaks of thunderstorms. That combination suppressed the formation of hurricanes. In up cycles, those conditions were reversed: the water was warmer, and the high-level winds weak—ideal for nurturing big, strong hurricanes.

The previous up cycle, they noted, had culminated in 1969, when Hurricane Camille's tightly focused knot of 190-mph winds glanced by New Orleans and swept a twenty-four-foot storm surge over the Mississippi Gulf Coast, killing more than 250 and obliterating many towns. It was then only the second time in recorded history that a Category 5 storm had struck the North American continent, but for more than forty years before that, powerful hurricanes had been a regular summer event in the Atlantic and Gulf of Mexico.

Then, starting in 1970, the North Atlantic's hurricane breeding ground mysteriously turned quiescent. With a few notable exceptions such as Hurricane Andrew in 1992 (another

Category 5), tropical storms were more likely to remain weak. If the flux of warm ocean water and atmospheric currents was favorable and a storm matured into a hurricane, it was less likely to strengthen into a superstorm.

A quarter of a century later, the lull came to an end just as abruptly as it had begun—"like somebody flipped a switch," Max Mayfield later described it. Suddenly, the Atlantic was once again awash with tropical waves making their way westward, their growth fueled by warm ocean temperatures. Weak winds in the upper atmosphere let storms rise higher and vent heat more efficiently. The 1995 hurricane season had nineteen named storms, then the second-busiest on record. Eleven of them became hurricanes, second only to the 1969 season. In 2004, Atlantic storms killed more than three thousand people, most in the Caribbean. Four hurricanes and a tropical storm hit Florida—two striking in virtually the same spot within three weeks. (With the November election approaching and Florida a pivotal battleground, President Bush and Democratic challenger John Kerry made ritual visits to storm-ravaged areas to commiserate with victims and hand out food and supplies.)

For decades, scientists had struggled to discover the climatic sources of those ups and downs. Stanley Goldenberg, who was also in Emanuel's audience that day, had obtained one piece of the puzzle. He had established the link between less active hurricane seasons and the El Niño Southern Oscillation—the cyclical pattern of warmer sea temperatures in the eastern Pacific Ocean. There was, not surprisingly, a corresponding link between La Niña, the mirror pattern of cooler eastern Pacific temperatures, and more active seasons.

Scientists have since found evidence for the multidecadal oscillation cycle—including rainfall patterns discerned from tree rings—going back more than one thousand years. They believed it would take a lot more than a few degrees of extra heat to stop it.

Part of the conflict between the two scientific viewpoints was a long-standing divide between meteorologists and atmospheric scientists. Meteorologists like Landsea spent their careers combing the historical record looking for subtle patterns. They used computer forecasting models every day and were well acquainted with their quirks and limitations, and thus suspicious of attempts to build bold theories on their outputs. (Still, many meteorologists did take seriously the evidence on global warming and hurricanes. The fact that Landsea and Max Mayfield, a fellow skeptic on the issue, held prominent positions at NOAA and shaped the U.S. government's public stance on the question caused consternation among scientists who disagreed with them—not to mention environmentalists.)

Emanuel and other atmospheric scientists, meanwhile, operated on a more rarefied, theoretical plane. They used many of the same computer models the meteorologists did, but without the risk of being proved wrong tomorrow. Instead, they did impossibly ambitious forecasts, gazing decades or centuries into the future.

The stark differences between the two scientific viewpoints were nowhere more apparent than in the ways Landsea and Emanuel interpreted 1995—the year of the upswing in hurricane activity that eventually spawned Katrina began.

Landsea and his colleagues interpreted that year's "flipped switch" as the culmination of a complex dance of ocean and atmospheric circulation, playing out over years and decades—something that it would be hard for any single factor, like warmer temperatures, to significantly disrupt. But Emanuel saw 1995 as the year global warming first began powerfully fueling hurricane formation, altering decades-long swings already under way in the process. "You had a combination of two things," he said. "First, we were just starting a big decadal time scale change when the Atlantic started responding to greenhouse gases. Plus, it went from an El Niño year to a La Niña year, and it was the superposition of the two that caused a jump in the number of storms."

And maybe, he provocatively proposed, the Atlantic Multidecadal Oscillation was a chimera, a fiction.

"I have come to believe this is largely an artifact of the way the analysis of the data was done in the past," Emanuel said.

"People have assumed that they're looking at stable climate and there are no changes in forcing [i.e., large-scale outside influences such as global warming], and interpret that as a cycle." Since scientists had good data for only two peaks and troughs of the oscillation, he suggested, maybe it was the relative stability of a cycle that was anomalous, not the recent explosion of superstorms.

"If there is no natural cycle, and you come to believe the evidence of one is tenuous," Emanuel said, "then there's no reason to believe that on a decadal time scale you'll see a downswing in activity."

In other words, there might be nothing to keep hurricane activity from spiraling indefinitely upward. If he was correct, Katrina was not a peak but a precursor.

Whether it lasted another ten years, forty, or indefinitely, the era of superstorms was going to pose vexing problems for the planet. More giant hurricanes would stir to life in the eastern Atlantic, gather force, and slam into the North American coast's communities. In the Pacific, typhoons would hurl themselves at Japan, Taiwan, China, Australia, and the Philippines.

Global warming was having another dangerous side effect that would compound the danger of violent storms. Sea level was already inching up worldwide. One study showed that shrinking Antarctic ice caps were adding 0.24 millimeters per year to sea levels around the world—a small amount, but it was likely to accelerate and mingle with the quickening flow from other sources. Over the long term, the picture was gloomy. In 2001, the Intergovernmental Panel on Global Climate Change cited scientific estimates saying that by 2100, sea levels could rise anywhere from about four inches to more than two and a half feet (and those projections did not account for more recent reports of melting ice). As powerful hurricanes proliferated and moved across higher seas, they would invariably generate storm surges that would make Katrina's wave look like a gentle summer swell.

When seas rose, people living in New Orleans and the

world's other low spots would need mighty fortresses to keep out towering walls of water rolling in off the ocean. On the Mississippi delta, when some projections of higher seas were combined with the downward velocity of sinking land, the result in 2100 was as much as four to six feet of extra water, enough to inundate most of the beleaguered towns on the delta and send water lapping against the urban levees—and that was with no hurricanes in sight. If it was still there at the time, and nothing were done to offset the rising sea level, New Orleans would finally, literally, become an American Venice.

But the problem wasn't restricted to the Louisianas of the world. Most coastal cities—and many lying miles inland but still accessible to the sea—would also be at risk. London, for example, was vulnerable to North Sea storm surges flowing up the River Thames. In 1984 the government completed the Thames Barrier, a giant system of sixty-five interlocking gates, ten feet high, across the river to the city's east. It was a striking engineering achievement, but it was only a Band-Aid: it was expected to last only until 2030, when higher sea levels would force Londoners to seek another solution. Their predicament was not unique: given that levees and barriers built to last decades or centuries could not constantly adjust to the rising sea levels, each millimeter of rise increased the odds that they would be overtopped. In the English port town of Immingham on the North Sea, for example, a study showed that by 2100, a once-in-a-hundred-years storm surge would become a once-every-eight-years event.

The one place in the world that seemed to offer some hope to places like New Orleans was the Netherlands. Like New Orleans, it was one of those odd places where people had long ago chosen to live in a state of near-constant peril, and yet somehow endured. "There the ocean throws itself, two times a day, daily and nightly, in a tremendous stream over a wide country, so one doubts if the ground belongs to the land or to the sea," wrote Roman philosopher Pliny the Elder, who served there as an imperial soldier in the first century CE. "There lives a miserable people at the highest known levels of the tide and here they have built their huts, living like sailors when the water covers their environment and as if shipwrecked when the water has gone."

Starting with windmill-driven pumps, first used a thousand years ago to keep farmland dry, the Dutch had devised flood defenses of uncanny brilliance. There wasn't much difference, technically speaking, between New Orleans's levees and Dutch dikes. But the thought, planning, and meticulous expertise that went into the Netherlands's modern system was unparalleled. The Dutch demonstrated that engineering could indeed be married to sound public policy to protect the population—if, that is, there was enough money and will to do it.

Large areas of the Netherlands were, of course, below sea level, including its most densely populated region, which reached a depth of twenty-two feet below at its nadir. Moreover, the nation's modern era had been defined by a single event: a devastating storm surge flood. In February 1953, a winter storm on the North Sea drove a thirteen-foot wave into southern Holland's estuaries, where the high water overflowed and breached dikes in hundreds of places. Tens of thousands were caught by surprise and forced onto rooftops to await rescue. Others were trapped or simply disappeared. More than two thousand people died, and the national psyche was permanently scarred.

In the aftermath, the nation reassessed the philosophy behind its dikes and decided to invest billions of Dutch guilders to make sure that another flood of the same magnitude would never happen again.

The old system had been a variation on that flawed idea that so tormented the Corps of Engineers: "levees only." Dikes had run for miles inland fronting three major estuaries (formed where the Rhine, Meuse, and Maas rivers flowed out to the sea). As in New Orleans, that design offered multiple potential entry points for rising floodwaters, so after some debate, the Dutch decided to junk it and set out to shorten the line of defense. The Delta Works, as the system was called, would consist of giant barriers across the openings where the estuaries flowed out into the North Sea. Initially, they tried dams, but the water behind them turned stagnant, fish and oysters died, and fisher-men suffered. After more debate, the plan was adjusted, and gates and sluices were installed to let water flow in and out—reducing but not eliminating the environmental fallout.

The largest of the Delta Works was the Eastern Scheldt storm surge barrier. When completed, the 7.8-billion-dollar structure snaked for five miles over the estuary, its distinctive white pylons visible from great distances across the water. The barrier consisted of sixty-two floodgates ensconced between gi-ant concrete piers, each weighing twenty thousand tons. Most of the time, the gates were left open. But if forecasters pre-dicted a potentially dangerous storm surge of three meters (about ten feet) or more—something that happened about once a year—the gates were shut until the danger passed.

The barrier and the Delta Works as a whole are among the world's great engineering achievements. "For a hydraulic engi-neer, this was like putting a man on the moon," said engineer Tjalle de Haan, who helped design the barrier while working for the Rijkswaterstaat, roughly the Dutch equivalent to the Corps of Engineers.

Where the Corps had stubbornly stuck with their hoary de-sign methods, Dutch designers melded technology with their structures, especially the last Delta Works project, the Maeslant storm surge barrier across the New Waterway, a shipping chan-nel heading into the heart of the busy port of Rotterdam. Com-pleted in 1997, the Maeslant barrier resembled a cross between butterfly wings and a Tinker Toy, blown up to monstrous size. But its most noteworthy feature was automation. Government storm surge warnings were automatically transmitted to the bar-rier's computers, triggering a closing sequence. Motors kicked on and rolled the gently curving white steel gates—turning on thirty-five-foot ball bearings—into the middle of the waterway, where they met and sealed it off.

The Dutch also had legal benchmarks for flood protection that were rigorously enforced. As a result, government agen-cies, politicians, and the public all kept close track of the mov-ing targets that pushed up flood risk—development and rising seas. Dutch engineers and bureaucrats obsessively tracked sea level rise, rainfall, and spring river stages to keep updating their standards.

With New Orleans's very existence in doubt after Katrina, many residents and experts seized on an obvious solution: do what the Dutch did after 1953. Design a new levee system, better than the one before. Build gates, this time environmentally friendly ones. Build higher, sounder levees. Construct state-of-the-art pump stations and move them out of residential neighborhoods. And make sure all of this can withstand the worst that any Category 5 hurricane could dish out—a thirty-foot storm surge or better. The most critical parts of the Dutch system were rated to withstand a once-in-ten-thousand-years flood, making them approximately fifty times safer than the failed levee system had been. Why not something similar for New Orleans?

"If we don't do that, there's no hope of rebuilding the city of New Orleans," Randy Hanchey, a former Corps official and assistant secretary of Louisiana's Department of Natural Resources, told the *Times-Picayune* not long after Katrina struck. "And there's only one way we can do that: build a barrier system strong enough to withstand the storm surge of a Category 5 storm. And we can't take our time doing it. We have to start now."

But the Corps wasn't quite ready to start. It set its bureaucratic wheels in motion, launching a long-delayed feasibility study on expanding protection. It was expected to be ready in 2008 and to offer an array of options to Congress, price tags attached. If a proposal passed muster and went forward, it likely wouldn't be finished for decades—a big window of vulnerability for the city while the Atlantic and Gulf were active breeding grounds for superstorms.

If doing nothing spelled doom for New Orleans, building such a system posed risks, too—chief among them its impact on a giant marsh restoration project also deemed necessary to preserve the Mississippi delta and the human settlements on it. While the Corps claimed it knew how to build levees that would let water flow freely, barely affecting the delicate wetlands around them, if people were to be protected indefinitely, the Corps would have to build a veritable Great Wall from Mississippi to Texas. More clashes with environmentalists seemed inevitable.

Still, the biggest concern raised by the plan was its cost. The initial guesstimate for New Orleans–area sea gates and higher levees was a hefty 23.5 billion dollars. With coastal restoration added in, that meant a forty-billion-dollar price tag. That was still far less than Katrina's total damages, which topped one hundred billion dollars, or the cost of the Iraq war, roughly double that. But given the nation's chronic deficits and the billions already spent just to rebuild the levees back to their pre-Katrina standards, it wasn't clear if Congress or the president would even consider the issue. If they ultimately did, and the appropriations flowed, it wasn't clear the state could afford to pay its share.

One mid-September evening after the storm, President Bush gave a speech in Jackson Square in the center of the French Quarter. With the St. Louis Cathedral lit up behind him, the president vowed that New Orleans and the Gulf Coast would be rebuilt. And he made an additional promise: "Protecting a city that sits lower than the water around it is not easy, but it can and has been done," he said. "City and parish officials in New Orleans, and state officials in Louisiana, will have a large part in the engineering decisions to come. And the Army Corps of Engineers will work at their side to make the flood protection system stronger than it has ever been." But of course, the system had never been particularly strong to begin with, so that promise could mean anything.

In the Netherlands, flood defense equaled national defense. It was part of the national identity. In the United States, it was just another local issue among a thousand to be hashed out in subcommittee hearing rooms. The tragedy of Katrina and its aftermath was, of course, a result of the never-ending dialectic between American society and the natural frontier that had nurtured it: mankind's alterations to the Mississippi delta, with development its own kind of treacherous flood; government decisions to offer insurance policies and other incentives that made it easy to forget about risk; changes in individual perspective and faith. To a great extent, we make our environment and our environment makes us. A storm is an act of nature—but of human nature, too.

With the economic resources that had sustained it for three hundred years greatly diminished, its weary population scattered and skeptical, and its political clout at a low ebb, New Orleans would have to fend for itself. If another storm hit, Venice would not be the model. Instead, washed away for good, this once-grand city of spice and jazz and good times and hard work would vanish beneath the sea, the first but possibly not the last American Atlantis. And those who will look back on it, and on other cities that meet a similar fate, will scratch their heads and wonder why we let it happen.

NOTES ON SOURCES

THIS BOOK DRAWS on an array of sources—interviews and on-scene reporting, news accounts, government studies, scientific papers, and legal documents, in addition to the original reporting done for our 2002 *Times-Picayune* series "Washing Away: How south Louisiana is growing more vulnerable to a catastrophic hurricane."

CHAPTER 1

Kam-Biu Liu's paper "Paleotempestology: Principles, Methods, and Examples from Gulf Coast Lake Sediments" in *Hurricanes and Typhoons: Past, Present, and Future* (New York: Columbia University Press, 2004), provides a useful introduction to the emerging study of ancient hurricanes. Alan Wexelblat graciously shed some light on his view of the perverse nature of modern disasters. Our account of the early history of Louisiana draws on various sources, among them Gwendolyn Midlo Hall's *Africans in Colonial Louisiana: The Development of Afro-Creole Culture in the Eighteenth Century* (Baton Rouge, LA: Lousiana State University Press, 1995) and *New Orleans 1712–1812, an Economic History*, by John G. Clark (LSU Press, 1970). For tracing Louisiana's repeated encounters with hurricanes, David Roth's report "Louisiana tropical cyclones" (available online at http://www.srh.noaa.gov/lch/research/lahur.php) and David Ludlum's *Early American Hurricanes: 1492–1870* (Boston: American Meteorological Society, 1963) are essential texts. The account of Reverend McAllister's experiences during the last Last Island flood comes from a summary prepared by the Thibodaux First Presbyterian Church and posted on its Web site (http://lafourche.com/presbyterian/lastisland.htm).

CHAPTER 2

The history of the Army Corps of Engineers and its efforts to control the Mississippi River is well documented on various Corps publications and Web sites. We drew on other sources as well, including John M. Barry's masterful *Rising Tide: The Great Mississippi Flood of 1927 and How It Changed America* (New York: Simon & Schuster, 1998) and the PBS *American Experience* series "Secrets of a Master Builder: How James Eads tamed the mighty Mississippi." Benjamin Franklin's letter on the storm that struck Boston is reproduced on numerous Web sites. John Magill's article "On Perilous Ground" (*Louisiana Cultural Vistas*, Winter 2005–06) surveys the history of flooding in New Orleans. Our narrative of the evolution of meteorology and hurricane forecasting draws from Jack Williams's and Bob Sheets's *Hurricane Watch: Forecasting the Deadliest Storms on Earth* (New York: Random House/Vintage, 2001) and Ivan Ray Tannehill's *Hurricanes, Their Nature and History* (Princeton, NJ: Princeton University Press, 1945). Isaac Cline documented his own experiences in *Storms, Floods and Sunshine* (Gretna, LA: Pelican Publishing Company, 1999). *Isaac's Storm* (New York: Random House, 1999) by Erik Larson is an engaging latter-day account of the storm and of Cline's role in it.

CHAPTER 3

Our recounting of the 1927 flood owes much to Barry's *Rising Tide* and also to "Disaster Response and Appointment of a Recovery Czar: The Executive Branch's Response to the Flood of 1927," a 2005 Congressional Research Service report with an informative analysis of Herbert Hoover's innovative role as the nation's preeminent emergency manager following the disaster. The subsequent history of New Orleans's federal hurricane levees employs information from various sources, including contemporary news accounts and Corps documents. President Johnson's visit to New Orleans after Hurricane Betsy could be reconstructed in some detail thanks to documents and recordings from the Johnson presidency organized by the University of Virginia's Miller Center for Public Affairs. Valuable political context and additional detail can be found in historian Edward F. Haas's article on the response to that hurricane: "Victor H. Schiro, Hurricane Betsy, and the 'Forgiveness Bill'" (*Gulf Coast Historical Review* 6, Fall 1990). Additional insights on the post-Betsy scene in New Orleans were gleaned from Miller Center historian Kent Germany's article "'They Can Be Like Other People': Race, Poverty, and the Politics of Alienation in New Orleans' Early Great Society" from *The New Deal and Beyond: Social Welfare in the South Since 1930* (Elna Green, ed. Athens, GA: University of Georgia Press, 2003).

CHAPTER 4

Our description of the legal battle over the Corps's plan to place gates and levees across Lake Pontchartrain is based on contemporary accounts, interviews, and Corps documents. The interesting tale of A. Baldwin Wood's invention of the pumps that New Orleans still relies on is contained in "The A.B. Wood Low Head High Volume Screw

Pump," a 1974 report by the American Society of Mechanical Engineers and the New Orleans Sewerage and Water Board. A more exhaustive history of the New Orleans pumping stations and drainage system can be found in the "National Register Evaluation of New Orleans Drainage System, Orleans Parish, Louisiana" by Benjamin D. Maygarden, Jill-Karen Yakubik, Ellen Weiss, Chester Peyronnin, and Kenneth R. Jones, done for the Corps of Engineers. The story of the canal floodwalls draws mostly on our own reporting, as well as studies by forensic engineering teams: the "Preliminary Report on the Performance of the New Orleans Levee Systems in Hurricane Katrina on August 29, 2005" by the American Society of Civil Engineers and National Science Foundation–sponsored teams (available at http://www.berkeley .edu/news/media/releases/2005/11/leveereport_prelim.pdf), the "Investigation of the Performance of the New Orleans Flood Protection Systems in Hurricane Katrina on August 29, 2005" by the University of California at Berkeley–led National Science Foundation team (available at http://www.ce.berkeley.edu/~new_orleans/), and various reports and documents released by the Corps's Interagency Performance Evaluation Task Force (available at https://ipet.wes.army.mil/).

CHAPTER 5
A concise history of the Indians of Isle de Jean Charles, drawn from their oral tradition and tribal documents, can be found on the Web site of the Biloxi-Choctaw-Chitimacha tribe (http://www.biloxi-chitimacha .com). Chief Albert Naquin provided additional details. A wealth of information on the Cheniere Caminada hurricane, including photographs and contemporaneous accounts, is available in the state of Louisiana's report on coastal restoration (http://www.coast2050.gov). Though somewhat dated after almost fifty years, Kolb and van Lopik's report, "Geology of the Mississippi River deltaic plain, southeastern Louisiana" (Technical Report 3-483, Vicksburg, MS: U.S. Army Corps of Engineers Waterways Experiment Station) is an excellent introduction to the peculiar geography of the Mississippi delta.

CHAPTER 6
The story of Louisiana's evolving hurricane response plans is based on our own reporting over the years. Elba Urbina's master's of engineering thesis, "A State-of-the-Practice Review of Hurricane Evacuation Plans and Policies" (Baton Rouge, LA: Louisiana State University, 2002) also proved useful. Many academics have explored the growing problem of disasters; the works and insights of these three were of particular help: Dennis R. Mileti's *Disasters by Design: A Reassessment of Natural Hazards in the United States* (Washington, D.C.: Joseph Henry Press, 1999); Mary Comerio's *Disaster Hits Home: New Policy for Urban*

Housing Recovery (Berkeley, CA: University of California Press, 1998); and Rutherford Platt's *Disasters and Democracy: The Politics of Extreme Natural Events* (Washington, D.C.: Island Press, 1999). The paper by Roger Pielke Jr. and Christopher Landsea, "Normalized Hurricane Damages in the United States: 1925–95" (Boston: American Meteorological Society, 1998), documents the role of economic development in the increase in hurricane damages. The Williams and Sheets book mentioned in the notes for chapter 2 provided interesting background on the latter-day evolution of hurricane forecasting.

CHAPTERS 7–15

We based the narrative of Katrina and its aftermath, beginning with the creation of the Department of Homeland Security, on interviews, news accounts, congressional testimony, and the two excellent reports put out by congressional committees: "Hurricane Katrina: A Nation Unprepared; Report of the U.S. Senate Committee on Homeland Security and Government Affairs" (2006) and "A Failure of Initiative: Report of the Select Bipartisan Committee to Investigate the Preparation for and Response to Hurricane Katrina, U.S. House of Representatives" (2006). The *Times-Picayune* staff deserves copious credit for providing on-scene reporting that brought terrible suffering to light; Brian Thevenot's articles proved especially useful to us, as well as his long piece on the paper's Katrina coverage, "Apocalypse in New Orleans" (*American Journalism Review,* October–November 2005).

CHAPTER 16

Our examination of global warming and its effects on hurricane activity is based on interviews and scientific papers, including Thomas R. Knutson and Robert E. Tuleya, "Impact of CO_2-Induced Warming on Simulated Hurricane Intensity and Precipitation: Sensitivity to the Choice of Climate Model and Convective Parameterization" (*Journal of Climate,* Sept. 15, 2004); Kerry A. Emanuel, "Increasing destructiveness of tropical cyclones over the past 30 years" (*Nature,* Aug. 4, 2005); Roger A. Pielke Jr., "Are there trends in hurricane destruction?" (*Nature,* Dec. 29, 2005); Christopher W. Landsea, "Hurricanes and global warming" (*Nature,* Dec. 29, 2005); Stanley B. Goldenberg, Christopher W. Landsea, Alberto M. Mestas-Nuñez, and William M. Gray, "The recent increase in Atlantic hurricane activity: causes and implications" (*Science,* July 20, 2001); and Peter J. Webster, Greg J. Holland, Judith A. Curry, and Hai-Ru Chang, "Changes in tropical cyclone number, duration and intensity in a warming environment" (*Science,* Sept. 16, 2005).

ACKNOWLEDGMENTS

THIS BOOK CAN ONLY BEGIN to document the efforts of hundreds of people trying to protect and later to rebuild New Orleans. We hope that readers find it useful, at least as a starting point, in understanding what led to the grievous blow that befell a beloved city, and as a cautionary note in efforts to ensure that such a disaster does not happen again.

This book would not exist without the *Times-Picayune*'s important willingness to support in-depth explanatory journalism. The paper's support for our series "Washing Away"—produced under the tutelage of the paper's editor, Jim Amoss, and shepherded to publication by editor Tim Morris—helped shape our reporting into a compelling anatomization of New Orleans's predicament. Dan Swenson's and Emmett Mayer's maps and illustrations and Ellis Lucia's photographs dramatized the sweep of the hurricane threat to the entire region. Many thanks also go to the paper's Pulitzer Prize–winning staff for its heroic work on reporting Hurricane Katrina, from the hours before landfall through the long, difficult months afterward, including James O'Byrne, David Meeks, Pamela Coyle, Brian Thevenot, Michael Perlstein, Gordon Russell, Bob Marshall, Bruce Alpert, Bill Walsh, Michael DeMocker, Ted Jackson, Nancy Burris, Danny Gamble, and Brenda Bell. Thanks also to Linda Fibich and the staff at Newhouse News Service for providing lattes and moral support in the weeks after the storm. A special thanks to Friends of The Times-Picayune (http://www.friendsofthetimespicayune.com), the relief fund for the paper's displaced families, and its creators Susan Feeney, Nan Varoga, Bridget O'Brian, and Wendi Schneider.

Thanks to Geoff Shandler at Little, Brown for his skillful editing and enthusiasm for this project; to Junie Dahn and Jen Noon for smartly assembling all the elements on a tight time frame; and to our agent, Kris Dahl at ICM, for helping two novice authors negotiate the shoals of the publishing business.

Many people directly caught up in the chaos after Katrina took time to speak with us, recounting sometimes difficult experiences.

They include Robert Green, Jaime Cooper, Bill Quigley, Harvey Miller, James Seaberry Jr., Craig Ratliff, Byron LaChance, Rickey De-Jean, and Louis Trachtman, along with David Lewald and Kimberly Foster of the Coast Guard. Thanks also to current and former public officials who spoke with us, including Mayor Ray Nagin, Governor Kathleen Blanco, Jeff Smith, Terry Ebbert, Denise Bottcher, Walter Maestri, Jesse St. Amant, and Mike Brown.

Over the years, many have contributed to our knowledge of hurricanes and emergency response. Those issues often defied easy understanding, so their help and patience with our elementary questions was essential. At Louisiana State University, Joseph Suhayda, Ivor van Heerden, Hassan Mashriqui, and Greg Stone provided countless insights and ideas. At the National Hurricane Center, Max Mayfield, Lixion Avila, James L. Franklin, Richard Knabb, Stacy Stewart, Christopher Landsea, and Frank Lepore all provided key insights and details. At the Corps of Engineers, Major General Don Riley, Colonel Richard Wagenaar, Dave Hewitt, James H. Taylor, Robert Brown, Ed Link, Lewis Setliff, and Don Resio all graciously answered our questions, as did Admiral Robert Duncan and Susan Blake of the Coast Guard. Thanks also to Chief Albert Naquin of Isle de Jean Charles, Windell Curole, and Madhu Beriwal.

Special thanks to Bob Bea, Ray Seed, and Dave Rogers for explaining the mechanics of levee failures, to Lee Butler for his deep understanding of storm surges, and to Jurjen Battjes for a fascinating tour of Dutch flood defenses and perspective on the New Orleans system.

Extra-special thanks go to our wives. Diane Schleifstein dealt with the logistics of finding, buying, and furnishing a new house to replace a flooded Lakeview home. Trish Clay uncomplainingly shouldered extra child-care duties and put up with the odd working hours that book writing sometimes requires. Thanks also to Ka Shin Zendo, Dr. Warren Bourgeois III, and to Rabbi Ted Lichtenfeld for being there during the worst, even though half a continent away. And finally, thanks to Matthew and Hannah McQuaid for putting up with their dad's sometimes frustrating unavailability.

ABOUT THE AUTHORS

WINNERS OF THE PULITZER PRIZE, John McQuaid and Mark Schleifstein were coauthors of the New Orleans *Times-Picayune*'s award-winning series "Washing Away," the definitive account of the Gulf Coast's grave hurricane risks. McQuaid is based in Washington, D.C. Schleifstein abandoned his Lakeview home in the flood but remains in the New Orleans area.